Human Security

This book traces the key evolutions in the development of the concept of human security, the various definitions and critiques, how it relates to other concepts, and what it implies for polities, politics, and policy. Besides charting the territory and structuring the debate on a concept that is rapidly gaining importance in international policy making circles, it responds to an intellectual need. In a globalizing world, in which threats become transnational and states lose power, security can no longer be studied in a one-dimensional fashion. Instead, it must be conceptualized from an interdisciplinary point of view, taking into account a variety of variables as well as their interactions. This book contributes to this new multidimensional conception of security, showing its strengths and weaknesses, and its implications for analysis and action. Case studies from different regions (Afghanistan, Central Asia and South Asia) are presented throughout so as to elucidate the arguments which centre on the following questions:

- Does the concept of human security introduce a fundamental shift in approach or is it a new name for old solutions, another popular label affixed to conventional policies?
- Why are there so many definitions and critiques?
- Is the concept utopian or does it have practical implications? How can we evaluate policies using a human security framework?
- What is the added value of a human security approach in re-examining theories of security, development and human rights?
- What are the roles, responsibilities and capacities of the state and the international community within a new security vision?
- How to reconcile calls for a global vision of security versus national sovereignty and cultural relativism? Do ethical norms have a role in international relations?
- How does foreign aid help or hamper the provision of human security?
- As a concept born out of the end of the Cold War, is it still relevant in the post September 11th reactions and the revived focus on national security?

Shahrbanou Tadjbakhsh is the Director of the CERI Program for Peace and Human Security at l'Institut d'Etudes Politiques (Sciences Po) in Paris, where she teaches courses on human security and on international organizations and is editor of the *Human Security Journal*, an online publication. She has also taught on human security as an Adjunct Professor at Columbia University in New York. Between 1995 and 2002, she was a staff member of the United Nations Development Programme, and currently continues to work as a consultant with teams preparing national Human Development Reports. She has written numerous articles on human development, human security and gender issues as well as on the application of these discourses in Central Asia and in Afghanistan.

Anuradha M. Chenoy is Professor in the School of International Studies, Jawaharlal Nehru University New Delhi, where she has been the Chairperson and Director of the Area Studies Program for Russia and Central Asia. She has also been on the governing bodies of several institutions in India and internationally, and has served as a specialist for various meetings of the United Nations. She writes extensively in journals and newspapers on international relations, gender and social issues.

Routledge Advances in International Relations and Global Politics

1 **Foreign Policy and Discourse Analysis**
France, Britain and Europe
Henrik Larsen

2 **Agency, Structure and International Politics**
From ontology to empirical enquiry
Gil Friedman and Harvey Starr

3 **The Political Economy of Regional Cooperation in the Middle East**
Ali Çarkoğlu, Mine Eder, Kemal Kirişci

4 **Peace-Maintenance**
The evolution of international political authority
Jarat Chopra

5 **International Relations and Historical Sociology**
Breaking down boundaries
Stephen Hobden

6 **Equivalence in Comparative Politics**
Edited by Jan W. van Deth

7 **The Politics of Central Banks**
Robert Elgie and Helen Thompson

8 **Politics and Globalisation**
Knowledge, ethics and agency
Martin Shaw

9 **History and International Relations**
Thomas W. Smith

10 **Idealism and Realism in International Relations**
Robert M. A. Crawford

11 **National and International Conflicts, 1945–1995**
New empirical and theoretical approaches
Frank Pfetsch and Christoph Rohloff

12 **Party Systems and Voter Alignments Revisited**
Edited by Lauri Karvonen and Stein Kuhnle

13 **Ethics, Justice and International Relations**
Constructing an international community
Peter Sutch

14 **Capturing Globalization**
Edited by James H. Mittelman and Norani Othman

15 **Uncertain Europe**
Building a new European security order?
Edited by Martin A. Smith and Graham Timmins

16 **Power, Postcolonialism and International Relations**
Reading race, gender and class
Edited by Geeta Chowdhry and Sheila Nair

17 **Constituting Human Rights**
Global civil society and the society of democratic states
Mervyn Frost

18 **US Economic Statecraft for Survival 1933–1991**
Of sanctions, embargoes and economic warfare
Alan P. Dobson

19 **The EU and NATO Enlargement**
Richard McAllister and Roland Dannreuther

20 **Spatializing International Politics**
Analysing activism on the internet
Jayne Rodgers

21 **Ethnonationalism in the Contemporary World**
Walker Connor and the study of nationalism
Edited by Daniele Conversi

22 **Meaning and International Relations**
Edited by Peter Mandaville and Andrew Williams

23 **Political Loyalty and the Nation-State**
Edited by Michael Waller and Andrew Linklater

24 **Russian Foreign Policy and the CIS**
Theories, debates and actions
Nicole J. Jackson

25 **Asia and Europe**
Development and different dimensions of ASEM
Yeo Lay Hwee

26 **Global Instability and Strategic Crisis**
Neville Brown

27 **Africa in International Politics**
External involvement on the continent
Edited by Ian Taylor and Paul Williams

28 **Global Governmentality**
Governing international spaces
Edited by Wendy Larner and William Walters

29 **Political Learning and Citizenship Education under Conflict**
The political socialization of Israeli and Palestinian youngsters
Orit Ichilov

30 **Gender and Civil Society**
Transcending boundaries
Edited by Jude Howell and Diane Mulligan

31 **State Crises, Globalisation and National Movements in North-East Africa**
The Horn's dilemma
Edited by Asafa Jalata

32 **Diplomacy and Developing Nations**
Post-Cold War foreign policy-making structures and processes
Edited by Justin Robertson and Maurice A. East

33 **Autonomy, Self-governance and Conflict Resolution**
Innovative approaches to institutional design in divided societies
Edited by Marc Weller and Stefan Wolff

34 **Mediating International Crises**
Jonathan Wilkenfeld, Kathleen J. Young, David M. Quinn and Victor Asal

35 **Postcolonial Politics, the Internet and Everyday Life**
Pacific traversals online
M. I. Franklin

36 **Reconstituting the Global Liberal Order**
Legitimacy and regulation
Kanishka Jayasuriya

37 **International Relations, Security and Jeremy Bentham**
Gunhild Hoogensen

38 **Interregionalism and International Relations**
Edited by Heiner Hänggi, Ralf Roloff and Jürgen Rüland

39 **The International Criminal Court**
A global civil society achievement
Marlies Glasius

40 **A Human Security Doctrine for Europe**
Project, principles, practicalities
Edited by Marlies Glasius and Mary Kaldor

41 **The History and Politics of UN Security Council Reform**
Dimitris Bourantonis

42 **Russia and NATO since 1991**
From cold war through cold peace to partnership?
Martin A. Smith

43 **The Politics of Protection**
Sites of insecurity and political agency
Edited by Jef Huysmans, Andrew Dobson and Raia Prokhovnik

44 **International Relations in Europe**
Traditions, perspectives and destinations
Edited by Knud Erik Jørgensen and Tonny Brems Knudsen

45 **The Empire of Security and the Safety of the People**
Edited by William Bain

46 **Globalization and Religious Nationalism in India**
The search for ontological security
Catrina Kinnvall

47 **Culture and International Relations**
Narratives, natives and tourists
Julie Reeves

48 **Global Civil Society**
Contested futures
Edited by Gideon Baker and David Chandler

49 **Rethinking Ethical Foreign Policy**
Pitfalls, possibilities and paradoxes
Edited by David Chandler and Volker Heins

50 **International Cooperation and Arctic Governance**
Regime effectiveness and northern region building
Edited by Olav Schram Stokke and Geir Hønneland

51 **Human Security**
Concepts and implications
Shahrbanou Tadjbakhsh and Anuradha M. Chenoy

Human Security

Concepts and implications

**Shahrbanou Tadjbakhsh and
Anuradha M. Chenoy**

LONDON AND NEW YORK

First published 2007
by Routledge
2 Park Square, Milton Park, Abingdon, Oxon OX14 4RN

Simultaneously published in the USA and Canada
by Routledge
270 Madison Ave, New York, NY 10016

*Routledge is an imprint of the Taylor & Francis Group, an informa
business*

Transferred to Digital Printing 2009

© 2007 Shahrbanou Tadjbakhsh and Anuradha M. Chenoy

Typeset in Times by
HWA Text and Data Management, Tunbridge Wells

British Library Cataloguing in Publication Data
A catalogue record for this book is available from the British Library

Library of Congress Cataloging-in-Publication Data
Tadjbakhsh, Shahrbanou, 1965–
    Human security : concepts and implications / Shahrbanou Tadjbakhsh
and Anuradha Chenoy.
        p. cm. – (Routledge advances in international relations and global
        politics series)
    Includes bibliographical references and index.
    1. Security, International. 2. World politics–1989– I. Chenoy, Anuradha
    M. II. Title.
JZ5588.T353 2006
355′.033--dc22   2006022001

ISBN10: 0–415–40727–3 (hbk)
ISBN10: 0–415–47338–1 (pbk)
ISBN10: 0–203–96595–7 (ebk)

ISBN13: 978–0–415–40727–4 (hbk)
ISBN13: 978–0–415–47338–5 (pbk)
ISBN13: 978–0–203–96595–5 (ebk)

What difference does it make to the dead, the orphans and the homeless, whether the mad destruction is wrought under the name of totalitarianism or the holy name of liberty or democracy?

Mahatma Gandhi, *Non-Violence in Peace and War*

This book is dedicated to our students at l'Institut d'Etudes Politiques (Sciences Po, Paris), Columbia University (New York) and Jawaharlal Nehru University (New Delhi) whose curiosity on what is human security deserved an answer.

Contents

List of figures	xi
List of tables and boxes	xii
Acknowledgements	xiii
List of abbreviations	xv
Introduction	1

PART I
Concepts: it works in ethics, does it work in theory? **7**

1 Rationale and political usage	9
2 Definitions, critiques and counter-critiques	39
3 A paradigm shift in security studies?	72
4 Human security and human development: shadow or threshold?	98
5 Debating dignity: human security and human rights	123

PART II
Implications **141**

6 Underdevelopment and conflict: a vicious cycle?	143
7 The state and its domestic responsibilities	166
8 Intervention, engagement and the responsibilities of the international community	185

x   *Contents*

  9 Externalities of human security: the role of international aid   208

10 Concluding thoughts: whither human security?   235

    Bibliography   244
    Index   263

Figures

2.1   Definitional mapping tool   47
2.2   Hampson's triangular definitions   51
2.3   Human security as the nexus between safety, rights and equity   52
2.4   Definitional mapping tool based on indirect/direct threats and
      thresholds   53
2.5   Definitional mapping tool depicting key elements of narrow/broad
      conceptualizations of HS   54
2.6   Human security as the securitization of human development
      (growth) to protect from threats and failures of development
      (downturn).   55
2.7   The need for HS: insufficient human development and protection
      of human rights   55
2.8   The security pyramid: human security and traditional notions of
      security   56
2.9   Human security, threats and relative thresholds   57
4.1   Human development as progress, human security as a static
      threshold   118
4.2   Human security threshold and the crisis: downturns in development   118
4.3   Human security and human development as mutually reinforcing
      dynamics   119
4.4   Human security as the response to crisis   120

Tables and boxes

Tables

1.1	Human-centred approaches to security and economic growth compared	22
1.2	Comparing political definitions of human security	32
2.1	State versus human-centred security compared	41
3.1	Comparing common, collective, comprehensive and human security	75
3.2	Differences in security models	94
3.3	Analysing security variables	96
4.1	Rostow's five stages of economic growth	102
4.2	Comparing and contrasting human development and human security	107
4.3	Summary of the added values of HS to HD framework	112
4.4	A threshold approach to gradual human security indicators	121
5.1	Human security components embedded within human rights treaties	128
8.1	Humanitarian intervention and human security engagement	201

Boxes

2.1	Classification of academic definitions of human security	42
2.2	Conceptual critiques	59
9.1	Positive and negative externalities of human security interventions	221

Acknowledgements

The book is a collection of three years of research and teaching on human security and owes much to the hard work and persistent questions of our students. First and foremost, credit goes to the students of Tadjbakhsh's Human Security master's level classes at l'Institut d'Etudes Politiques (Sciences Po) in Paris (Spring 2004, Spring 2005 and Spring 2006) and the School of International and Public Affairs at Columbia University (Spring 2003, Fall and Spring 2004). Their as yet unpublished works appear in the bibliography. In fact, the first outline of the book and some of its content was drawn by Alex Amouyel, Maya Mailer, Werner Schäfer and Jeremy Shusterman as a textbook that would help students digest the many readings and discussions in the Spring of 2005. They helped us design many of the charts and tables and wrote some of the copy. From JNU, Chenoy solicited the diligent help of Rajan Kumar throughout the project.

Jeremy Shusterman is notably thanked for his persistence in human security studies and for the innovative charts that he drew for the book. We are grateful for his Tables 4.1, 4.3, 4.4 and Figures 2.2, 4.1, 4.2 and 4.3. In the Spring of 2006, the team that continued the work consisted of Carron Beaumont, Fairlie Jensen, Terrence James McDonald, Kate Noble and Maya Olek. They are credited for their help in putting together Boxes 2.1, 2.2 and for the inventive Figures 2.1, 2.3, 2.4, 2.5, 2.6, 2.7, 2.8 and 2.9. Terrence James McDonald is thanked for Figure 4.4. Leonardo Castillo, Katie Miller and Elena Zelenovic are thanked for Table 5.1; Alex Amouyel Maya Mailer, Simon Wells for Table 8.1; and Naomi Burke and Anna Wagner for their help on Box 9.1.

Additionally, we would like to express our appreciation to Jill Alpes, Betsy Annen, Laurene Chenevat, Celia Keren, Stephanie Kleschnitzki, Jeremie Kohn, Faye Leone, Anne Lise Reve, Renaud Rodier and Hanna Schmidt among the students whose ideas pepper this book. They are credited in the text and in the bibliography. We hope they keep on contributing to scholarship in their careers.

Besides students, we would like to also express our gratitude to a large number of colleagues, friends and families for their support during this project. We are both grateful to A.K. Shiva Kumar who introduced us, encouraged our collaboration, and when the end was not in sight, intervened with a reality check. At Routledge, we thank Omita Goyal of the Indian office who had sufficient faith in the initial proposal to draw it to the attention of Routledge UK, Dorothea Schaefter of the

South Asia desk in the UK for taking it up, and Tom Bates, also of the South Asia desk for his valuable help and for bearing with the questions and delays. We thank Shreemoyee Patra and her team of co-editors Parul Goyal and Manisha Bajaj Malik in New Delhi for a marathon edit of a first draft under pressure. The staff of the India Habitat Center showed superb hospitality in New Delhi during the frequent periods of hibernation which the writing induced.

We used for this book materials that had gone into research for two previous publications: one is the *UNDP Human Development Report for Afghanistan: Security with a Human Face*, for which Tadjbakhsh was the editor-in-chief and worked with a team of Afghan writers between 2002 and 2004. We are grateful to the then Country Director of UNDP, Ercan Murat, and to the team of Daud Saba, Omar Zakhilwal, Abdullah Mojaddedi and Fakhriddin Azizi for the creation of that report. The other is materials which appeared in the *Etudes du CERI* (Centre d'Etudes de Recherches Internationales) of Paris (No. 117–118, September 2005), which Tadjbakhsh produced as a pre-publication entitled 'Human Security: Concept, Implications and Application in Post-Intervention Challenges in Afghanistan'. We thank Christophe Jaffrelot, Director of the CERI and Judith Burko for the opportunity.

Chenoy would like to thank Kamal Mitra Chenoy for his constant support and companionship. She is grateful to Ayesha and Archit, her children, for their understanding and love. Tadjbakhsh owes much of this book to Coralie Bryant, the former Director of the Economic and Political Department of Columbia University who plucked her out of the UNDP in 2002 and continued to inspire and mentor her in her new teaching career at Columbia and at Sciences Po. She thanks Sakiko Fukuda-Parr, former Director of the Human Development Report Office of UNDP who let her go and followed suit later by joining Harvard. In Paris, she would like to thank especially Bertrand Badie, Director of the International Relations of the Doctoral School for supporting the study of human security and Christophe Jaffrelot, Guillaume Devin, Ewa Kulezsa, Laurent Bigorgne, Francis Verillaud, Silvia Da Rin Pagnetto, Martine Papacostas and Ambrosio Nsingui-Barros for allowing her to set up shop at Sciences Po. Sophie Guerbadot, the assistant of the Program, has been a genuine support in the final stages as has been Florence Basty who was writing a thesis on human security. Finally, Tadjbakhsh would like to thank her parents Guity and Gholamreza who, throughout a revolution and immigration, taught their children the value of education and of not being afraid of change.

Abbreviations

ASEAN	Association of Southeast Asian Nations
CCPR	International Covenant on Civil and Political Rights
CESCR	Covenant on Economic, Social and Cultural Rights
CHS	Commission on Human Security
DAC	Development Assistance Committee
DFID	Department for International Development (UK)
EU	European Union
EC	European Commission
ENP	European Neighbourhood Policy
FDI	Foreign Direct Investment
G77	Group of 77
GDP	Gross Domestic Product
GNP	Gross National Product
HD	Human Development
HDI	Human Development Index
HDR	Human Development Report
HS	Human Security
HSN	Human Security Now
ICC	International Criminal Court
ICISS	International Commission on Intervention and State Sovereignty
ICG	International Crisis Group
IFI	International Financial Institution
IMF	International Monetary Fund
LSE	London School of Economics
MDGs	Millennium Development Goals
MSF	Médecins Sans Frontières
NAM	Non-Aligned Movement
NATO	North Atlantic Treaty Organization
NGO	Non-governmental organization
OAU	Organization for African Unity
ODA	Overseas Development Assistance
OECD	Organization for Economic Co-operation and Development
OED	Oxford English Dictionary

OSCE	Organization for Security and Co-operation in Europe
P-5	Permanent Five
RTPR	Responsibility to Protect Report
SC	Security Council
SADC	Southern African Development Community
SARS	Severe Acute Respiratory Syndrome
UDHR	Universal Declaration of Human Rights
UNAMA	United Nations Assistance Mission in Afghanistan
UNDP	United Nations Development Programme
UNESCO	United Nations Education Sciences and Culture Organization
WB	World Bank

Introduction

The Human Security concept evolved at a time of great international shifts: the disintegration of the Soviet Union ended the Cold War, lifting the shadow of bipolar politics that clouded relations between countries, but gave way to the recognition of new threats and conflicts in addition to the many unresolved ones. Simultaneously, globalization changed international rules for facilitating the faster flow of capital and technology by breaking down national barriers. New non-state actors came to play a critical role in the international political system, some as threats, and others as bridges between communities and nations. In these circumstances, the role of the state started undergoing transformation and the traditionally accepted conception of power was contested. These shifts necessitated new thinking that would address problems and trade-offs linked with the age old question of development and security. Human security theorizing was a step in that direction.

When the decade of the 1990s began, the world was not quite the same anymore. Just a few years earlier, people had been shot trying to cross the wall that divided the city of Berlin. An American president had spoken of an 'evil empire' and poured billions of dollars into the development and acquisition of new, ever more powerful weapons. Two superpowers had dominated world politics and international relations had developed in the shadow of their competition. But suddenly, everything changed: no more Communism, no more Soviet Union, no more arms races. The wind of change blew through Moscow and much of the world. Everything seemed possible; peace in our time had become an unexpected reality. The concept of Human Security emerged in this environment. The world was at a crossroads, and road maps were in high demand. In 1994, the United Nations Development Program first identified Human Security as a 'way to go from here.' Thus, its *Human Development Report* sought to broaden the traditional notion of security focused on military balances and capabilities to a concept that included 'safety from such chronic threats as hunger, disease, and repression' as well as 'protection from sudden and hurtful disruptions in the patterns of daily life.' Human security thus implied economic security, food security, health security, environmental security, personal security, community security, and political security.

Since then, human security has become somewhat of a buzzword. Countries like Canada and Japan have proclaimed it as the guiding principle of their foreign policies. Both have encouraged other countries to join them in international forums to promote the goals embodied in the concept, giving rise to a number of international conferences, networks, and commissions. Numerous reports have been published, elaborating the concept and applying it to specific situations. Academic authors have joined the fray, trying to incorporate human security into theories and developing measurements to make it useful for empirical analysis. Activists have made it a rallying cry to unite diverse hopes, ideologies, and interests.

What has evolved in recent years is thus a jungle of ideas, declarations, reports, analysis, and critiques that is often difficult to traverse. This book is intended to make the journey through this jungle a bit more manageable. It is inevitably difficult to catch up with this literature. When Tadjbakhsh started teaching human security at Columbia University in the Spring of 2003, there was not much material available. In 2004, with the apparition of a Special Issue of the Journal *Security Dialogue*, devoted to 'What is human security? Comments by 21 authors' (Vol. 35, September), various academic definitions were proposed. Since then, the literature is growing steadily. In this book, we try to present and analyse a comprehensive overview of the existing literature on human security while posing our own challenges to the field.

The book tries to show the key evolutions and events in the development of human security, explain how it relates to other concepts, and what it implies for polities, politics, and policy. Besides charting the territory and structuring the debate on a concept that is rapidly gaining importance in international policy making circles, the book tries to respond to an intellectual need. In a globalizing world, in which threats become transnational and states lose power, security can no longer be studied in a one-dimensional fashion. Instead, security must be conceptualized from an interdisciplinary point of view, taking into account a variety of variables as well as their interactions. This book seeks to contribute to this new multidimensional conception, show its strengths and weaknesses, and its implications for analysis and action.

These shifting and contrasting priorities beg the following questions, which the monograph tries to answer:

- Does the concept of human security introduce a fundamental shift in approach or is it a new name for old solutions, another popular label affixed to conventional policies?
- Is the concept utopian or does it have practical implications? Do ethical norms have a role in international relations?
- What are the roles, responsibilities and capacities of the state, and the international community within a new security vision?
- Does human insecurity get resolved by traditional methods of security or is an alternative required?
- How can we reconcile calls for a global vision of security versus national sovereignty and cultural relativism?
- As a concept born out of the end of the Cold War, is it still relevant in the post September 11 reactions and the revived focus on national security?

Structure

For the purpose of this book, we broadly define human security as the protection of individuals from risks to their physical or psychological safety, dignity and well-being. An environment that is said to provide its members with human security is one which affords individuals the possibility to lead stable, self-determined lives. Analysing social phenomena – be they wars, post-conflict situations, financial crises, or developmental models – from a human security perspective, thus means to focus on the consequences they have on the stability and dignity of the lives of individual human beings.

The book is divided into two main parts, a first part concerned with theoretical and conceptual debates within the field, and a second one which looks at implications for the actual provision of human security at the national, regional and international levels.

We begin Part I with two chapters on the elaboration of the various definitions policy-makers (Chapter 1) and scholars (Chapter 2) have given the concept of human security. Chapter 1 looks at the political implications of adopting the concept by international and regional institutions as well as by intermediate powers. Chapter 2 then charts the various definitions, as well as the various types of criticism that have been levelled against the concept of human security. Three chapters then compare and contrast the notion with established fields of analysis: Chapter 3 explores a comparison with more traditional conceptions of security, namely those of realist, liberal, constructivist and radical/alternative theories of international relations. The following two chapters juxtapose the human security perspective with two other concepts that have structured thinking about international and development policy in recent years, namely human development (Chapter 4) and human rights (Chapter 5).

In Part II we pose the question of how human security can actually be guaranteed. In this context, we first look at how it has transformed the debate on the linkages between conflicts and underdevelopment (Chapter 6). We then focus three chapters on the transformation of various responsibilities. Chapter 7 considers the role of the state in providing, threatening and protecting human security as both an external and internal actor. In Chapter 8, we look at humanitarian intervention, one of the ways in which states and international organizations have tried to 'impose' human security in certain areas of the world. What are its shortcomings, but also what are the possibilities it offers? How can we reconceptualize the idea of a responsibility to protect through intervention with one of long-term engagement? Chapter 9 then addresses the implications of the human security framework for foreign aid. How can aid harm or hinder? How can it ameliorate the human security situation in target countries? In the conclusions (Chapter 10), we present a summary of human security as a theory and in practice before opening up to identify new questions of research that this new field requires.

Throughout the book, we present case studies from areas with which we are mostly familiar, namely transition countries of Central Asia where Tadjbakhsh lived and worked between 1992–2000, Afghanistan, where she worked on producing the first National Human Development Report (2002–2005), and India and South Asia, an area of expertise of Chenoy. Although regional generalizations are not useful, they are presented here as examples of issues that have come on to the global scenes from the particular realities of a region.

The idea of the human security book: a collaboration based on common values

Note from the authors

The book, we hope, will serve as a useful introduction and overview for academics, policy makers, students, development practitioners and civil society interested in the contemporary problems and challenges facing the international community. It may raise more questions than it answers, and that is what it intends to do: encourage interest in further research.

When we began our reflections, each in different parts of the world, we were both faced with what we can term as an epistemological misunderstanding. In the United States and the Anglo-Saxon world, the idea of human security has always created a puzzle. Security, after all, was automatically associated with strategic dealings, defence, military, deterrence, etc. 'What was human security?' we were asked repeatedly. Wasn't that an oxymoron, the imposition of two words from two different worlds: 'human' and 'security'? In France however, the surprise was ours when students would not understand our insistence at explaining the deconstructive approach. 'La sécurité' or better yet, 'la sureté' for them already embodied the idea of social security and students seldom understood our imaginary frustration. Wasn't human security obvious and did we need a new term? This was not simply a matter of speaking to two different communities, of 'defence' scholars or 'development' practitioners. We came to understand that the inherent understanding of 'human security' was embedded in our interlocutors', in this case students', worldview from their own experiences, one that had grown up in a Cold War atmosphere of supremacy of power, and another in a welfare state.

But what about the Third World? Inevitably, the debate around human security was seen as an interventionist idea, as yet another concept coming from the 'North' with a punitive stick. But wasn't it obvious that it was precisely in the developing societies of the South that an emphasis on security of individuals, and the security of development, had to take root? The apprehension we came to understand was the collective experience with a number of mistrust: first with concepts that came from international organizations, which to the South, were often seen as institutions led by powerful Northern nations. Whether it was democracy, human rights and now human security, the discourses smacked of power in the construction of the terms. Second, we realized, was the collective experience with security being associated with arms build-up, with many societies of the South falling victim to becoming unwittingly consumers of defence paraphernalia and arms sold by state and non-state arms merchants. Security was far from the connotation of the French welfare state. It was more like the Anglo-Saxon idea of all things deadly.

Thus came the idea of exploring these connotations, and the collaboration between two professors, one at l'Institut d'Etudes Politiques (Sciences Po) in Paris, and one at Jawaharlal Nehru University (JNU) in New Delhi, in probing what was after all behind the many meanings of human security.

The idea of the book came to Tadjbakhsh as a result of her professional and intellectual engagement with human security, combining a career in academia with development policy and practice. After a PhD from Columbia University, where she had studied core–periphery relations in nationalities questions in the Soviet system and Central Asian republics, she went to work for seven years at the United Nations Development Program in the field in Central Asia, Eastern Europe, CIS and finally at the Bureau for Human Development Report in the headquarters of UNDP in New York. It was through her engagement with economists and political scientists preparing National Human Development Reports in such diverse places as Iraq, Afghanistan, India, China, Kuwait, Mongolia, Tajikistan, Uzbekistan and Kazakhstan that she came to empathize with the relationships between concepts and implications. After leaving the UN in 2002, this engagement was then taken to the classroom where she began teaching human security first at Columbia University and then at Sciences-Po in Paris, where she currently directs a Program for Peace and Human Security at the CERI.

Anuradha M. Chenoy teaches at the School of International Studies, JNU, where she has been chairperson and currently the director of the programme on Russia and Central Asia. She has written *Militarism and Women in South Asia* (New Delhi, 2001) and *The Making of New Russia* (New Delhi 2000) and been a consultant and spoken at various international meetings, including the United Nations, on issues linked with gender and security. This book is part of Chenoy's intellectual engagement with Tadjbakhsh, and a meeting of minds on their common concerns with security of people rather than that of states. The need for an alternative concept of security that can be inclusive and reach out to people's everyday concerns, gave the direction to this. Issues of insecurity that confront people's lives, whether it is their next meal, the lack of shelter, or search for a political framework for their aspirations, confront all intellectuals in developing societies, especially one like India. The question that remains is how one responds to these issues. Which side does one locate one's theoretical understanding? It is this that attracted Chenoy to the idea of human security.

We are scholars who want to change the world. This may seem like an oxymoron. As the research community tells us, scholars describe, analyse and predict and policy makers change. But as Marx continues to prophesize on student banners at JNU, there is a need to change the world rather than just interpret it. Thus, the collaboration brought together one Iranian woman who had been educated in American universities and had worked in the UN before moving to teaching, and an Indian woman steeped in the tradition of activism that, fortunately, does not escape the faith of intellectuals in India. A number of factors united us: we both had a responsibility to educate students for the future, and we chose to take it up by clarifying concepts, engaging students, and ultimately, allowing them to change the world. For this book, we engaged many students whose names appear in the acknowledgements. We also both believed in a strong sense of justice and ethics, and were united in our principled approached to politics. In this collaboration we posed three contentions:

First, the study of human security reminded us of the cliché: 'it works in practice, but will it work in theory?' As this book will show, much has been written about the many definitions and critics as a theory in what we can only recognize as being a paradigmatic war among security scholars themselves on one side, and security and development specialist on the other. And yet, it is an undeniable truth that human being beings live decidedly complex lives while threats to their perceptions and to their existence come in a highly inter-related multi-dimensional package. Why then have we fretted so long in trying to determine and explain what matters in the final analysis?

Second, the study of human security could be driven by a conceptually driven approach which looks at how the concept co-exists with existing fields of study or a policy-driven approach that focuses on practical implications. In this book, we have begun engaging with both. Yet, because of our strong belief in human dignity, what mattered to us in the final analysis was the ethical approach which colours all practical and conceptual dimensions. Human security to us was ultimately about human welfare, justice and dignity. Ethics and morality, then, should guide our behaviours *vis-à-vis* securing (as in ensuring and insuring, which is different from securitizing) human dignity.

There was also however a fourth approach to human security, which was action-oriented and focused on concrete policies and urgent measures. As teachers and researchers, we have not been able to engage in this most important aspect, which should be the work of practitioners and policy planners. We have only tried to present elements that should guide that search for concrete solutions and the impetus for mobilizing the will 'to do something'. Yet, we recognized the discomfort that divorcing theories from practice creates and empathized with Chourou when he wrote in a 2005 publication on human security in the Arab World for UNESCO:

> While we sit discussing our reports, our land is churned into a dust bowl, our resources are depleted, our children are in despair, our best brains in exile, our women in seclusion and our intellectuals in reclusion … Our intellect tells us this, and if our conscience does not spark us into action, what will?
>
> (Chourou, 2005: 95)

Part I

Concepts

It works in ethics, does it work in theory?

1 Rationale and political usage

Simply put, human security debunks the question of 'security' from its traditional conception of the safety of states from military threats to concentrate on the safety of people and communities. Once the referent object of security is changed to individuals, it then proposes to extend the notion of 'safety' to a condition beyond mere existence (survival) to life worth living, hence, well-being and dignity of human beings. Thus, poverty, for example, is conceptualized as a human security threat – not because it can induce violence which threatens the stability of the state, but because it is a threat to the dignity of individuals. This is human security in a nutshell.

In a case where politics precede academia, mounting interest in the concept by international organizations, regional bodies and national states has led to a number of international conferences, networks, and commissions. Numerous reports have been published, elaborating the concept and applying it to specific situations. Activists have made it a rallying cry to unite diverse hopes, ideologies, and interests. Academics and policy analysts have now joined the discussion in trying to incorporate human security into theories and developing measurements to make it useful for empirical analysis.

Yet, there is no single definition of human security today. The EU, Canadians, Japanese, UNDP and scholars have all come up with different definitions for the term, ranging from a narrow term for prevention of violence to a broad comprehensive view that proposes development, human rights and traditional security together. What has evolved in recent years is thus a hybrid of ideas, declarations, reports, analyses, and critiques that is often difficult to traverse. Despite its straightforward claim, and active engagements by institutions and scholars, human security – its concept, framework, or policy agenda – has no consensual definition. Each proponent of the concept has his or her own definition, vindicating the critics' view that 'the content of human security really is in the eye of the beholder' (Paris, 2004: 36) Does this elasticity of definition detract or add to the concept and its practice?

Can human security be a useful paradigm shift – as human development was the early 1990s – for policy makers and academics, or is it simply a rallying cry: a 'glue that holds together a jumbled coalition' of middling powers and development agencies that want to exist on the international scene (Paris, 2001)?

It is often described as a vague concept with no analytical or practical utility; so broad that it includes everything, and therefore, nothing; a new nemesis from northern countries, wrapped in an excuse to launch just wars and interventions in weak states. Does Human Security signify any conceptual added value or is it just an attempt to 'securitize' issues belonging to the fields of development, human rights, or conflict resolution? Are the various definitions irreconcilable, or do they converge into a concept that can be studied and implemented?

The authors aim to establish that human security is an idea of our time, an idea worth exploring, cajoling, comparing and using as a policy tool. Before tackling the myriad of definitions and criticisms of human security in Chapter 2, this chapter concentrates on the two factors in its favour. First, it is an idea that answers many of the new questions that have been raised in the past decade. Second, whether or not it is justified, or valid as an academic concept, today human security is on the political agenda of a number of states, international organizations and the UN. For these reasons alone, human security is worthy of examination within the context of international relations in the twenty-first century.

What are we defining and how do we judge human security as a concept?

Security itself, as Smith puts it, is 'an essentially contested concept' (Smith, 2002). While Buzan refers to security as ultimately a political process, 'when an issue is presented as posing an existential threat to a designated referent object' (Buzan *et et al.* 1998), it is also helpful to recall, as King and Murray do, the definition from the *Oxford English Dictionary (OED)*: 'The condition of being protected from or not exposed to danger; safety ... Freedom from care, anxiety or apprehension; a feeling of safety or freedom from an absence of danger' (King and Murray, 2001). Thus, while Buzan explores the political nature of labelling an issue as security, the OED definition emphasizes the subjectivity inherent in security as a 'feeling'.

The concepts of 'security' and 'insecurity' have relative connotations in different contexts. For some, insecurity comes from sudden loss of guarantee of access to jobs, health care, social welfare, education, etc. For others insecurity stems from violation of human rights, extremism, domestic violence, spread of conflicts, displacement, etc. To be meaningful, therefore, security needs to be redefined as a subjective experience at the micro level in terms of people's experience. For example, 'security' for a farmer in a Kashmir valley is the livelihood he gains from selling his crops, but this form of security is very different from the 'security' interests of Pakistan and India who are keen to become nuclear powers. For a school teacher in Jalalabad, Afghanistan, security is the possibility to educate his children and invest in the construction of his house, confident that the little he has today would not be taken away from him tomorrow – a different matter from that of the coalition troops in Paktika, fearful of a suicide attack or a renewal of insurgency by the Taliban or Al Qaeda. We therefore begin by submitting that security is, in fact, in the eye of the beholder.

The history of trying to define and refute human security as a concept has been a battlefield in itself. In international relations and development studies literature, it has been referred to variously as a new theory or concept, as a starting point for analysis, a world view, a political agenda, a policy framework, and even a new paradigm. How important is it to arrive at a consensual definition? As Stoett, advances, 'defining words is a fundamental act' (Stoett, 1999). The necessity of understanding such keywords serves to delineate reality, framework and priorities. Definitions can simultaneously restrict or broaden concepts and solutions. More importantly, defining is an act, performed by an actor, and never something neutral or objective, at least where concepts are concerned. It is therefore paramount when attempting to answer 'What is human security?' to bear in mind how the definitions emerge from or against past theories, who is defining, for what purposes, and what consequences the definitions entail in terms of action. The concept of human security is anything but neutral from a political or an intellectual point of view, as it implies a renewed look at existing paradigms and responsibilities. Its definition is thus a stake of power among various actors: this would help understand both the proliferation of definitions and the numerous criticisms.

To judge the malleability and usability of a concept, we may consider various questions before attempting to analyse definitions advanced in the political and academic arena.

Is it relevant to the changes of international politics today?

The answer is in the affirmative. The human security approach responds to the need to address the major changes in international relations and, above all, to the increased inter-dependency of nations and individuals. The end of the Cold War did not result in the expected peace dividend. While conflicts continued unabated, new insecurities confronted states and individuals. Security, in this sense the sustainability of development, in itself is questioned because of the persistence of pervasive poverty, lack of entitlement and gender oppression to which societies and individuals are subject. As Kofi Annan notes, the world has changed profoundly since 1945, when the United Nations was created.

> Geopolitical patterns, economic trends, technological change and other developments are severely straining the system of collective security that has been in place for the past 60 years. Today's threats – familiar ones with added potency, and some entirely new dangers – are borderless, highly connected, and capable of crippling, and even destroying societies everywhere.
>
> (Annan, 2005b)

The genesis of human security was thus conditioned by the new possibilities and new threats emerging with the end of the bi-polar power blocks. If during the Cold War, security, in the tradition of national security, was the prerogative of the state through military defence, and peace was the absence of war, the end of bi-polar competition precipitated powerful transnational actors – private companies, international organizations, NGOs and non-state entities – and enabled them to become relevant actors in international relations. Democratization and globalization heralded 'power to the people' through increased activism of global civil society that sought debt relief and fairer international institutions. The flip-side was the rise of networks of discontent, as witnessed in the rise of Al Qaeda (post-September 11) and organized terrorism penetrating borders and making unprecedented use of the Internet. The end of bi-polar competition changed the very nature of threats and their conception. While on the one hand, the risks of a global confrontation and major inter-state conflicts decreased, the shift from a polarized to a globalized environment meant increased awareness of intra-state conflicts, ethnic confrontations, terrorism, migration and forced displacements, extreme poverty, marginalization and exclusion of groups and communities, HIV/AIDs and new diseases, etc. Beyond the opportunities and challenges of the end of the Cold War, the process of globalization enabled the unfettered movement of capital and technology as national barriers were removed for rapid financial movement. This unrestricted movement led to financial meltdowns and economic downturns as seen in the Asian (1997) and Russian (1999) crises, as well as increased trafficking of drugs, people and arms – all with devastating human impacts. Within the various definitions of human security are acknowledgements of these threats as well as the urgent need to address new insecurities that affect millions of people, and which the dominant realist conception of security has failed to explain.

In the post-Cold War period, while conflicts seemed to settle down, the score card on post-conflict rehabilitation and long-term peace-building has yet to prove sustainable gains in international interventions in Bosnia, Kosovo, East Timor, Afghanistan and Iraq, especially because of continued inattention to inequality between groups and denial of justice – the very reasons for conflict or regime repression in the first place. In the post-September 11 world, the traditional state-based security interests are challenging individual liberties as a global 'war against terrorism' is launched to the detriment of war against socio-economic injustices such as poverty. Interventions in Afghanistan and Iraq propagate the use of force for regime change with an increasingly violent backlash of insurgencies and terrorism, while preventive measures such as understanding the root causes of grievances are bypassed in favour of national security concerns. While the decline in the authority of United Nations and its struggle for legitimacy continues, the return of military expenditures and conditionalities as well as the continued trade-off of guns over butter bear witness to the sustained militarizing of the international political system.

Liberal values such as open societies and open markets, although intended to lift millions out of poverty while setting them on paths towards 'freedom and liberty', are also marred by increasing gaps between the haves and the have-nots, with the silent majorities becoming more distant and marginal. Liberal-based interventions may also have exacerbated disillusionment with structural adjustments, shrinking responsibilities and capacities for the states in transition countries, along with fragmentation and localization based on ethnicity, religion and geography in much of the Third World. The uneven pace of economic growth, both in the world and within countries and regions, has resulted in major economic disparities that have increased over time and caused economic insecurities.

It is obvious that innovative international approaches are needed to address the sources of insecurity, remedy the symptoms and prevent the recurrence of threats. Technological innovations, increased wealth, disappearing borders and the end of bi-polar competition have not alleviated our insecurities. These issues and phenomena defy state regulation – in fact, many of them actually result from the states' failure to provide for people's security. The traditional lexicon of sovereignty and statehood is inadequate when it comes to security in the twenty-first century. These changes have prompted policy makers and scholars to think about more than military defence of state interests and territory, to include 'welfare beyond warfare'.

Does it pose new questions?

We argue that the added value of the concept of human security lies in the new questions it poses as regards the problem of 'security'. The shift from state-based to individual-based security introduces three new answers to the questions: 'security of whom', 'security from what' and 'security by what means'.

Security of whom?

Human security's contribution to security studies is to designate the individual(s) rather than the state as the 'referent object' of security, although this does not abrogate the security of a state, which, in turn, can protect its individuals. Thus, the community, the nation, and other groups are referents of security as long as the security 'trickles down' to people. Human security promises a focus on individuals and peoples, but more widely, on values and goals such as dignity, equity and solidarity. But this new paradigm involves more than just setting the individual up as the centre of a constellation of threats, actors and programmes. It changes the very status of the individual, who is no longer consubstantial to the state – an infinitesimal part of an organic whole – but an equal subject and actor in international relations. Graham and Poku relevantly stress that 'rather than viewing security as being concerned with "individuals qua citizens" (that is, toward their states), [the Human Security approach] views security as being concerned with "individuals qua persons"' (Graham and Poku, 2000: 17). The individual has reached the status of a 'whole', a 'unit of account' in himself. With human security, he/she becomes the ultimate actor taken into account. His/her security is the ultimate goal, to which all instruments and peripheral actors are subordinated. Elevating the person as the ultimate end is made possible by defining this new actor in terms of his/her vulnerabilities on the one hand, and his/her capacity to affect change on the other.

Security from what?

Because it concentrates on the well-being and dignity of individuals, another added value of the human security approach is that it recognizes menaces beyond violence to include a host of other threats. Human security does not explain threats, but recognizes new ones together with their inter-dependence. The approach identifies agency-based, as well as structural causes of insecurity, i.e. those that are deliberately orchestrated, such as genocide, or drug related crimes, and those that arise inadvertently or structurally, e.g. under-investments in key social/economic sectors such as education and health care. The threats therefore both include unstructured violence that often accompanies many aspects of non-territorial security such as violence emanating from environmental scarcity or migration, as well as violence inflicted by nature such as natural disasters, in addition to threats by the states themselves. Human security threats include both objective, tangible elements, such as insufficient income, chronic unemployment, dismal access to adequate health care and quality education, etc., as well as subjective perceptions, such a the inability to control one's destiny, indignity, fear of crime and violent conflict, etc. They can be both direct (those that are deliberately orchestrated) and indirect (those that arise inadvertently or structurally). Thus, human insecurity is comprised of a multitude of different threats beyond military or traditional security risks.

Socio-economic threats are those which pertain to security of employment and income or access of individuals to major public services such as health care, adequate housing, and education. Beyond the more traditional threats of under-development (poverty, hunger, access to food, disease, pollution, etc.) structural violence is also included in the definition of insecurity. Food security, defined as not only the availability of food, but also the capacity to gain access to it through livelihoods could also be in this category. This dimension, which can be measured quantitatively, is generally associated with 'freedom from want' in the broadest sense.

Personal security threats are those which are attributed beyond criminality, to individual perceptions and fears; for example, fear of losing access to health services in the process of health insurance reform, or fear of losing a job in the process of restructuring contribute to personal levels of insecurity. They encompass threats from the state through physical torture, threats from other states (wars), from international or cross-border terrorism, from other groups (ethnic or religious conflicts) and from individuals or gangs (street violence), domestic violence, violence against children (abuse, prostitution, labour) and even violence against one's self (suicide or drug abuse). Hence, this dimension is generally associated with 'freedom from fear' and best measured through proxy indicators and qualitative perception studies.

Environmental threats are defined in this framework as not only threats to the environment (degradation) but how these impact on people and increase their vulnerability (e.g. pollution and man-made or natural disasters such as floods, earthquakes, etc.).

Political threats include civil and human rights violations, violence stemming from conflicts, as well as arbitrary behaviour, a corrupt civil service, the unpredictability of institutional settings, a poorly functioning judiciary, the lack of enforcement of the rule of law, etc., generally associated with 'freedom from fear'. In this category could also be included the UNDP 1994 definition of 'community security' dimension, which designates both the security of the community as regards its identity and practices, and the security of the individual against possible threats from the community such as discriminatory practices.

The 1994 UNDP *Human Development Report* (HDR) (UNDP, 1994) synthesized threats to human security in seven components: economic, food, health, environmental, personal, community and political security as follows:

1   Economic security, where the main threat is poverty, requires an assured basic income – either from productive and remunerative work (through employment by the public or private sector, wage employment or self-employment) or from government financed social safety nets.

2   Food security, where the threats are hunger and famine, requires that all people at all times should have both physical and economic access to basic food – that they should be entitled to food, by growing it for themselves, by buying it, or by using the public food distribution system. The availability of food is a necessary but not a sufficient condition for food security. People often go hungry because they cannot afford to buy food, not because food is unavailable.

3   Health security, where the threats include injury and disease, requires access to health care and health services, including safe and affordable family planning. The threats to health security are greater for poor people in rural areas, particularly women and children, who are more exposed to disease.

4   Environmental security, where the threats are pollution, environmental degradation and resource depletion, requires a healthy physical environment, security from the degradation of the local ecosystems, air and water pollution, deforestation, desertification, salinization, natural hazards (e.g. cyclones, earthquakes, floods, droughts or landslides) and man-made disasters (e.g. due to road or nuclear accidents or poorly built slum buildings).

5   Personal security, where the threats include various forms of violence, requires security from physical violence and from various threats. People are increasingly threatened by sudden, unpredictable violence (e.g. threats from the state through physical torture inflicted by the military or police), threats from other states such as wars, threats from international or cross-border terrorism, threats from other groups of people such as ethnic or religious conflicts, threats from individuals or gangs against other individuals or street violence, from hostage-taking, threats directed against women such as domestic violence, abuse or rape, directed against children such as child abuse, neglected child labour, or child prostitution, and threats to one's self such as suicides or drug abuse.

6   Community security, where the threat is to the integrity of cultural diversity, requires security from oppressive traditional practices, treating women harshly, discriminating against ethnic or indigenous groups and refugees, group rebellion and armed conflicts.
7   Political security, where the threat is political repression, requires respect for human rights, protection from military dictatorships or abuse, from political or state repression, from the practice of torture, ill treatment or disappearance, and from political detention and imprisonment.

One may postulate that most of these 'threats' had already been highlighted by the human development approach. The novelty of reconceputalizing these as human security threats is that political repression, identity and various forms of violence are included in the definition of 'personal security'. The 'community security' dimension is also innovative, to the extent that it designates both the security of the community as a whole, as regards its identity and practices, and the security of the individual against possible threats from the community, such as structural violence. It thus points out that HS exceeds states to include the widest possible range of actors studied in their interconnectedness and network-functioning – from the individuals to the ecosystem – through groups, communities, societies, transactional linkages, international organizations, NGOs, financial fluxes, and so on. Finally, 'political security' refers to human rights, protection from military dictatorships or abuse, from political or state repression, from torture or political detention. It is an open condemnation of the hegemon and the former colonial powers supporting authoritarianism throughout the world in order to expand their soft power and influence networks (Annen, 2005).

Because of its concern with the quality of life beyond survival, and an existence with dignity, the human security framework postulates three assumptions about threats: that equal weight has to be given to under-development and human right violations as 'threats' alongside traditional insecurities, that threats are inter-linked and inter-connected, and that these linkages mean that they should not be prioritized.

Threats are interlinked and interconnected: threats to human security are inter-connected in two ways. First, they are mutually linked in a domino effect: health insecurity could lead to poverty, which could lead to education deficits, etc. Responses to insecurities stemming from environmental degradation could contribute to population movement into other fragile ecological settings, a deteriorating health situation, hunger, loss of livelihoods, and so on. Second, the various threats can spread within a given country (with impoverished areas, for example, threatening the stability of more progressive ones), bleed into other regions (through massive employment migration, export of arms, environmental degradation, health epidemics, etc.), and negatively impact global security (through breeding discontented armed groups, drug exports, etc.). The concept of 'mutual vulnerability', coined by Jeorge Nef (Nef, 1999), relates to the inter-connectedness of systematically related security threats: dysfunctionality in one sphere is structurally and sequentially expressed in other sub-systems and leads to a vicious circle of causes and effects. Human security is, at the same time, an independent and dependent variable, and the interactions between the treats are mutually reinforcing. They could evolve into a virtuous or a vicious spiral of interlinkages and consequences. Threats to human security are, thus, no longer just personal, local or national; they are global. Drugs, disease, terrorism, pollution, poverty and environmental problems respect no national borders. Their consequences travel the world, leading to inter-connectivity and inter-dependence among states and international systems on the one hand, and mutual vulnerability among communities on the other. Political communities are not only affected by the activities of other territorial states, but also by other local communities and individuals. Weak communities have direct ramifications on powerful ones. No region in the international system, argues Nef, is immune to the risks that affect the human security of others.

The inter-dependence of threats means, ultimately, that they should not be prioritized. If adopting a security language is an attempt to draw attention to the urgent need for priorities for action and policy, which of the many threats deserves more attention? To the question of priorities, one could answer that the fallacy lies in assuming that policy is made by top 'political actors' eager to sift through competing demands to choose specific targets of their attention and resources, while reality may, in fact, be a circular multiplication, rather than consolidation of priorities. Policy making is not a vertical process but a networked, flexible and horizontal coalition that needs a complex paradigm (Makaremi, 2004). Furthermore, to 'hierarchize' and prioritize among HS goals may be a futile exercise as the concept actually rests on the postulate that all threats are interdependent: the eradication of one is of little effect without the implementation of comprehensive security to restore the individuals' dignity.

For example, it is often noted that security is a pre-requisite for development. The human security threat analysis, however, shows that development concerns can themselves create insecurities, and are just as urgent. Poverty and inequality, for example, can both lead to insecurity and conflict, in addition to being 'inhumane' by themselves. The imperative is, therefore, to simultaneously work on 'freedom from fear', which entails provision of security and a violence-free day-to-day life for everyone, and 'freedom from want', which calls for providing not only the basic needs of food, shelter and services, but also the more strategic needs that support long-term, sustainable development. Perhaps then it is less a question of prioritization among competing goals for policy makers than about identification of thresholds, below which welfare, dignity and survival cannot be tolerated. Thresholds and measurements of human security are especially complicated, given the distinction between objective (real) and subjective (perceived) fear, because security, on any scale, will remain a feeling, and because thresholds of tolerance can be different and culture/ space/ time/ circumstance specific.

Security by what means?

Another innovation of human security lies in its recognition that none of these threats and forms of violence can be addressed in their singularity; that all threats, actors, instruments and potential solutions to the challenges stressed above are deeply interconnected and interdependent in a global context in which national borders and sovereignty have lost much of their relevance.

Human security posits that security is not just the end of war, but also the ability to go about one's business safely, in a safe environment – to have a job, to participate in political processes, to have choices for the education of one's children, to live a healthy life and to do all this with the knowledge that one's family is safe and unharmed. Insecurity, therefore, is not only a problem of physical safety, but also of deprivation and restricted access to health and education facilities, legal and political rights, and social opportunities. Hence, insecurity should not be dealt with through short-term military solutions, but a long term comprehensive strategy that abides by promises of development and promotion of human rights. It should promote public policy and state-building efforts that reduce local incentives that trigger insecurities in the first place.

Since the peace treaty of Westphalia in 1648, the Hobbesian model of the state has been said to provide security for people living within its borders in exchange of the monopoly of the legitimate means of use of physical force within this territory, that is to say in exchange for state sovereignty. No authority can be imposed above the sovereign state and no supranational organization can regulate inter-state relations, so the state has to assure its own security (to assure the security of its people) and survival against the military threats posed by other states (self-help). However, the major failure of state-centred security, a tenet of the realist school of thought, is to not take into account that a large number of states today are partly or completely failing to fulfil their social contract to protect people. Some states are the very actors that threaten their people through repression, genocide or massacre: As Mack claims, 'in the last one hundred years, far more people have died at the hands of their own governments than have been killed by foreign armies' (Mack, 2004). Some states are so weak, failing, failed, collapsed or inexistent, that they are incapable of providing this broadened concept of security.

If the human security approach considers human beings as the fundamental basis of security, then by implication international security depends on the security of individuals. The international system is only as strong as its weakest link, and since weakness is contagious, failures on the periphery can threaten the entire network of international interdependence. As Neff states, if the safety of individuals is the key to global security, then if this safety is threatened, so is international security (Nef, 1999). In this perspective the status of the individual is transformed from that of a simple citizen of his state into that of an actor involved in international relations. The individual becomes an 'agent' who can be actively engaged in defining potential security threats, and who can participate in efforts to mitigate them. The survival, well-being and dignity of the individual become the ultimate goal, and constructs such as the state, the institutions of political democracy, and the market are relegated to secondary status as simply means to achieve that goal. If primary threats stem from economic failures, violations of human rights, and political discrimination, then the guarantee of national security no longer lies in military power, but in favourable social, political and economic conditions, the promotion of human development, and the protection of human rights.

Does it constitute a paradigm shift in international relations?

According to Thomas Kuhn, scientific revolutions consist of the emergence of a paradigm that challenges, defeats, and eventually displaces the previously accepted view; therefore, the distinct mark of an emergent paradigm is its direct attack on the nucleus of the conventional wisdom (Kuhn, 1962). Although critics chided him for his imprecise use of the term, Kuhn was responsible for popularizing the term 'paradigm', which he described as essentially a collection of beliefs shared by scientists, a set of agreements about how problems are to be understood. In *The Structure of Scientific Revolutions* (1962), he presented the idea that science does not evolve gradually towards truth, but instead undergoes periodic revolutions which he called paradigm shifts. Paradigms, Kuhn suggested, are the basis of all science. Indeed, a paradigm guides the research efforts of scientific communities, and it is this criterion that most clearly identifies a field as a science.

Paradigm and theory resist change and are extremely resilient, hence crises provide the opportunity to retool and loosen rules for normal research. As this process develops, more attention is devoted to the new proposition which was viewed as an anomaly by the field's eminent authorities. The field of study transforms as scholars explicitly dispute, the paradigm is criticized and competing articulations proliferate. A new candidate for paradigm emerges, and a battle over its acceptance ensues. To be accepted as a paradigm, a theory must seem better than its competitors, but need not explain all the facts with which it can be confronted, thus making research possible. New assumptions require the re-evaluation of prior facts and theories. This is often strongly resisted by the established community. Indeed, Kuhn observed that 'novelty emerges only with difficulty, manifested by resistance, against a background provided by expectation.'

Social scientists such as sociologists, economists and psychologists in particular took up Kuhn with enthusiasm. There are primarily two reasons for this. First, Kuhn's notion of 'science' appeared to permit a more liberal conception which could also be applied to disciplines such as sociology and psychoanalysis. Second, Kuhn's rejection of rules as determining scientific outcomes opened the doors to admitting that other factors, such as social and political factors, could influence the outcome of scientific debates. Social constructivism took this influence as central, not marginal, to the very content of accepted theories. Furthermore, the fact that Kuhn identified values as guided judgements opened up the possibility of applying ethics to scientific theories.

Every 'new' paradigm has its predecessors. Human development came to debunk traditional views of economic growth as will be discussed in Chapter 4.

Similarly, human security came to represent an ethical and methodological rupture with the existing conceptualization of state-based security in international relations. The 'security for what' debate postulates an ethical rupture that poses new questions about the end goals of security, and proposes a different way to achieve development and security in its various dimensions through multilateralism and agency. The paradigm posits a set of values that guides scholars and practitioners in assessing contemporary world arrangements and methods through which to envision more humane arrangements.

The ethical rupture

The dominant conception of theories of security deals with facts, not with values; with explaining things as they are, not with finding out how they ought to be. Human security raises doubts among political scientists that remind us that a social science term should not 'do' anything, that theories and disciplines cannot be based on a normative, value-laden framework. Contemporary social and political science deals with the factual (the 'being'), and, occasionally, with the feasible, but not with the desirable (the 'should be') (Gómez Buendía, 2002). Yet, in the field of economics, Amartya Sen led the rebellion in challenging utilitarianism as the conceptual basis of economic theory and by re-opening economics to ethics, he brought values back into the core of social science. Sen's theoretical revolution, in the technical language of 'functionings', and 'capabilities' was in tandem with the practical dictates of Mahbub Ul Haq, the Pakistani planner associated with the foundation of the UNDP Human Development approach, who posed a simple statement that the purpose of all public policies is to increase people's choices. In his 'Development as Freedom', Sen elaborated on why and how freedom is at the same time the main goal and the main means to achieve development. In other words, development is the increasing of human freedom by means of human freedom.

Human security poses a similar moral challenge to realism. Underlying human security are normative ethics, or moral standards that regulate right and wrong conduct in the international system. Human security offers the definition of an end point towards which all politics have to strive, i.e. the ethics of ultimate ends, which holds a transformatory potential for actors and institutions at all levels of international governance. For realists, the moral argument is the raison d'état itself (Campbell and Shapiro, 1999). Faith in the notion of the raison d'état is an acceptance of the priority accorded to the security of the state. Human security redirects the focus to the well-being of people: there no longer is a raison d'état beyond the raison d'être of the security of people.

Behind the three main shifts that human security proposes is a new normative framework of world politics advocating an ethical idea of how human beings might best achieve security (Alpes, 2004). The first shift – from state to individual security – implies that human security accords moral priority to the security of individual human beings, and rejects the Cold War view that sovereign states are the paramount moral community of international society worth preserving. Human security directly confronts the moral dilemma of national security, a dilemma that expresses a conflict between the rights of states and the rights of human beings by giving priority to individual security (Bain, 1999). Thus, human sufferings cannot be ignored in the cause of state sovereignty. The second shift – linking the individual with global stability – proposes a society of humankind above a society of states and a global consciousness on the interdependence of all actors and scales in international politics. The third shift – from national to universal values – advocates a world in which all human beings are 'freed from want' and 'freed from fear,' a world where fundamental rights, dignity, the rule of law and good governance are respected. These three shifts call for a wider ethical concern into international politics: the insecurity of individuals anywhere in the world should take precedence over state sovereignty.

The methodological rupture

Sen and Ul Haq's human development approach had proposed a methodological rupture from theories of development and economic growth by suggesting that the best strategy to increase national income is not to accumulate capital, but to develop people. Human security similarly claims that the best way to achieve security (both for the state and the international system) is to increase that of people. This re-conceptualizing of means of security alters Cold War conceptions about the international order, not only in its understanding of the main threats to international peace but also for solution for how best to secure it. (Hampson *et al.* 2002). Indeed, during the Cold War, the international order was dictated by state-centred mechanisms, be they the realpolitik approach to balance of power and security dilemmas or the liberalist and constructivist views of interdependence and international institutions. The human security approach builds on the linkages between the individual and global security in a new world order: a threat to the individual is seen as a threat to international security. This rupture has implications for how security strategies should be designed, as an opportunity to protect people and empower them so that they, in turn, desist from violating the security of the state (by not engaging in conflict that could destabilize it), and by not threatening other states and sub-systems (through migration and movement of disease) etc. The moral deserves to be repeated: securing people is not just an ethical imperative; it is the best strategy to secure the state and the international system.

Convincing realists and neo-realists of the need to broaden the concept of security from that of the state to include that of the people within, is similar to the challenges that human development had *vis-à-vis* mainstream neo-liberal economics. Consider Table 1.1:

Table 1.1 Human-centred approaches to security and economic growth compared

	Neo-liberal economics	Human development	Realists, neo-realists and state-centred security view	Human security
End/goal	Economic growth (which is supposed to then 'trickle' to wealth of all).	People + growth (because growth does not automatically trickle down).	State sovereignty/strength (which then is supposed to protect people).	People + state (protection is not automatic – what happens when the states are weakened, or are perpetuators themselves?)
Means to achieve goal	Growth policies (liberalization, privatization, macroeconomic stability, etc).	Growth policies + social policies + human rights at the same time.	Policies that strengthen military might.	Military + good economic policies + governance policies.
Assumptions about 'people'	Homo-economicus, 'the rational man' making decisions vis-à-vis the market.	This 'rational man' as an entity is in fact comprised of women whose behaviour is affected by their varying needs, ethnic identities, means of livelihood etc. that affect their behaviour etc. The 'rational man' has to be unpacked.	State and people are not divorced. If WMD are launched, they annihilates both.	State and people are like a married couple whose individual interests are not necessarily served in congruence. Sometimes there are trade-offs, some elements can affect one more than other (For example, a country can have a strong military but with large pockets of poverty).

Human security as a political discourse

A stake of power

Having set out our position as to why human security is worthy of examination, we turn to the various ways in which international organizations and states have adopted the concept. As Chapter 2 will demonstrate, human security is a complex paradigm that has spawned many debates. Ultimately, as Smith argues, no 'neutral definition' is possible (Smith, 2002). Because it implies new responsibilities, defining human security has become a stake of power for a variety of actors, each adapting or criticizing its definition in line with their own interests and fears.

The concept of human security has been around within the international system for at least a decade now, ever since it was coined in the 1994 UNDP *Human Development Report*, which described it as 'freedom from fear and freedom from want'. Since then, it has been adopted by a number of states, regional and international organizations. Chronologically, we can establish three broad stages of its engagement with international politics: First, a world début was in the global *Human Development Report* of the UNDP in 1994 that sought to seize the opportunity provided by the end of the Cold War, but was met with scepticism from the G77 for fear it would lead to violations of state sovereignty. The UNDP definition was snubbed in the Copenhagen Summit in 1995. In the meantime, a coalition of 13 'like-minded' countries – Austria, Canada, Chile, Costa Rica, Greece, Ireland, Jordan, Mali, the Netherlands, Norway, Switzerland, Slovenia, Thailand, with South Africa as an observer, came together to form the Human Security Network (HSN) in 1999. Throughout their years, their collective efforts has led to notable successes in the form of ad hoc campaigns which led to the the signing of the Ottawa Convention to ban anti-personal landmines (1997) and the creation of the International Criminal Court. The HSN also held a number of ministerial meetings during which issues such as human righs, conflict prevention and HIV/AIDs and health security were raised at high level. In 2000, UNESCO opened a global discussion revisiting security and peace by launching an international network for the promotion of peace and human security (SecuriPax Forum). Second, between 2001 and 2003, the concept was revived in the debate on the 'responsibility to protect', spearheaded by the Canadian International Commission on Intervention and State Sovereignty (ICISS), and in the discussions on the 'responsibility for development' initiated by the Japanese Commission on Human Security (CHS), with the two governments – Canada and Japan – providing the necessary leadership and funding for including human security in the global agenda. Third, In the years 2004–2005, as the need to readjust to the new realities of the twenty first century, and in particular, to find means of mounting concerted, collective responses to new threats became increasingly clear, human security, conceived of as the linking of security to development, became a topic of reform agendas at the UN and in such regional organizations as the European Union. In the meantime, UNESCO, which, since the late 1990s had sought to put it on its broad agenda for peace, began looking at the particularities of human security through a series of regional consultations in East Asia, Central Asia, Latin America, Europe, etc.

The UNDP debut: human security as peace dividend

Much of the literature on human security attributes the official 'launch' of the concept in global politics through the UNDP *Human Development Report* of 1994, which saw it as an extension of the human development paradigm into security discourses:

> For too long the concept of security has been interpreted narrowly as security of territory from internal aggression, or as protection of national interests in foreign policy or as global security from the threat of nuclear holocaust … Forgotten were the legitimate concerns of ordinary people who sought security in their daily lives.
>
> (UNDP 1994)

Human security was broadly defined as 'freedom from fear and freedom from want' and characterized as 'safety from chronic threats such as hunger, disease, and repression as well as protection from sudden and harmful disruptions in the patterns of daily life – whether in homes, in jobs or in communities' (UNDP, 1994). The UNDP's people-centred approach to security was developed with seven universal and inter-dependent components, namely, economic, food, health, environmental, personal, community and political security. These were seen as universal concerns, as their absence was a threat common to all. Going beyond the traditional weaknesses associated with underdevelopment (poverty, hunger, disease, pollution, etc.) an attempt was made to define insecurity as a form of structural violence. This human development approach to human security was not only concerned with gross violations of human rights, armed conflicts, and natural disasters, but encompassed wide-ranging aspects of underdevelopment: inequality, public health, international crime, population growth and environmental degradation. These were to be the new focuses of development assistance for the international community as preventing them would be less costly than having to deal with their consequences.

The UN agenda: rethinking collective security

Within the UN, the concept seems to have been initiated in the 1992 *Agenda for Peace* which stressed the special and indispensable role of the UN 'in an integrated approach to human security' as part of the new mandates proposed by Boutros Boutros Ghali in relation to peacemaking, peacekeeping and post-conflict management (United Nations, 1992). But it was Kofi Annan who adopted the human security agenda in a quest for a new UN mandate in the 1999 Millennium Declaration. Defining peace as 'much more than the absence of war', he called for human security to encompass economic development, social justice, environmental protection, democratization, disarmament, and respect for human rights and the rule of law (Annan, 2001). The adoption of a human security agenda by the UN stemmed from a recognition of the failure of its peacekeeping efforts and its desire to compensate for these failures by involving the UN in a more global forum where NGOs could dialogue with, or exert pressure on, governments in order to implement more feasible and comprehensive development agenda.

By the end of 2005, two documents tried to clarify further human security threats and what the international community should do about them. One was the report from the UN High-level Panel on Threats, Challenges and Change entitled *A More Secure World: Our Shared Responsibility*, and the other was the reform agenda proposed by Kofi Annan in *Towards All Freedom*. The High-level Panel on Threats, Challenges and Change was established in late 2003 by the Secretary General to look beyond traditional security threats of the era: first were the post-Iraq realities that required operative definitions for terrorism, the doctrine of preemptive intervention, and humanitarian intervention in the name of human security. Second, here was the need to find a position for the UN, whose responsibility was challenged by both globalization and the emergence of one superpower prepared to use force for its national interests. *A More Secure World: Our Shared Responsibility*, released in December 2004, advanced the cause of human security in two ways: it set a broad framework for collective security to address new and exacerbated threats, grouping today's threats into six clusters: economic and social threats, such as poverty and deadly infectious disease; inter-state conflict and rivalry; internal violence, including civil war, state collapse and genocide; nuclear, radiological, chemical and biological weapons; terrorism; and transnational organized crime. But beyond recognition of the threats, it also identified interconnections: poverty, infectious disease and war feeding on one another in a deadly cycle. Poverty was strongly associated with civil wars that disrupt and destabilize societies and their economies. Diseases such as malaria and HIV/AIDS continued to cause large numbers of deaths and reinforce poverty. Thus, the High Level Panel recognized development as the indispensable formulation of the new collective security, where greater intergovernmental cooperation and partnership with national, regional and civil society actors were essential.

The High Level Panel prompted a reform package that Kofi Annan proposed to the member states in March 2005, aimed at restoring UN credibility and relevance for this new era of collective security. Although the Report, entitled *In Larger Freedoms*, did not technically mention the term 'human security' for fear of definitional questions over a concept not yet debated in the General Assembly, it clearly underscored the linkages between human rights, development and security as three imperatives that reinforce each other.

> While poverty and denial of human rights may not be said to "cause" civil war, terrorism or organized crime, they all greatly increase the risk of instability and violence ... And countries which are well governed and respect the human rights of their citizens are better placed to avoid the horrors of conflict and to overcome obstacles to development.
>
> (Annan, 2005a)

The Report stressed poverty, deadly infectious disease and environmental degradation, which could have 'equally catastrophic consequences' as civil violence, organized crime, terrorism and weapons of mass destruction. Alluding to the global preoccupation with failed states, the report stressed that these threats could undermine not only people's survival but also states as the basic unit of the international system. Stopping short of enforcing a policy framework, the document, nevertheless, made four important institutional reform proposals that have endured years of inconclusive debate: expanding the UN security council, defining terrorism, increasing foreign aid, and a new proposal for replacing the UN Commission on Human Rights with a new Human Rights Council. Thus, 'human security' saw its mention in the outcome document of the High-Level plenary meeting of the General Assembly during the September 2005 summit. In paragraph 143, the document noted 'we commit ourselves to discuss and define the notion of human security in the General Assembly.'

Underlying these proposals was the basic problem of how the UN could effectively learn from its failures in places like Bosnia and Rwanda a decade ago, and Darfur and Congo today. In the meantime, the need for collective action proposed by the UN was challenged by new interventions, especially unilateral, as seen in Iraq, on the basis of national interests, but using a human security cover. For example, among the many arguments used for the invasion of Iraq were the supposed existence of WMDs, which threatened the security of the Americans, followed by the need to 'bring democracy' as a strategy of peace and prosperity for the Iraqis – both human security arguments, but used to justify what many considered illegal and immoral unilateralism. In order to counter such temptation to instrumentalize the concept, the UN had to to position itself as the authority capable of organizing multilateralism and network-functioning as a neutral supra-national body.

Global commissions: defining the contours of intervention and engagement

One of the most salient critiques of a human security approach, especially when promoted by states on behalf of people of other states, becomes the fear of *carte blanche* for intervention. To alleviate fears and clarify the conditions and modalities for intervention, the Canadian government launched an International Commission on Intervention and State Sovereignty (ICISS) co-chaired by Gareth Evans, ICG Director and Mohamed Sahnoun, the Algerian Special Advisor to the Secretary General. By the time the Commission began its work in November 2000, the international community had been faced with a number of ineffective interventions: the legitimacy of the intervention in Kosovo, the failure to intervene in Rwanda, a withdrawal before the job was completed in Somalia, and a failure to protect vulnerable communities in Bosnia; failures that prompted the need to rethink interventions in general. Responding to the Secretary General's challenge of the meaning of people's sovereignty within state sovereignty, the ICISS was to examine new actors/institutions, new security issues (competition over means of violence by non-state actors, vulnerability of civilians, small arms, weak states, etc.), new demands and expectations (human security as a conceptual framework, technology and globalization, etc.), and new opportunities for common action.

The final report, called *Responsibility to Protect* in answer to critics of military interventions for humanitarian purposes in sovereign states, had a number of important impacts: it first redefined the meaning of sovereignty to include dual responsibility – externally to respect the sovereignty of other states and internally to respect the dignity and basic rights of all people within the state. The report echoed Annan's formulation of sovereignty on the basis of responsibility. Second, it redefined interventions as actions taken against a state or leader, with or without its consent, for purposes which are claimed to be humanitarian or protective. These could mean both military interventions as well as alternatives such as sanctions, criminal prosecution, etc., used as preventive measures (to avoid the need for the military) or as reactive (as alternatives to the military). However, the Commission also put a number of conditionalities around intervention that would, in fact, put severe limitations on the military ones. Responsibility to protect also entailed a responsibility to prevent (through early warning, root cause prevention, etc.), a responsibility to react but also a responsibility to rebuild (by clarifying post-intervention obligations: peace building, justice and reconciliation, security, development, local ownership and limits to occupation, etc.).

Contrary to fears, it was not a report that endorsed military interventions in the name of human security. The decision to intervene fell only to extreme cases where other measures, such as arms embargo, economic sanctions, diplomatic pressure, etc., had not been effective coercive measures. The report identified six criteria to justify military intervention: the right authority (obtained by the UN Security Council), a just cause of large scale loss of life or large scale ethnic cleansing, the right intention to halt or avert large scale human suffering, carried out as a last resort, with proportional means and reasonable prospects of success. Although the report intended to address the causes of conflict, making prevention the single most important dimension of the responsibility to protect, its reactive pillar received most attention due to timing. The launch of the report coincided with new security interests in the immediate aftermath of September 11, when world attention moved to the rapid reactive and preemptive strikes by the United States in Afghanistan and Iraq. The occupation of Iraq then led to even more suspicions of any doctrine that could be used to justify ill-conceived northern-led military interventions and ignore the fine lines of conditionalities and costs and benefits of intervention.

The timing of the post-September 11 world also led to a lukewarm reception of the April 2003 Report of the Global Commission on Human Security which had tried to argue for human security as public goods, especially for people in the aftermath of conflict situations, to be provided by states and communities instead of through military interventions by the international community. The Commission on Human Security (CHS), co-chaired by Sadako Ogata, former head of UNHCR, and Noble Prize laureate Amartya Sen had been created by the Japanese Government in 2001 as an attempt to examine new responsibilities with a focus on development communities and states. In its final Report, *Human Security Now*, the Commission described human security as the necessity to protect vital freedoms by building on people's strengths and aspirations (Sen's approach to capabilities), and protecting them from critical and pervasive threats and situations (Ogata's approach) (Commission on Human Security, 2003). The CHS had two ways of reconceptualizing security: one in a negative way, as the absence of threats to various core human values (such as survival, dignity and livelihoods), and the other in a positive way, as the opportunity to safeguard the 'vital core' of all human lives from critical pervasive threat without impeding long-term human development. Each word within the CHS definition was carefully chosen: safeguard required a protective approach – institutionalized not episodic; responsive not rigid; preventative not reactive. 'Vital core' referred to fundamental human rights, basic capabilities and absolute needs. Critical and pervasive threats referred to sudden, deep, large scale and recurrent, direct or indirect threats.

The Human Security Commission offered two general strategies for achieving human security: protection and empowerment, which were mutually reinforcing and required in most situations. The Commission's Report, though it received a lukewarm reception for its failure to add clarity to definition questions of human security, became the backbone of the largest trust fund in the history of the UN, established by the Japanese government to finance human security projects. It also gave an impetus for coordinated action among UN agencies and civil society organizations for advocating alternative understandings of security. Ultimately, it gave the Japanese Government a leading role in lobbying for alternative modalities of power distribution in the UN Security Council.

Capture by middle power states

Although the human security concept proposed to debunking state-centred security interests, it has primarily been adopted as a foreign policy tool by states (Canada, Norway, Japan), while civil society organizations have been slower in welcoming it on the global scene. It is also ironic that the few states that have adopted it have done so in their foreign policy mandate rather than their domestic national security or development agendas. What interest does human security serve as a foreign policy framework? From the specific perspective of the Canadian and Norwegian governments, human security represented an opportunity of enhancing their status and influence in the international arena (Suhrke, 1999: 268). Paris describes human security as the 'glue' holding together a coalition of 'middle power' states, development agencies and NGO, which together seek to adjust policy goals and resources (Paris, 2001: 88).

The reasons why some states have adopted human security as their foreign policy option, and others have not, are twofold. One is the dynamics of the state's domestic politics, and the other, the desire by elite sectors of society to adopt the policy as a way to enhance the role of their country on the international scene. Human security as foreign policy is an opportunity to draw attention to states with middle-power influence and status in the international arena. Yet, how can a people-centred approach to security be promoted by a state as foreign policy without becoming an interest-based agenda used as a vehicle for furthering national power, demonstrating as it does, the government's interest in the well-being of people of *other* states, rather than its own, especially given that the state in question pursues its own 'traditional' security concerns for itself. Japan presents a good example. While supporting a human security mandate for its Overseas Development Assistance (ODA), national military expenditures remained high and the country built a substantial nuclear power industry to reduce its reliance on imported oil. Although Japanese citizens were economically well taken care of, human rights practices such as racism and discrimination remained concerns in Japanese society as did the issue of capital punishment.

Ultimately, when human security is adopted as a government's diplomatic policy, and thus endorsed by the state, the paradigm is redefined so as to serve particular state-centred national interests. This has been the course taken by Canada and Norway, who have seen in the issue of human security an opportunity for 'middle-power' states to gain greater independence *vis-à-vis* international institutions, greater influence in the United Nations, and increased credibility on the international stage, particularly (in the case of Canada and Japan) *vis-à-vis* the United States. For Japan, a contribution of approximately $170 million to the Trust Fund for Human Security through the UN Secretariat cemented its status as a primary donor to Overseas Development Assistance and reinforced the country as an economic power, not only regionally but internationally. Through the Ottawa Process, Canada focused on gaining recognition for its handling of post-conflict situations as peacekeepers – an area in which it had already established a reputation. For Norway, international power lies above all in the promotion of powerful ideas (Suhrke, 1999). Thus, in essence, the differing focuses of Japan's and Canada's human security policies reflect different histories and attempts to capitalize on already-existing strengths and capabilities.

Japan: freedom from want

In December 1998, in the context of the 'Intellectual Dialogue on Building Asia's Tomorrow', Prime Minister Keizo Obuchi launched the Japanese programme on human security, citing it as a foreign policy based on 'comprehensively seizing all the menaces that threaten the survival, daily life and dignity of human beings and strengthening efforts to confront threats'. To add credibility to its initiative, Japan established a Commission on Human Security and set up the largest trust fund in the United Nations. Japan has been one of the leading countries to provide leadership and funding for human security, prompted by its desire to attain a permanent seat in the UN. The Japanese government endorsed the more comprehensive definition of human security based on 'Asian values' and greater focus on 'freedom from want'. The Japanese approach to human security promotes measures designed to protect people from threats to their livelihoods and dignity while supporting self-empowerment. Article 9 of the Japanese Constitution prohibits the use of force to solve disputes, leaving Japan with self-defence forces only for international security purposes. Japan hence used its engagement in developmental assistance as a way to circumvent its military limitations, while at the same time, playing an important economic role in the region in the aftermath of the 1997 crisis.

The Asian crisis began as a monetary crisis, quickly became a financial crisis, then broadened into a full-scale economic crisis that had socio-political consequences that threatened regional security – proof, if needed, of the inter-dependence of threats. The events of 1997 made the Japanese government aware of the fragility of the region's economic base and the need for Japan to play a greater role in stabilizing the area's economy by adopting a long-term agenda which the human security concept was in a position to provide. Through the trust fund, Japan also sought to open up the region, one that held out great economic promise with China's entry into the WTO, but which was also fraught with danger due to North Korean nuclear proliferation. The Japanese human security policy took as a model a ministerial-level programme which had proved successful in the area of ODA, and which was very popular with the Japanese public (Yeo, 2004). The Japanese diplomatic *Bluebook* claimed that human security, as defined by the CHS's *Human Security Now* report, was very similar to the concept of development assistance which Japan had been implementing. Yet, Japan's foreign aid, based on reciprocal agreements and reliance on multiple credit sources, has drawn criticism from those who see it as a way to promote Japan's own economic status. Furthermore, despite Japan's official claim that its foreign policy is based on human security, it continues to pursue traditional security interests in the region, especially since the beginning of the North Korean nuclear threat in 2002. Thus, the human security agenda in Japanese foreign policy is a complement and not a replacement of traditional security concerns. Nevertheless, the funding and leadership on human security issues provided by Japan has stimulated the emergence of programmes concerned with development especially in post-conflict situations.

Canada: freedom from fear

While initially criticizing the UNDP definition of human security as so all-inclusive as to render it 'an unwieldy policy instrument because of the breadth of its approach', Canada, as of 1996, concentrated on the goal of 'freedom from fear', calling for 'safety for people from both violent and non-violent threats [...] a condition characterized by freedom from pervasive threats to people's rights, their safety, or even their lives' (Axworthy, 1999). Much of Canada's interest can be attributed to the efforts of Lloyd Axworthy, Foreign Minister from 1996 to 2000, who recognized the need to revamp Canada's foreign policy with new measures needed to deal with post-Cold War problems: the situation of children caught in the war zones, the dangers of terrorism, the increase in drug traffic, and the circulation of arms. He called for addressing these issues through rapid humanitarianism-inspired interventions for which responsibility would be shared. Canada's adoption of the human security concept was considered by some as an attempt to rescue the country from military irrelevance. As a middle power with limited military capacity, Canada had to carve out for itself an international role so as to stand apart from its powerful neighbour in the south. The inclusion of human security in the foreign policy agenda was an attempt to combine a strong tradition of non-intervention with the ambition of playing a more important role in international affairs, while at the same time reducing threats to its own security by curbing immigration. Canada's stance was also taken in response to the pressures exercised by a broad coalition of NGOs that, in formal partnership with the government and through Axworthy's efforts, successfully lobbied for the adoption of the treaty banning landmines and for the creation of the ICC.

Canada's human security policy is based on five priorities: (a) public safety (building international expertise with the capacity to counter growing cross-border threats posed by terrorism, drug trafficking and spread of crime); (b) protection of civilians (establishment of legal norms, reduction of the human costs of armed conflict, human rights field operations, and deployment of military forces in extreme situations to control atrocities and war crimes; (c) conflict prevention (strengthening the capacity of the international community to resolve violent conflicts, building national and local capacity to manage political and social tensions without resorting to violence, by using targeted economic sanctions to reduce the chances of civil war breaking out); (d) governance and accountability (fostering improved accountability of public and private sector institutions, with emphasis on building an effective International Criminal Court (ICC) and promoting reform of security institutions including military, policy and judiciary, reducing corruption, promoting freedom of expression and encouraging corporate social responsibility), and (e) peace support operations (bolstering international capacity to undertake peace missions, dealing with issues related to women, providing policy and civil experts to undertake complex missions). To reach these objectives, the Canadian government launched a human security programme for the amount of $10 million per year until 2010.

A human security agenda allowed Canada to play a leading role in the campaign banning the deployment of landmines; the Ottawa Process, which led in December of 1997 to the signing by 122 countries of the 'Ottawa Convention on the Prohibition, Use, Stockpiling, Production and Transfer of Anti-Personnel Landmines and their Destruction'. Other results were the creation of the International Criminal Court, the Kimberley Process on conflicts in the diamond trade, and the launching of the International Commission on State Sovereignty and Intervention with its landmark report, *Responsibility to Protect*, which addressed some of the criticisms of the interventionist elements of its 'freedom from fear' approach.

Table 1.2 summarizes the various definitions used by international organizations and states in terms of the values and strategies that they propose.

Table 1.2 Comparing political definitions of human security

Who?	Definition	Values, angle, focus	Conception of threats	Usability potential (purpose of definition)	Strategies
CHS	To protect the vital core of all human lives in ways that enhance human freedoms and human fulfillment. The authors also acknowledge that this definition might vary across cultures: 'The vital core of life is a set of elementary rights and freedoms people enjoy. What people consider "vital" … varies across individuals and societies.'	Survival, livelihood and dignity (freedom from fear, want and a life of dignity).	Protecting people from critical (severe) and pervasive (widespread) threats and situations. Joint focus on poverty and violence.	Political agenda, 'operationalization'	Making such freedoms possible requires protection from critical and pervasive threats and empowerment, i.e. building people's strengths and aspirations. This needs to take place in the political, social, environmental, economic, military and cultural spheres of life.

UNDP 94 definition	Safely from such chronic threats as hunger, disease and repression and protection from sudden and hurtful disruptions in the patterns of daily life, whether in homes, jobs or communities.	Freedom from want, freedom from fear.	Includes 7 components: economic, food, health, environmental, personal, community, and political security.	Peace dividend.	Coordinated action by states, international community and people's groups.
Government of Canada	'Freedom from pervasive threats to people's rights safety or lives'.	Focus on freedom from fear. Rights, safety, Lives.	Truly people-focused, but with no major revolution in the definition and lists of threats, those being somewhat traditional: armed conflict violence, human rights abuses, public insecurity and organized crime.	Lessen impact of conflict on people, ban on landmines, creation of a criminal court, protection of civilians and reduction of the costs of conflict: – peace operations viewed as human security missions – conflict prevention – good governance and political accountability as part of the basic human rights aspects of the concept of public safety.	Public safety, protection of people, conflict prevention; governance and accountability; peace support operations; small arms and light weapons; international plan of action; humanitarian intervention; responsibility to protect; international campaign to ban landmines; Ottawa Coalition.

Table 1.2 (Continued)

Who?	Definition	Values, angle, focus	Conception of threats	Usability potential (purpose of definition)	Strategies
Government of Japan	'Comprehensively seizing all the menaces that threaten the survival, daily life and dignity of human beings and to strengthen the efforts to confront threats.'	Freedom from fear and want: lives, livelihoods, dignity.	Poverty, environmental degradation, illicit drugs, transnational organized crime, infectious diseases such as HIV/AIDS, the outflow of refugees, etc. The focus is thus primarily on physical and material well-being.	To offer durable solutions for the region in the aftermath of the Asian financial Crisis. To emphasize a set of goals that seemed compatible with so-called Asian values.	Concentrated on protection from threats to livelihoods, dignity and everyday life, and sought empowerment to bring out the potential (capabilities, empowerment).

For the 'South': a nemesis from the north or an appropriate paradigm?

It is unfortunate that the so-called southern countries, especially the G77 group, express criticisms against the human security paradigm, fearing it as a tool for the West to impose its values and order and for big powers to justify their interventions abroad. In their views, instead of being implemented as a tool for a new global social contract to protect individuals, it seems to have served mainly as an excuse for intervention. Southern countries also particularly fear that human security might be used as a new conditionality for receiving aid. In this case, they point to the hypocrisy of double standards, as human security will become a measuring rod against which only recipients of aid would be judged. The fact that it proposes to be debated within the General Assembly as part of the general framework of the responsibility to protect also adds to the fear of the South.

Yet, the advent of human security should be seen, instead, as the triumph of the South to put development concerns into global security discussions. It can be seen as a continuation of the historical concerns and interests of the South within international relations and organizations. The popularization of development economics after the mid-1970s was in response to the collective demand by developing countries, who, under the banner of Group of 77 in the United Nations, demanded more equitable terms of trade at the international level. It was emphasized that differences in power and wealth, steeped in history, would lead to 'perpetual inequality' (Tucker, 1977: 3). Connections between underdevelopment and security were already at the heart of the demands of the South which argued that a more stable and just world order warranted a search for new ideas to match their needs, and some level of equity, safety and rights could be building blocks for such a construction. The intellectual response from the emerging international community came in the form of the North-South Report by an Independent North/South Commission chaired by Willy Brandt, that stated:

> Our Report is based on what appears to be the simplest common interest: that mankind wants to survive, and one might even add has the moral obligation to survive. This raises not only traditional questions of peace and war, but also how to overcome world hunger, mass misery and alarming disparities between the living conditions of rich and poor.
>
> (Independent Commission on International Development Issues: Brandt Report, 1980: 13)

The underlying focus was that hunger, economic crisis and terrorism led to the breakdown of peace as much as military aggression. This was followed by the Independent Commission on Disarmament and Security chaired by Olaf Palme, that raised the question of morality in the international economic and political systems, again placing threats other than military ones on the table, especially in the Third World, where they argued that hunger and poverty were immediate challenges for survival (Independent Commission on Disarmament and Security Issues. Common Security: A Blueprint for Survival, 1982: 172*)*.

These reports indicated that traditional security, especially in the South, was not providing the security necessary for development. They called for common security, a concept that was largely ignored at the time of divided international alliances behind the two rival super powers, the Soviet Union and the USA. In the meantime, between the two confrontationist ideologies of the superpowers was a third voice – softer, if not ignored in the international realm – that of the group of Third World countries that had joined together in the late 1960s as the Non-Aligned Movement (NAM) – a movement of ex-colonial countries like India, Indonesia, Egypt and others that looked for international space and assertion of independent foreign policy away from the military blocs and superpower politics. Jawaharlal Nehru, India's first prime minister and a key figure behind NAM, had argued that: 'Security can be obtained in many ways. The normal plea is that armies protect security. This is only partly true; it is equally true that security is protected by policies' (Nehru, 1961). Since the non-aligned countries at that conjuncture were experimenting with independent development, and looked for a 'middle path', they were not looked upon favourably by Western powers, who felt that their independence drew them into the Soviet camp. The Soviet Union, on its part, was happy to provide them the aid and assistance they required for key projects. In the realm of international relations, given their relative lack of military strength, the NAM however exercised little more than an independent yet moral voice, often lost in the reverberations of Cold War rhetoric of the superpowers.

However, it was from these voices that the concept of development, the need for solutions to the problems of the South, and non-military security gradually emerged. Fora formed by these nations within the United Nations, like the G77 that gradually expanded as more countries became independent, asked for a North-South dialogue and lobbied for more equitable development moving beyond war and peace. By the early 1990s, the South Commission, chaired by Julius Nyerere, argued in its report *Challenge to the South* that insecurity stemmed from poverty, de-institutionalization, environmental degradation and deficit of democracy (South Commission, 1990: 11).

Yet, when the UNDP proposed a human security approach to the peace dividend, the G77 countries rejected the 1994 report for fear of intervention and as a reinforcement of the North-South divide. To many G77 countries, human security is seen as yet another conditionality that poses a moral challenge to state sovereignty and its role by threatening intervention by the international community on behalf of the people. Its focus on the individual has created discomfort for proponents of the societal values of the Asian Model of Development, while others fear a double standard usage, where rich Western nations would use human security as punitive measure against developing countries, without abiding by it themselves. For many G77 countries, human security is yet another ethnocentric paradigm that emphasizes subjective aspects and values while reinforcing the economic might of the North, another attempt by the West to impose its liberal values and political institutions on non-Western societies. Their alarm is especially compounded by the liberal view that economic and social underdevelopment in the South will breed political instability or spill over to the North, which will require further militarization, as has been witnessed in the current global war against terrorism. They argue that it is precisely this security dilemma and militarization that threatens a South already weakened by interventions, economic sanctions and debt crises.

Despite the fears, however, human security is exactly the paradigm needed for the South today, and it would be best divorced from the notion of 'responsibility to protect' as the prerogative of northern states bent on military interventions. As this book will argue further, a human security approach for the South would allow it to shed international light on the concerns of underdevelopment and individual dignity at a time when state-based interests are increasingly being used in the global war against terrorism. Rallying around a human security agenda would be an alternative to two positions: first to promote multilateralism and networking among like-minded countries to combat unilateral actions by states such as the US, and second, to define new threats such as poverty, diseases, lack of education, the culture of impunity, uncontrolled population movements, global warming, small arms, etc., on the global agenda as alternatives to the current over-focus on terrorism, WMDs and threats emanating from so-called 'rogue states'. These kinds of discussions would equalize the voice of the South and the North. It is not only the South that is dangerous, but the North also has a large responsibility to curb its dangerous practices, such as the arms trade, pollution inducing industrialization, etc. For southern countries, global discussion on human insecurities, emanating not only from failed states, but also from such non-traditional threats as HIV/ AIDs, natural calamities, uncontrolled population movements, massive under-development and poverty is an imperative. After all, people are more threatened by so-called 'soft' threats in their everyday lives than 'hard' threats such as being attacked by terrorists or with weapons of mass destruction. Conflicts in the South are also increasingly of a private and criminal nature. As such, they are not solved by mere political agreements of power-sharing, but through considering economic and social factors that can curb the opportunities that conflicts provide for entrepreneurs of war. As stressed by Mahbub ul-Haq, human security is a means to instituting a:

> new partnership between the North and the South based on justice not on charity; on an equitable sharing of global market opportunities, not on aid; on two-way compacts, not one-way transfers: on mutual cooperation, not on unilateral conditionally or confrontation.
>
> (Ul Haq, 1998:5)

Ultimately, with all kinds of insecurities in their back yards, the so-called global South needs to take a collective decision about what the main insecurity threats are today and how they can be prevented. It cannot afford to reject the paradigm on the basis of its provenance from other spaces. At a time when the global security discourses are becoming more realist, and political agendas, driven by the war against terrorism and WMDs, mean that resources are being diverted from development priorities to geo-strategic and national interests in wars over oil, the South should take up this opportunity to challenge priorities. When aid and national budgets are diverted to the war on terrorism at the expense of the war on poverty and development goals, the question is, can the South and the North afford such a view of state, national and international security *vis-à-vis* their obligations towards their populations?

Conclusion

In conclusion, the concept of human security on the global political scene has been adopted by various organizations to conform to different political agendas. International organizations and commissions have used their moral authority to encourage states to improve their citizens' lives. They have sought to revive collective and individual conscience. Yet, as Grayson, trying to find a 'workable' definition for human security is a question of politics and search for power (Grayson, 2004). In fact, endorsement of well-defined acceptances of human security by Canada (freedom from fear) and Japan (freedom from want) was determined by policy-utility. While Canadian conception of human security as 'freedom from fear' and the focus on human rights served as justification for interventionist foreign policy, Japanese support for human security as 'freedom from want', which concentrates on human development, had the advantage of allowing the pursuit of economic interests without confronting Asian systematic opposition to Westernized human rights.

Making a concept applicable to reality means allowing prioritization and distribution of resources; in one word, shaping a political agenda. This is perhaps why some organizations, like the OSCE, have shied away from adopting the concept: It would mean reflecting it in priorities, then budgeting, etc., and finding mechanisms for monitoring. At the same time, choosing a broad definition for human security can also be politically oriented: international organizations such as the UN or UNDP, because they gather states that represent people with different concerns, had to include all kinds of threats in their agendas. This universal rationale is exemplified by the High-Level Panel on Threats, Challenges and Change's claim that all threats have to find mutual recognition and should be equally addressed by the UN in order to avoid all feeling of discrimination and double-standard agenda (High-Level Panel on Threats, Challenges and Change, 2004: 12).

2   Definitions, critiques and counter-critiques

If human security first saw light within international organizations, and then states, it has increasingly become a subject of interest in the academic world, where it does not suffer from a deficit of definitions. Defining it has been an art reminiscent of the blind men who each tried to describe an elephant according to the part they were able to feel. An elephant was described as a long narrow soft column by the one who had touched the trunk, a massive circular bulk by he who had felt its body and a hard pointed objected by the blind man who had felt the ivory. The myriad of academic definitions on human security, and the fact that one definition has not been coined so far, similarly reinforces the view that the 'truth' about the definition is in the eyes of the beholder.

Proponents of a broad definition in the meantime argue that instead of lamenting the lack of definitions, research should be concerned with what the act of defining within security studies inherently says about power relations based on political, moral and ethical choices. The lack of an agreed-upon definition is not a conceptual weakness but represents a refusal to succumb to the dominant 'political trappings of the disciplines' definitional project' (Grayson, 2004: 357). A broad definition is, therefore, critical to transforming the ethos, raising questions that are peripheral to security studies and encouraging comprehensive measures to be applied to issues that affect the everyday lives of people, subjective as they may be, but of paramount importance. If security is ultimately a feeling, then human security must be a felt experience.

The art of definitions

What is human security in the final analysis and why are there so many definitions and critics?

The simplest definition of security is 'absence of insecurity and threats', i.e. freedom from both 'fear' (of physical, sexual or psychological abuse, violence, persecution, or death) and 'want' (of gainful employment, food, and health). Human security, therefore, deals with the capacity to identify threats, to avoid them when possible, and to mitigate their effects when they do occur. This broadened use of the word 'security' encompasses two ideas: one is the notion of 'safety' that goes beyond the concept of mere physical security in the traditional sense, and the other, the idea that people's livelihoods should be guaranteed against sudden disruptions. Defining human security therefore begins with its juxtaposition with the traditional stato-centric definition of 'security' from the realist and neo-realist school. A simplified table (Table 2.1) can illustrate the differences between a state-centred and a human-centred approach to security.

Scholars and policy makers have variously viewed human security as: (a) an attractive idea but lacking analytical rigor; (b) limited to a narrowly conceived definition; and (c) an essential tool for understanding contemporary challenges to people's well-being and dignity. Among academics, the debate is, first, between the proponents and detractors of human security, and second, between a narrow, as opposed to a broad conceptual theorization of human security.

In 2004, to mark ten years of definitional deliberations on the concept of human security, the journal *Security Dialogue* brought together 21 of the most vocal academics who had expressed their opinions on the subject. The results were published in a special issue devoted to the question of 'What is human security?'. Box 2.1 classifies the various definitions of these authors according to their opinions on the academic usability, the political implementations and the possible strategies that were identified.

The minimalist (narrow)/maximalist (broad) debate

Stoett's gradient of minimalist to maximalist definitions illustrates the vastness and complexity of the human security debate (Stoett, 1999). Using the maximum/minimum gradient, Figure 2.1 presents an attempt to class some of the better known definitions of human security in relationship each other based on the characteristics that distinguish them.

Listed vertically at each end of the spectrum are different traits a definition is more likely to reflect, being located nearer either end of the scale. A definition located nearer the centre can be considered to reflect all or some of these aspects in varying degrees. How much each definition incorporates the language of fear/want/dignity can be read according to the horizontal measure at the top of the frame. The measure is cumulative. Thus, for example, the Toda definition is understood to be based on the language of fear, as well as want, as well as dignity, and not solely on dignity. Along the horizontal measure at the bottom of the frame, a cumulative measure indicates the referents or actors any definition is likely to incorporate. Because the scale is again cumulative, it can also be understood as measuring the degree to which a definition focuses on empowerment of the individual.

The most minimalist approach to human security, i.e. 'freedom from fear', seeks to ensure individuals' safety from direct threat, their physical integrity and satisfaction of basic needs. Threats to be addressed remain relatively traditional: armed conflict, human rights abuses, public insecurity and organized crime. Such a narrow definition is justified by its analytical quality and its policy-applicability, in opposition to the all-encompassing definition of human security that is deemed to be a useless 'shopping list of threats' (Krause, 2004).

Table 2.1 State versus human-centred security compared

	State-centred security (a neo-realist vision)	Human-centred security
Security referent (object)	In a Hobbesian world, the state is the primary provider of security: if the state is secure, then those who live within it are also secure.	Individuals are co-equal with the sate. State security is the means, not the end.
Security value	Sovereignty, power, territorial integrity, national independence.	Personal safety, well-being and individual freedom: 1 Physical safety and provision for basic needs; 2 Personal freedom (liberty of association); 3 Human rights; economic and social rights.
Security threats	Direct organized violence from other states, violence and coercion by other states and from non-state actors.	Direct violence: death, drugs, dehumanization, discrimination, international disputes, WMD; gendered violence. Indirect violence: deprivation, disease, natural disasters, underdevelopment, population displacement, environmental degradation, poverty, inequality, ethnic/sectarian oppression. Threats from identifiable sources (such as states or non-state actors) or from structural sources (relations of power ranging from family to the global economy).
By what means	Retaliatory force or threat of its use, balance of power, military means, strengthening of economic might, little attention paid to respect for law or institutions.	Promoting human development: basic needs plus equity, sustainability, and greater democratization and participation at all levels. Promoting human rights. Promoting political development: global norms and institutions plus collective use of force as well as sanctions in case of genocide, cooperation between states, reliance on international institutions, networks and coalitions, and international organizations.

Source: Author's chart adapted from Bajpai, 2000.

Box 2.1   Classification of academic definitions of human security

Amitav Acharya

Acharya argues that we need to avoid casting the HS debate within the existing paradigms of IR. Instead, HS is in itself a holistic paradigm which offers opportunities for creative synthesis and theoretical eclecticism. As for its policy utility, the concept addresses issues that the narrow definition of security no longer reflects in terms of real world developments. 'Governments can no longer survive – much less achieve legitimacy – solely by addressing economic growth; nor can they maintain social and political stability solely by providing for defense against external military threats. Democratization empowers new actors, such as civil society, that must be accounted for in the security framework'.

Sabina Alkire

As one of the theorists of the Commission of Human Security, she crafted their conceptual definition 'to protect the vital core of all human lives in ways that advance human freedoms and human fulfillment'. The definition disciplines the content of human security by focusing only on the 'vital core' – the 'freedoms that are the essence of life' – and by selecting only critical (severe) and pervasive (widespread) threats. Yet, while the concept aims at creating a viable security framework to allow for policy responses to non-state threats, defining clear policy priorities is needed.

Lloyd Axworthy

While national and HS interests are complementary, the challenge lies in finding the meeting place 'between global rights and national interests'. 'This kind of security is based on the emerging, growing body of law and practice that establishes the authority of international humanitarian standards to challenge the supremacy of national state sovereignty – a fundamental shift from the state-based balance of power of the Cold War.' Policy-wise, viewing concerns from those focused on national interests to those affecting the individual offers a different lens through which to understand and implement policy. The concept recognizes the inter-connectiveness of our security on that of our neighbours on the one hand, and the fact that basic rights of people are fundamental to world stability on the other. The development of HS science and governance solutions must be based on thorough research, training and education in a cross-cultural context.

Kanti Bajpai

Threats to security and capacities to deal with them vary according to time, so a universalist conceptual definition is a misguided idea. HS study as a policy science must focus on audits of threats and possible responses. Having commissioned a yet unpublished public opinion survey among 10,000 people in India on national and human security and how insecure Indians feel, Bajpai proposes to draw a Human Security Index based on eleven measures of threats.

Barry Buzan

No clear analytical value is derived from the concept of HS which confuses international security with social security and civil liberties. HS thus presents a reductionist vision of international security and hence has limited academic usability. The concept collapses the differences between international and domestic security agendas without analysing existing linkages. Yet, the concept may allow for discussion of human rights issues which were previously considered sensitive, but this amounts to little more than 'political pandering'.

Paul Evans

HS highlights issues of state responsibilities, sovereignty and intervention. Reconciling national security and development is necessary in developing countries. Individual must be at least one of the referent points for determining security for whom, from what and by what means.

Kyle Grayson

The act of definition is an act of power which marginalizes some and empowers others. As no workable definition exists, HS enables broader and deeper questioning of subjects usually and unjustifiably peripheral to security studies. HS ultimately subverts the power relationship upheld by security studies in order to question the legitimacy of established paradigms. HS makes new, different and better policy orientations possible by including options that were excluded before.

Don Hubert

Definitional issues are unlikely to be resolved but should not stand in the way of effective international action to improve HS. Lack of agreed definition may however impede scholarly work. The major moral question relates to the legitimacy of international intervention or military action against atrocities such as genocide. The concept has both policy relevance and policy impact, for instance, it was successfully used for advocating the banning of landmines and establishment of the ICC.

Keith Krause

Krause advocates for a focus on freedom from fear because a) broad definition is simply an itemized wish-list, and b) there are no clear gains from linking security and development. Thus, the narrow definition of HS allows for clear policy goals and actions to combat direct threats to the individual (such as organized violence).

Jennifer Leanning

For Leanning, the concept of HS includes social, psychological, political, and economic factors and encompasses psychosocial needs and individuals' relationships with location, community and time. In addition to basic needs like food, water and shelter, and a degree of protection, people also have psycho-social needs such as identity, participation, and autonomy, for which they need a home, identity, a network of social and family support, and relationships with time (an acceptance of the past and a positive grasp of the future). It is therefore important to define and measure HS at the local level and to develop models of early warning and evaluation.

P. H. Liotta

The multiplicity of conflicting issues should not lead to dismissal of the concept but to an examination of what forms of security are 'relevant and right' at community, state, regional and global levels. HS is an attractive mandate for middle power governments.

Keith Macfarlane

There exists no intrinsic reason to favour broad definitions and no analytical value or normative traction in re-labeling human development as HS. The wider definition makes the establishment of policy priorities difficult. Narrower protection-focused definitions have had more success in implementation of agenda.

Andrew Mack

According to Mack, 'if the term "insecurity" embraces almost all forms of harm to individuals – from affronts to dignity to genocide – it loses any real descriptive power. Any definition that conflates dependent and independent variables renders causal analysis virtually impossible. A concept that aspires to explain almost everything in reality explains nothing'. While a broad definition of the concept may not have analytical value, Mack nevertheless sees value in broadening the security referent away from the state. If it is states that threaten citizens, how can they also protect them? Ultimately, the concept indicates shared political and moral values between diverse groups of actors.

Edward Newman

HS highlights what traditional views of security leave out, which is a useful normative project. Yet, a broad definition of HS may not be useful because it generates an unworkable number of variables. Much human insecurity results from structural issues, beyond the influence of individuals. Human security holds normative implications for the evolution of state security, especially, 'conditional security': 'the international legitimacy of state sovereignty rests not only on control of territory, but also upon fulfilling certain standards of human rights and welfare for citizens'.

Osler Hampson

Hampson classifies the various definitions of Human Security into a triangle of 'freedoms: Natural rights/rule of law, humanitarian concerns and sustainable development'. 1) Natural rights/rule of law, based on fundamental liberal assumption of basic individual rights to live, liberty and purpose of happiness and international community's responsibility to provide this and promote it. 2) Humanitarians: International efforts for war crime, intervention, protection, peace building and conflict prevention. 3) Sustainable Development: survival and health of individuals. He argues that improved research efforts are critical in order to provide effective guidance to IO/ NGO and national governments seeking to incorporate HS into their agendas. Effective action to improve HS must address the restructuring of legal, political and economic institutions.

Rolland Paris

The HS discourse is currently dominated by 'circular discussion' deliberating definition. Yet, the vagueness is very problematic for academic study given the inability to analytically separate the components of the concept, rendering a determination of causal relationships impossible. Ultimately, the vagueness of the definition serves a political purpose in uniting diverse coalition of actors.

Astri Suhrke

Suhrke argues that HS has been a useful tool for middle powers (such as, Canada and Norway) and the countries that form the Human Security Network. As an agenda, however, it has been crowded out of the international forum by post-9/11 concerns over terrorism. Academic interests were generated as a result of funding provided by the policy community as well as new interest in an emerging concept. Whether that interest will survive however remains unclear. 'The critical question for survival is hardly definitional coherence or strong disciplinary anchors. Rather, at issue is whether an academic discourse in a policy-related area can mobilize sufficient resources and intellectual momentum to sustain itself independently of the shifting priorities of states'.

Ramesh Thakur

Human security is improved when the 'quality of life' of people in a society can be upgraded, that is, the enhancing of what he calls 'human welfare'. It is threatened when this 'quality of life', which is left open to definition, is degraded by threats such as unchecked demographic growth, diminished resources and scarcity, or access issues, and other global reaching threats. The reformulation of national security into HS has 'profound consequences' for international relations, foreign policy and people's conception of other peoples and cultures. Traditional security conception privileges military in terms of resource allocation but non-traditional concerns merit the gravity of the security label.

Caroline Thomas

Human security is an integrative concept allowing for bridging and interconnection of sector specific threats to people in the international system, rather than states. For Thomas, HS means the provision of basic material needs and realization of human dignity, including emancipation from oppressive power structures, global, national or local in origin or scope. A distinction is made between quantitative aspects of HS, which are the basic needs (food, shelter, healthcare and education), and the qualitative aspects, encompassing dignity: personal autonomy, control over one's life, participation in the community, chance and opportunities. The concept provides a language and rationale for raising the concerns of the majority of humanity. The ultimate utility of the concept is in the practical application of knowledge to interconnections between threats. For policy purposes, bottoms-up participatory approaches to politics are necessary.

Peter Uvin

HS provides a bridge between humanitarian relief, development assistance, human rights advocacy and conflict resolution and allows for insights and strategies about the overlaps and intersections between these fields. 'Increasingly, scholars and practitioners from different professional disciplines are seeking to go outside the confines of their usual professional boxes to develop a better understanding of the relations between the different fields of social change.'

Donna Winslow and Thomas Hylland Eriksen

As anthropologists, they do not limit their definition to the 'traditional' definition of human security as freedom from fear and freedom from want. Rather, they examine 'how security is defined in different social and cultural contexts, through symbolic and social processes, and how security and insecurity are dealt with through social institutions'. Because security in HS is not a static concept, it offers potential for new theories to make it possible to examine processes of signification and meaning in relation to other issues, 'thereby connecting the quest for security to issues of identity'.

Source: Based on these authors' expressing their views on the definitions, academic and policy utility of human security in *Security Dialogue* vol. 35, no. 3, September 2004.

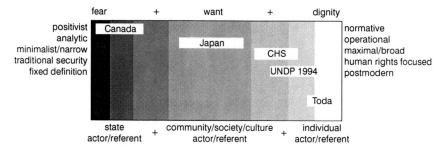

Figure 2.1 Definitional mapping tool.

Canada endorses this understanding of human security and defends 'freedom from pervasive threats to people's rights, safety or lives'. The December 2001 Report of the International Commission on Intervention and State Sovereignty, *A Responsibility to Protect* also defends this narrower view of human security, based on direct physical violence organized around a classical epistemology of threats as open conflict and war: 'The fundamental components of human security – the security of people against threats to life, health, livelihood, personal safety and human dignity – can be put at risk by external aggression, but also by factors within a country, including "security forces"' (ICISS, 2001: 15). Authors such as Krause, Mack, and MacFarlane also advocate the narrow concept for reasons of conceptual clarity and analytic rigour. Krause supports the human security concept as a key to a powerful agenda, but wants it limited to freedom from fear, since including freedom from want would make it an endless list, a 'potential laundry of bad things that can happen'. For instance, he does not understand why explaining illiteracy as human security should be helping policy formulation (Krause, 2004: 367). Freedom from fear, on the other hand seems to him a coherent and manageable agenda, which has an intellectual tradition that rests on Weber and Hobbes and on limited institutions that can make safety their mandate. MacFarlane similarly opposes broadening of security since it would makes prioritization difficult and ultimately unmanageable (Macfarlane, 2004: 368). For Mack, the concept is less an analytical concept than a signifier of shared political and moral values (Mack, 2004: 366). For Murray and King, the 'essential' elements are those that are: 'important enough for human beings to fight over or to put their lives or property at greater risk' (King and Murray, 2001).

The broadest category of definitions adds 'a life of dignity' to 'freedom from want and fear'. Defended by the Human Security Network as well as UNDP, the combination of security, development and dignity encompasses both material and quantitative aspects of human security. The rationale behind the Japanese view of human security, for example, 'preservation and protection of the life and dignity of individual human being', is the essential indivisibility of human security components, the presence of a wide range of non-classical issues affecting individuals and the interconnectedness of threats (individuals' insecurity causes global instability). Japan thus underlined the need of a malleable cultural definition of the 'vital core of all human lives' to make the concept adaptable to Asian values and not a replica of the Western human rights agenda.

Academics supporting the broad view of human security recognize the maximalist definition with its added value including going beyond classical violent threats. MacLean highlights for example that

> human security does not merely 'envelope' matters of individual benefit (such as education, health care, protection from crime, and the like) [...] but rather denotes protection from the *unstructured violence* that often accompanies many aspects of non-territorial security, such as violence emanating from environmental scarcity, or mass migration.
>
> (MacLean, 2002)

Supporters of the broad conception, exemplified by the 1994 UNDP definition and embraced by the government of Japan, include academics such as Leaning, Alkire, Thakur, Axworthy, Bajpai, Hampson, Winslow and Eriksen, as well as Kofi Annan. For Jennifer Leaning, the concept 'includes the social, psychological, political and economic factors that promote and protect human well being through time' (Leaning, 2004: 354). Thakur refers to human security as 'the quality of life of the people of a society or polity. Anything which degrades their quality of life – demographic pressures, diminished access to or stock of resources, and so on – is a security threat' (Thakur, 2004: 348). Similarly, Acharya bases his understanding on the human costs of violent conflict and the need to focus on human needs and the rights dimension, that may be a base for conflicts but are not the only reason for accepting human security (Acharya, 2004: 355). Uvin believes that there is 'urgent need for insights and strategies about the overlaps and interactions between the fields of humanitarianism, development, human rights and conflict resolutions (Uvin, 2004: 352).

To their proponents, broad definitions also provide 'integrated solution for multifaceted issues' (Hampson, 2004), and imply useful inter-disciplinary dialogue. The Commission on Human Security thus proposed a more expansive and maximalist definition of human security around 'a vital core of all human lives' in the *Human Security Now* report of 2003, enlarging the concept to a new epistemology of threats and structural forms of violence, i.e. 'violence built in the structure and [showing] up as unequal power and consequently unequal life chances' (Galtung, 1969), as well as structural inequalities and distributional injustices. Structural inequalities and distributive justice issues are well-beyond pure direct violence and military threats according to the Commission on Human Security, which calls for instance for the reform of intellectual property rights regimes on pharmaceuticals, arguing that these regimes lead, in developing countries especially, to major health problems which can be seen as built into the structure, thus being threats to global human security issues.

Converging definitions

The various definitions of human security differ according to the nature of threats, values and priorities to be pursued, and strategies for prevention, yet, there are commonalities to be found, the foremost being that security is seen beyond the prerogative of the State, but as that of individuals within them. Second is the interdependence between the security of individuals and that of systems. Human beings therefore become a point of national and global interests. Third is the expansion of the notion of violence, which goes beyond physical threats to such outcomes as extreme under-nourishment, human rights abuses, etc., echoing the structural violence in the writings of Galtung. To traditional threats of conflict, violence, nuclear weapons, military threats and terrorism are added non-traditional ones, i.e. economic, social, environmental, etc., in other words, quality of life.

Hampson's *Madness in Multitude* analyses the various definitions of human security as built on three distinct pillars: the natural rights/rule of law approach, the safety of people/humanitarianism approach and the sustainable development approach. The 'human rights' view, focusing on universal, inalienable 'natural rights', presupposes the protection and promotion of human rights an obligation of the international community, linked as it is with international security. The question of minority rights is an important and much contested aspect of this approach. An example of the advancement of human security under the banner of human rights is the building of international institutions such as the ICC – but this approach remains quite focused on national-level human rights law. Threats are considered in terms of the absence or the violations of norms, laws and codes. The safety of people approach focuses on people in conflicts, emergencies and situations of 'dire need'. It is also called the 'humanitarian approach', because it focuses on international law in order for the international community to take charge in situations of genocides, war crimes and humanitarian crisis. It is a conflict-based approach and stems from international efforts to set norms and limits to wartime behaviour and the effects of conflicts on civilians. And, perhaps most importantly, it is an interventionist approach as it paves the way for the internationally legal use of force to ensure the safety of peoples. This is obviously a very contentious path as some arguments insist that interventions, be they military or non-military, can in fact exacerbate conflicts rather than resolve them or alleviate their harm. Some branches have begun to consider the need for economic and structural causes of war to be assessed. In this way the UN recognized that 'non-military threats sources of instability in the economic, social, humanitarian, and ecological fields have become threats to peace and security' (1992 Security Council).

The economic interpretation of human security is an offshoot of economic and developmental studies that have established the efficacy of the market and the fact that the welfare state is not economically viable except in post-industrialized countries and cash-rich oil states. Yet, the restructuring of several welfare states under International Monetary Fund and World Bank guidelines have resulted in a worldwide community of transition states that are rapidly privatizing, and thereby, causing economic disruption, namely, unemployment and reduction in state benefits. These have caused widespread economic distress and insecurity by seriously jeopardizing livelihood options and thus denying many a life of fair means of survival with dignity. Human insecurities are thus classified into various types corresponding to the various aspects of life affected by them. These are economic, food, good health, employment, personal security/safety, dignity, cultural integrity, environment, and political security. This approach is considered to be consistent with the UNDP report. It differs radically from the other approaches as it seeks to construct human security on broad and comprehensive terms which go beyond human rights violations to wide aspects of underdevelopment, inequality, disease, international crime, population growth and environmental degradation for example. One of the key features of this approach is its marginalization of military matters and the emphasis placed on sustainable development as being crucial to global security. As opposed to jurisdiction and intervention, this approach focuses on development, distribution and social justice and the means to ensure people's security. Under this approach, the other categories are blurred: the right to development becomes a human right; health becomes a security priority; refugee flows become an international responsibility.

Visualizing human security

Hampson sums up the various definitions as triangular interrelations, resting on three interconnected pillars: 'safety of people (freedom from fear) – equity and social justice (freedom from want) – rights and rule of law (liberty)' whose communion might be achieved through conflict prevention, human development and human rights. The three variables depend on each other to exist, expand, and probably, even act. Hampson's trident is directly linked to the CHS's concerns for values: survival, quality of daily life and dignity. The broadest way of looking at HS seeks to ensure that people have the security to *live* – beyond the ceasefire, beyond the next ration of rice, etc. A want-based or development-based approach focuses on subsistence: keeping people alive with the minimum of provisions; it is a relatively long-term form of being. Adding security to a want-based approach brings in *survival*, especially with regard to sudden downturns such as conflicts and economic crises. Pure existence not being enough, people also need to have dignity, livelihood and enjoyment as well as survival. The concept of universal *dignity* is perhaps the most contested value within this definition – perhaps one that ultimately distinguishes human security as a fresh concept.

Yet, by categorizing each as an angle for entry point, however, Hampson does not explain the relationships between them, nor the interlinkages. As it is apparent above, most definitions end up being associated with the broadest SHD approach

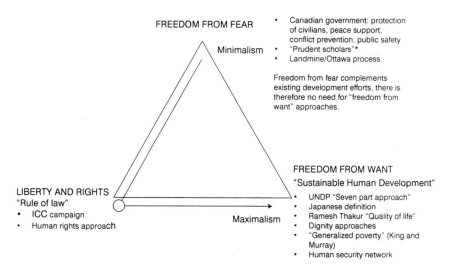

FREEDOM FROM FEAR

Minimalism

- Canadian government: protection of civilians, peace support, conflict prevention, public safety
- "Prudent scholars"*
- Landmine/Ottawa process

Freedom from fear complements existing development efforts, there is therefore no need for "freedom from want" approaches.

LIBERTY AND RIGHTS
"Rule of law"
- ICC campaign
- Human rights approach

Maximalism

FREEDOM FROM WANT
"Sustainable Human Development"
- UNDP "Seven part approach"
- Japanese definition
- Ramesh Thakur "Quality of life"
- Dignity approaches
- "Generalized poverty" (King and Murray)
- Human security network

* Lincoln Chen, Edward Newman ("normatively attractive, analytically weak"), Keith Krause ("a key concept if properly delimited"), Lloyd Axworthy (former Canadian Foreign Office minister)

Figure 2.2 Hampson's triangular definitions.

(the UNDP, the Japanese definition, 'dignity' approaches …), while Canada seems to represent on its own the minimalist 'safety of peoples' angle, and the 'rule of law' pole remains somewhat trapped between those two extremities, with no definitions specifically attached to it. Indeed, rather than polarizing the issue in a triangle organization which in the end does not seem to fit the real picture, it would probably be best to go beyond Hampson's categorization in a triangular model. Instead of a triangle model, we propose a variety of graphs that suit better the understanding of the concept of human security and its relationships with other paradigms.

Figure 2.3 is loosely based on the divisions expressed in Hampson's triangle but reinterprets the overlap between the three areas identified as a potential threshold for action based on consensus over what constitutes a threat to human security. This central area is also the point where human security becomes distinct from other concepts such as traditional security concerns and human development. The diagram illustrates the relationship between human security and other concepts while pointing out that the area of overlap varies and is not always easily discernable.

Figure 2.4 maps some well-known definitions of human security in comparison to each other to show the relationship between them. The vertical axis ranks the

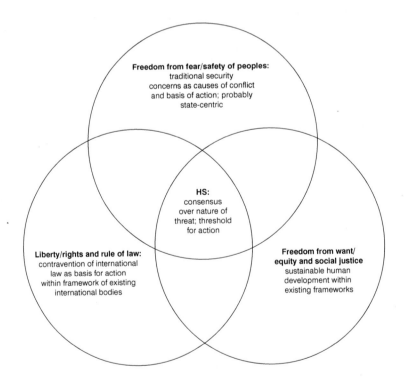

Figure 2.3 Human security as the nexus between safety, rights and equity.

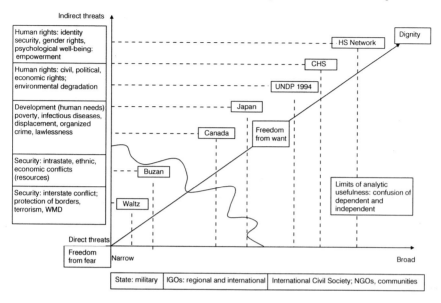

Figure 2.4 Definitional mapping tool based on indirect/direct threats and thresholds.

definitions according to whether the threats they cover can be considered only direct or also indirect. The diagonal axis converts this ranking into a scale of the language of human security as popularized in discussion of the concept: 'freedom from fear' (at the beginning), 'freedom from want' (towards the middle of the scale) and 'dignity' (at the end of the scale). Finally, the horizontal axis measures the how narrow or broad each definition can be considered to be and concurrently which actors might be implicated in security issues according to the definition in question. The irregular line that crosses the central axis represents the 'limit of analytical usefulness' of a definition of human security according to some of its critics; it separates relatively narrow definitions considering direct threats from broader definitions thus reflecting the idea that a broader definition makes a distinction between dependent and independent variables impossible.

Figure 2.5 situates various important aspects of the most well known human security definitions in relationship to each other. Reading from the centre outwards in the direction of the arrows, it shows that a narrow definition corresponds to a more objective, narrower, more security focused definition that concentrates on 'freedom from fear' while within the outer square the broadest kind of definition would be read as the most subjective, most focused on the individual and integrating a dignity approach. The arrows show that the facets of the definition are cumulative so that the process of moving from a smaller square towards a larger one shows that what was included in the narrower definition is integrated into a new focus on a new aspect. The boundaries of the squares can move freely according to the specificity of the definition they reflect.

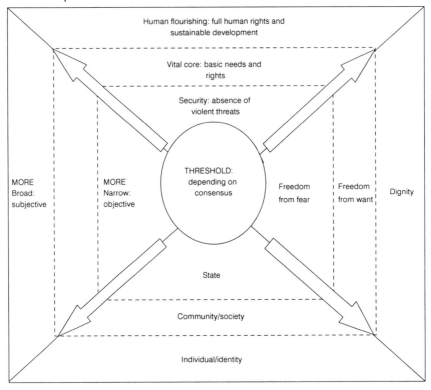

Human flourishing: full human rights and
sustainable development

Vital core: basic needs and
rights

Security: absence of
violent threats

THRESHOLD:
depending on
consensus

MORE
Broad:
subjective

MORE
Narrow:
objective

Freedom
from fear

Freedom
from want

Dignity

State

Community/society

Individual/identity

Figure 2.5 Definitional mapping tool depicting key elements of narrow/broad conceptualizations of HS.

In concert with successful human development (growth), the need for human
security is represented in Figure 2.6 as the threats posed by the absence or failure
of human development (economic crisis, downturns). The relativity of both
human rights and human security concepts, is depicted with circular thresholds, or
boundaries, that can be expanded or contracted according to the values reflected in
the particular conception being employed to define a threat. This also shows how
narrow and broad definitions of human security vary according to the number of
sources of potential threats they identify and the fact that a broad definition is also
likely to be more relative. Human security here is depicted as the 'securitization'
of development and related protection against threats, i.e. growth with equity and
the capacity to face downturns with security.

In Figure 2.7 the two largest circles represent the entire agenda of human
development and human rights respectively. Within each of these circles, specific
aspects of development and human rights are identified by smaller concentric
circles. The size of the circle represents the degree to which these aspects can
be considered critical to individual survival and well-being. Consequently, the
absence of any of these components is equivalent to a threat more or less critical
in nature. The square in the centre reflects the need for human security as the

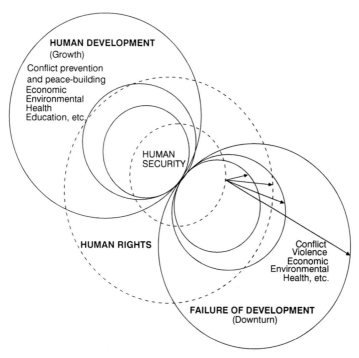

Figure 2.6 Human security as the securitization of human development (growth) to protect from threats and failures of development (downturn).

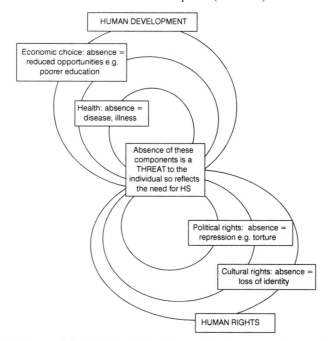

Figure 2.7 The need for HS: insufficient human development and protection of human rights.

threats posed by the absence of successful development or viable human rights. The square can expand or contract according to the perception of threat, and thus, can also be read as a threshold for action conceived of as a consensus about the nature of a threat. It should be noted that this diagram inherently infers a hierarchy of rights and development goals by ranking different aspects as more critical than others according to the nature of threat they pose, direct physical threats being considered the most critical.

In Figure 2.8 the triangle represents one way of looking at human security in relation to traditional versions of security. The apex, corresponds to the narrowest conceptions of security as state based and focused on exterior, direct threats. The first dotted line represents the transition from traditional security concepts to human security. Moving down, the triangle becomes broader as does the definition; moving from a 'freedom from fear' emphasis towards the broadest conceptions which include 'freedom from want' and dignity. The range of security referents also increases as communities are added to the definition (Buzan) moving towards an exclusive focus on the individual. Read from the base upwards, the image

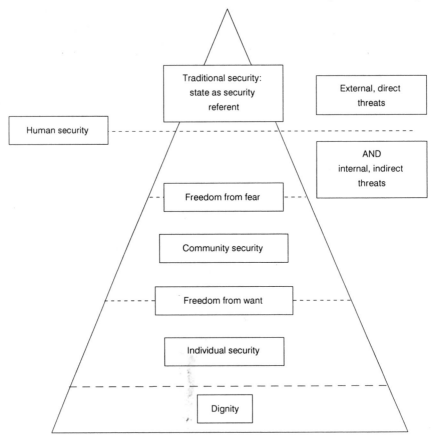

Figure 2.8 The security pyramid: human security and traditional notions of security.

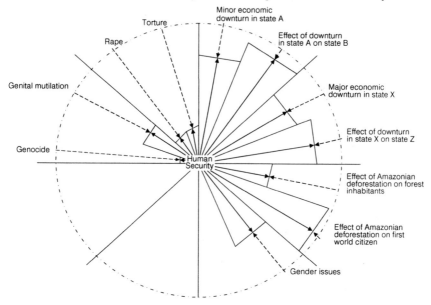

Figure 2.9 Human security, threats and relative thresholds.

shows that human security is based on the individual and includes all the above components; traditional security considerations are thus justified only as a state-based means to individual security.

In Figure 2.9 the circle illustrates the broad variety of threats that can be considered under a human security framework while also demonstrating the subjectivity inherent in threat assessment and the ingenious way that human security can integrate both subjective and objective security threats. The point where the arrows meet is the threshold of the threat and as the examples show, this can be different according to who is affected by what threat and how. The nearer the threshold falls to the centre of the circle the more likely it becomes that there will be a consensus over the threat threshold as in the example of genocide. Equally, as the threshold approaches the outside of the circle, the more subjective the perception of that threat is likely to be. The consensus over any given threat will be greater if it is more generally considered to be very serious; in this case it is also likely to be considered more objective thus the circle can also be read to reflect a relationship between the gravity of a threat and its status as subjective or objective.

Typology of critiques

If definitions are abundant, so are critiques based on theoretical, analytical and policy-oriented arguments. The main critique is the alleged vagueness of the idea and the broadness of its epistemology of threats. The entire agenda is presented as first conceptually hollow, and, second, of very little use theoretically. Human security is envisioned by Roland Paris for instance at best as a 'rallying cry' and at worst as unadulterated 'hot air' (Paris, 2001: 88, 96). The 'securitization' of economic, social, political and environmental and human rights issues is criticized by many commentators, who see it as, variously, a broadening of the term security to the point that it loses its signification, a gimmick to give credence to a vague movement, and a dangerous form of jargon that could easily fall prey to political manipulation by governments in the name of security.

To better understand the various critiques of this relatively new concept, we have grouped them into five clusters, each offering their own insight into the questions that human security raises.

1   The *conceptual critiques* look at how the very definition (or lack thereof) of human security impedes its progress. These sets of critiques mostly argue against the broad definition of human security, accusing it to be too vague to act against threats, understand causalities and explain behaviour.

2   From an *analytical point of view*, the concept challenges the existing academic disciplines by denying the traditional rules and realities of international relations and driving towards a reductionist understanding of international security. Among these critiques, the problem of over-securitization is questionable not only on moral grounds but also intellectually.

3   The *political implications* of a human security agenda is also criticized on the grounds that it challenges the traditional role of the sovereign state as the sole provider of security as well as the very sovereignty of the state in the international context.

4   Building on these arguments, a number of criticisms is diverted to the *moral implication* of the human security agenda. Southern countries worry about industrialized countries, notably Western-based, imposing their own social and economic values upon the weak. For critics from the so-called North, the moral dilemma exists when it fails to distinguish between individual and universal security concerns.

5   Those interested in operationalizing human security point to a number of *implementation* difficulties in creating a bridge between rhetoric and policy. To these critics, the complexity and subjectivity makes prioritization difficult, measurements of success are unclear and human security represents a short-term response to threats without providing long-term solutions.

We argue in Box 2.2 that each of the points raised could be challenged by counter-critiques that deserve examination. Despite the challenges, human security still appears to be a useful and innovative concept that inspires a new worldview and political agenda but also a powerful tool for research and analysis in both existing academic fields as well as for cross-disciplinary potentials.

Box 2.2 Conceptual critiques

Conceptual critiques

Lack of precision makes defining impossible

Critique

If the term insecurity embraces almost all forms of harm to an individual, it loses any real descriptive power.

Counter-critique

- A process definition allows for recognizing political, economic, social, environmental and cultural threats. A broad-based concept is operational in multiple situations and lends itself to progressive, dynamic and evolving visions (Grayson, Suhrke).
- The lack of a firm definition for a concept does not necessarily bring down its utility. The notion of 'development' received (and still does) much of the same criticism but over time categories were established and policy was constructed using more concrete, and prioritized, tools.

Vague definition hides casual relationships

Critique

Vague definitions lend themselves to analytical blunders whereby independent and dependent variables are conflated (Mack; Paris; Foong Khong; Krause). Human security proponents make dangerous attempts to prove false causal assumptions linking socio-economic issues to political outcomes.

Counter-critique

- Defining is an act of power so human security, given its very lack of a structured definition, gains a certain suppleness of dimensions which makes it a powerful conceptual tool free from analytical prejudice (Grayson).
- Given the breadth of analytical freedom that studies of human security enjoy any threat can be studied as a dependent or as an independent variable because insecurity can be both a cause and a consequence of violence (Owens).

The concept is too broad to focus on how to act against threats

Critique

The notion of human security includes everything from substance abuse to genocide (Paris), making it impossible to determine where policy attention is most required and priorities for action to be established (Foong Khong). Human security is less an analytical concept than a signifier of shared moral and political values (Mack).

Counter-critique

- Human security studies recognize that threats are multiple and inter-linked and it identifies the thresholds below which welfare, dignity and survival are threatened intolerably. These thresholds are necessary because subjective nature of security perceptions can make human security a relative concept.
- Human security can be perceived as an 'organizing concept' or principle (King and Murray).

'Grand theory' nature of concept means lack of academic utility

Critique

Human security as a concept aspires to explain almost everything and consequently, in reality explains nothing (Buzan). It is academically confusing because it seems to support all hypotheses and their opposites at the same time (Paris). If theory building is difficult enough in security studies with 200 states, what are we to learn from the behaviour of 6 billion diverse people (Foong Khong)? It therefore seems to add complexity without extra-explanatory power.

Counter-critique

In the post-Cold War world system, individuals are faced with real security threats that are very different from concerns of traditional security. Human security classifies different types of threats and their relationship to traditional security while illustrating the inter-connectedness of threats. Human security's large field of action directly draws upon situations of individuals in insecure environments.

Lacks a concise research agenda

Critique

Critics contend that human security as a field is too wide to generate a specific research agenda.

Counter-critique

The field of human security is vast enough for much needed inter-disciplinary research. Thresholds and their operationalization are at least one example of possible research directions. Measurements are another field, as are causalities between threats. In addition, case studies drawn from concrete situations can identify typologies.

A political science concept should not be an ethical stance

Critique

Human security should be neutral. A social science concept should not propose ethical choices.

Counter-critique

Social sciences are normative by nature. Ethics in social sciences is not new and the field has already been explored by economists such as Amartya Sen. Traditional security, when it refers to security of the state from military threats, is already a normative concept.

Inter-disciplinarity and inter-sectorality are unworkable

Critique

Academia and policy institutions are specialized along defined fields of study and sectoral lines. Lack of methodological know-how on implementing inter-disciplinary approaches within existing administrative structures impedes policy formulation within the inter-sectoral and pluralistic human security framework. This difficulty is compounded by inter-disciplinary opacity among donors and governments, dictated strictly by 'mandates' and sectoral ministries respectively.

Counter-critique

The post-Cold War world faces unprecedented threats that provide the most urgent reasons for inter-sectoral and pluralistic approaches to ensuring human security. The High Panel and Threats and Challenges final report highlights this very aspect and condemns the lack of coherent interconnectedness between institutions. It is important to study how interventions in one sphere can actually have externalities, both positive and negative, on other areas, and what causalities could be in order to better design human security interventions.

Academic implications

Human security as misfit in international relations theory

Critique

Human security is an exclusive paradigm that denies the traditional rules and realities of international relations and 'drives towards a reductionist understanding of international security' (Buzan). In the traditional state-centred conception of security, it is the sovereign state that alone can provide for its own security, while liberal approaches allow for collective security through interstate cooperation, for example through international institutions.

Counter-critique

- The international system is only as strong as its weakest link: if the safety of individuals is critical to global security, a threat to individual security is a threat to international security (Nef). Given mutual vulnerabilities, the North is vulnerable to events in less secure and underdeveloped regions of the globe. Weaknesses in the periphery can render the entire configuration of an inter-dependent system.
- The international order depends not only on sovereignty and the viability of states, but on individuals and their own sense of security as well (Hampson). An interconnected world makes individual state security impossible, so it is necessary to look beyond traditional approaches to security (Stoett).
- Most realists fail to take into account the causes of civil wars which constitute 90 per cent of armed conflicts (Mack).

The problem of securitization

Critique

Securitization means prioritizes an issue, making it worthy of special attention and resources, including an immediate resolution through possible military means. Consequently, prioritization of 'soft' issues takes away from the urgency of traditional security issues (Foong Khong). Over-securitization risks destroying the intellectual coherence of the field, overcomplicating solution-finding (Buzan). In any case, securitization is a political act that should not be idealized: security is a negative issue pointing to the failure of politics and 'desecuritization' would be preferable.

Counter-critique

- The critique of excessive securitization lies within the traditional view of security based on military force, yet broadening the concept of security should forestall the need for later military intervention.
- Military power is not a guarantee of well-being. If we accept economic and group security, threats are to well-being, capacities and opportunities: including these issues leads to a democratization of security and an empowerment of people to solve these problems. HS in reality, addresses issues left out in the 'desecuritized' public sphere and aims to desecuritize the state in the long run.

Political implications

A challenge to the role of the state

Critique

Human security challenges the role of the sovereign state as the sole provider of security. It is a new tool for existing governing agencies to shape and control civil populations. Any expansion of security definitions will result in an increased use of force, justified by the international community as their 'responsibility'. Human security remains state-centric despite the supranational dimensions of the concept, allowing for a prominent role of the state as a necessary condition for individual security (Buzan).

Counter-critique

- A state is not the only 'policy actor'. A state may in fact threaten its own people, rather than assuring their security (Mack). Refusal to acknowledge the multiplicity of actors responsible for security demonstrates a 'clear lack of imagination' (Mack).
- Human security as a concept leads to a democratization of security and international relations. People become stakeholders in a common security and the state supports this empowerment (Axworthy, Osler Hampson, Evans). Yet, structural factors and the distribution of power at the root of insecurities are beyond the reach of the individual (Newman).

- Securitization internationally does not automatically imply militariz- ation (Owen). 'Interventions' include longer-term engagements, includ- ing incentives such as trade expansion and delivering on promises of aid and debt relief, as well as sticks such as judicial prosecutions, economic sanctions, and diplomatic isolation.
- Security should be and indeed can be provided through a network of diverse actors, a 'jumbled coalition' made up of states, the UN, NGOs and the empowered individual (Paris). Adoption of human security on domestic and foreign policies allows for an increased participation of middle power states on the international scene (Liotta). While agenda- based action is an inevitable consequence of human security, it is not necessarily a reason to discredit the concept; it is the results, not the means, which are important.

Human security is a threat to state sovereignty

Critique

Viewing underdevelopment as a source of conflict provides justification for continued surveillance and engagement, used by dominant powers to legitimize self-interested interventionism. The concept of human security may be used to justify military interventions and may impose military solutions to problems of the welfare state. It can become a new excuse for interventionism in areas where sovereignty was previously respected (Bain).

Counter-critique

- Sovereignty is increasingly being viewed as conditional on the ability of the state to provide security to the individual.
- Military intervention is but one of many forms of intervention under the human security banner. Human security as a discipline favours largely non military solutions to threats, ideally addressing root causes of tensions and conflicts before the war or massacre ensues, which might then require military intervention.
- While the international community recognizes a 'responsibility to protect', guidelines for intervention, including prevention, have been created by the United Nations to prevent misuse. The failure of past military interventions encourages a move towards preventive, non- military enforcement of human security. If a truly human security agenda were thus adopted, with focus on prevention, the 'responsibility to protect' would be less likely to be enforced. The concept could

be seen as a remedy to illegitimate intervention, and as a check to Western imperialism and instrumentalization.

Securitization as 'responsibilitization'

Critique

Linking suffering in other countries to one's own national security could lead to 'wall-building' instead of 'bridge-building' (Krause). Critics fear that that the result of expanding the definition of security will be an increased use of force considered as the 'responsibility' of the international community.

Counter-critique

- Human security is not based solely on the changing behaviour of various actors and 'bridge-building' capacities: sufficient conditions for a 'sustainable human security' involve restructuring legal and political institutions, reconstruction of the economy and redefinition of prevailing social norms (Hampson).
- Securitization should not be taken to mean militarization but a responsibility for engagement at all levels and in various stages, not as last resort.

Moral implications

Human security is a reinforcement of global division

Critique

It is commonly asserted that human security reinforces the North-South divide: economic and social underdevelopment in the South are said to breed political instability which may spill over to the North, requiring interventions in the name of 'responsibility to protect', sanctions and pre-emptive action. Yet, the G77 for example argues that human security is essentially an ethnocentric paradigm from the North. It is a 'means by which the West imposes its own views on the world' and applies double standard or a 'hypocritical use of the concept as a punitive measuring rod by rich nations' (Daudelin).

Counter-critique

- The South needs to develop its own concept of human security. Root causes for insecurities sometimes stem from the North within this asymmetrical world of power relations. Ballistic missiles and arms trade from the North have proved enormously dangerous for the South, as have sanctions and unfair trade rules. The question is whether HS will provide a bridge ('a grand bargain') to ensure North's cooperation with the South to reinforce their security concerns while addressing the South's development deficits.

- Human insecurity of people in one region is not relative to that of others. Urban violence in Europe and immigrants' precarious situation in urban slums in America is as much an issue of human insecurity as food and job shortages in Ethiopia. Human security is about differences among people not among states, therefore the North/South division discourses are artificial and irrelevant.

Individual and universal?

Critique

- The human security concept is too universal to distinguish the differences between people, and in that it undermines pluralism. At the same time, measuring individual security is too complicated: security on any scale is a feeling, so how do we differentiate perceived and real fears? Thresholds of security being culture, space, time and circumstance specific, are too diverse and complex to identify through a standard methodology.
- Put at the centre of analysis, people are seen as critical to international security and thus people are instrumentalized as international security becomes dependant on individual security (Nef). This instrumentalization can be used for the foreign policy purposes of other states.

Counter-critique

- All security needs are not the same, therefore the broadness of the concept allows for circumstantial factors in the definition of these needs.
- Society can be ruled by respected international rules limiting state sovereignty and instituting the rule of cosmopolitan rights for the citizens. Human security can be a means to make states aware of 'the law of peoples' (Rawls) by which populations give themselves rules forbidding their state to use war as a continuation of politics, thus reinforcing 'just war' theories.
- Human security should be 'universal, global and indivisible' (Ul Haq). The 'freedoms' should be promoted because of their close connection to human rights (Evans).

Implementation critiques

Complexity and subjectivity make prioritization difficult

Critique

Human security's complex nature does not allow policy-makers to prioritize between competing goals and security needs (Paris).

Counter-critique

- The concept postulates that all threats are complex, interconnected and interdependent. Thus, the creation of a hierarchy of security needs is at best a futile exercise and at worst dangerous because complex threats must be addressed via integrated policies designed and carried out by networked, flexible and coalitions of actors not one homogeneous 'policy maker'.
- The strength of the human security approach lies in its flexibility, which allows individuals and communities to prioritize the different components of human security according to their needs. Since policy making is a networked, flexible, and horizontal practice between different actors, each with their own hierarchy of security needs and capacities to react, priorities can thus be determined via a process of negotiation and exchange between different actors (Uvin), recognizing that political actors' priorities are a factor of individual contexts.

Measurements are unclear

Critique

The concept's subjectivity limits effective measurement and analysis, which is necessary given that existing resources for intervention are limited.

Counter-critique

Individual or societal perception of gravity can trump quantitative evaluation of needs by the international community, so the usefulness of such quantitative tools is overstated. The objectivity of indicators can vary according to the human security definition employed (Booysen). A Human Security Audit or measurement will always be context-specific (Bajpai, Thakur, Hampson). More generally applicable indicators and norms will emerge as concept is integrated into policy making.

Human security simply re-labels existing issues and tools

Critique

The 'securitization' of human development issues is an attempt to draw attention and change their status in the international policy hierarchy (Foong Khong).

Human security simply re-labels old tools without proposing new policy mechanism. It represents a short-term response to threats without providing long-term solutions (Foong Khong).

Counter-critique

- The myriad of internal conflicts and war against poverty since the 1980s reveals the links between development, poverty and war, thereby justifying the treatment of development and human rights issues as questions of security.
- The goal of human security is to shift security focus to the individual level rather than provide instant solutions. Yet, it does offer new tools for evaluation and prevention by shifting the focus to individuals and communities. Applying these preventive and evaluation tools can yield to numerous long-term positive externalities on other domains.

The threshold solution

Does this highly controversial debate mean that we should end our quest to define human security? No. Beyond debates on concepts and definitions is the need for establishing thresholds, below which welfare, dignity and survival cannot be tolerated. Owen's suggestion of a threshold-based conceptualization is particularly relevant as it aims towards bringing together as much as possible the narrow and broad conceptions of human security, while allowing for flexibility. His platform, which proposes to reconcile advocates of narrow freedom from fear approaches, advocates of broad freedom from want, and those dismissing the concept altogether, is to present human security as a threshold: 'A threshold-based conceptualization, one that limits threats by their severity rather than their cause, allows all possible harms to be considered, but selectively limits those that at any time are prioritized with the security level' (Owen, 2004: 384).

This proposition attempts to strike a balance between those who feel that human security should encompass all threats, and those who feel that it needs to be more narrowly defined by creating a threshold defining the *severity* of each threat as the basis to determine whether or not international attention is required.

Nonetheless, to identify these thresholds, beyond which survival, livelihood and dignity cannot be tolerated is hardly a simple task. Many recognize the possibility of existence of universal and objective basic minimum standards as minimums to achieve, but these have not, so far, been in evidence. Thresholds, once human development is under way, should evolve as a function of the level of development, but because security remains a feeling and ultimately subjective, determining these is next to impossible, if we are to take into account levels of development but also particularities of culture and circumstances. Perhaps it is less a question of prioritization among competing goals for policy makers than about identification of thresholds of minimal welfare and human dignity. Such thresholds, which involve setting up criteria for the measurement of human security, are difficult to establish given the distinction between objective and subjective factors. Security, at whatever level, will always remain in part a subjective feeling, and thresholds of tolerance will be different in different cultures, at different times, and in different places.

Where is the bar to be set then? The answer depends on the impact these thresholds have for national and international policy. A threshold-based approach to human security requires choosing policies on the basis of their concrete effects on people's welfare and dignity. They cannot always be quantitatively monitored, for example through such indicators as the cost of living, life expectancy and mortality rates, wage scales, etc., as they are qualitatively defined in terms of what is intolerable and inhuman. At the same time, the exercise is political as it points up a wide range of issues for the national and international actors who are responsible for providing human security as a public good. A threshold-based definition recognizes that certain threats cannot be dealt with by traditional institutions but are severe enough to require immediate action, both in the short term to handle the crisis and in the long term to prevent reoccurrence.

Another way of searching for thresholds is to take the de-centred or collective approach. Communities that face insecurity or are threatened need to identify these risks based on threshold limits and how to address and prioritize them. These risks need to be addressed by the state and if the state itself is part of the threat, the international community needs to be involved. This approach requires a recognition that needs beyond the basic minimum will vary from region to region and that thresholds can change as aspirations and expectations of people change. Supporters of the broad view of human security would have to concede that not all threats constitute international attention, while proponents of the narrow view would have to concede that physical violence only falls into one category of human security and thus is not enough to cover the entire concept. The threshold-based solution tries to find a common ground while offering policy makers something that they can work with.

Conclusion

Human security thus seems to appear as an endless debate between its proponents and critics, and even among its advocates, who have not agreed on a single unified definition reconciling maximalist and minimalist understandings. However such quarrels and disagreements should not be seen as damning flaws of the concept, which remains new and still on the course of reaching its matured form. What is most relevant however is not how new human security is, but rather what *makes* it a new concept in both the theoretical and practical realms, considering possible policy perspectives and implications. By designating the individual, rather than the state, as the 'referent object of security', it has, in its short history, become a concept that realists have to engage with and to contest, if not accommodate.

No straightforward answer can thus be given to the question of what human security in the end embodies as a concept, research agenda and policy tool. Yet it would be unwise to dismiss it immediately. Rather, it is perhaps a general problem within social sciences of not being able to deliver 'definitive' definitions of its most sophisticated concepts, because the objects of study are in constant motion, and there can be no methodological posture of objectivity. Thus, in the end the best way to 'define' human security would be to acknowledge this insurmountable obstacle of subjectivity characteristic of social sciences, and apprehend it as a concept in motion tailored to moving situations, rather than sticking to motionless approaches of security as static in an ever more mobile world.

Beyond the perpetual definitional challenge, the debate on human security unearths two difficulties within the academic and policy community. First, as an interdisciplinary concept, it forges a dialogue between specialists to find common ground in three separately evolved fields of study, i.e. Development, Human Rights and Security Studies. Inter-disciplinary thinking is compounded with tangible difficulties given the compartmentalization of disciplines rigid administrative structures in universities and a multitude of 'mandates' and ministries in policy administrations and institutions. While multi-disciplinary or multi-sectoral approaches have been experimented with, for example through the creation of commissions on cross-cutting issues such as poverty or gender, the real difficulty is lack of experience and methodological know-how in this domain. Second, the question here is not really of choosing a broad-based or narrow-based definition of human security, but the lack of complementarity between academic researchers and policy makers. Can there be a successful marriage between research and policy? Are policy decisions taken on theoretical grounds, or do we act first and then adjust the theory later? Is it simply the availability of funds and the attraction of innovating concepts that stimulates academic research, unconnected to any practical application? Human security is in an uncomfortable position, caught between the normative and positivist approaches – between the pragmatic and the theoretical.

Therefore the main challenges in answering the only apparently simple question of 'what is human security?', lie in the defence of its one utility, in particular when compared to human development, human rights and their interrelations, in an attempt to synthesize positions on the maximalist-minimalist gradient. It seems these challenges can best be overcome using the intrinsic link between human security and human development (Chapter 4) and the consubstantial relation between human security and human rights (Chapter 5), for it seems that through the scope of these linkages most of the uncertainties on the concept can be cleared and a synthesized definition can be thought as an answer to what human security basically is.

The question that remains is whether human security can be successful in challenging traditional security paradigms, or will it simply remain a marginal concept? In other words, can human security serve as an operational basis for action? The later chapters address these issues as we argue that human security begins by asking the right questions. It proposes a framework that puts individuals at the centre of both analysis and action. It can serve as a means to evaluate threats, foresee crises, analyse the cause of discord and propose solutions entailing a redistribution of responsibilities. In this respect human security is not only an analytic concept, it signifies shared political and moral values (Mack, 2002b). Although human security analysis may not have provided explanations of how insecurity originates, it has called attention to the importance of recognizing the interconnections between a host of factors that in combination produce insecurity. Whatever its weaknesses may be as an analytic tool, it provides an effective means for preventing the degradation of people's well-being and dignity as well as diminishing the consequences of 'insecurities', be they man-made conflicts or natural disasters. Human security should not be given a narrow definition, but should remain flexible enough to develop as our understanding of the roots of worldwide insecurity deepens as does our capacity to address them.

3   A paradigm shift in security studies?

Within the field of security studies, the debate has raged on the need or not to expand the concept of 'security' beyond the prerogative of the state to defend itself from military threats. In a bipolar world, security essentially meant the concern with the territorial integrity of the state to be confronted by military means. Within the 'realist' framework, the state would exchange loyalty of its citizens with the protection it would provide them from external aggression. The possibility that the security of the individual and the state need not coincide or that the state might be a threat to its citizens was not contemplated. Despite its major interest in war, realist theory showed little interest in civil conflicts.

Approaches to such a notion of security are contested today by constructivists, critical theorists, and feminists, all of whom seek an alternative framework from the realist assumption and distinguish between the security of people and that of the state. The human security approach similarly reviews conventional knowledge on security.

In this chapter, we sketch the evolution of security studies within the traditional frameworks, before highlighting what the human security approaches brings to the debate each time. The debate about expanding security is fuelled by the shortcomings of these theories and their inability to comprehensively address contemporary evolutions in an increasingly inter-related world.

What is, ultimately, security and whose security is it anyway?

Traditional security studies, especially in North America, have been concerned with the phenomenon of war and the use of military force, with scholarship focusing on relationships that can be altered by deliberate acts of policy. Walt however called for a distinction between scientific theories, which explain why the world works in a certain way, and normative frameworks, which project how particular agents should act (Walt, 1991). Walt described neo-realism as 'scientific' and denounced other theories as idealist or esoteric. He noted the danger of linking scholarship to policy issues, thus decreasing the integrity of ideas. Yet, new theories expanded and converged together towards increasingly ethics-based normative principles. Among them, human security cannot aspire to be a scientific theory given that ultimately, its goals are humanitarian and its methodology moves away from positivism to one that brings scholars from different fields together. In doing so, it constitutes a normative break with realism.

The field of 'security studies', compartmentalized in itself and ranging from peace research to strategic studies, has also been characterized by an absence of a common understanding of theory-building and discipline building in the 'security puzzle' (Haftendorn, 1991). Strategic studies chose a limited thematic approach and focus on military dimensions of security, with special attention to nuclear strategy. It reworked the thesis of geopolitics popularized by Mackinder on the geographical context and reach of power (Mackinder, 1904). Mackinder's approach, critiqued for its ahistorical generalizations and rejected because of its adaptation by the Nazi Party in Germany, saw a re-emergence when strategic studies were popularized in the 1980s and remained a conceptual tool during the Cold War. Conflict studies became prominent with decolonization and after the Cold War. The field focused on civil wars and more recently on weak and failing states with an eye to understand root causes of war and to develop early warning systems, preventive tools and preventive diplomacy. Peace studies, in the meantime, became popular at European sites and universities, building its quest around notions of 'peace', 'security', and 'violence'. Influential peace studies by Galtung and his group replaced the monopoly of security in the field of international relations, and brought in ideas that looked at more than just negative or positive peace. Within this stream, the idealist and liberal approaches, as also the normative paradigm and behavioural approaches to critical theories, worked out methodologies for alternate strategies to war. Boulding proposed the status of a 'stable peace' as better than 'negative peace equated with an absence of war' (Boulding, 1991). He argued that genuine peace and security presupposes elimination or reduction of structural violence.

Policy makers adapted these alternate visions of security to the world of international and regional alliances. In a situation of accumulation of weapons of mass destruction, there was a clear need for new strategies of reassurance rather than deterrence. Instead of nuclear and arms-control efforts, security strategies sought new tools to prevent war. Simultaneously human rights and humanitarian intervention were accepted as part of security needs. The term 'Common Security' (also called cooperative, reciprocal, or mutual security) was coined in the early 1980s by Bahr and discussed in the Palme Commission's 1982 Report, which recommended arms control. Common security did not propose a new type of security but cooperation among nations as a way to prevent conflict. The objective was for joint survival rather than the threat of mutual destruction, and the means were proposed through cooperation. 'Collective security' strategies in the meantime concentrated on the transfer of power to international authorities such as the UN and the OSCE to not only restore peace between states but also within them, through safeguarding of human rights. Humanitarian interventions, therefore, were legitimized as ways to promote security. Within this view, the new world order was seen as one where international politics were superseded by domestic politics of a global scale. A third stream, that of 'Comprehensive Security' included threats other than those to territorial integrity and political order, and concentrated on non-state actors and natural catastrophes. In the mid-1980s, a South East Asian concept of security was developed based on this, which saw states and ruling regimes as the security object of political stability, economic development, and social harmony. While no common perceptions of external threats were adopted, threats to individuals were seen as a threat to the comprehensive security of the states. The approach called for cooperation within the region based on sovereignty and a policy of non-interference.

All three approaches are similar to human security in two ways. First, they recognize a larger array of threats beyond military threats; second, they share similar views about the need for multilateralism as a way of dealing with this expanded set of threats. The main difference, however, is that these strategies concentrate on the needs of security for the state – order and stability. Human security, on the other hand, concentrates on human needs and is geared towards justice and emancipation. Therefore, state security becomes a means and not the end of security objectives Table 3.1 displays a rough comparison between these strategies.

Central to making the individual rather than the state the referent object of security, which the human security approach proposes is the argument that traditional security paradigms do not adequately demonstrate how personal insecurity and lack of freedom cause interstate conflicts. First, the state-centric paradigm of realism cannot explain the civil wars that are today the most prevalent form of armed conflict. Second, privileging the state as the entity to be secured deflects attention from the fact that the pursuit of state security is too often at the expense of individual security. Third, the idea of people-centric security has an important historical genesis in the Universal Declaration of Human Rights, the UN Charter, and the Geneva Conventions. Security has been acknowledged as a right in liberal discourse since Hobbes and Locke. The American and French declarations at the end of the eighteenth century reaffirmed the need to insure a 'right to safety'. Therefore, security is a fundamental right, or more precisely a 'degree 0' of human rights, which comes before the three different generations of rights – political rights, social and economic rights, rights of difference. Human security appears as a renewed focus on people's safety tending to promote their other rights.

Human security arises from the lacunae in existing security paradigms and encompasses multidimensional aspects, becoming increasingly compatible with other disciplines. It is distinct from Westphalian security that focuses on military threats to states in a condition of international anarchy. It is also separate from common security (defensive realism) which focuses on states and military threats and considers that states' natural aggressiveness can be mutually restrained by the constitution of a community of states. It is distinct from liberalist security which retains trust in the possibility of an international society based on states as the primary referents. Human security thus stems from the obsolescence of these paradigms due to the declining relevance of the traditional state-based security system, changing notions of sovereignty, transnational threats (such as terrorism), the growing moral imperative to intervene in cases of massive violations of human

Table 3.1 Comparing common, collective, comprehensive and human security

	Common security	Collective security	Comprehensive	Human security
Values	Security for all states	Security by transfer of powers to international authorities, partial relinquishment of sovereignty	For all states and actors	Human needs
Security for whom? And what threats?	Nations to prevent conflict by cooperative means; role of the UN; security to include economic, social, and political terms too. Joint survival rather than threat of mutual destruction	States safeguarded by UN and OSCE which not only restore peace between states but within them; safeguarding of human rights	Threats other than military to territorial integrity and political order; non-state actors and natural catastrophes	Security for people and not just states; threats not just from conflicts but structural; models of development; from economic and social systems and biases; from states; etc
Towards what ends?	Development and disarmament	New world order, where international politics superceded by domestic politics of a global scale	Security to state and people	Empowerment, dignity; and human rights, no unilateralism

rights; and other changes in the international discourse. Ultimately, if human security is the objective – the ultimate ends – of all security concerns, then other forms of security, such as military security, are not ultimate goals but means for achieving the ultimate objectives of human security. The state has thus a privileged position to ensure that people should enjoy without discrimination all rights and obligations, including human, political, social, economic and cultural rights that belonging to a state implies.

Broadening and widening security and its implications

The crisis of security is linked to the crisis of the role and the nature of the state. States are more threatened by internal factors in the globalizing capitalist economy and internal constraints have meant that people turn to ethnic or religious communities for identity and protection. Further, states often have to share power with businesses, international organizations, NGOs, and others. The role of the state as provider of security has thus increased; there has been a rearrangement in its priorities; its role has decreased in social sectors and increased in security and surveillance. In this changed situation, the security dilemma needed envisioning. The security dilemma model assumed the absence of the state and is thus of little help in explaining the reasons for its collapse. It focused on elements which contribute to the escalation of civil wars, once the state has collapsed. The view that human insecurities are interconnected, and that human rights and development needed to be linked with security issues brought the human security idea into salience, popularizing it with agencies that were engaged in alleviating human suffering in instances where the state did not take responsibility for securing the dignity of its citizens. It is in this context that the debate on broadening the concept of security takes place.

Security studies have until recently either followed a narrow trajectory or have expanded their arena to be more inclusive. Waltz's realist security studies is a leader of the narrow concept and restricts its study to wars, threats to the state, military control, and national interest (Waltz, 1979). Buzan, whose definition of insecurity is confined to 'existential threats', concedes to expanding the analysis to possible non-military threats to the existence of groups and markets (Buzan *et al*. 1998). Thus, for the past two decades, security studies itself has been engulfed in the debate on its expansion and contraction.

Broadening of security is based on considerations of non-military security threats such as environmental degradation, spread of disease, overpopulation, mass refugees, terrorism, nuclear catastrophes. Buzan *et al*. broadened security by including economic, social, and political sectors (Buzan *et al.*, 1998). *Deepening* security considers the security of individuals and groups, rather than of states and examines other referents as units of analysis. Buzan, for instance, uses the international system, international sub-systems, units, sub-units, and individuals. Broadening of the security discourse started with the Brandt Commission's Report on Common Security (1981). In the 1990s, those who advocated broadening had won and analysts who wanted to limit security to military issues retreated to strategic studies as a branch of IR. The idea was best promoted through various World Commissions: the 1980 Commission on International Development chaired by Willi Brandt (*North/South Report*) and the Independent Commission on Disarmament and Security Issues, chaired by Olaf Palme (*Common Security*), the 1995 Commission on Global Governance (*Our Global Neighbourhood*), with concern for the security of people and security of our planet.

The logic for expanding the notion of security was its inability to explain insecurities caused by states themselves. For a comprehensive view of security, civil wars and human rights violations have to be explained. Further, security should be able to factor in values such as 'freedom', livelihoods, and dignity. Thus broadening of security arises not entirely because of a critique of traditional paradigms, but also because of the historical conjuncture and change in international relations. After the Cold War, it became necessary to look at new threats within states, at failed states, new humanitarian issues, and local conflicts. It was realized that these multiple security threats that arose from the state to the individual required engagement from two angles, one to prevent them from spilling over regionally and globally and second from the humanitarian point of view. It was from these debates that thinking on human security took a serious turn.

There are two groups of 'scholar-activists' that conversed on the common interest to promote security for all, that is, responsibility of various institutions for security (responsibility view) and the view that each government should worry about non-military threats to its citizens, but not those of other states (non-interventionist view). In this debate, Del Rosso argued that it was not only violence, but harm to human, material, and natural resources on a potentially large and disruptive scale that is an issue of concern. These 'harms', even if they did not lead to violence, could produce extensive disruption and thus ramifications on security (Del Rosso Jr., 1995). Others, like Myers (1998) and Brown (1989) used environment and demography as entry points to talk of responsibility. The environment was also a logical entry point as it had global implications and its degradation was not initiated deliberately by foreign actors. Renner (1996) focused on disparate concerns as peace, environment, human rights, democratization, and social integration, the argument being that the environment is superior to military security as it is positive, inclusive, protective, and restoring. The debate between the approaches intensified when writers like Mack concluded that state-centric methodologies did not adequately explain civil wars that increasingly became the prevalent form of armed conflict in the 1990s.

The importance of people-centred security however has a historic genesis. As Rothschild noted, the historical antecedents of human security are associated with the centrality of the individual in the evolution of liberalism (Rothschild, 1995). The involvement of the 'new' development community added the idea of individual freedom to basic needs based on the assumption that these comprise the core values that make individuals secure. They added the idea that violence is not the only bad outcome, but that structural violence (such as extreme discrimination and inequality, and poverty) is equally damaging, as both lead to a decline in the quality of life, which is the aim of both security and development. This argument proposed to move resources away from military to human development but it faced critics and challenges. The first challenge came from the question of what are the limits to the inclusion of such huge questions as structural violence. In this broadening of the security discourse, it is important to understand that all threats cannot be included, because it would make security and its responsibility so broad as to lose meaning. Further, there has to be a balance and no trade-off between security of the state and that of the people.

This debate was systematized by Møller (2001), who argued that not to widen security would marginalize the field. Yet, the direction and extent to which security is widened is a matter of political choice and analytical convenience. Specifically, he identified three stages of deepening/broadening: the first stage in the international system is a state-centric understanding where the system is anarchic and the main concern is the balance of power. A moderate alternative is in the theories of common and collective security. It is believed that interdependence may serve as a powerful inhibition against war. The limitation of this argument is that it sacrifices other human values for those of sovereignty and territorial inviolability, in other words national security is posited at the expense of human security. The central theme at this stage is that state security means regime security and international politics means domestic politics on a global scale. The second stage is when societal security enters the discourse in international politics. Threats are diversified to include identity (as identified by the Copenhagen school and Buzan) and non-traditional threats. Human collectivities are placed as possible referent objects of security. International security acknowledges matters of identity. The third stage then is the one that recognizes human security. At this stage, threats can come from direct or structural violence including for instance intentional threats, for which the state is to blame, for example, human rights violation or violence by one group against another. In this expansion, the views of the realists are not totally disregarded or considered invalid, but that they are no longer sufficient, and other threats and other actors must be taken into consideration.

Critics of broadeners

Thus, while a consensus emerged on the need for widening of security within the field of international relations, disagreement remains as to where to draw the line. Smith for example described the extension of security downwards, i.e. security of nations to groups and individuals; upwards, that is from nation to biosphere and globally; and horizontally, that is to include military, political, economic, social, and environmental threats, and ultimately, he saw security as diffused in all directions, to include individuals, NGOs, public opinion to press and abstract forces of nature and the market (Smith, 2002). In the broad or narrow conceptualization, there have been many interventions and many have opposed broadening the concept. In this debate, Keller (1996) wanted to restrict threats that led to traditional security problems and which could be responded to most effectively by the military. Suhrke (1996) argued that the securitization of migrants would render them as threats rather than victims or assets. Others believed that it is inappropriate to 'securitize' the environment as the result would be militarization instead of greening. Del Rosso (1995) called the broadening debate the 'new gospel of security', that was trying to fill a vacuum, but no singular widely accepted new paradigm was found acceptable. There was thus a division between those who sought a change and those who resisted a change in the concept of security itself.

Amongst those who argued against change, many continue to believe that the fundamental realities and the nature of international relations have not changed. The possibility of war and the need for military preparation remain the defining conditions of international relations and divisions on the broadening of security naturally relate to how threats are viewed for states to tackle and guard against. The danger of excessive 'securitization' implies that anything under the label of security carries a strong presumption of priority and is related to well-funded military institutions. Buzan and Waever believed that the security field must be seen as a complex 'speech act' or 'language game'. Thus, caution is needed since there is a risk of elevating too many issues to the level of a 'security problem'. First, it may lead to abuses by those in power. To label an issue as a 'security problem' can make it off-limits from discussions and opposition as everybody must remain loyal to 'the common cause' of national security. Thus the need for 'desecuritizing' some issues arises. Second, institutions that are traditionally in charge of 'security' can benefit from securitization of new issues. For instance, this provides justification for the armed forces to make claims on national resources. Third, a security problem carries a label of urgency. It has absolute first priority and becomes a matter of 'existential' importance.

This speech act however, has its own limitations and has to be overcome, otherwise national security can be used to curb the debate. This issue is addressed by the question of morality in national and human security. The argument is that national security can be morally objectionable since it is insufficiently responsive to claims of justice. At the same time, human security can be morally objectionable if it means it is corrosive of liberty. Each one separately is not sufficient as a guide to the practice of statecraft and they should be considered depending on the context. There are moments when our responsibility towards other human beings is more important than state sovereignty (for example, ethnic cleansing in Kosovo). However, intervention may not always be right as it may be violating the right of states to try and fail, which is a unique process of development. How then, can issues of critical importance like environment or poverty be brought into the security discourse?

Security theorists would argue that unless human security threats have the potential to lead to violent conflict, endanger the integrity of the state, or involve the threat or use of the military, they should not be labelled as security concerns. Even if they put the well-being of citizens as a top priority, the means to accomplish this is the architecture of a strong state. Thus, security analysts are most comfortable with threats that can be resolved by the use of force and involve distress to the power of the state alone. Conflict is central to their focus, and remains an entry point to security studies. Environmental issues also illustrate a state-centric focus.

For the state, competition over scarce resources has always been a concern. Like individuals, states know their dependencies and they arrange their priorities to prevent vulnerabilities. Human security receives attention from security analysts when individual issues reach a crisis proportion.

The context: theories of international relations

To understand better the shifts that human security proposes to the field of international security, it must be compared to existing fields of study and how they are being debunked (adapted from Reve, 2004b).

The 'classical' security paradigm: realism

The realist approach to security focuses on states and military means to achieve maximum security in an anarchical context. Realism's unchallenged area of dominance coincides when the state becomes the principle actor and is traced to the Peace of Westphalia in 1648. Realism is a broad umbrella with a wide variety of 'schools': classical realism, neo-realism, structural-realism, defensive, cooperative, state-centric realism, reflections in terms of balance of power or unipolarity are all grouped together under this common denomination. The reason for such diversity is the attempt by new scholars to reconcile the classical realist paradigm which is considered an appropriate framework of analysis of international relations with their observations in a changing world. Classical realism can be summed up in five basic points.

1 It is strongly linked with Hobbes' thought, according to which, men in a state of nature are in a constant state of war in the absence of a superior sovereign power able to ensure their security. Hobbes derived this argument from Thucydides and later Machiavelli, who advised the 'prince' (the sovereign power) that power had no morality and self-interest for the state was supreme. Clausewitz projected these individual conditions to the international community of sovereign states. The state of nature that Hobbes talked about is now the state of the international system.

2 In this paradigm, the state is considered the only unitary rational actor whose aspirations are constant: states always prefer maximum security. This paradigm focuses on material resources which ensure the power of the state. Security policies rest on two pillars: diplomacy and force described in military terms, both of which aim at national security and domestic 'order' in a context of international 'anarchy'.

3 Anarchy implies that uncertainty defines international relations. A state can never be sure of the intentions of others. In this context, security is synonymous with the security of the state against external threat, to be achieved by increasing military capabilities.

4 States have no choice but to pursue power as an overriding imperative to ensure security. This gives rise to a security dilemma and a permanent state

of rivalry, tensions, and wars. Security in this model is a zero-sum game. As Tickner puts it, 'What are justified by one state as legitimated security-enhancing measures are likely to be perceived by others as a threatening military build-up' (Tickner, 1995: 176).

5 The stability of the entire system derives exclusively from its structure and from the distribution of military capacities between states. The key factor in ensuring stability is the balance of power. It is a mechanism of selective intervention, where states engage in conflict to support the weaker of the belligerents to preserve the *status quo* and prevent any state from achieving hegemony.

On a theoretical basis, classical realism derives elements from 'just war' (St Thomas Aquinas), 'necessary war' (Machiavelli), as well as Clausewitz's thought. Their influence on classical realists is profound with regard to the submission of the military to the political sphere, the unquestioning acceptance of the unitary, all-powerful state, and foundational belief in practical reasoning. The theorists of the transnationalist school believe in a 'post-Clausewitzian' world after the Cold War. They criticize the realist analysis on the following grounds: first, it is too conceptual and its conception of war ignores cultural and historical characteristics. War is not necessarily the Clausewitzian continuation of politics anymore. Second, war today is not an expression of power as it was during the nineteenth century. It is mainly the fact of a disintegration of states rather than their projection in the international sphere. Third, the frontiers between war and peace, national and international, soldiers and civilians have been blurred by new forms of conflicts which do not fit into the realist scheme. It thus seems that the Clausewitzian paradigm is poorly adapted to deal with new forms of conflicts or the fact that the principle of sovereignty is increasingly undermined by human rights, international organizations criminal jurisdictions or humanitarian interventions. Neo-realism is a theory that does not necessarily overlook the safety of citizens, rather, it assumes this as given. Waltz for example makes a clear distinction between thought (which a collection of realists present) and theory (which makes a bold conjecture) (Waltz, 1990). Neo-realist conceptualization has been questioned from within the realist school and more consistently by critical/radical theorists and feminists, strengthening the position of advocates of human security. The strength of realism lies in that it has been able to accommodate new challenges by ensuring the state as the only possible actor in the internationally anarchic system, where power has to be maintained through military means. This pessimism was endorsed by classical theorists as well as by later day realists like Metternich, Bismarck, and Kissinger who used this as strategic action, and whose theories are seen as classics. It is from this that neo-realists derive their legitimacy.

The structural determinism of neo-realism

Neo-realism sought an advance from realist perspectives by adding the 'scientific' element into its theory, in addition to rational choice. It maintained continuity with realism in the importance it gave to the state, military power, and the polarity of the international system. There are however other differences within the overall continuity between the two.

1   One difference is in the approach to the security dilemma. In the 1980s, neo-realist theorists such as Gilpin and Waltz wondered whether the security dilemma and the free rider phenomenon in the international anarchical system could be challenged. Their answer was 'no'. For Gilpin, the system cannot be emancipated from the rivalries which stem from the search for power by individual states (Gilpin, 1981). As a consequence, wars of hegemony shall always be repeated. For Waltz too, no transnational movements could prevent wars between hegemonic powers and the subsequent redistribution of power. He promoted the bipolar model as the most stable one because the two superpowers would have sufficient material power to reduce uncertainty about the enemy's intentions, to keep their allies from defecting, and to not rely upon them too closely (Waltz, 1979). The neo-realist paradigm fits extremely well with the Cold War period. For Waltz, security was ensured by nuclear deterrence and nuclear power-balancing while bipolarity produced a balance of power which assured a considerable measure of security.

2   Two, like classical realists, structuralists and neo-realists believe that the fundamental feature of the international system is anarchy and lack of control. Therefore, it is a system of self-help through military build up or alliances. In other words, you might not be interested in war, but war may have an interest in you, which you as the state must defend against. Threats may also come from inside but this state is characterized by a monopoly over the use of force. Waltz's third image is that it does not matter if you are democratic or authoritarian. It is not the character of the state, but its relative position in a structure that determines outcomes and proclivity to war. All states can go to war. Systems do not matter (democracy or dictatorship), culture and history, or individuals do not matter, and competition between states is eternal and universal. In these circumstances pre-emptive war is accepted. The security dilemma however is that war is a constant possibility. Interest in individuals is limited to collateral damage.

3   Three, neo-realists claim to have found a scientific principle of conflict independent of its historical representation. In the post-Cold War period, the neo-realists reformulated this structural determinism in reaffirming the state as an exclusive unitary actor and in denying the influence of international organisations because they required an unacceptable loss of sovereignty. For them, security exclusively means 'order and international

boundary maintenance, to be achieved by the preservation of a hierarchical international system in which the great powers act as the world's policemen' (Tickner, 1995: 185). The neo-realist school also emphasizes economic interests. However, it does not do so a priori. States make threats in sectors where they have the best options, and when reacting to threats, they choose their means on the basis of comparative advantage. Lodgaard argues that if the focus of discussion is on security concepts with a claim to universality it would be consistent if this stays within the realm of common denominators (Lodgaard, 2000).

4   Four, in classical realism, balance of power occurs because of conscious effort of states; for the neo-realists it occurs despite and outside the effort of states (Sheehan, 2006: 19). The neo-realist framework emphasizes the primacy of the state in addition to 'new security thinking' by writers like Buzan. Neo-realism has been criticized for 'its insistence on the sameness effect and on the unchanging, structurally determined nature of international politics' which 'makes it unhistorical perhaps anti-historical' (Brown *et al.*, 1995: 461). It could not anticipate the peaceful end of the Cold War and the break-up of the Soviet Union. Moreover, it promotes a concept of the international system focusing on exceptional cases of relationships degenerating into war whereas in most cases international relations are peaceful.

Buzan defined security as existential threat to a designated referent object which justifies measures to handle the use of force, and/or provokes a situation where rules can be broken. He argued that the straightjacket militaristic approach to security that dominated the Cold War led to the underdevelopment of the concept. He broadened the security concept to include political, economic, social, and environment threats and proceeded to examine security from three perspectives of the international system, the state, and the individual. However, in his analysis, the state should remain the main, though not necessarily the sole, referent of security. For Buzan, it remains primary because it is the only agency that can safeguard the individual. Buzan states that to maintain security, the state has to be strong. For this he equates the fate of human collectivities as the primary object of security. The state becomes the reference of security as the representative of human collectivities. The choice is between the lesser of two evils, threat from state or from others. Threats from state are lower than those that would arise in its absence. In seeking security, the state and society are sometimes in harmony, sometimes in opposition. The bottom line is survival. For Buzan, the degree of weakness of states is correlated to socio-political cohesion, but that of strength is traditional (military). The state is not secure if constituent parts are insecure and state security invariably leads to individual security.

Contemporary realist writers contest this neo-realist structural determinism that postulates that states shall necessarily wage wars. Defensive realism theorists such as Walt or Taliaferro (Taliaferro, 2000/1) challenge the fatality of conflict and believe that states' expansionist tendencies can be restrained and that states can build mutual trust to reduce the security dilemma which fuels the constant state of war. They believe that conflict is avoidable through a 'balance of threat' with nuclear power and mutual deterrence on the one hand and through alliance networks on the other hand. Besides, state-centric or neo-classical realists shift the realist focus from interstate behaviour to intrastate decision. They still consider that material conditions and search for power are key elements of security but they introduce the idea that public opinion and domestic factors do influence the priorities accorded to security policies. Thus they attempt to broaden the scope of the realist definition of security.

The problem in such theorizing is that states are identified with governments that are made up of people with their own interests, and it is necessary to question the different types of states that were unable to provide security. Moreover, new threats to security which defy boundaries cannot be solved by one state alone. The uneven development and a global capitalist economy have contributed to an 'insecure' and unjust situation where the security of the rich seems to be increasingly diminishing that of the poor. Further, while strong states can withhold the pressure, weak states cannot, since the integrated economy is not to their advantage. Paradigms that focus entirely on the capabilities of the state are unable to explain the necessary internal dynamics of security. Despite these gaps, neo-realism continues to influence international relations theory and its logic continues to lure governments and international policy makers. It wills them to concentrate more on their role in the international balance of power than on their primary function, that is extending authority, law, and security, and thus fostering the conditions necessary for the prosperity and well-being of their citizens.

The human security difference/objection

Human security advocates criticize neo-realism in four main ways: on the question of the referent object, on values, on pereception of threats and on means to protect (adapted from Kleschnitzki, 2003).

Referent object: the central tenet of all human security writings is that an excessive focus on state security comes at the expense of the well-being and security of individuals. This is overlooked in traditional security studies that ignore the history, culture, economic relations, and political orientation of states. Neo-realists homogenize states because in the international system states become part of the club regardless of their history. Yet, neo-realism is a systems theory that overlooks domestic conditions and focuses solely upon the structures of the international system created by the capabilities of states.

Values: in many human security readings there is the assertion that sovereignty and territorial integrity are values in the state-centric, neo-realist doctrine (example of Bajpai, 2000). These values come instead from the policy of states that may use neo-realism or any other theory as a means of promoting their interests. Neo-realism, in fact, strives to be essentially value-free by design. It is interested only in discerning structures of power that affect state behaviour in a condition of anarchy. To further clarify this issue, 'sovereignty' and 'territorial integrity' are not 'inherent' in states' values. Neo-realists acknowledge the existence of these concepts but believe that what the human security advocates call 'values' are actually 'institutions'. According to Mearshimer, 'Realists also recognize that the state sometimes operates through institutions. However, they believe that those rules reflect state calculations of self-interest based primarily on the international distribution of power'. Sovereignty and territorial integrity then, are 'institutions' that states have mutually agreed or promised to uphold, due to their mutual interests in preventing attack (Mearshimer, 1994/5: 13). The liberal institutionalists accept the basic premises of realism but believe that institutions can play a useful role in changing the 'contractual environment' to help states cooperate. Institutions 'provide information, reduce transaction costs, make commitments more credible, establish focal points for coordination and, in general, facilitate the operation of reciprocity' (Keohane and Martin, 1995: 42). In this way they may mitigate fears of cheating and exploitation by other states. Buzan understands this distinction well as he explains that security is about survival. The securitization of an issue is when something 'is presented as posing an existential threat to a designated referent object'. And this, Buzan says, 'has opened the way for the state to assume special powers to handle existential threats' (Buzan *et al.*, 1998).

Perception of threat: following Buzan's point, human security advocates, in addition to *deepening* the debate on referent objects, have also *widened* the perception of threats. Taking the viewpoint of the individual however can be absolutely overwhelming – the range of potential threats may affect freedom, dignity, or well-being. As the UNDP shows, there can be threats that endanger the economic, food, health, environment, personal, community, and political security of individuals. In contrast, neo-realists limit their investigation to the threat and use of force, conflict, and war. Thus, they remain focused on relations between other actors – not on background conditions or environmental states. Similar to Nef's ideas of mutual vulnerability, it is recognized that poverty or underdevelopment in one state can lead to unstable conditions that threaten other states' security (Nef, 1999). Such underdevelopment however, is not addressed unless it leads to competition or conflict. These limitations are difficult for many to accept. The neo-realists defend their territory by insisting that they are concerned with structure. Background conditions may cause important problems for policy makers but they are not threats in the sense of violent conflict. In the end, policy makers can turn to neo-realism to interpret other states' behaviour but it may not provide the most salient advice for crafting domestic policies.

The means to protect: human security advocates promote the idea that their interests can be promoted through soft power (as opposed to the hard power of the military), long term cooperation (in contrast to suspicious relations in anarchy), and preventive measures (as opposed to the use of coercion) (Bajpai, 2000). They indirectly attack the assumed power that realists give to military force, and express a concern that the accumulation of military might can actually decrease the security of citizens (by diverting valuable resources from other projects) and the security of mankind (by proliferation and diffusion of lethal technologies).

Human security thus proposes a departure from realism and neo-realism by focusing on the individual and redefining both violence and threats to go beyond their physical military significance. It is consequently a radical condemnation of the realist paradigm which only considers interstate military threats, the stability of the international order, and the security dilemma.

The liberalist claims

The second traditional approach that was inherited from the Enlightenment influenced by Grotius, Kant, etc., was classical liberalism. In the context of breaking down bipolarity and economic challenges after the oil shocks, liberalism stressed the role of institutions, political relationships, and economic interdependence as a means to strengthen peace and cooperation among nations. While neo-realism is strongly pessimistic, liberalist theoreticians emphasize the possibility of overcoming the natural tensions between states. The basics of this extremely broad theory might be summed up in six major points.

1   Like the realists, liberalists believe that the international system is anarchic. However, they assume that there is room for regulation and that states can be constrained by means other than the use of force.
2   As opposed to realists, they consider that security does not comprise only military and material capacities but also institutional, economic, and political factors.
3   Since the 1970s, they have taken interdependencies and globalization into account and have built a radically new paradigm known as institutional liberalism. Whereas before they focused on interstate relationships, now theorists think in transnational terms. Security is not a zero-sum game anymore but a network in which all actors and all factors are strongly interrelated. This paradigm does not consider only states but also groups, NGOs, international organizations, and transnational movements.
4   Whereas neo-realists believe in the fatality of conflict, liberalists consider it possible to reduce the natural aggressiveness of states through the establishment of common values, the harmonization of norms, and the creation of networks and multilateral institutions. They believe that the notion of commonality and sharing might become superior in IR to the notion of power.
5   They promote the institutionalization of security in international organizations to submit states to common values. Through such networks and institutions, liberalism and democracy shall spread, together with their culture of compromise and negotiation instead of conflict. This point is intimately linked with the 'democratic peace' theory first propounded by Kant in 1795, who argued that democracies were less warlike than other forms of government, and in recent times promoted by Doyle. This theory

contends that democracies do not fight against each other: first because they have a propensity to settle their tensions peacefully, and second, because, in a democracy, citizens influence decisions about going to war. However, this theory states that democracies and other states are equally prone to wars.

6   Finally, commerce has a tremendous importance in achieving international peace because it consolidates egotistical interests to found a common interest. This reasserts the role of interdependence, globalization, free trade, and transnational financial networks in security. It argues that as the commercial interdependence of countries grows they will avoid conflicts in order to protect their commerce.

The human security debate

Human security breaks with the liberalist view of security that still adopts a too narrow state-centric vision of international relations. There is, however, a common line between the two paradigms in that the liberalist one introduces economic, political, and commercial dimensions alongside military concerns, and considers international organizations, NGOs, representatives of the civil society, and transnational fluxes alongside states. The system is seen as multi-centric, the threats and actors interacting, the institutionalization of security possible. Liberalists highlight the advantages of cooperation and stress the fatality of conflict. Human security stands in the tradition of these liberalist innovations; expanding the threats and broadening the range of actors taken into account. But it revolutionizes these sober novelties by moving the cursor to the individual's perceptions that are freed from their realist state-centric chains.

The constructivist approach

In the 1990s, a group of theoreticians contested the traditional realist and liberalist theories in an effort to free themselves from the usual focus on the state as the *one* security actor. In the new approach, individuals, groups, NGOs, and the emerging transnational civil society actors became the centre of focus. Realism and liberalism were criticized for their over-emphasis on material, objective rational factors, and for failing to take into account subjective, psychological, and 'human' elements.

This constructivist approach is defined by four key points:

1   Wendt opposed both realists and liberalists by arguing that the international system is not the reflection of power relationships and desires to dominate but of concepts and images (Wendt, 1987, 1992). Thus security is only a question of what he calls 'inter-subjective' perceptions. Onuf contests the ahistorical, mono-variable realist view of security and points out that there is no single truth, for truths are linked to the arguments with which they are justified (Onuf, 1995).

2 As a consequence, anarchy and the security dilemma can be deconstructed. There is no *fatality* of tensions between states. Even though the liberalist paradigm argues that they can be overcome, it postulates that there are some tensions due to the anarchical structure of society and the security dilemma. Constructivists consider that tensions between states flow from values, aspirations, and perceptions that change from time to time. Such shifts do not stem from material conditions as realists think but from self and subjective representations.

3 Constructivists like Adler point out that not only are the security dilemmas socially constructed but also the whole structure of the international system: anarchy, competition, search for power, constant tensions are not objective realities (Adler, 1997). They are 'inter-subjective constructs' integrated by states since the Westphalia treaties in 1648. Wendt thus says that 'anarchy is what states make out of it' (Wendt, 1992).

4 Finally, the determinants of security are not material conditions (military for the realists and economic or financial for the liberalists) but ideas and norms. States' interests are not exogenously given. They are constantly evolving and, therefore, they make it possible to change security and to challenge the determinism of realism in changing representations. For constructivists, the end of the Cold War was due to a cognitive reformulation of the external environment by key elite decision makers, for instance, Gorbachev.

These are the basic concepts shared by all the writers who conduct extremely diverse researches under the 'constructivist' denomination. Katzenstein (1996) studies the impact of cultural identity on security policies and on the construction of perceptions and values, stressing that power and culture should not be separated as distinct phenomena or causes. Finally, Finnemore (1996) reconciles liberalism and constructivism in studying how norms can be socially 'reconstructed' and how international organizations reshape state behaviours. As a response to the failure of traditional realism, the constructivist paradigm focuses on endogenous factors determining security policies. Although it may not provide a coherent theory of security and often interprets case studies which cannot always be generalized, it does propose a clear theory of agency that orients actors' behaviour and dictates strategies and choices.

Similarities with human security

The break from state-centric approaches was undoubtedly made possible by the works of the constructivist theorists who built a vision of security starting from the individuals and their inter-subjective perceptions. They showed that cultural identity had an impact on conflicts (Katzenstein, 1996) and that norms could be reconstructed by international regimes (Finnemore, 1996), opening a field which was further explored by human security. Human security can thus be read as an attempt to reconstruct the interpretation of the roots of insecurity; to place underdevelopment, poverty, and humiliation at the top of the structure. Some of these themes have also been examined by critical and radical theories. Constructivist international relations theory is not a single unified movement, but its significance lies in its assumption that behaviour, interests, and relationships are socially constructed and can change. This has value for human security because it broadens international relations by bringing in actors other than the state. Constructivism explains phenomena to which realism is blind, like the assumption that threats are constructed, not inevitable, and they can be altered or mitigated. It has thus been used in theory building and critiquing. But human security is wider than the constructivist approach, since culture and perceptions are only some of the multiple aspects considered by human security.

Alternative theories

The critical theory approach

Critical theory, inspired by the philosophical underpinnings of the Frankfurt School and the leftist scholar Gramsci, seeks to provide an alternative to the realist paradigm of security and structure. It stands for social transformation in a world which, in its view, supports a powerful few and reinforces th status quo. Critical theorists maintain that the realist security framework preserves the existing system managed by powerful countries at the international level and elites at the domestic level (Harshe, 2005). They argue that the realist preoccupation with the security of the state overlooks the insecurity of individuals, groups, and communities. The basic points of critical theory have been summarized by George (George, 1993): critical theory explores the connection between the dominant idea and its impact on the practice of power. It examines the relationship between the wealth, knowledge, and the perception of reality. It sees the present in terms of the past; the present is an outcome of continuous historical process. Critical theory further challenges the existing system and favours a fundamental change in the institutions and power structure.

Radical theory

The radical theorists, similar to critical theorists, contest realist epistemology from a Left position. Their strength lies in their critiques of realists and their focus on world systems. They object to the realist premise that the objective of international relations is to study relations among states, because states hold ultimate political and military power based on sovereignty (Teschke, 2003: 300). This definition is deliberately restricting, since it excludes other actors, communities, and systems and presents the international system and the state as unalterable entities. In reality, alternative theories exist and international laws can be changed. Preiswerk shows that realism covers an elaborate network of power relationships often based on extreme inequalities and injustices (Preiswerk, 1981: 8).

Vanaik argues that 'By its basic premise, political realism is incapable of theorizing the relationship between intra- and trans-state actors, actions processes and inter-state behaviour and occurrences' (Vanaik, 2005: 411). Realism then, is 'obsessed with stability' and how to manage this. Its treatment of the source of state power/ interest is necessarily crude and unproblematic since order is established in the international system through 'balance of power'. So, fewer the big actors, the more manageable the balance of power, whereas the nature of international system i.e. capitalism or the global expansion of capital and its implications are ignored (Teschke, 2003: Chapter 2). Radicals argue that realists see power as the aggregate of territorial size, population, valued natural resources, political cohesion, national morale, economic strength and productivity, and above all military strength. The key aim of state power is enhancement of security of one's state. Military security is geared not for a nation's own needs but to intentions or perceptions of security of other nations. This is what leads to the arms race. The radical writers focus on policies of imperialism and see globalization as a negative phenomenon. Human security accepts the people-centred premise of the radical approach, however, it focuses on development rather than developing a critique of imperialism as the dominant factor of international relations. Further, radical theory uses class rather than the individual as the basic unit of analysis.

Postmodernists' look at security

Postmodernists factor in the dramatic changes of the contemporary period into their world view, so international relations too should be based on an understanding of new structures. The most influential amongst the many postmodernists are Lyotard, Foucault, and Derrida, who reject modernity and do not accept normative positions that they believe are grounded in privileged ethical assumptions (Sheehan, 2006: 135). They argue against meta narratives and grand theories of knowledge on the grounds that there is no single truth, ideology, or text. Similarly, there can be no single authority or value system as these are all interest driven. For the postmodernists, security is part of the linear narrative characteristic of the modern Western understanding and self-interest. The Cold War is a triumph of Western capitalist values. Modernity is linked to war and its brutality and those who reject it, postmodernists argue, are seen as obstacles to development.

Postmodernists essentially attempt to dislodge the state as the primary referent of security, and place emphasis on the interdependency and trans-nationalization of non-state actors. This is reflected in the work of Booth (Booth, 1995, 1998), and others who also broaden the security concept, expanding it horizontally and vertically, making human security more important than state security. States are neither effective nor adequate since they have become the primary source for insecurity. The postmodern approach asserts that national sovereignty is unravelling and that states are proving less and less capable of performing their traditional tasks. Global factors impinge on government decisions and undermine their capacity to control either external or domestic policies. Carim has argued that if state sovereignty has not ended, it is under severe challenge (Carim, 1995).

The logical alternative to the modern state as the unit of analysis is the diffusion of power from states to local or regional communities so as to cater to cultural diversity. The strength of postmodernism lies in its challenge to the realist and neo-realist generalizations but the problems are equally severe because it does not believe in providing alternatives. It is against regional integration, even though regional integration can deal with some common problems of human security. Further, the existence of strong non-state actors does not mean end of the state. Human security approaches that show the interconnection of phenomenon and construct a larger theory are at variance with the constructivist approach.

The feminist contribution to engendering security

There are many strands of feminist theories, ranging from liberal, radical, socialist, and essentialist feminists. However, they all argue for women's equality and see patriarchy as an overriding part of the social system that permeates every other institution. Their critique of the traditional approaches of realism has contributed to alternate paradigms of security. Feminists challenge the realist doctrines of the state where the central figure and main actor is the 'sovereign man' or the 'hero warrior' who is the symbol of power, they fault the realists for endorsing a 'masculinist' understanding of the world that favours the power and status of men. In this system 'sovereign man' can make a rational choice to legitimize violence, while women are excluded and controlled either through direct physical violence or indirectly by conceptions and ideology that endorse role differentials. The state is complicit in this through its laws and policy of non-intervention in domestic violence. Exclusion of women and all minorities is similarly challenged by the human security framework. Feminists believe that the realist and neo-realist emphasis on anarchy is really a subterfuge that keeps women from discerning the recurrent patterns of patriarchy and denies the inter-connection of things and prevents visualizing reality in all its complexity (Sylvester, 1994: 140). Human security does not deny the existence of patriarchy but privileges all individuals rather than women. Feminists like Tickner believe that national security has been an almost exclusively male domain (Tickner, 1992). Feminists have challenged the view of the military as a defender of a pre-given 'national interest'. Security of the state does not automatically bestow security to its members, especially those outside its priorities and boundaries. Strategies must encompass non-militarist methods of negotiations. Feminist geopolitics is not an alternative theory of geopolitics, but an approach to global issues with feminist politics in mind.

The human security convergence with alternative theories

There are some commonalities between the radicals and critical theorists, the feminists, and human security approaches. For all three, the individual is the prime referent of security. Second, they are inclusive and comprehensive in their approach. All focus on the interconnectedness of international relations and see the systemic links of domestic and international events and policies. All three link the domestic to the external and the constant impact of one on the other. Third, all are based on a commitment to social and economic justice, and not just the absence of social and economic rights as threats. All three base their theoretical postulates on the combination of the theories of rights, human rights, development, and equity. The feminists go further by engendering all institutions and questioning patriarchal theory and practice. The feminist conception of power is specifically 'power to engage with' rather than 'power over the other'. The radical theorists want power for the people, whereas human security argues for empowerment for all and protection for the marginalized and vulnerable.

Radical theorists advocate social change, challenge the national status quo, and build strategies for counter hegemony. They advocate internationalism which is an alliance of counter-hegemonic forces. Feminists look for an alliance of women's movements and other excluded forces. They oppose militarization and see it as an aspect of masculinity. Feminists, however, believe that the human security concept needs to be gendered (Chenoy, 2005) because, even within radical frameworks like 'people's security' it is men who get privileges and the special roles and needs of women are taken over by male agendas.

Critical theorists are closer to the human security approach in that they make vulnerable individuals and groups their primary referents. However, they differ from the latter since they focus mainly on the counter-hegemonic forces that aim to change the dominant security and development processes. Human security seeks to change how states and individuals think about security by gradually broadening security and raising the threshold of what should be the basis of human dignity and rights. The problem with radical and feminist theories is that while they remain useful critiques to traditional international relations, and open the doors to the inclusion of new actors and issues, they are unable to present complete alternatives to realist theory. They add to the consensus on the need to widen the international relations paradigm.

Paradigms compared

To sum up, for the realists, the key words are 'state', 'sovereignty', 'power', 'national interest', 'national security', and 'self-help'. Their paradigm is based on the assumption that human beings are innately bad, an assumption which is transferred at the state level and for which the resort to force is a natural way to increase power and to ensure survival. The liberals stress on norms, institutions, and moral issues promoted by international organizations and non-state actors in a multi-centric system. They believe that anarchical conditions can be mitigated by the expansion of liberal democracies, the growth of liberal trade, and by a network of transnational institutional linkages. Finally, constructivism argues that state interests stem from identities and international norms, rather than from the effects of international anarchy.

However, if attention shifts from theory to practice, one sees the growing role and significance of peace keeping operations, civil society involvement, the spread of democratic values, human rights considerations, the role of the media, soft power, the dissolution of state authority, etc., there exists no one paradigm capable of explaining the security behaviour of relevant actors. Rather, each of the paradigms has something potentially worthwhile to say and a watershed has probably been reached as regards the necessity to rethink security. Currently security in practice seems to evolve towards the critical paradigm expanding the notion of security to individuals, to social, economic, and environmental threats to human life and dignity.

The following two tables provide a complete comparison of the different international relations theories against human security variables. Table 3.2 reviews the potential differences in the four questions of security, while Table 3.3 provides a more extensive comparison of variables.

Conclusion

The debate between human security and other paradigms in international relations is not closed. The dominance of traditional theory as expressed by realists, neo-realists, and liberals has been systematically challenged by the critical, radical, and feminist theorists, but continues to hold its ground, because of its use value by powerful states, aspiring regional hegemons, and entrenched elites that are interested in retaining their power within the nation state structures. The proponents of human security see the value of the incremental approach, take the middle path, and propose an approach that uses the strength of public morality and brings back ethics into the international discourse. Human values that had been sacrificed for the sake of sovereignty and territorial inviolability of the state have become central in human security. The individual who is crucial in liberal theory, but was at the receiving end of state power, has become the main referent. This is a shift from the traditional theories and their methodology. Human security has a long history and derives its strength from many ideas and theories across disciplines. It can develop as a concept only by maintaining and advancing this plurality.

Table 3.2 Differences in security models

	Human Security	Realism – Neo-realism	Liberalism	Feminism/critical theory/constructivism
Referent object: security for whom/what?	People, communities, and state	State and state system	State, liberal values, state and liberal values International organizations, state	Women, civil society actors, and excluded people
Values: security of which values?	Human rights, human development, dignity. Security and protection of individuals Feeling of internal/personal security Freedom from fear and want, and dignity Freedom to make choices	Sovereignty Power Territorial integrity Markets Democracies	Democratic institutions; human rights, markets Cooperation, institutions Peace, security, democracy	Inclusion of women, civil society groups, feminist values Identity, context Critique of systems/values
Perception of threat: security from what?	Poverty, environmental degradation, violation of rights by states and non-state actors Natural disasters, man-made violence, economic decline	Other states and non-state actors Threats to state integrity	Illiberal values and state and non-state actors and threats Rogue/failed states	Masculinity and militarism Internal/external (environment)

| The means to protect: security by what means? | Ensuring human rights, human development
Engagement with states and non-state actors; sanctions etc.
Development
Empowerment
Local ownership
Diplomacy/military
Human rights
Empowerment of individuals
Protection of state | Power, military force, diplomacy and deterrence, alliances, collective security | Power negotiation and military force
Diplomacy, multilateralism
International economic regimes | Multilateralism, negotiation and inclusion of women, communities, and groups as stakeholders at every level |

Table 3.3 Analysing security variables

Questions/Focus	Human security	Realist approach	Liberal approach	Constructivist approach	Feminist approach
State of the international system?	Insecurity from inequity, injustice, poverty, health and environmental hazards, denial of human rights and justice	Anarchy, competition, and self-help system Balance of power	Anarchy, competition but some space for regulation through multi-lateralism	Anarchy as an 'inter subjective' construct that can be deconstructed The international system is based on communal interaction	A system based on the exclusion of women and masculinity
Central referents of security?	Individual and communities	The state and its expressed national interest	States and international institutions, NGOs and civil society as well as transnational groups	Individuals, groups, NGOs, the civil society	Women and feminist values
Determinants of security?	Economic, health, and food security; environmental, personal, community and political security	State and national security and military security	State and market security; and security for institutions	Security of cultural identities, ideas and norms	Security and empowerment of women and all subaltern classes
Aims/interests of the state?	To empower and protect its citizens	To ensure stability and maximum power States' interests	To reach military, economic and political interdependence	To change the aspirations and perceptions of the population	To create gender equity and a justice based peace loving state

		determined by material conditions	States' interests are based on values and institutions	States' interests determined by identity and culture	Feminist interests representing civil society to replace elitist patriarchal state interests
Security through which means?	Prevention, protection, provision of human security, empowerment of people	Protection of the state, a zero-sum game	Cooperation; institutionalization and interdependence	Peaceful norms and perceptions, reconstructed security through international organizations	Security through gender rights, equity, and empowerment
Role of actors in security?	People and civil society should be empowered and responsible for human security	State executives, military commanders and selected experts oversee national security	Actors that emerge from and use democratic processes to build trust	Multiple actors who work on the basis of trust	Women to be empowered as equal citizens and actors.
Notion and role of power?	Power as collective principle and people's power	State has ultimate power based on legitimate force and military strength. Between states there is a balance of power	Power sharing based on values and ideals	Power is based on 'inter-subjective' perceptions	Power needs to be feminized and negotiated.

4 Human security and human development

Shadow or threshold?

Among the development community, it was Mahbub ul Haq, former Economy and Finance Minister of Pakistan and founder of Human Development Reports, who first viewed human security as a supplement to the human development debate in the 1994 UNDP *Human Development Report*. The concept was introduced as a 'natural extension of human development in the security field' in the context of post-Cold War opportunities for the peace dividend. Ever since, however, conceptual overlap with human development has spawned confusion. This chapter tracks the evolution of the human development concept, its distinction from human security and the additional values in the overall field of analysis, keeping in mind their inter-linkages and the scope for reconciliation between the two concepts. Is human security ultimately a parallel shadow of human development or is it a way to determine its threshold? The first question that can be posed is why was there a necessity to expand the human development agenda to human security? Was this a mere attempt to rephrase development concerns in a security language, or an opportunity to cover the shortcomings of the paradigm of human development that had been conceived in early 1990s?

The problem of paradigms

The previous chapter dwelt on the necessity to broaden the scope of 'security' horizontally to include non-traditional threats, and to deepen it vertically to include referent objects beyond the state, with a focus on individuals, thus laying the groundwork for the intrusion of development thinking into security studies and *vice versa*. Human security further addresses the need to explain 'threats' to development neglected by the human development discourse. Three cogent reasons now follow for the emergence of the human security concept within development thinking based on practical considerations:

First, development is not enough for protecting individual's lives and well-being. Development gains can be undermined by conflicts and wars (through social, physical and material destruction), extreme situations such as natural disasters (as the 2004 Tsunami showed in South Asia), and sudden downturns, or in Amartya Sen's terminology, 'sudden destitution', which cannot be addressed solely through human development. Even when a society is witnessing growth (development), or growth with equity in a manner that involves people in the process (human development), sudden downturns can erase those gains. In Asia for example, where there had been considerable achievements in human development (increase in life expectancy and adult literacy, access to health care and nutrition), the 1997–1999 crisis led to severe budget cuts on government social sector programmes, resulting in unmet needs of the poor and impoverishment of people. As a result, poverty made a comeback among population groups that had moved above the threshold, while affecting some groups for the first time. People became poorer, both in terms of assets and opportunities for health, education, etc. Human development had not been enough to mitigate the harm done by sudden crisis.

Such extreme situations show that it is not only difficult to maintain progress but also that the progress recorded may be seriously eroded. The Asian crisis proved that during the economic crisis, social protection systems (or social safety nets) were inadequate to meet the needs of the affected people. Safety nets needed to be institutionalized as part of development. As the crisis demonstrated in Thailand, Indonesia and South Korea for example, governments need to have the institutional capacity to deal adequately with layoffs and find formal mechanisms to protect people from unemployment and its consequences, retrenched workers in state-owned enterprises, or a sudden influx of returning overseas contract workers. This involves not only identification of structural impediments to policy (i.e. adequate macroeconomic management required for growth, its adequate distribution for human development), but also risk identification and prevention, adequate responses as well as protective measures in response to crisis situations.

Second, traditional development can undermine human security in both the short and long term. Within this argument, development itself holds the seed of the *raison d'être* of human security. The risks that human security is meant to protect against attest to weakness of the development process. Development is transitional by definition and therefore gives rise to instability and insecurity. The overall growth experienced in a developing country may not only fail to improve life for the poorest groups, but it can also undermine longer term opportunities for them. Traditional development models have had a flawed record for being a 'catch-up' process that favour Western models based on individualistic consumerism and industrialization, which can endanger the modes of life in developing countries. Although the models have since been readjusted in response to failed policies and widespread criticism, the by-products of much of development strategy are still environmental damage, disempowerment of women, and increasing inequality between the rich and the poor, leaving the majority of the people to suffer for the profits of a few. Traditional development models promulgated by the Bretton Woods Institutions have undermined human security by enriching a powerful few while impoverishing and disempowering the majority. The roles of the state are reduced to promoting economic growth and unleashing private initiatives, while their capacities diminished to compensate for the associated marginalization affecting large population groups in most developing societies.

Just as risk and instability are part of societal changes in the process of development, the transition towards a political system that increases human security is also bound to be characterized by uncertainty and increased vulnerability. In Sen's words, this 'simple recognition of vulnerability in growth makes it absolutely obligatory to see security as a central part of development' (Sen, 1999: 28). Even democratic changes and accelerated development can undermine human security, as the experiences of transition countries attest. Individuals are able to take advantage of the options presented by development to the degree that they are able to shape social processes. In many transition countries of the former Soviet Union and Eastern Europe, while regime changes opened up new avenues for democratic participation, many people were unable to participate because of the accompanied retrenching that occurred in the economy, costing them their means for livelihoods. The risks, however, are not only in the short-term. Traditional development can also undermine human security by setting up a dependent relationship *vis-à-vis* donors, by undermining local capacities, and forcing trade-offs in social and human spending under the weigh of conditionalities, as Chapter 9 will argue.

Third, the changing global order and new threats have led to the merging of development with security imperatives. As Nef argues, much of the assumptive scaffolding underpinning development studies and international relations and securities studies have lost their relevance in the aftermath of the Cold War (Nef, 1999). Between 1945 and 1989, development and security were compartmentalized, both conceptually and in practice. National security was framed within an East–West debate, while the North–South was a 'development' problem. After 1989, with the shift of security focus to internal dynamics, civil wars, ethnic competition, natural resources, etc., security and development needed to be seen not from a zero sum perspective, but from a negative score card perspective, with the possibilities for winning and losing together. On the one hand, mainstream orthodox models saw backwardness as the result of the legacy of a traditional society, to be overcome by modernization based on Western models. On the other, according to the dependency theory, backwardness was the negative consequence of Western domination over the Southern periphery. Both models saw development as a unidirectional and irreversible historical continuum: developed regions were secure, while 'insecurity' came from the other world. With the advent of trans-border threats such as uncontrolled migration, health epidemics, global criminal networks, environmental disasters, etc., the seemingly secure societies of the North came to be increasingly vulnerable to the events in the less secure and underdeveloped regions of the globe in a way that international relations and development theories had failed to recognize. Changes after the 1990s needed to be increasingly understood through comprehensive, dynamic conceptualization that would require inter-disciplinary approaches beyond security and development in order to explain better the complex interdependence.

Nef proposed to reconceptualize the North/South development and East/West security paradigms with the core–periphery model, based on the idea of mutual vulnerability. His concept of the world system portrayed better the type of dominant and integrated pattern of global production, distribution and power. As he saw it, relations in the present system are not so much those between territorially defined centres and peripheries (national, regions or settlements) as among concrete social actors: groups, classes and individuals. The model relies on an unequal and asymmetrical exchange between a developed core and underdeveloped semi peripheries and peripheries, in which systemic and sub-systemic development and underdevelopment are functionally and historically, but not deterministically, interrelated. The 'core' constitutes the elite socio-economic groups, trans-nationally integrated, and the 'centre' of developed geographical regions with their own elites and non-elite social periphery. Power became the ability of one actor or group of actors to induce compliable behaviour in others. Within this model, the Western core consists of an interdependent and stratified bloc of dominant trading partners, while the other two worlds collapse into one heterogeneous conglomerate of newly industrializing, development and transitional countries, increasingly 'insecure' in their path to development.

Given these reasons, there is need for new approaches and policies to 'secure' development gains. What however is human development in the first place and how did it evolve?

Evolution of development thinking towards human development

Human development evolved in response to the theoretical and practical needs of preceding decades. Thus, before the Second World War, progress was still seen as a trickle-down effect of economic growth. The Great Depression of the 1930s and decolonization were the push factors that led to the articulation of a development approach to economic growth. Progress became associated with a model of economic growth defined by the kind of commodities produced, the number of people and the social class of people benefiting from the developmental efforts. Throughout the developing world, the colonial legacy had led to low incomes, low savings and investments, appalling health, low literacy, and primary production with little manufacturing and total dependency. A school of economic thought, known as development economics, emerged in the 1950s and the 1960s with a specific plan to improve conditions in poor countries through economic measures as well as industrialization and investment mechanisms (Sen, 1988: 10–24). Development economics of the 1950s and 1960s was traditionally associated with Walt Whitman Rostow's five-step theory of industrialization to attain prosperity, in a model considering only the advantages of purely-economic oriented growth, most of the emphasis being concentrated on raising levels of basic economic indicators such as GNP, investment, savings and industrial output (see Table 4.1).

However, notwithstanding the appeal of this easy recipe for development through economic growth, the expected results never came to fruition, and rather than durable development, emphasis on industrialization and investment often led to no more than countries scattered with 'white elephants' – huge state-of-the-art plants often lost in the middle of the landscape, which had no triggering effect for any form of development. The 'growth only theory' also fell under the criticism of 'dependency theory', which underlined that economic growth was not necessarily

Table 4.1 Rostow's five stages of economic growth

Traditional society	⇨	Preconditions for take off	⇨	The take off	⇨	The drive to maturity	⇨	High mass consumption
• Low output rural economy • Ad hoc innovations • Hierarchical society with low vertical social mobility.		• New ethos: risk taking, enterprising investment • Greater emphasis on education. • Wider scope for trade (internal and external).		• Remnants of the traditional society are overcome. • High investment, savings and profit. • Innovations • Higher output and industrialization.		• Sustained fluctuating progress. • Steady investment • Successive waves of industrialization.		• Shift of production towards durable consumer goods • Development of services industries • Increased resources for social welfare and security.

Source: Adapted from Rostow 1960.

synonymous with improvement in human life conditions due to oft-neglected distribution problems, which resulted in unemployment, underemployment and vicious circles of poverty. Not only was the human dimension neglected, but the terms of trade between First and Third World countries deteriorated, furthering higher outside dependency.

The 1970s saw challenges to the growth-only agenda, with the focal indicators for development shifting from the traditional economic approach to Gross National Product (GNP), to socio-economic indicators such as employment rates, or quality of redistribution of economic growth. The 1970s also brought about the 'Basic Needs' approach in a further move towards human-centred concerns, focusing on a range of basic goods and services required for decent quality living for the poor. This approach and definition of development was devised inside the World Bank and the International Labour Organization, and by scholars such as Ghai, Streeten, and Stewart, but was criticized for its paternalism, with institutions from the North often deciding what were the good decisions for the South and its poor. Amartya Sen also disapproved its materialistic reductionism, utilitarianism and commodity fetishism (Sen 1988). At the same time, the widening of social differentiation, research on Third World women and pressures from the growing women's movement, led to a new model that sought to 'integrate' women into the development model known as the 'Women in Development' (WID) movement (Momsen, 1991: 3; Newland, 1991: 123). The approach ultimately led to only marginal gains for women, and to a selected improvement in some countries and amongst specific classes and races. The approach was thus revised to include an analysis of gender relations that affected social and economic outcomes, and came to be known as the 'Gender in Development' approach (GAD).

The 1980s was a harsh decade for development theory, with most Third World countries crushed by the debt crisis after the policy shift from soft to hard dollar at the United States Federal Reserve Bank in 1979. The ongoing system of North–South petrodollar loans with an effective negative interest rate, was suddenly reversed with the interest rate hike, implying unsustainable debt repayments for major Third World countries, which were often forced into default. The answer to that crisis was the Structural Adjustment Program, led by the International Monetary Fund, whose prescriptions often could be summarized as increasing the role of the market, opting for export orientation while downsizing the role of government and cutting back on many, if not all, social expenditures. This combination was (almost) foolproof for these countries to get back on the track of regular debt repayments, but meant a heavy toll on the people, and women especially (Mitter, 1986). Adjustment and stabilization programmes, which had called for the shrinking of the role and size of states and increased the role of markets, led to increased inequalities and poverty, exposing further the chasm between growth-only approaches and the necessities of *human* development, leading UNICEF to launch an appeal in 1987 for 'adjustment with a human face' Cornia *et al.*, 1987).

The 1990s' human-centred approach to development was thus a natural extension of failed efforts of the past – a marriage between a philosopher (Amartya Sen) and a practitioner (Mahbub Ul Haq). It set itself apart from previous development theories by arguing that economic growth does not automatically trickle down to benefit the well-being of people, and other approaches, such as basic needs, did not hand over the reigns of decision-making to the beneficiaries themselves.

Mahbub Ul Haq, credited for bringing the approach to policy circles through the publication of annual reports, summarized the goal of development with a simple revolutionary statement: 'The obvious is the most difficult to see: the true wealth of a country is its people.' Sen, for his part, introduced ethics to economics by transforming this science from the study of national accounts to a search for freedom.

The concept thus advocated putting people back at the centre stage, encompassing an 'evaluative aspect', namely, improving human lives as an explicit development objective with emphasis on equity as a policy objective, as well as an 'agency aspect', emphasis on people as ends and means of development (see Fukuda-Parr and Shiva Kumar, 2005). In his *Development as Freedom* (1999), Sen expanded on individual freedom as a social commitment that builds on entitlements and enhances people's capabilities and quality of life. Freedom is not only the primary end of development but also the constitutive means of bringing it about. Sen's work on capabilities and functioning provided the strong conceptual foundation for the new paradigm. The purpose of development was said to expand the range of things that a person could be or do, in other words, to expand the freedom for functioning and capabilities to function, such as to be healthy and well-nourished, be knowledgeable to participate in community life, etc.

'Human development' thus came to rethink the purpose of development as well as the way development is carried out to put emphasis on how individuals play fundamental roles as subjects and objects. Human development thus posed an ethical, theoretical and methodological rupture from mainstream development thinking (Gómez Buendía, 2002): ethically, it placed people's well-being as the ultimate end goal and proposed that development was not for increasing capital but for advancing people's choices, to give them freedom. Theoretically it posed different questions about why development had failed or why it was at a certain level. Methodologically it proposed new ways to 'do' development by exploring the role of people as agents of change. It was a rupture from mainstream economic growth models as well as the basic needs welfare model.

Human development was hence conceived as an alternative to purely economic development by emphasizing the diversity of human needs. It argued that economic growth centres exclusively on the expansion of only one choice – income – while a holistic development approach must embrace other choices that people value: greater access to knowledge, better nutrition and health services, more secure livelihoods, security against crime and physical violence, satisfying leisure hours, political and cultural freedoms, sense of participation in community activities, and ultimately, self-respect and dignity. Economic growth, therefore, is only a *means* to improving human welfare, not an *end* in itself. The causal link between economic growth and improved well-being is not given automatically, but rather, has to be created consciously through public policies. Development as freedom was thus not just about shifting to people's material needs, but expanding on the needs to include dignity and participation. It meant achieving both basic material needs (food, shelter, education, health care) and achieving of human dignity (personal autonomy, participation, etc.).

Conceptual distinctions and added value of human security

What does human security concretely add to the human development discourse? The idea of human security as a guarantor of the continuation of human development, as well as a prioritization of its most urgent variables, was introduced in 1994 by Mahbub ul Haq in the annual UNDP *Human Development Report*. He proposed that human security was not just about safety during conflict but also maintaining and safeguarding development gained. Gasper argues that the human security language revives a basic needs notion under a new label of 'security' (Gasper, 2005b). If human development is about well-being, human security concentrates on the security of development gains. This enhanced concept of human security brings a number of new elements within the human development debate.

First, if development leaves some groups of people particularly vulnerable to downturns, then human security is a framework for protection against the worst harm to the most vulnerable. As Sen argues, 'human development is "growth with equity", whereas human security is "downturn with security". When a crisis hits, different group ... can have very divergent predicaments. United we may be when we go up and up, but divided we fall when we do fall' (Sen 1999: 28). Human development focuses primarily on improving the conditions of the world's poor, but falls short of action strategies when situations deteriorate, as highlighted by the Asian economic crisis. Fukuda-Parr highlights this different perspective by stating that human development focuses on absolute levels of deprivation whereas human security emphasizes the risk of sudden changes for the worse (Fukuda-Parr, 2003: 8). Human insecurity results directly from existing power structures that determines who enjoys the entitlements to security and who does not (Thomas, 2000). Some people survive and some people fall and have shattered lives. Shocks and insecurities make the poor poorer and engrain poverty and vulnerability, depending on the entitlements of different groups. A bit of insecurity can wipe out the poor completely. If human development is about equity and distributive justice, human security would like to ensure the presence of a social safety net to respond to sudden destitution.

Second, if human development is about people and expanding their choices to lead lives they value, human security recognizes the conditions that threaten survival, the continuation of daily life and the dignity of human beings, such as extreme impoverishment, environmental pollution, ill health, illiteracy, etc. Human security, therefore, becomes both the prerequisite of human development, as well as a guarantee for its sustainability and continuation. Gasper notes that human security is an addition that concerns the 'stability' of the goods provided within the human development framework, as opposed to their levels or trends (Gasper, 2005b). As the UNDP 1994 HDR argued, while human development is a process of widening the range of people's choice, human security means that people can exercise these safely and freely while being relatively confident that the opportunities they have today are not lost tomorrow.

Third, whereas human development expresses the purpose or main goal of people's existence, human security stresses the essential conditions for achieving that purpose. The Commission on Human Security for example proposed that human security activities may at times have a much shorter time horizon, and include emergency relief work and peacekeeping as well as longer-term human and institutional development (CHS, 2003). Human security includes development as one, but not the only, variable for a dignified existence. Human security acts as a guarantee of the progresses brought about by human development. According to Alkire, 'the objective of human security is to safeguard the vital core of all human lives from critical pervasive threats, in a way that is consistent with long-term human fulfillment' (Alkire, 2002: 2.1). Her approach is deliberately protective – 'to offer protection that is institutionalized, not episodic or reactive' (Ibid.: 2.2).

Fourth, as Gasper argues, human security helps in the prioritization of human development by concentrating policies on those goods that are needed for the basic minimum and which can improve both well-being and security (Gasper, 2005b). Reducing some kind of human insecurity can improve well-being or improve security or improve both. If human development is a long list of capabilities to be achieved, human security prioritizes the more urgent ones: those related to survival, livelihoods and dignity.

Fifth, in contrast to the 'freedoms to' potentials in the capability approach (freedom to do what one wants to do and be what one wants to be), human security concentrates on 'freedoms from', which as Gasper argues, 'concern definite absences not just potential absences'. As Ul Haq lamented in the 1994 HDR, 'Human security is not a concern with weapons. It is a concern with human dignity. In the last analysis, it is a child who did not die, a disease that did not spread, an ethnic tension that did not explode, a dissident who was not silenced, a human spirit that was not crushed' (UNDP, 1994: 22).

Sixth, human development and human security are both people centred, but while human development is more aggregative and carries within it the potential justification to sacrifice the individual for the majority, human security is a more personal, contextual concept. Human security is therefore more disaggregative: it is more about the feelings of insecurity that individuals express, more personalized, and seeks to establish guarantees for all individuals, one a time.

The Table 4.2 is a compilation by the authors on the differences between the two concepts, using, among others, Sen's writing in the Commission on Human Security's *Human Security Now* Report.

The human security debates with human development

Similar to the narrow and broad debate within the field of security studies discussed in Chapter 3, two debates are raging in the field of human development. The first one also concentrates on the narrow/broad scopes: is human security broader than

Table 4.2 Comparing and contrasting human development and human security

	Human Development	Human Security
Original definitions	Human development aims at widening people's choices. Amartya Sen equates the notion of 'choices' with that of 'freedoms'. Enlarging people's freedoms is thus the means and the end of development Mahbub Ul-Haq underlines that human development 'embraces the enlargement of all human choices, whether economic, social, cultural or political' (Ul Haq, 1995)	Human security aims at enabling people to exercise choices offered by human development, allowing these choices to made safely and freely, while also guaranteeing that the opportunities brought today by development will not disappear tomorrow (UNDP, 2004)
Values	Well-being	Security, stability, sustainability of that well-being
General objectives	About people, about expanding choices to lead lives they value, through expanding opportunities (growth/ expansion with equity)	Emphasis on prevention: means going beyond coping mechanisms to avoiding poverty and potential conflict and preparing for disasters Downturns with security require social minimums, safety nets, etc. Assurance of continuity: guarantee against risk, probability that gains made in one sphere not taken away suddenly
Orientation	Moves forward, is progressive and aggregate: 'together we rise'	Looks at who was left behind at the individual level: divided we fall (even growth with equity does not provide protection to those who are thrown to the wall)
Scope	Broad and multi-faceted	Can also be relief and preventive oriented, as a matter of urgency, but also deals with root causes of potential insecurity (poverty, inequality, etc.). Identifies and prepares for recessions, conflicts, emergencies and the darker events of society

continued ...

Table 4.2 continued

	Human Development	Human Security
Time-scan	Long term	Combines short-term measures to deal with the risk, but also long term prevention efforts. For example, during conflicts, spans from emergency relief work and peacekeeping to longer term human and institutional development to prevent new cycles of violence
View of role of people	People are seen as both ends and means. Emphasizes on participation and empowerment of people	Also emphasizes protection of people, in addition to their empowerment
View of society	Aggregative: development for all society	Emphasizes more on individuals, because any larger unit can discriminate (example of women in households)
Measurements	The human development indices measure quantitatively the levels of human development achieved in society based on indicators of income, education and health care	Although there is no human security index devised yet, indicators that are most likely able to determine human security levels are qualitative, as human security is more of a subjective feeling of the satisfaction received, the feeling of being 'secure'
Policy objectives	Removing the various hindrances that restrain and restrict human lives and prevent its blossoming	Actions needed to secure what is safeguarded, and to prevent the spiralling down which could create conflicts, crisis(including man-made and natural ones)
Policy goals	Prescribes four policy goals: Empowerment, sustainability, equity and productivity.	Insists on the promotion of human 'survival' and 'daily life' and the avoidance of indignities that can result in injury, insult and contempt (Sen, 2002).
Policy example	Promoting Health for All	Preventing and coping with a sudden growing pandemic, HIV/AIDs, malaria, etc.

Commonalities:
HS and HD are both human-centred and share concerns with lives of human beings, longevity, education, participation. Both are basic freedoms that people can enjoy. Both are based on introducing ethics into academic disciplines and policy choices.

human development or *vice versa*? The second debate concerns the sequential, what we shall call the 'chicken or egg dilemma'. Is human security a prerequisite of human development or *vice versa*?

Debate 1: the narrow/broad debate

The case for human security as broader than human development

Proponents of this view see the human security angle as an opportunity to broaden human development debates to include not only 'freedom from want' and 'a life of dignity' but also 'freedom from fear'. While the development community is increasingly interested in taking into account the specificities of development in conflict situations, the human security approach is inherently oriented towards taking conflict (in its larger meaning) into its core of conceptualization. Given its position at the intersection of development *and* security, it can allow for both a developmental analysis of conflict situations and priorities, as well as a conflict analysis of developmental efforts and programmes. Human security makes the critical acknowledgement that underdevelopment can be dangerous and conflict prone, and that conflict is necessarily dangerous for overall and long-term development, even though economies may very well strive on conflict. The added value offered here pertains also to the interconnectedness of issues human security puts forward: economics and development cannot be dissociated with peace and war contexts, and managing conflicts cannot be done without tight scrutiny on the economics and developmental outcomes of war and violence.

Besides including risks from conflicts, however, human security can be seen as broader than human development as it can be described as the self-perception of human individual and collective vulnerability levels, and is a function of the human development levels achieved. It can be a subjective and analytical indicator of human development, especially if we find a sound way of measuring it through a composite index. It requires tolerance and quality of life in every day life, at home, in the work place and in the environment, but it requires sufficient income earned with dignity. It means historical and cultural conditions of existence specific to the society in question. In this sense human security deals with social exclusion and poverty, with equity and inclusive economic development, and above all with the quality of the social fabric, i.e. relationships among people and the ties of solidarity. In this view, the sum of indicators within the human security approach are larger than those of human development. A state of human insecurity in this sense reflects a subjective sentiment of malaise or unease in one or several realms of one's quality of life which affect attitudes towards others and towards society. In this sense human security can be defined as the subjective reflection of the state of human development in a society and it is at the same time the 'raw material' for the construction of human development.

The case for human security being narrower than human development

On the other hand, human security can appear more focused, centred and thus narrowed down to specific situations, making it altogether a narrower concept than human development. It acknowledges a core range of issues that are paramount and should be priorities, over the overall list of issues that human development may want to tackle. The adversity of persistent human insecurity is much more for those whom the growth process leaves behind while human development is an aggregate measure and is not expected to be of the same level for every person in a population. Human security may be said to focus on individuals rather than societies or groups. This recognizes inter-group oppression and marginalization of minorities-within-minorities. Human security seeks to protect those left out of the 'growth with equity' equation, rectifying, at least in theory, the inadvertent injustices of both traditional development and human development. In this sense, human security may be seen as narrower, as it is geared towards the individual and personal context, while human development tends to be more aggregative. Development thinking still relies on an overall conception of well-being, focused often on groups, communities and so on, while human security is completely disaggregated, geared entirely towards insecurities felt by the individual.

Moreover, human security can be seen as narrower from a perception point of view. Because it relies much on the individual experience, individuals' understanding and regard for security depends on their immediate surroundings. Security becomes an issue only when one feels threatened, similar to the way in which few give a thought to the health system until they get ill. What people are concerned about includes whether or not food will be on the table, their jobs will be secure, if their children's access to basic health and education will be easy, if they will be discriminated against because of race, sex, social status or membership or participation in social/economic/community group, and the safety of their homes and communities. These are the immediate needs of individuals. Human development can allow for larger conditions that policy makers need to think about in order to provide for those needs. While human security can exist without human development, human development cannot exist without human security.

From an operational point of view, human security as a policy imperative allows a focus on the most imminent risks. In this sense, human security is a necessary but maybe not sufficient condition for human development. For development agencies, this linkage implies that they need to avoid compartmentalizing their thinking and programmes, or segregating between immediate security issues and longer term development issues. From a human security perspective, efforts to build a road or other investments may be used as a leverage to re-establish law and order in a community. Operationally, the human security approach enables development practitioners to focus better attention on personal and community issues regarding security and development. In a way, human security is closer to home, and to people's immediate concerns, and human development may be the broader societal framework of these concerns.

The verdict

Establishing whether human security is broader or narrower than human development may be of little relevance in the end. Human security may have a broader angle which includes want, fear and dignity, but it has a pinpointed focus on those elements in these three agendas that matter the most, thus narrowing down the list of themes and areas to work on. Instead of a debate on the broad or narrow concepts, it may be preferable to look at the added value of the human security approach to human development, and this added value may ultimately be a question of prioritization. As he was striving to propose an enlarged human development paradigm, Mahbub Ul-Haq saw the need of a 'priority zone' which would allow for more immediate policy relevance to the human development approach. The clear added value of human security is its utilization as a tool for better prioritization: human security in the end is about security, while human development overall is about well-being, which is endangered by insecurities. Human security can thus help the human development angle to identify what are security downturns hampering human development and well-being. Simply put, if human development is geared towards the belief of a long run and optimistic trend of development going upward, human security recalls the 'downturns in security'. The ultimate added value is that no progress is taken for granted, and risks and threats are better integrated in overall human development / human security thinking.

Therefore, if originally in the 1994 UNDP report human security was equated with 'an extension of human development', this assertion can go both ways: human security is just as much an extension of human development, as human development is a complementary angle to human security. Human security is narrower and defensive in terms of overall conceptual ambitions (defending the fruits of development), is broader in terms of contexts covered and issues taken into account (conflict, freedom from fear, dignity), but is narrower, only to be more pragmatically effective in identifying vital capacities that human development should adopt as its priorities (Shusterman, 2005).

Debate 2: the chicken and egg debate

The second debate asks whether human security is a prerequisite of human development or *vice versa*. This debate, which, we shall call the chicken or egg debate, embodies two different discourses – one that is the traditional 'security first or development' debate, which concentrates on the freedom from fear, and the other the more nuanced one which attempts to concentrate on the values of human security versus those of human development.

The first sub-debate, of course, is easier to dissect as it simply asks which comes first, development or security? Among development circles, there is an increasing recognition that security is a fundamental co-condition, if not pre-condition for development, and that conflict management and sound governance in the security sector are critical to achievement of development. This linkage has come in a

Table 4.3 Summary of the added values of HS to HD framework

	Human development	Human security
	Widening people's choices	Enabling these choices
Conceptual objectives	Broader	Narrower
	Added value: Human security acts as a 'guarantee' for the progress made by human development. Widening people's choices could be said as 'moving forward', while human security's concern here is 'defensive': making sure that no steps are made backwards.	
	Freedom from want	Freedom from want, freedom from fear, right to live with dignity
	Narrower	Broader
Contexts and range of issues	Added value: Human security underlines the interconnectedness of issues in the three agendas of want, fear and life in dignity, furthermore the platform of freedom from fear allows for better conceptualization of development/security efforts, in bringing in conflict analysis in developmental fields.	
	Improving all capacities	Defending vital capacities
	Broader	Narrower
Policy and operational prescription	Added value: In identifying the 'vital core' of human lives, human security adds to the human development paradigm what it lacked in prioritization of efforts and issues to tackle.	

context where the understanding of socio-economic development focuses on the neglected everyday insecurities faced by the poor and marginalized that gradually add up to form collective insecurities. Insecurities and inequalities are seen as increasingly dangerous as they can lead to conflict, and poverty is seen as bad for development. While the means for achieving security may incorporate human development practices, the human security framework proposes that development in areas with security concerns is different.

The case for human development as a pre-requisite for human security

Human development can be argued to be the necessary pre-condition to human security for several reasons. At the theoretical level, since human security is preoccupied with 'downturns', this implies logically that a certain amount of development has to have been achieved for downturns to occur. Furthermore, fragile and low development levels, combined with weakened state institutions and economic crises naturally lead to growing human securities. For instance, the Latin American countries, recently facing a major economic and developmental downturn, were witness to soaring crime rates, signifying a fall in overall human security because of a downturn in development. Decrease in development indeed induces social stress as the countries of transition demonstrated. In Moldova for example, when the economic crisis reached its apex in 1998, the Moldovan Council for National Security found itself discussing issues related to growth, economics and development, for the consequences of the downturn had led to 'rising personal insecurity [and] social tensions' (UNDP, 1999c: 10).

Overall, the argument to put human development before human security simply states that sources of insecurity stem from lack of development. Indeed, progress in economic development and especially in human development (growth with equity) reduces the risk of conflict situations and the temptation to wage war for greed. When a population is empowered and has opportunities for its own personal and human development, then reasons to go to war can no longer play on the greed or economics model, this applying especially within states, and being particularly relevant in times where conflicts are mostly intra-state and no longer opposing states. Sen, therefore places human development before human security, underlining that poverty strongly influences the likelihood of conflict. As Sen argues, even though deprivation does not necessarily lead immediately to revolt, it can produce strong effects on collective memories and impact the unfolding of future events. Poverty is obviously a fertile recruiting ground for 'foot soldiers' for terrorism and ethnic wars. The crying injustices of poverty can lead people to better accept terrorism as a means to fight, if it is perceived as the path to fight these crying injustices. Overall deprivation can lead to moral alienation from collaborative and peaceful values and approaches to the world.

Hence, human development or lack thereof, is critical to sustain certain levels of human security, downturns in development and extreme poverty almost systematically triggering conflict, whether open through warfare, or through growing social unrest, tensions and stress. Progress in human development will enhance the chances of progress in human security, while failure in human development will increase the risk of failure in human security. From a practical standpoint as well, most aspects of the maximalist definitions of human security simply cannot be delivered without a certain level of pre-existing development. Indeed, definitions that emphasize the need within human security, for instance, for 'social safety nets' to mitigate downturns, must acknowledge that setting up such institutions needs an already relatively significant level of development and state stability to finance such social security and economic security schemes. Only progress in the developmental field can bring the capacities to then make sure, through human security, that no steps are made backwards, and no one lags behind.

The case for human security as a pre-condition for human development

On the other hand, however, a case can equally be made to present human security as a pre-condition for human development. Human security deals with tackling extreme situations and urgencies, beyond overall goals of general development. Human security is about priorities and how to face them: conflicts, natural disasters, economic depressions, pandemic outbreaks. In a sense, before talking about human development, one must be assured that, minimalistically, human survival is guaranteed. Under the conceptualization that human security is a component of development, security is the dependent variable and development the independent one. However, if we hold security as the necessary condition for development, it is implied that development cannot occur in conditions of insecurity.

Security, hence, is not entirely a component of development. Security is more appropriately the environment of development. Security conditions determine in an indirect way whether development will take place or be stopped, but it does not determine how development takes place. The Commission on Human Security Report also describes insecurity as a different and a much starker issue than uneven development. Threats to human security can emerge at any level of social development, in rich or in poor countries. For example, minority ethnic groups did not feel secure despite living in the developed state of the former Yugoslavia. Minority rights are as important as development for social cohesion, as this case revealed. In a country with weakened state institutions, lacking in rights and values and feeling of justice to all communities, the threats to the human security of the population naturally grow, and these insecurities can revive memories of historical oppression and lead to the construction of 'the other' as enemy. Threats can arise not only from certain individuals or groups or from political parties but the state itself. At the same time, decrease in human development can cause social stress. For example, in many transition countries, the dramatic and critical deterioration of economic and social indicators, which affected human potential, increased social inequalities, have given rise to symptoms of social stress. In these instances development cannot not be sustained without human security.In societies where the minimal conditions of human security are not met, human development is difficult to achieve and to sustain. Human security is an essential contribution to the development process and for the success of development policies and assistance. There are many types of insecurities that affect both the well-being and the safety and security of people. By decreasing them, the quality of both human security and human development can be affected. An example to envision how then human security is critical and comes as a pre-condition of human development would thus be to launch an education programme of building schools within a community, not making sure before that children can go to these schools safely, without fear, and that the community is sufficiently pacified to promote peaceful values within the education system. If a child cannot simply walk safely to school, then there is often no point in even having the school. This argument in favour of presenting human security as an *a priori* necessity to human development thus introduces the concept of a threshold under which human development is not sustainable and too easily jeopardized.

To summarize this position, without human security, there can be no or little *ability* for development, as there are also risks to the *sustainability* of existing levels of development. Human development cannot be realized without ensuring human security. The absence of human security calls into question the ability to implement human development, since it is virtually impossible for people to expand and realize choices in an environment of war, want, crime, rape, political repression, the absence of free expression and fear or chronic threats. Freedom from fear and from want, if not achieved, bring further impediments to sound human development. If human development is about choices, human security is about making these choices possible. Another layer of explanation for human security to be a pre-condition to human development relates directly to this concept of choice: not only can choices not be guaranteed in an environment of human insecurity, they are in fact prevented from being made, or are warped by the overall context. Indeed, people's perceptions of security impact on their optimism and pessimism and influence their choices and courses of action, and ultimately impact on their lives. Hence, everything from demographic behaviour to participation in political economic and cultural life comes into consideration. People suffering from constant fear do not contemplate long-term development.

Reconciling both perspectives: common roots, co-conditions

Rather than oppose human security and human development, it is better to envision them as intersecting one another. Instead of a shadow approach, therefore, a threshold approach suits better the overall parameters of this debate. Human development and human security are indistinctly linked given that progress in one enhances the choices of progress in another, while failure in one increases risk of failure of another. Human security is a necessary condition for both development and human development. Beyond a certain threshold of human security crisis, development may get disrupted. Development on the other hand, is only a sufficient condition for human security. In severely deteriorated human security conditions, human development conditions also regress and *vice versa*. Human security is therefore a condition defined by an approximate threshold of security conditions.

Beyond these threshold conditions, there is high insecurity and increased threat to life and existence for humans, it is here that human security acquires its greatest relevance. Human development, meanwhile, is a gradient of human condition measurable by indicators. Conditions generated by development are conducive to the enhancement of human security. They may actually contribute positively to a fragile security situation. There is positive reinforcement from enhanced human security to development again.

Lack of development and the prevalence of insecurity have common roots in horizontal inequalities – unequal allocation of economic, cultural and political resources among identity groups defined by characteristics such as class, ethnicity, profession, geographic origin or religion. Human security is necessary but not sufficient for human fulfilment and should be consistent with ongoing human development by supporting participation, freedom, institutional appropriateness and diversity. Human rights can be seen as a bridge between human security and human development. Neither human development nor human security can occur where human rights are routinely violated. But at the same time, development cannot ensure horizontal equality, without which insecurities remain as do potential conflicts.

The debate therefore seems pointless, as the most relevant way to conceptualize human security and human development is to see them as co-conditionalities. Human development and human security are both concerned with human freedoms, and they both seek to address the same root causes: horizontal inequalities, human insecurities. 'Same goals, different scopes', as the *Human Security Now* report states (CHS, 2003). Human development and human security thus appear as two parallel processes that go hand in hand. Progress in one enhances the chances of progress in the other, when failure in one enhances the chances of failure in the other. Human security and human development are therefore overall sister-concepts with mutually beneficial cross-contributions. Narrow human security is the pre-condition for development, the initial impetus of development then helping to widen human security concerns, while human security is also a way to prioritize efforts, which is sometimes lacking in strict development thinking.

The added value of a threshold-based analysis

Ultimately, the chicken and egg debate may also be a futile exercise as both sides may be true at the same time (Shusterman, 2005). Frances Stewart for instance acknowledges the difficulties in a comparative definition of security and development (Stewart, 2004), for security indeed appears as 'an intrinsic aspect of development', in the sense that human development or lack thereof can breed human insecurity, while human security or lack thereof has very high developmental costs. Instead of thinking in terms of pre-conditions, Stewart refers to a 'security-development-security nexus', with human security and human development belonging to the same cumulative process (Stewart, 2004). Indeed, 'societal progress – human development – requires reduced insecurity [… and the] more inclusive and egalitarian development is [the more is it] likely to lead to greater security' (Stewart, 2004: 24). This integration of issues between human security and human development is precisely why both concepts should not be seen as competing one with the other, but as mutually reinforcing. It is important, however, to note Stewart's observation in this context that one does not always come with the other, as there are many cases of 'security cum stagnation' (in Latin America for instance) or non-inclusive insecure growth (in Asian countries). The 'security-development-security' nexus could thus be envisioned as a virtuous circle requiring particularly well adapted fine-tuning to be set in motion.

The idea of a 'nexus' thus represents the first attempt to bridge the false antagonism between human security and human development proponents, and to show interconnections rather than opposition. Owen, for example, proposed a threshold-based definition of security threats and human security (Owen, 2004: 381–5). His proposal of a 'hybrid definition' using a threshold for *defining* contextually what is human security can be conjugated to define how human security and human development are related to one another, giving an integrated picture.

This first graph (Figure 4.1) is a conceptual representation of a holistic response on human security and human development, assuming first that human development is synonymous with a rising trend of societal progress. Second, we assume that human security is a static threshold. The overall picture would thus be as presented in Figure 4.1. This graph shows the integration of both concepts, and how they cannot be separated or thought of independently, testifying to the validity of an integrative approach rather than a chicken and egg debate. This representation may nevertheless seem biased in favour of those defending the view that human security is a pre-condition to human development, but such an interpretation would be incorrect.

Indeed, while Figure 4.1 underlines that below a certain human security threshold there can be no development, de-development can be equally adverse in its impact on human security (see Figure 4.2). Figure 4.2 represents the interconnectedness of development and security from a general theoretical standpoint, which can be easily contextualized and exemplified. It thus identifies a generic 'crisis' provoking a reversal of development trends, a downturn or even general de-development, which then triggers reverse dynamics endangering levels of human security below the threshold. There can be many examples of such crises: the general economic downturn experienced by Asia in and after 1997 which extended beyond an economic crisis to food insecurity, or changes in Latin America where similar economic crisis have provoked extended social unrest and a rising wave of criminality.

The 'generic crisis' can also come from outside the developmental sphere and be a human security crisis which impacts on human development, which in turn, impacts on human security, recalling here the reality of the nexus inter-relating both concepts. Indeed, the crisis considered can equally be the outbreak of armed conflict, which has development costs and security costs at the same time. Stewart uses Amartya Sen's concept of 'entitlements' to underline how conflicts impact human well being through entitlement failures. They can cause fall in 'market

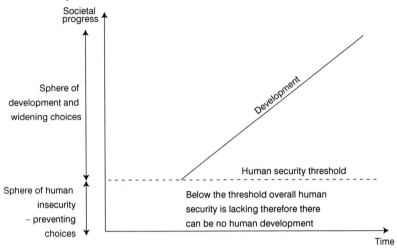

Figure 4.1 Human development as progress, human security as a static threshold.

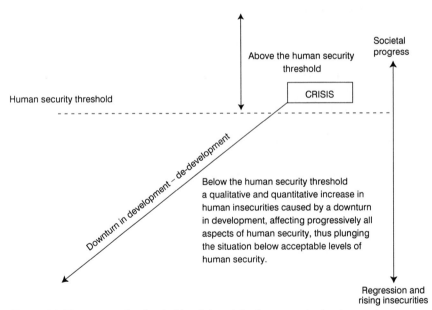

Figure 4.2 Human security threshold and the crisis: downturns in development.

entitlements' (through spiralling inflation and budget deficits and consequent drop in real wages), as well as in 'public entitlements', through decrease of social expenditures. Extrapolating from Stewart's work, there also exists a 'development – security – development' nexus alongside the security development security nexus, with certain overlaps (Figure 4.3).

This conceptual integration can be extended even further. Instead of assuming human development as a dynamic variable and human security as static, both can be viewed as mutually reinforcing *dynamics*. Indeed, the question of the chicken and the egg in human security and development stems precisely from the idea that both concepts are *dynamic* and not static. They both reinforce each other and connections are three-way rather than two-way. In this sense therefore human security should not be considered as simply a threshold, but should be theorized as a *moving threshold* responding to varying levels of human development. A narrow human security threshold, based essentially on freedom from fear, is indeed a necessary pre-condition to trigger the driving force of progress which human development represents. However, once this has been set in motion, human development represents an impetus that can be tapped into for the raising of the human security threshold to levels covering freedom from want and freedom to live in dignity.

To expand and develop better the idea contained in Figure 4.3, while summarizing previous contents, we have seen that 'narrow' human security, freedom from fear and from the effects of direct physical violence, be it contexts of armed conflict, rampant crime or massive social unrest and instability, is instrumental for human development, which cannot build sustainable trends of societal progress on shaky and human-insecure foundations. As far as the first threshold is concerned, human security is understood along its narrow definitions, setting it as a precondition for human development. The second threshold that is 'freedom from want' is at the cusp of the human security and development overlap, wherein securing certain freedoms from want are pre-conditions to human development, others being potential by-products of human development. Indeed, freedom from a pervasive threat, such as generalized hunger or lack of access to water, belongs to the human security pre-conditions for human development. Achieving these goals means people in turn can switch from a survival mode to better prospects and developmental self-empowerment. On the other hand, the establishment of social safety nets, essentially a part of the human security agenda, appear instead as by-products of progress made in human development. It is through the development of the economy that tax revenues can yield enough resources to set up social security schemes, the impetus of development serving to raise the threshold of

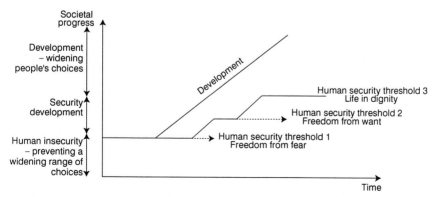

Figure 4.3 Human security and human development as mutually reinforcing dynamics.

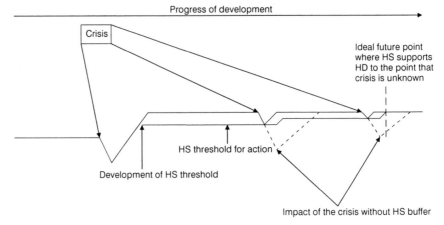

Figure 4.4 Human security as the response to crisis.

human security to the level of want, cushioning threats not only to the lives and survival, but also to well-being of the people.

Another way to map the relationship between human development and human security can be visualized as Figure 4.4 which shows that human security develops in response to a crisis as a way to support human development. After the crisis has occurred, the institutions for human security are developed to help prevent future crises from occurring and to limit their effects and speed up recovery in case they do. Furthermore, when the next crisis occurs, agents providing human security learn from the crisis and its institutions are strengthened to cope better with future crisis situations. This continues until a point is reached where human security supports human development to the extent that the possibility of a crisis is rendered remote and its effects, if one does occur, are negligible. It also shows the effect that a crisis might have without the existence of human security to act as a buffer and to help speed up recovery.

Conclusion: a threshold approach to human security policies

Policy-wise, the idea of a moving threshold and an integrative approach interlinking human security levels and human development trends could be useful for a holistic approach to crisis situations and for prioritization of efforts. In concrete terms, these moving thresholds of human security/human development could be envisaged through composite progressive indicators pertaining to levels of freedom from fear and want and freedom to live in dignity (Table 4.3).

Policy-wise, therefore, acting conjointly in human security and human development would mean assessing the situation at hand, identifying which thresholds need to be upheld, and acting accordingly, giving priority either to development or security objectives. In a situation of conflict and widespread fear, human security must take precedence over human development concerns, because the primary issue is ensuring short-term *survival* of the populations.

Table 4.4 A threshold approach to gradual human security indicators

Threshold one ⇨ Critical fear	Threshold 2-A ⇨ Critical want	Threshold 2-B ⇨ Enlarged want	Threshold 4 Dignity
Facing violence	Facing great hardship	Building choices and dignity	Living in a secure environment
Violent deaths rate	Access issues and distributive justice: water, food security	Education rates	Corruption levels and good governance indicators
Infant mortality	Nutrition levels: calories per/day	Social safety nets	Nature of the rule of law and judicial security
Displaced population statistics	Health statistics	Unemployment rates	Environmental issues
Rape/gendered violence levels	Critical access and Health issues: water, fast spreading pandemics	Income distribution, inflation, purchasing power measures	Equality levels, satisfaction, overall well-being, happiness

When recovering from conflicts, which have tremendous development costs, survival remains an issue, and falling back into conflict dynamics is to be avoided absolutely. Hence once again, human development should reach out to human security systems of thought while engaging in 'conflict-development' thinking.

Human security could be said to be a three-dimensional agenda, encompassing security, development, and rights, echoing freedom from fear, want and freedom to life in dignity. For policy purposes, these agendas can then be translated into imperatives to 'protect and restore', to 'prevent and improve' and to 'change mindsets and perspectives'. In emergency or crisis situations, conflict related or natural disasters, which have entailed fall-outs below the threshold level of freedom from fear, human security would be concentrated on the protection of populations, and aimed at restoring previous levels of security. Human security therefore becomes *reactive,* guided by humanitarian and assistance concerns in a pre-development mindset, because once again in dramatic situations, what matters first is survival rather than empowering people to widen their choices. The second tier of the human security agenda would be to *prevent* downturns and *improve* situations overall, this time with human development being the driving force and human security following the impetus. Improvement of contexts and environments would essentially be the objective of development, but applying a human security focus on the efforts made would guarantee that development is accompanied by distributive justice, inclusive growth and income generation, this aiding overall social cohesion and preventing fall outs back into conflicts. Instances can be drawn in this context from post-conflict recovery strategies for development, or considering economic tissues which have been disarticulated by natural disasters, and whose distortions could lead to violence even though peace reigned beforehand. Here human security would be truly an extension of human development, and would shift from a *reactive* to a *defensive* and preventive stance, being truly the safety net guaranteeing the societal progresses achieved through regular development. Operationally this could be translated by empowerment through *peace* education in conflict-recovery contexts, the setting up of microfinance schemes, etc.

All in all then, this segment of the paradigm would be geared towards the identification of situations where human security levels are below an acceptable threshold, yet not necessarily as a consequence of a particular or identifiable downturn in security, but rather as consequences of shortcomings of development-only thinking. Efforts would be broader than strict protection and restoration, including capacity rebuilding and empowerment at the individual level as well as at the community and state levels (upholding the rule of law, implementing state-level safety nets). Finally, such efforts to improve can also build upon and follow up previous efforts concerned with protection and restoration of human security, focusing, for instance, on reconciliation efforts, and in turn, improving human security could help prevention of human security downturns. The last platform for human security is constructed around changing mindsets and perspectives at global levels, for many definitions of human security identify forms of structural violence built in the overall system, and which need, therefore, to be addressed at high levels. The Commission on Human Security, for instance, called on the need to reform intellectual property rights regimes because of their impact on the provision of medicine for pandemics which affect wide segments of world populations. Hence, human security at this level would be oriented towards the creation of a globally favourable environment for the development of human security, even without specific field missions or crisis situations (Shusterman, 2005).

5 Debating dignity

Human security and human rights

As seen in previous chapters, the human security additional value to the security debate poses new types of questions as to whose security it is and security from what. To the human development discourses it brings forth answers to why a minimum threshold is necessary to secure development gains. *Vis-à-vis* the human rights framework, this chapter argues, the paradigm engages in a discussion on how human security can be promoted as a right-cum-obligation and how the human rights framework formalizes the ethical and political importance of human security. By their moral imperatives and their normative quality, human rights might prove to be the way of more clearly defining the threats, the actors and the duties that human security should be addressing.

There is extensive overlap between the areas of human rights and security which are mutually re-enforcing and indispensable for each other. For some, such as the UN human rights expert Bertrand Ramcharan, human rights actually define human security, 'To be secure is to be safe, protected. Security is a secure condition or feeling. It is respectfully submitted that international human rights norms define the meaning of human security' (Ramcharan, 2002: 9). To him, the *essence* of human security is to respect human rights and fundamental freedoms while 'upholding human rights is the way to achieve individual, national and international security.' Whether it is for citizens or non-citizens, migrants or displaced persons, members of a minority or an indigenous community, the essence of human security is to respect the rights and fundamental freedoms that have been distilled and articulated by the international community (Ramcharan, 2002: 5). For Hampson, human rights (associated with the rule of law) is only one of the components of the tripartite categorization of human security. Human rights/rule-of-law is the 'fundamental liberal assumption that individuals have a basic right to "life, liberty and the pursuit of happiness" and that the international community has an obligation to protect and promote these rights' (Hampson *et al.*, 2002: 5). According to this definition of human security, 'the denial of fundamental human rights [is] the main reason for human insecurity' (Ibid.: 18). For Seidensticker and Oberleitner, human rights and human security are mutually enriching; for example, human security can help refocus international law onto people-centred concerns.

What are the points of intersection between the concepts of human security and human rights and how do the two complement each others? We begin the chapter with a general introduction on the terms of the human rights debate before comparing the commonalities and differences between human security and human rights. We then examine how the two frameworks reinforce each other, first conceptually and then operationally. We conclude with an examination of the thorny question of universality in both debates and the criticism that has entangled human security, like human rights, in a cultural relativism debate.

The terms of the human rights debate

Human rights are basic rights grounded in the dignity of each human being, whether their foundational basis comes from human nature, human reason, a divinely sanctioned spirit, natural law or what Dallmayr refers to as the practice of 'humanization', that is, the 'steady cultivation of the sense of justice and fair-mindedness' or whether they are historically and contextually contingent or wilfully constructed or fabricated (Dallmayr, 2002). Human rights first had an official standpoint in world politics when the Universal Declaration of Human Rights (UDHR) was created in 1948, as a response to massive human rights abuses during World War II. Henceforth, they were contained in a corpus of international treaties, among them the International Covenant on Civil and Political Rights (CCPR, 1966), and the Covenant on Economic, Social and Cultural Rights (CESCR, 1966). These declarations collectively included several clusters of rights: first, personal rights (right of life, recognizable before the law, protection against cruel or degrading forms of punishment, protection against racial, ethnic, sexual or religious discrimination); second, legal rights (access to legal remedies for violations of basic rights, right of due process, including fair and impartial public trials, protection against arbitrary arrest, detention, exile); third, civil liberties (freedom of thought, conscience, religion); fourth, subsistence rights (food, basic standards of health and well-being); fifth, economic rights (right to work, rest, leisure, social security); and finally, political rights (the right to take part in elections and participate in government).

At the start of the Cold War, there was a split between the consensus over the unity of civil and political rights and economic, social and cultural rights. It was not until 1993, in the Vienna Declaration and Programme of Action at the World Conference on Human Rights, that there was an attempt to place civil/political and economic/social rights on an equal plane. Thus, human rights need to be seen in an expanded sense that includes all three generations of rights without privileging one set over the other. For human rights to be universal, economic, social, and cultural rights have to be a part of the human rights agenda.

The strength of human rights lies in their morality and values. There is a moral argument for poverty eradication, beyond the instrumental need for growth and for reducing conflicts. Pogge for example bases his argument for social and individual responsibility for eradicating poverty on the fact that Western nations have substantially contributed to it. Not only is the state responsible, so, too, are 'all and only those who participate with this person in the same social system' (Pogge, 2002: 66). He moves from the libertarian notion of human rights, which requires that humans simply do not inflict harm onto others, towards an institutional understanding that bridges the gap between civil and political rights, and social, economic and cultural rights by emphasizing negative duties across the board:

> Human agents are not to collaborate in upholding a coercive institutional order that avoidably restricts the freedom of some so as to render their access to basic necessities insecure without compensating for their collaboration by protecting its victims or working for its reform.
>
> (Pogge, 2002: 69)

This notion of human rights requires a guaranteed access to certain goods and rights. Thus, Pogge's arguments on poverty eradication and human rights oblige developed countries to assist in ensuring secure access of rights to non-citizens. This dispersal of responsibilities makes the human security agenda more feasible. In fact, human security becomes truly people-centred when the individual is both the referent of security and an important contributor to ensuring that security.

Human rights also require fulfilment or under-fulfilment as opposed to violations. Human rights shift from the negative to positive where human right to life is fulfilled for certain persons if their security against certain threats does not fall below specific thresholds which differ across human rights and threats (Pogge, 2002: 47–8). The emphasis here is on enjoying not only the substance of a right, but also the secured access to that right, which is as imperative to this conceptualization of human rights as it is to the definition of human security. This understanding of human rights helps defend against criticisms of human security by explaining the 'vagueness' of the concept and contextualizing it to rights with dignity.

Commonalities and differences

However we look, there is an undeniable link between human rights and human security. These similarities are examined here first from the theoretical/conceptual viewpoint before discussing how the two frameworks are operationally linked.

First, the major characteristic of both human rights and human security is that they are people rather than state centred and both aim at guaranteeing human well-being (Oberleitner, 2002). The people-centred approach both in human security and human rights is not limited to individuals but equally encompasses communities. Human rights treaties after World War II were the first documents explicitly recognizing a person as a subject of international law. This, in turn, has an important implication for the human security debate, providing a stronger status to people through their legal personality.

Second, the two frameworks share defining features: the components that make up both the human rights and human security frameworks are said to be inter-dependent and interrelated. Furthermore, both human rights and human security approach their problems in a holistic way (as provided by UNDP 1994 report and international human rights law), both promoting the interdependence of 'security' and 'rights', thus abandoning the more traditional sector-based approach under which actors worked independently and issues were addressed separately. Similarly, threats are interconnected and security is indivisible. Both concepts emphasize virtuous circles: one right advances another right and so on. (e.g. economic security for families enables children that would otherwise have had to work to receive an education that in turn leads to empowerment etc.). Human security also highlights vicious circles: loss of one form of security endangers other forms.

Third, they both share a focus on freedoms and both pursue dignity. Amartya Sen contends that the vital core of life is a set of elementary rights and freedoms that people enjoy (Sen, 2000a). Both human rights and security involve the pursuit of dignity. Human rights developed in response to violations of human dignity. Human security emerged from threats to human rights and the use of national security to curb rights, making it an extension of the pursuit of dignity. Human rights developed in response to the emerging modern state and markets, which threaten human dignity. In this sense, both human rights and human security are protected in the pursuit of human dignity and both have a basis in morality.

Fourth, both frameworks stress on the universality and indivisibility of their components. Specific rights and security components are not universally defined. Human rights' language of indivisibility and interdependence, i.e. rights, methods and objectives, are mutually reinforcing. Human security orientated policies will promote human rights; violation of human rights will undermine human security. The strength of human rights lies in their morality and ethical position and values. Human security, by defining threats and duties, helps identify the rights at stake in a particular situation and provides the descriptive nature of considerations of security in human lives. Human rights designs correlative duties and then gives effectiveness in determining obligations.

Most importantly, the content of human rights and human security is undeniably similar, even though they may be phrased slightly differently. There is a strong correlation between 'freedom from fear' and first generation human rights, the civil and political rights. Second generation human rights incorporate 'freedom from want' – social and economic rights that were backed by the former socialist states and appear relevant to people's movements' today. Third generation rights – cultural and collective demands – correspond to the rights to development, health and environment and are about a life of dignity. Table 5.1 (see p. 128) contextualizes the various components of the HDR 1994 definitions of human security with their corresponding elements within the human rights framework, as identified in three major international human rights treaties (UDHR 1948, CCPR 1966 and CESCR 1966) to show how content of human rights overlaps with that of human security.

Human security has transposed most of the major human rights into its own framework by putting the emphasis on the threats. Nevertheless, the preoccupation is with the same rights. Therefore, the existing human rights normative framework and in particular those human rights treaties which have been ratified by a majority of the world's states, would be very useful for operationalizing the concept of human security.

Although we can argue that the human rights framework is the closest to human security from among those studied in Chapters 3 and 4, there are nonetheless a number of important differences. Human rights are substantiated by a body of legal norms and international conventions which do not exist for human security. Human rights also have more than a century's worth of experience while the human security framework is in its formative years since its entry into the international arena a decade ago. The two are not competing discourses, and human security is not just about securing human rights. It tries to understand potential sources of threats to these rights and the types of institutions and governance arrangements required to sustain them. States were protected from international scrutiny under the shield of sovereignty and thus often got away with violations of human rights. Human security argues for the responsibility to protect both citizens and states, whereas human rights impose the duty on others. Human rights are not an analytical tool, and even though human security has been criticized for its analytical shortcomings, it does have an explanatory power that supports human rights. Human security provides the framework for analysis of interconnections and causal links between different threats and weaknesses. Importantly, human security explores the terrain before and beyond human rights: using a language identifying threats, it highlights the insecurities that arise when human rights are lacking and beyond human rights to emancipation.

Human security implies immediate reaction in the face of crises where human rights violations are possible but not inevitable, e.g. conflict situations, natural disasters, inter-community tensions. Human security's mantra of prevention/ mitigation of crises implies measures not covered by human rights, e.g. social safety nets, community coping measures. Human rights tend to focus (in theory and practice) on protection from public authorities i.e. state (as explained by Berlin's concept of negative liberty (Berlin 1969)). Human security is a broader concept with a series of implications: human security goes beyond the private-public distinction to identify a range of threats where the state and non-state actors are not sufficiently bound by international humanitarian and human rights law. Human security also identifies new opportunities for countering these threats, i.e. highlights the role of non-state actors in providing human security. Human rights are legalistic and open to interpretation, while human security has important non-legalistic aspects. It focuses on the daily lives and communities of individuals. This non-legal, contextual character could help expand human rights and also provide a basis for the prevention of the violation of human rights. The human security paradigm creates the most conducive environment for rights and reduces unwarranted state discretion in the realization of rights. As Seidensticker argues, human rights cannot be neglected/violated in the name of security (Seidensticker, 2002). The deconstruction of the national security paradigm exposes such violations.

Table 5.1 Human security components embedded within human rights treaties

Components of human security as per the HDR 1994 report	Human rights	Articles and rights from human rights international treaties
Economic security = an assured basic income Threats: unemployment, temporary work, precarious employment, self-employment, low and insecure income, leading to poverty	Social and economic rights	UDHR – Art. 17 (right to property), 22 (right to social security), 23 (right to work), 24 (right to leisure), 25 (right to social services), 26 (right to education) CESCR – Art. 6 (right to work), 7 (just work conditions), 8 (right to form trade unions, strike), 9 (right to social security), 10 (protection of the family), 13-14 (right to education)
Food security = physical and economic access to basic food Threats: poor distribution and lack of purchasing power	Right to food	UDHR – Art. 25 (right to food, housing, clothing and medical care) CESCR – Art. 11 (right of adequate standard of living – right to food)
Health security Threats: infectious diseases coming from poor nutrition and unsafe environment Threats are greater to the poor, women and children	Right to health	UDHR – Art. 25 (right to food, housing, clothing and medical care) CESCR – Art. 12 (right to highest standard of health)
Environmental security = healthy physical environment Threats: degradation of ecosystems: water (depletion), land (salinization), air (pollution), natural disasters and lack of warning system	Right to a healthy environment	CESCR – Art. 12 (right to highest standard of health)
Personal security = security from physical violence Threats: from the state (torture), other states (war), groups of people (ethnic tension), individuals or gangs (crime),	Civil rights	UDHR – Art. 3 (right to life), 4 (prohibition of slavery), 5 (prohibition of torture), 6 (right to juridical personality), 7 (equality before the law), 9 (prohibition of arbitrary arrest) 11 (principle of legality and presumption of innocence), 12 (protection of privacy), 13 (freedom of movement),

	against women or children. Also industrial, workplace and traffic accidents. Women and vulnerable	14 (right to asylum from persecution), 18 (freedom of thought, conscience and religion), 19 (freedom of opinion), 20 (freedom of association),children are particularly CCPR – Art. 2 (equal protection of the law), 6 (right to life), 7 (prohibition of torture), 8 (prohibition of slavery), 9 (right to liberty and security), 10 (treatment of prisoners), 11 (prohibition of arrest due to debts), 13 (non-refoulement), 15 (principle of legality), 16 (juridical personality), 17 (protection of privacy), 18 (right to freedom of thought, conscience and religion), 19 (right to hold opinions), 20 (prohibition of war and racist propaganda), 21 (right to assembly), 22 (freedom of association), 23 (protection of the family), 24 (protection of children), 26 (prohibition of discrimination)
Cultural rights	Community security = safe membership in a group. Threats: from the group (oppressive practices), between groups (ethnic violence), from dominant groups (e.g. indigenous people vulnerability)	UDHR – Art. 1 (equality between man and woman), 2 (prohibition of discrimination), 7 (equality before the law and prohibition of discrimination), 16 (equal rights in marriage), 27 (right to participate in the cultural life) CCPR – Art. 2 (prohibition of discrimination), 3 (equality between man and woman) CESCR – Art. 3 (equality between man and woman), 15 (right to participate in the cultural life)
Political rights + democracy	Political security = living in a society that honours basic human rights Threats: human rights violations, e.g. state repression, etc.	UDHR – Art. 21 (right to political participation) CCPR – Art. 1 (right of self-determination), 25 (political participation) ESCR – Art. 1 (right of self determination)

How both frameworks re-enforce each other: added values

Given the comprehensive nature of human rights, why do we require human security at all? How can the two frameworks enforce and strengthen each other?

Conceptual complementarities

On the one hand, human rights enrich the concept of human security as they provide a sound conceptual and normative foundation of human security and make human security more practically operational. As Seidensticker emphasizes, 'hitching human security concerns onto human rights vocabulary can enrich both' (Seidensticker, 2002).

If there is a right, there must be a duty and if there is a duty, there must be a responsibility. This moral and logical obligation to fulfilling human rights can be applied to human security. Moreover, while human security has re-directed human rights vocabulary towards the threats mode, it has not fully taken the correlative duty component of human rights. This human rights' emphasis on obligation which is inextricably linked to each right, would be useful to human security and allow it to be more practical and operational (Seidensticker, 2002). Human rights can mobilize the language of duties and responsibilities to facilitate implementation of human security. Given that human security is only a decade-old concept and is weakly institutionalized, it can benefit from the well-established human rights many of whose treaties have been adopted by members of the United Nations. It can draw on human rights' legal regimes, conventions, sanctions that compel actors (essentially states) to fulfil their responsibilities.

On the other hand, human security is also of use to human rights. Within the UN Charter, tension exists between principles of state sovereignty (Article 1) and protection of human rights (Article 1.3). Thus states that violate human rights protect themselves by invoking the principles of sovereignty, territorial integrity and non-intervention. Hence, by focusing attention on the protection of people, human security can readjust the political balance in favour of the human rights principle and has the potential to reconcile two conflicting principles of the UN Charter and have an impact on international law and UN action (Oberleitner, 2002).

Furthermore, human security, as a holistic concept, can help overcome the divide between different generations of human rights as well as to solve conflicts between human rights (Oberleitner, 2002). The human security paradigm argues for equity, right to economic, social and cultural rights, and advocates for duties and obligation by the state to ensuring these. Within this paradigm then, the balance between civil-political and socio-economic rights states is restored and given focus. For example, some countries have democratic systems with regular elections but ignore severe poverty which denies dignity to people. Human security brings such denials into focus, arguing for their inclusion. It is argued that there has been a trade-off between economic and social rights and human rights and that liberal democracies promote political rights while neglecting economic rights since market economies cannot guarantee these. Human security sees the reconciliation between the economic safety nets that freedom from want proposes with the rights that are necessary for freedom from fear. It is a rights-based political system that reconciles economic/social rights with human rights. The human security framework reconciles the differences by seeing them as trade-offs: violation of one set leads to the abuse or denial of the others and insecurities have to be recognized for their inter-dependence.

Human security is not necessarily a challenge to state sovereignty but redefines it as a responsibility of the state to protect its citizens. It identifies the role of non-state actors in providing security in the international legal order, thus reducing unwarranted and 'excessive' state discretion in the realization of rights (Seidensticker, 2002). Because of its emphasis on other actors and the move away from the traditional notion of security, centred on the state, human rights offers a framework of state accountability. State responsibility is the inherent strength of human rights, and can give credence to the idea of human security by ensuring that there is an accountable actor to ensure that the claims of human beings – freedom, welfare, safety – are indeed realized (Seidensticker, 2002). States also have tremendous flexibility on the pace at which they instil economic, social, and cultural rights. These rights are often subjected to "progressive realization" in terms of duties and obligations. Human security can reduce the discretion of the states in delivering these rights by eliminating the 'way out' that the progressive realization has left open.

Operational implications

The linkages between human rights and human security have their own set of implications. By putting security, human rights, and development into a single human security framework, the goals of each separate agenda are more effectively achieved. Further, the moral argument of human security helps fulfil interrelated human rights. Security, development, and rights – civil and political, economic, social, and cultural – must be pursued together.

Limits of state action

Dignity-related rights have their limitations and lack consensus, but they need to be protected by citizens and the state. Writers like Glendon (2000) and Donnelly (2002) believe that this assumption was underlined in the Universal Declaration of Human Rights. Thus by extension, modern notions of human rights that emphasize freedom grounded in dignity are linked with notions of responsibility and solidarity. Article 1 of the UDHR states that '[a]ll human beings are born free and equal in dignity and rights. They are endowed with reason and conscience and should act towards one another in a spirit of brotherhood' (Glendon, 2000: 153–4). Donnelly further clarifies that human rights developed in response to emerging markets and the modern state, both of which threatened human dignity (Donnelly, 2002: 64). Specifically, modernized market economies destroyed the social bases of traditional communities and created individuals who came to bear 'human rights' because of the new range of related threats to human dignity. Likewise, the modern state was empowered with new institutions to 'invade the lives and threaten the dignity of a rapidly increasing number of people in new and increasingly ominous ways' (Ibid.: 64).

As human rights emerged from threats to human dignity, human security emerges because of new threats to human rights (such as predator and weak states). Human security can be conceived as an extension of the pursuit of human dignity that offers an alternative to the concept of human security as an expansion of state security. The human rights approach focuses on the realization of rights legally and morally, whereas human security adds a third dimension whereby the potential for external threats is a supplementary motivating factor in fulfilling political and economic rights.

There have been some encouraging test cases in national jurisdictions in India and South Africa. In April 2001, a petition was filed by the People's Union for Civil Liberties (a national NGO) in the Supreme Court of India. It demanded that federal institutions and local governments be responsible for the mass malnutrition of people in the concerned state. In an interim order, in July 2003, the Supreme Court affirmed that, where people are unable to feed themselves adequately, governments have an obligation to provide for them. Such a model of judicial activism can be followed by other countries with active and independent judiciaries. But promoting human rights is not enough. The misuse of interventions for national interest as opposed to humanitarian intervention through international law is viewed by the human security approach as a possible way for securing rights when violated in the most extreme cases. Can we separate human rights from the last two concepts? Humanitarian efforts and development are increasingly guided by human rights. Human security reinforces human rights and so strengthens its claims. Under human security, the state shifts from militarist concerns towards empowerment of its people.

The state plays a role in ensuring human rights and three international documents focus on this relationship. The United Nations Charter (1945) formed the basis of state recognition of the idea that human rights are integral to international peace and security. The Universal Declaration of Human Rights (1948) enshrined individual security as 'life, liberty, and security of a person'. The Helsinki Accords of 1975 reaffirmed human rights as a key element of international security, and stated that respect for human rights would no longer be a matter of domestic jurisdiction. Human security can bring accountability mechanisms beyond state borders.

Civil and political rights set the limits on the state, especially when states consider national security as a priority. It is argued that for reasons of state, and especially during emergency situations, human rights practice may be curbed since it jeopardizes the interests of the state. Human rights advocates respond to this by stating that states use emergency situations to legitimize opportunities to withhold certain rights. According to human rights law, even a state party with no reservation to the International Covenant of Civil and Political Rights (ICCPR) could derogate from a significant number of articles within the Covenant, as long as they are not designated under Article 4 as 'non-derogable in times of public emergency.' According to the ICCPR, among the list of rights which can be legally withheld during a state of unrest are the rights of self-determination, judicial remedy, peaceful assembly, freedom of movement and the prohibition on war propaganda. The existence of some rights as derogable – or able to be withheld as emergency measures, has traditionally meant that national security concerns as claimed by states can limit rights enjoyed by their people.

Human security builds on the human rights model by shifting the concept of security from the state to individuals and collectivities. By doing so, it deconstructs the popular justification that states' violation of rights (civil and economic) on grounds of national security are necessary to protect national interest. When states justify curbs on dissent, use secret surveillance, arbitrary detention, and torture in emergencies, human security contests national security considerations by showing the diversity amongst people on the issue of security and by contrasting people's security with state security. Similarly, when defence expenditure far exceeds social sector spending by states on the grounds of national security, human security shows the skewed nature of priorities by focusing on people's security. The idea of the state's responsibility in governing its people and guaranteeing them security is part of classical political theory as argued by Locke. Foucault wrote that from the eighteenth century onwards, security increasingly became the dominant component of modern governmental rationality (Gordon, 1991). Duty and responsibility is what the human rights framework adds to the field of security.

Stemming from the universality of rights is the idea of 'responsibility to protect' that can imply a motivation and duty for intervention – whether through preventive development assistance or relief from the devastating effects of an internal conflict or emergency (Lucarelli, 2003). State responsibility is the inherent strength of human rights and gives credence to the idea of human security by ensuring that there is an actor to ensure that the claims of human beings – freedom, welfare, safety – are indeed realized. Without accountability, human security truly will be another utopia, rather than a new paradigm. For the human rights field, the greatest challenge at the international level is that its accountability system is based on states' protecting their own citizens. Human security brings accountability mechanisms beyond state borders. It weakens the shield of sovereignty as an excuse for human rights violations, yet pushes the issue of state responsibility to an inter-state level. Thus while human rights offers a framework of state accountability, human security seeks to address the limitations of this framework by creating inter-state mechanisms that limit the national shadow of the law for violators of human rights. Human security has the potential to alter both why we promote rights and how we do it. This opens the door to a more subtle choice, the likely clash between rights and security which is appropriately described by Foucault when he says: 'Just as people say milk or lemon, we should say law or order' (Foucault in Faubion, 2000). Human rights and democratization accelerate acceptance of human security as an alternative to the state-centred approach. Well-defined human rights are integral to human security policy. Human security provides a framework of state accountability necessary for operationalizing human rights.

One area where human rights are not theoretically developed was how state and civil society was to be organized and how core values and processes should be reconstructed and strengthened to ensure that international humanitarian law was protected and propagated. This gap has largely been met by human security and especially its pro-people and egalitarian versions. The human security approach incorporates human rights into everyday practice by focusing on the interdependence of rights, development, and security to ensure dignity of citizens. The specifics of human rights are not universally agreed upon but conceptualizations of human rights use three general principles: first, the interdependence of rights; second, state obligations/duties to individual and societal responsibilities; and third, focus on fulfilment, not violations of rights. States have an obligation and duty to human rights by ensuring laws, legal frameworks and a culture of human rights that includes a social and individual responsibility for eradicating poverty. Various mechanisms can be arrived at for example: creating legal and political systems that would reduce inequity, but this is not adequate in itself. There is thus a disbursement of responsibilities to make the human security agenda more feasible. Human security aims at protecting human rights by preventing conflicts, addressing the root causes of insecurity, and establishing a global political culture based on human rights. The state is the agency for governance and human security argues for its humanization in order to ensure governance with a human rights lens.

However, in examining the concept of human security as a right, some have recognized the limits of the existing legal framework. Oberleitner concludes that because human security includes non-state actors and non-state threats, it is a broader concept than fundamental rights (Oberleitner, 2002). Ramcharan, although first defining human security as a right, also calls for 'human rights strategies of governance' (Ramcharan, 2002) i.e. recognition that the aim of governance is the advancement of human rights. He suggests incorporating both paradigms into concrete actions, as in peace-keeping/peacemaking operations, conflict prevention and humanitarian work. However, in his recommendations, he focuses on the strengthening of existing procedures such as the UN special rapporteur's reports on human rights violations, instead of imagining non-legal solutions.

Enforcement mechanisms

Human rights transgressions are punished by legal sanctions, international tribunals, courts of law, etc. Enforcement of human rights rests on a vertical relationship between the enforcing agent and individual. Human security emphasizes a horizontal relationship between individuals and their responsibilities. Human security implementation, therefore, goes beyond compulsion/sanction and reinforces the notion of empowerment of the individual and community. In international security, respect for human rights is linked to international peace and security. Hampson argued that the main threat to human security lies in the denial of fundamental human rights, including the right of national self-determination, the absence of rule of law, the right to development (Hampson *et al.*, 2002: 18). Human rights/

rule-of-law is the 'fundamental liberal assumption that individuals have a basic right to "life, liberty and the pursuit of happiness" and that the international community has an obligation to protect and promote these rights'. The method of such enforcement through military intervention however is subject of both debate and controversy to the extent of de-legitimizing rights themselves.

Strategies for enforcing these rights have evolved instruments to follow up monitoring mechanisms that include imposition of sanctions by the UN Security Council and pressure from the international community. Sanctions deny access to foreign goods, services, markets, and capital to states/industries that violate rights or treaties, for example: sanctions against Zimbabwe (Rhodesia) after the Unilateral Declaration of Independence by the Smith regime (1966–1979); against South Africa during apartheid; against Iraq when Saddam Hussein invaded Kuwait (1989) and Haiti when General Cedras overthrew Artistide (1993–1994).

The close monitoring of human rights violations by international bodies like the UN Human Rights Commission and Amnesty International pressurizes governments to stop and reverse violations of human rights to avoid negative press and a bad reputation abroad This, in human rights language, refers to 'shaming'. Co-optation is yet another method whereby international courts and commissions promulgate legal norms and suggest reforms for democratic practices. Examples are the European Court of Justice and European Convention on Human Rights. By re-conceptualizing legal protection, human security evolves ways for more acceptable means of enforcement of human rights.

A major problem facing the human rights movement is that of enforcement which requires the identification of an individual victim, violator, and remedy. This requires autonomous judicial bodies that are not in place in many countries either because of lack of political will, resources, or judicial culture (Burke, 2005). The enforcement mechanisms envisaged by international law are tailored towards the richer Western states. Further, the implementation method chosen by international human rights law is based on a specific political and economic model that cannot be easily transposed on all nations at the same time. Besides regime resistance, there is a risk that local people may not understand the complex procedural rules. In response to this problem, An-Na'im proposes 'a reconceptualization of legal protection as part of wider strategies of implementation, rather than as the primary means of realising respect for human rights' (An-Na'im, 2001: 95). By doing so, the concept of human security can contribute to human rights with positive consequences for governments, policy makers and the global protection of human rights.

Enforcement is difficult because the ratification of international instruments on human rights is left to the discretion of states. For example, the United States has not signed the Convention on of the Rights on the Child, the Ottawa Convention banning anti-personnel mines, and the Statute of Rome establishing the International Criminal Court. There is no way that these obligations can be imposed on it under international law. Even after ratification, the effective enforcement of such a treaty depends on the political will and judicial system of the state. States are also allowed to request that certain provisions should not apply to them. This system allows states to 'dis-apply' certain provisions of key human rights treaties in cases of or 'exceptional public danger threatening the existence of the nation' (see Article 4 of the International Covenant on Civil and Political Rights, Article 15 of the European Convention on Human Rights and Article 27 of the American Convention on Human Rights).

The human rights framework does not provide effective remedies for violations of economic, social, and cultural rights. Respect for state sovereignty blocks external imposition of economic and social responsibility on erring states. No international committee exists to guarantee these rights, though some states have social policies that give citizens some social and economic guarantees. Another problem with the existing human rights framework is its narrow definition of responsibility for rights violations: many obligations apply only to states, and exclude non-state actors. Given the power of multinational corporations, this is a serious oversight. For example, when Shell Petroleum Corporation was accused of serious environmental degradation of the Ogoniland in Nigeria, it took no responsibility and blamed 'rapidly expanding population, over farming, deforestation and industry' (Maier, 2000: 95). However, international law is gradually becoming cognisant of this non-state threat, for example, Security Council Resolution 1373 (28 September 2001) obliges states to freeze the assets of corporate entities which facilitate terrorist acts.

While it is apparent that in recent years, human rights have been politically manipulated for intervention and some states feel their sovereignty can be threatened, it does not imply that the idea of human rights itself should be rejected. Ul Haq, addressed the attacks on human security as an excuse for western intervention (Ul Haq, 1998). He suggested the creation of a Human Security Council (HSC) to work alongside the Security Council to provide leadership in tackling global crises. He urged that a far less interventionist stance would be to send development workers rather than soldiers into regions of potential conflict and to ensure representation of developing countries in the HSC.

Debating 'values' in human rights and human security

Apart from the above-mentioned similarities, human rights and human security have both been described as universal and have both been criticized on this basis. Thus, the question of universality and culture is an essential issue in this topic (Castillo *et al.*, 2005). Human security by its holistic view helps surmount cultural relativism. In this way, one of the main challenges of human rights, i.e. the accusation of not being truly universal, may be overcome through its connection with human security. In particular, Asian countries, which have traditionally rejected universality of human rights but are now increasingly accepting discourse on the broad definition human security because of its preoccupation with economic development, may now become more open to the issue of human rights because of its inherent link with human security. Consequently, they may thus contribute to strengthen the economic and social branch of human rights, which has traditionally been neglected by Western countries.

Universalism means that something applies to everybody without distinction. As far as human security is concerned, Ul-Haq maintained that 'human security will be regarded as universal, global and indivisible' (Ul Haq, 1998). The 1994 HDR proclaimed it to be a 'universal concern. It is relevant to people everywhere, in rich nations and poor. There are many threats that are common to all people – such as unemployment, drugs, crime, pollution and human rights violations' (UNDP, 1994). At the same time, the HDR recognized that 'their intensity may differ from one part of the world to another, but all these threats to human security are real and ongoing.' Moreover, the CHS's report *Human Security Now* recognized that what people consider to be vital 'varies across individuals and societies'. Nevertheless, both reports emphasized the need for human security to be applied universally.

Even though the universality of human rights is a highly contested issue, its proponents maintain it as one of its basic characteristics. This is also affirmed in international human rights law, for instance in the universal declaration of human rights 1948 and the Vienna 1993 World Conference on Human Rights. The preamble of the universal declaration of human rights proclaims the declaration as 'a common standard of achievement for all peoples and all nations'. For example, article No. 1 declares that 'all human beings are born free and equal in dignity and rights'.

Despite the above-mentioned proclamations of universality, there has been much well-founded critique on this issue. Dallmayr for example argued that 'property rights, for instance, may very well be a universal claim, but this leaves untouched questions of the amount of property and the rightness of its exercise' (Dallmayr, 2002). How realistic, applicable, flexible, and wide is indeed a particular right? How does it combine with other rights? A similar problem applies to human security: what thresholds can there be for freedom from want, for example, and how can they be applied in practice?

More importantly though, proclamations of universalism have been opposed by relativists who question the possibility of detaching rights from their social, historical and cultural context, especially as the majority of human rights proponents are citizens and emissaries of the 'West'. Dallmayr talks of the distinction between the quality of the message and the role of the messenger (Dallmayr, 2002). Obviously, the origin of the messenger would have something to do with its proposed/intended effect and/or consequences. Similar critiques are advanced for human security, which is perceived by some as both Western-dominated and easily manipulated against the interests of the developing world, particularly through the issue of interventions. Most prominent critics of the so-called Western universality are the proponents of what is known as 'Asian values' and 'Islamic values'. This is so even though in reality, as far as human security is concerned, disagreements about it are as much West–West and East–East as East–West (Acharya, 2001). Nevertheless, because of the importance of the cultural issue, the cultural critique has imposed itself as one of the most dominant of both frameworks.

Finally, certain criticism aimed at human security and human rights comes from particular cultures, namely those proponents of Asian values. Even though the criticism is not based on cultural relativism as such, it challenges universalism by the very fact that the critiques come from a specific culture and are thus based on that culture's interpretation of human security and human rights (Castillo *et al.* 2005). Proponents of Asian values have compiled a list of criticisms concerning both human security and human rights within it. This may explain why human security has had little impact on national or regional policy making in Asia, even though it has become a growing aspect of the regional discourse (Evans, 2003).

The debate started in East Asia, where Asian cultural values are projected as specific and relative to Asia and as distinct from the human rights framework that was identified with Western values. Unlike in the West where the focus is on individuals and empowerment, Asian values included goals like social harmony, supremacy of a community's good over individual interests, preservation of customs, respect for seniority and authority, and absolute respect for sovereignty. Acharya tried to distinguish human security of the East with that of the West (Acharya, 2001). East Asian countries are suspicious about human security because they see it as the West imposing its values and political institutions on non-Western society. There are also fears that human rights would be used for intervention and threaten state sovereignty, which is very important for these countries. Some Asian leaders have argued that human security is not new but the same as comprehensive security/cooperative security. However, Acharya argues that human security has an Asian pedigree because of contributions by scholars like Haq and Sen. Dallmayer states that the debate on Asian values indicates that rights are contextual, but this does not necessarily dilute their universality (Dallmayr, 2002).

Some East Asian leaders claimed that 'Asian values' were undermined by individualistic Western principles such as free speech. However, Robertson points out that people in these countries 'usually turn out to prefer the so called Western values, rights that in fact belong to everyone, everywhere' (Robertson, 2002: 519). People's movements often argue that their leaders critique the Western conception of rights in order to oppress local opposition and to shelter their regimes on counts of violations. These groups however, equally critique Western governments, for not guaranteeing social and economic rights and allowing multinational companies and other actors to violate rights in their subsidiary companies in the South (Burke, 2005). Asia has multiple philosophical foundations, for instance, Hindu values have plural trends, some that support and others that contest. Confucian and Islamic values have differences within these. Besides, secular values adopted by some Asian countries have led to universal understanding of rights. Human rights advocates and other progressive movements within these societies articulate these rights. For example, there is a movement for Dalit rights in India.

Many Asian societies have adapted Western ideas like democracy and federalism into their political systems, thus the adaptation of human rights is possible. Moreover, ideas and institutions are shaped by history and cross-cultural developments. Thus, to reject some ideas as 'Western' rather than examine them on their merit is inappropriate. Asians have contributed to the human security debate, not appropriated it. Connecting human rights with human security helps mitigate criticisms that human rights are falsely universal, e.g. Asian countries appear more willing to accept human security than the human rights discourse because human security focuses on economic/social security and links with development (especially post-Asian financial crisis, 1997).

Conclusion

The centrality of human rights in human security is underlined by writers like Axworthy:

> ([H]uman security) is, in essence, an effort to construct a global society where the safety of the individual is at the centre of the international priorities and a motivating force for international action; where international human rights standards and the rule of law are advanced and woven into a coherent web protecting the individual; where those who violate these standards are held fully accountable; and where our global, regional and bilateral institutions – present and future – are built and equipped to enhance and enforce these standards.
>
> (Axworthy, 1999b)

The real test of human rights is in their implementation and accountability mechanism. The current human rights model is based on violations by states. It is argued that in the case of economic rights, a state apparatus with limited economic resources can truly be in violation of its 'progressive realization' of such positive rights. For example, Article 2 of the International Covenant on Economic Cultural and Social Rights is weak in its emphasis on what a state actually must do to fulfil its obligations. States should 'take steps ... to the maximum of its available resources, with a view to achieving progressively the full realization' of economic rights. The other argument against the state as guarantor of economic rights is that like the earlier Soviet model – the state will became more powerful, curbing more rights than it grants. In this context, human security argues for the state to ensure more equity than the free market model advocates and to take up the cause of the dispossessed to give them dignity of livelihood.

The relationship between human rights and human security is symbiotic because human rights lead to human security as it empowers people to seek solutions in a right-based approach. 'Rights for' rather than 'power over' is the message and end goal. There is therefore extensive overlap between these areas which are mutually reinforcing. Thus the internal debate on human security is not just indices of growth or rights violations, but for empowering, egalitarian development, and liberating social systems. This makes it more than clear that human rights and human security are not only mutually reinforcing but necessary if such principles are to work as envisaged in their conceptualization.

Part II

Implications

Every gun that is made, every warship launched, every rocket fired signifies, in the final sense, a theft from those who hunger and are not fed, those who are cold and not clothed.

Dwight D. Eisenhower

6 Underdevelopment and conflict

A vicious cycle?

The Roots of Violence: Wealth without work, Pleasure without conscience, Knowledge without character, Commerce without morality, Science without humanity, Worship without sacrifice, Politics without principles.

Gandhi

This chapter extends the debate on the dynamic between human development and security as concepts, pursuing the debates on the linkages in one of human security's prime fields of concern: conflict situations. This chapter therefore aims at showing the main interconnection that human security brings to the overall field: seeing underdevelopment as dangerous and conflict prone, and securitizing the need for development to avoid conflict.

The post-Cold War era has been marked by a changing nature of conflicts that has significantly altered the contexts in which development operates as well as the factors which influence the effectiveness of development interventions. Conflicts are no longer predominantly between nations but within states. Fifteen of the 20 poorest countries in the world have had a major conflict in the past 20 years, and 22 of the 34 countries furthest away from the millennium development goals are affected by current or recent conflicts. The relationship between conflict and human security is two-fold: while conflicts can be caused by underdevelopment and grievances in the first place, they certainly contribute to the exacerbation of human insecurities once disintegration happens. Conflict de-humanizes people as it takes away their dignity, increases suffering and brings about new types of insecurities, which often continue even after the conflict has ended. Therefore the promotion of human security should figure among the priorities of post-conflict reconstruction processes. Post-conflict recovery phases, especially because they are vulnerable to renewed cycles of violence, are opportunities to promote change, heal fragmentation, erase inequalities, and fundamentally recast social, political and economic bases of power. An understanding of conflict analysis, prevention and re-construction is imperative for aid development actors to devise conflict-sensitive strategies for programme planning, implementation and evaluation.

Increasingly, development actors stay engaged in situations which were once the pejorative of humanitarian, diplomatic and military actors: conflict and post-conflict situation. The continuous engagement stems from a conceptual shift in the 1990s that pitched underdevelopment as a 'danger' both to the stability of a country and to the global and regional countries which become recipient of not only the unemployed or the poor, but also diseases, drugs, arms, environmental hazards, and other risk factors that travel borders without passports. Hence, development became increasingly associated with a conflict prevention agenda. This conceptual shift led to increasing numbers of development agencies (such as the OECD/DAC, the World Bank, and UNDP) to incorporate operational means for altering aid and development in conflict contexts.

In this chapter, we look first at the conceptual shifts that have led to merging of security and development discourses. We then review the various models that explain the causes of wars, stemming from those that attribute conflicts to economic opportunity, to those that factor in social and political grievances. After evaluating these from a human security point of view, we look at the operational aspects of how international organizations are working in conflict situations. We finally use the human security approach to review the challenges of peace-building before concluding on some recommendations of why an HS approach is desirable for understanding, measuring and dealing with conflicts.

Insecurity and underdevelopment: the critical linkages

While the causality links between war and underdevelopment still remain to be fully explored, evidence confirms that the economic, social, political and environmental costs of war can slow down, hold or even reverse development processes. Obviously, this holds particularly true for poor countries whose development processes are incipient and slow. Moreover, poor countries tend to suffer on average more internal conflicts than richer countries. From this evidence came the consensus over a potential causality between poverty and conflict, or the fact that poor countries had a higher probability to suffer a war (Rodier, 2004). Conflict in the 'periphery' was the result of and resulted in development malaise. While conflict was seen as a de-developing process, then underdevelopment was also dangerous, because it not only potentially led to intra-state conflicts, but also to the 'export' of new threats, such as the migration of the unemployed and poor, diseases such as HIV/AIDs and SARS, drug trafficking and criminality, etc., to more affluent societies. If underdevelopment was seen as potentially 'dangerous', then development should be about conflict prevention. From this thinking came the reconceptualization of development as a security strategy (Duffield, 2001).

The redefinition of development also coincided with changing global norms and paradigms along the liberal peace model. The break-up of the Soviet Union, and with it the end of the Cold War, saw a demise of alternatives to the neo-liberal economic model. The triumph of liberalism meant a shift from isolated national policy making to networked solutions concocted by global actors and national elites linked through common outlooks and experiences. While war was a 'de-developing' phenomenon, peace could be brought through promoting intensified inter-dependence and economic linkages among states. The end of the Cold War thus provided an optimal opportunity for a re-conceptualization of 'development' as social transformation of the entire society based on new liberal norms. Societies had to be changed to ensure that past patterns would not be repeated, and, attitudes shifted to embrace the opening of systems that affected every day life.

The liberal peace model, born within the context of the merging of development and security, came to argue for the accountability of liberal economic instruments and democratic practices of 'open' societies as a means of enforcing peace. The consensus among international organizations, be they the UN or international financial institutions (IFIs) by the mid-1990s, was based on the Kantian call for the simultaneous opening of political and economic systems and the interaction between growing economic interdependence and mutual democracy as a fundamental instrument of promoting international peace. By the mid-1990s, democracy as the best form of governance to fight poverty and encourage development, and therefore promote peace and stability (given that democracies were not supposed to fight each other), became a norm by itself within the UN system. If underdevelopment was dangerous, the type of development that was needed was based on the liberal model: a transformative development, conceived as the self-management of liberal markets, transforming social processes. By addressing the root-causes of violent conflict and supporting local and national capacities for peace, development could help mitigate against violent conflict.

The consensus on the merging of development and security around liberal norms had a number of practical implications. The notion of underdevelopment as dangerous and destabilizing provided thus a justification for continued surveillance and engagement. As a result, humanitarian concerns were increasingly used to provide a moral justification for international interference. Military engagement lasted throughout the stages of conflict (pre, during and post). Aid conditionality could be based on security objectives and development became increasingly part of national security strategies. Peacemakers understood the need for development for sustainable peace. Development practitioners recognized the risks of their intervention in exacerbating conflict. Humanitarian agents appreciated the need for long-term interventions. Economists sought to include a political economy approach to post-conflict rehabilitation frameworks. Post-conflict situations were seen as opportunities to promote change, and to fundamentally recast social, political and economic bases of power, to include the excluded, heal fragmentation and erase inequalities. This consensus also meant a continuum between relief-development-reconstruction in a reconceptualization of development as conflict prevention, which then would become synonymous with peace-building.

As the relationships between conflict and development became increasingly evident, there were attempts to incorporate the notion of 'security' in the global development agenda. In 1948, the Charter of the United Nations explicitly linked war, development and human rights. In the 1960s, the Universal Declaration of Human Rights included 'security of person' and 'social security'. In the 1970s, the Food and Agricultural Organization coined the concept of 'food security' further merging the notion of development and security. In 1980, the Brandt Commission explicitly connected insecurity in the world with global inequality and underdevelopment. In the late 1980s, the environment was a focus on development efforts. In the creation of 'sustainable development', conflict was a key factor of sustainability. This evolution shows how conflict and security have been an increasingly important factors in development efforts. This cumulated in the 1994 *Human Development Report* in which the concept of 'human security' emerged.

Such an explication of war had direct implications for the responsibilities of donor countries towards development. The merging of the development and security discourses also led analysts to look increasingly into economic and social factors as root causes of violence in their conflict models.

Approaches to understanding causes: greed or grievance

The securitization of development and the humanization of security meant a renewed look at not only the impact of underdevelopment on the likelihood of conflict, but also the impact of conflict (or risk of conflict) on development. Many reasons have been put forth to explain the causes of civil wars, including misperceptions and failures of communication, deep-seated ethnic, religious, cultural tensions and animosities and so on. Until very recently, however, the political economy of conflict was not an often-studied field in academic or policy circles beyond economic costs of conflict. An attempt to overcome this lacuna has been made in several studies by independent researchers, sometimes for clarifying the linkages for international institutions, especially those engaged in giving development assistance. Among the various trends of analysis on root causes of civil wars, the debate has been on theories of greed that have concentrated on economic opportunities in wars, and grievance, the more subjective perceptions of groups. These new trends have focused on social and economic processes, in contrast to the more traditional analysis on political factors that were said to contribute to conflicts.

The greed model

According to research by the World Bank and the International Peace Academy that tried to understand the economic agendas of armed factions, violence (and more precisely conflict in civil wars) is often seen as an opportunity for groups to grab booty (Collier and Hoeffler, 1998; Collier *et al.*, 2003; Collier in Berdal and Malone, 2000, etc.). The findings concluded that much of the post-Cold War civil conflict has been driven not for purely political reasons, but rather by powerful economic motives and agendas. Greed was seen as an opportunity to grab power and resources. Instead of regarding war, through traditional realist theories, as the continuation of politics by another means, the greed theorists concluded that conflict could be seen instead as the continuation of economics by other means. Warfare was to be better understood as 'an instrument of enterprise and violence as a mode of accumulation' (Collier in Berdal and Malone, 2000). Further findings of a World Bank research argued that three key economic factors make a country susceptible to civil war. Paul Collier's empirical/econometric research into the causes of large-scale civil conflicts from 1965 to the present for the World Bank concluded that the best predictors of conflict, all other things being equal, were low average incomes and the availability of a high proportion of young men with inadequate access to educational opportunities, low growth, and a high dependence on exports of primary products such as oil, timber, or diamonds (which could be 'lootable' resources). The first two factors produced a pool of potential rebel recruits amongst disaffected young men, while the third was a potential source of financing conflicts. Another important determinant of conflict highlighted in research by the World Bank was the 'conflict trap', whereby past conflict weakens economies and leaves a legacy of atrocities which tended to be repeated.

Based on the empirical evidence that a common factor among war-prone countries was their poverty, Collier demonstrated that inequalities, political repression and ethnic and religious divisions had in reality no importance in predicting rebellion and escalation of conflict. This model reasoned that war is waged by actors whose interest is not in seizing power but in gaining financially through the perpetration of the conflict, and civil wars occur only when rebel groups are able to build large organizations that can mobilize substantial financial resources (Collier, 2001: 151). Rebellion still uses the language of protest to justify its action and remains the basis for recruitment; while oppression, unfairness and victimization of the population referred to by the leadership in fact is responsible for the 'inculcation of grievance' (Collier, 2001: 155) by making people aware they are victims of injustices. David Keen argued that war should not be seen as a breakdown of development processes, but rather as an alternative system of profit as it confers a legitimacy on actions that in 'peacetime would be punishable as crimes' (Keen, 1997). In support of the greed model, Keen cited instances of pillage, control of trade, profit from arms, use of forced labour (as in Myanmar, Sudan), the depopulation of land and transfer of land to victors, and selective use of humanitarian aid to fortify his thesis.

For Collier, the secondary factors that assist war include geographical factors like a dispersed population and a difficult terrain that makes it hard for the government to control war, the risk of recurrence of war in regions with a history of wars as well as the existence of diasporas and their role in funding of rebellions because of their 'romanticized attachments to their group of origin and may nurse grievances' (Collier, 2001: 151). Collier also believes that ethnic or religious diversity can avert the risk of war because if no one group is big enough to dominate the country, inequalities are less felt and organizing a rebellion becomes more difficult. The greed-inspired model advocated that the government, with the assistance of the international community, could reduce important risk factors by making it more difficult for rebel organizations to get established. These steps included: (a) making the rebels unpopular by using revenues to provide effective basic services, which rendered the population less sensitive to the rebellion's promises of wealth; and (b) addressing financial viability of rebellion and making it more difficult for rebel groups to sell commodities. For instance, global efforts have been made to curb the trade in conflict diamonds by reducing the prices that guerrillas in Angola and Sierra Leone could charge for these gems and through a certification process to keep conflict diamonds out of reputable shops. Other ways include addressing the dependence on natural resource exports by promoting diversification and targeting international aid to these societies and by taking measures to increase low incomes and reverse economic decline the government could ensure economic growth and improve people's standards of living. Steps in preventing ethnic dominance by entrenching minority rights in the constitution and legislating either on group rights or on individual rights could also be taken. Good governance, the respect of human rights and democracy were seen as indispensable for ensuring peaceful coexistence of groups. The model also proscribed arms control policies which would prevent the diversion of weapons of security forces to the rebels. It was calculated that each average year of education reduces the risk of conflict by around 20 per cent; and that each 5 per cent increase of the annual growth rate also reduces the risk of conflict by 20 per cent (Collier, 2000: 97).

Collier warned against the generalization of political violence and the durable 'inculcation of grievance' during post-conflict recovery stages (Collier, 2001: 158). For this he advocated that policy-makers remove the military option through the demobilization of the rebel organization and its transformation into a conventional party. Here, donors could provide aid conditional upon the signature of a peace agreement. However, such an intervention is useless if looting is too lucrative. Other measures could include DDR (disarmament, demobilization and reintegration) that gives incentives to foot-soldiers to give up arms by offering them legal work. He argued for resolution of the political contest itself through addressing at least minimum grievances, the main purpose being the change of perceptions, rather than redistribution of assets. The international community could also provide insurance to the minorities through military presence and guarantees.

The World Bank based some of its analysis on Collier's work to profess that the financial gain that some minorities made from the conflict through war economy could lead to a lavish life style and contribute to sustaining the conflict (Collier *et al.*, 2003: 4). According to the World Bank, the prospects for stabilization and economic recovery in conflict-affected countries depended largely on the success of disarmament, demobilization and reintegration programmes, especially the latter phase of reintegrating ex-combatants into a productive and peaceful life. To operationalize its findings, the World Bank has increasingly become engaged in institutional and human capacity building and using initial aid to pay salaries, especially for security personnel. Other policy initiatives have included regionally agreed military spending reductions, policies to cushion resource-dependant countries from price shocks and greater openness and scrutiny of government use of natural resource revenues to diminish chances of grievances over allocation of profits from these.

However, researchers like Humphreys have not found evidence for a correlation between economic inequality and conflict, and further conclude that there is no evidence to suggest that structural adjustment programmes have led to an increase in conflicts (Humphreys, 2003). At the same time however, Humphreys agreed that horizontal inequalities defined as 'systematic inequalities between culturally formed groups' are aspects of conflict situations and that along with structural adjustment, the World Bank should also advocate education, affirmative action, creation of political institutions, etc. Most other studies agreed with Collier and Hoefler's assumptions that poverty in itself is a crucial structural cause of insecurity and violent conflict (Saether, 2001). Some contributors see democracy as a prerequisite for internal peace and recognize the vital role of the state in reconstruction and prevention.

Drawbacks of the greed model

The greed model, however, did not provide an answer to questions like how and at what historical conjuncture does ethnicity get converted into aggressive nationalism. How is nationalist consciousness organized and mobilized? When does a movement of ethnic nationalism get militarized? All these transformations are linked to subjective processes and an analysis of the cultures and their transformations in these regions, and none of them can be deduced from pure economic data of deprivation or greed. This kind of analysis would not touch on ethnicity, gender, the political economy, or the nature of militarized consciousness. It would gloss over the history of the conflict and the story of exploitation, colonialism and even rights. It is thus difficult to measure precisely emotions such as grievance and the motivations for greed through econometrics (Mack, 2002a: 296).

The greed analysis of conflict would logically dismiss movements and struggles based on genuine grievances of people that arise out of oppression and violation of rights, which may be morally justified, for example, the struggle for an independent East Timor; the pro-democracy conflict in Nepal, or the movement for a Palestinian homeland. Elements of criminalization and extremism do enter such movements, but do not necessarily distort their aims, ideas and goals. The greed inspired models however, homogenize them into one unsavoury club of 'criminalized politics' and legitimize the use of armed forces to suppress these, without looking at the deep structural causes that ignited these in the first place.

The reality of armed conflicts is that they are a confluence of subjective and objective forces. For example, can the Mohajir conflict in Pakistan be put into the compartment called 'greed' when it is a struggle for citizenship rights? How can this model account for the memories of Sinhalese nationalism that helped construct Tamil minority consciousness in the Sri Lankan conflict? (Coomaraswamy, 1986). Can this be put down to greed and organized crime? While many ethnic dissent movements in India's North East became degenerated insurgencies as they developed vested interests and a conflict economy was generated, they had started as movements for self determination. By clubbing all armed rebellion, wars and other forms of protest into one mass, Collier argued for the prevalence of the status quo against violent dissent, even if the state was predatory. He removed all legitimacy from rebellion and reduced the means for war (necessity for rebellion to be funded), the nature and the objectives of rebellion (seeking change/rights etc.)

and the motivation of rebels (greed) to 'organized crime'. By confusing legality and legitimacy, Collier's model could lead to unlimited support of a state, whatever responsibility it may have in the conflict. In Rwanda for instance, France until the end supported the Habyarimana regime while ethnic hatred and violence was an instrument of the state itself.

The greed inspired model interestingly focuses entirely on 'local' greed, leaving out as a consequence the greed of the transnational players in such conflicts that have a stake in many conflict regions over issues of resources. It has been repeatedly studied for instance that many multinational companies have an interest in natural resources and thus become stakeholders in the conflict. Further, it leaves out the role of the international shadow economy that plays a role in all conflicts. Nordstorm argues that a startlingly large proportion of the entire global economy passes through the shadows: 90 per cent of Angola, 50 per cent in Kenya, Italy and Peru. 40 per cent in Russia and between 10–30 per cent in the US economy enters into extra-state transactions (Nordstrom, 2004: 11). She shows in no uncertain terms that 'It is these 'extra state' exchange systems, what have come to be called 'shadow' networks, that are fundamental to war, and in a profound irony, central to processes of development' (Ibid.).

The danger of the greed model lies in suggesting narrow ways of conflict resolution that are restricted to improving conditions of the market, or giving aid to some groups without addressing the root causes. Such minimal interventions fail to stop a new spiral of conflicts. This narrow approach has led to the grievance models where justice plays a bigger role. It is thus clear that there is no such thing as one way causality between war and underdevelopment but that their linkages should be considered more dynamically by the human security approach, introducing the probable common root cause of horizontal inequalities.

Justice matters: the grievance approach

The grievance model based on the more traditional perceptions of the reasons for conflict was revived by Stewart and researchers at Oxford University, who concentrated on failures of the social contract between states and citizens like inequalities, weak institutions, poverty and lack of social services as root causes for conflict. They noted that while wars were essentially group activities, individual motivations could prolong conflict. In studying the economic and social causes of war and underdevelopment, they categorized group formations around religious, class, ethic, clan and regional interests and the political and economic sources of differentiations among each. Horizontal inequalities between groups with differentiated access to socio-economic opportunities, resources and power-sharing could lead to a feeling of 'unfairness' in distribution of development gains and deep-rooted conflicts when they associate identity with inequality in a historically or emotionally charged situation (Stewart, 2000). Power inequalities and asymmetries can include sources of long-term as well as short-term grievances ranging from economic inequality to gender, race, religion, ethnicity, etc. It is not the mere existence of these inequalities, but a collective feeling of 'unfairness'

,stemming from a skewed distribution of development gains and power sharing among different groups that could feed animosities. The failure of political structures to address inequalities and curb the dominance of particular groups leads to dissatisfactions that ignite conflicts.

Stewart *et al.* used Amartya Sen and Martha Nussbaum's concept of entitlements, legally-based claims to the goods and services supplied by the markets or derived from their own production, to show that the breakdown of the private and public economy during conflict leads to a decline in entitlements, which is countered by informal networks creating vested interests and victims in the conflict (Stewart and Fitzgerald, 2000). They identified five basic types of entitlements: market, direct (goods and services which are produced and consumed on a shared basis by the same household), public, civic and extra-legal. War implies that as distribution of essential supplies are disrupted, socio-economically marginalized groups are severely affected and suffer an increased economic vulnerability with changes in economic behaviour, leading to serious macroeconomic consequences (fall in GDP, domestic savings, investment or government expenditure, etc.).

Stewart argued that political leaders exploit group identity constructs, group cohesion and mobilization as powerful mechanisms in their competition for power and resources. Extending the idea further, Stewart and Fitzgerald stressed that 'the greater part of the human costs of war does not result directly from battle deaths and injuries, but rather "indirectly" from the loss of livelihoods caused by the dislocation of economy and society resulting from conflict'. They concluded that civilian deaths often outweigh military losses due not to physical violence, but a lack of access to food and health facilities. They cautioned against making a division between immediate human costs and long-term development costs, such as between 'humanitarian assistance' and 'development co-operation'. Human costs, like worsened nutrition and education also impact development and the destruction of infrastructure or declining exports also cause immediate human suffering. Given the negative impacts of conflict on poverty reduction and sustainable development, conflict prevention should therefore become central to effective long-term development efforts. Ostby suggested that vertical inequality as worked out by Collier and others does not cause armed conflict, whereas inequality between ethnic groups is often an input into conflict (Ostby, 2003: 8). He argues that it requires more than ethnic diversity and mobilization to cause conflict, and the true reason lay in structural relative deprivation.

The strength of the grievance model thus lies in that it takes into account the aspirations of communities, though does not adequately point to issues such as the violation of rights, the building of stereotypes and the biased nature of states in dealing with sensitive inter-community issues. Stewart and others focused on the group dimension of conflict rather than on specific individuals as civil wars are organized group conflicts. The grievance model contests the Bretton Woods institutions approach that conflict is the breakdown of normal economic growth. This model then indicates that the human security approach that re-examines the pattern of growth itself in order to view conflicts is a more holistic and effective way of preventing conflicts.

Horizontal iniquities are not sufficient to generate a conflict but provide the basis for the construction of group identity for political mobilization that political leaders may use. Given the complex mechanisms of group mobilization, the model of horizontal inequalities is not a direct causality for conflict. It should however, be one of the many inputs that the human security model should use for examining and preventing conflict, along with other variables that include absolute poverty, past history, regional and international contexts, etc. In this context it would be useful to look at some of the other models that have viewed wars and conflicts through such lenses.

Moving away: other models of conflict

Underdevelopment may not directly cause violent conflict but poor social, economic and environmental conditions as well as weak or ineffective political institutions certainly diminish a society's capacity to manage social tensions in a non-violent manner. Causality for exacerbated social stress and ultimately, conflict may lie in horizontal and vertical inequalities, lack of representation, social marginalization, political exclusion and a record of human rights violations.

The liberal peace approach to conflict prevention

By the mid-1990s, democracy came to be seen as the best form of governance to fight poverty and encourage development and therefore promote peace and stability. Liberal theorists such as Doyle believed that societies with democratic systems and free market economies based on neo-liberal patterns do not fight each other. The mutual benefit from trade and the force of public opinion led to avoidance of wars (Doyle, 1983). This model is based on the belief that the West has experienced long-standing peace due to the existence of democratic institutions and liberal economic instruments. The theory assumes that developing countries that are not democratic are dangerous, and the type of development that was needed was based on the neo-liberal model, conceived as the self-management of free markets that will transform social processes and help militate against violent conflict. Democratic countries have institutions that are more accountable to people and help resolve conflicts through negotiations and democratic change. Mack's *Human Security Report* for 2005 for example uses the arguments of liberal peace to show that conflicts have dramatically decreased from 50 armed conflicts in 1992 to 29 in 2003 as a result of dramatic increase in democratic countries [from 20 in 1946 to 88 in 2005] (Mack, 2005). The report however, acknowledges that development with equity, safeguarding minority rights, empowerment and the human security approach to understanding and resolving conflicts are the inputs that are most likely to resolve conflicts.

The liberal peace theory focuses only on inter-state wars, whereas contemporary conflicts are primarily within states and then have regional effects. Such a model cannot explain the secession movements in Northern Ireland, or the Catalan movement in Spain, to cite some examples. The idea that democracies do not fight each other became a norm by itself within the UN system, even though this is historically untenable and democracies have waged pre-emptive wars on other states. The Kargil conflict between India and Pakistan at a time when Pakistan had the democratically elected government of Nawaz Sharif, again showed that such wars occur. The liberal peace argument leaves out the fact that most countries engaged in current or past conflicts have often followed policies suggested by the World Bank and International Monetary Fund. As Chapter 9 will argue, simply approving the creation of liberal political institutions will not necessarily ensure a peaceful model. Equitable economic policies and state control of markets in order to ensure an element of justice in distribution are also necessary to ensure a lasting peace.

Other models of conflict analysis

Dependency theorists have argued that conflicts in the Third World are linked with the history of colonialism, with global inequality rooted in the unequal and exploitative international trade system, an imbalance of structures, and inequality of world systems. They advocate the 1970s alternative state based models that promote equity and better terms of trade. Radical critics continue to use the argument of the existence of finance capital and new forms of imperialism as one of the causes for conflict, for example, the US intervention in Iraq and their national interest based Middle East policy. Again, this model, like the greed model, can be over determined by its economic focus.

Other analysts argue that the new world order of economics, neo-liberal globalization and its effects have generated new conflicts and exacerbated old ones. Rising inequities as a consequence of policies of globalization are resulting in new threats and conflicts that are taking shape in the form of terrorism, water or environment related conflicts. The *Human Security Report* 2005 shows that while interstate conflicts have decreased over time, the privatization of security structures has increased vastly. In Asian countries, the ratio of military to civilians has risen. This indicates that militarization continues and democratic governance alone is not a sufficient incentive for peace. Kaldor and others show the fragmentation of violence at the national and state level, since the 1980s in the wars of the 1990s like Bosnia, Rwanda, Somalia and the break-up of the Soviet Union and the consequent economic collapse of Russia and the new states created by the break-up, have provided the basis for authoritarianism and regime change (Kaldor and Vashee, 1997).The Final Report of the Carnegie Commission on Preventing Deadly Conflict states: 'the rapid compression of the world through breathtaking population growth, technological advancement and economic interdependence, combined with the readily available supply of deadly weapons and easily transmitted contagion of hatred and incitement to violence' act as a multipliers of new forms of conflicts (Carnegie Commission, 1997). Most of these conflict models polarize around the greed or grievance models, and focus on the economic causes using a political economy approach.

Synthesis of the approaches

Most of the academic debate on the causes of armed conflict has become polarized around the greed versus grievance dichotomy, juxtaposing 'loot-seeking' with 'justice-seeking' rebellions, and, more generally, the significance of economic versus socio-political drivers of civil war. However, there is emerging recognition of the analytical limits that this dichotomy imposes on what are in reality extremely complex systems of interactions. While there is overall agreement that economic factors matter to conflict dynamics, there is no consensus as to how they matter relative to other political and socio-cultural factors. What therefore is necessary is a synthesis of these two approaches, since both models have some validity. Sen, for example, sees a correlation but no causal relationship between violent and persistent conflict and massive economic inequality and poverty (Sen, 2001). He warns against 'economic reductionism', that social and political strife is explained away by hidden economic roots. Yet, he concedes that conditions for conflict and poverty do co-exist. The memory of discrimination, inequity and political dissatisfaction can trigger conflict, and poverty can be a fertile recruitment ground for foot soldiers. Poverty can also increase tolerance for violence. Yet, the direction of causalities is not clear, and can go from war and violence to famines and destitution. For Sen, poverty reduction cannot be a sole policy instrument for conflict resolution. Avoiding war and removing deprivation are separate ends but can be means to each other. Sen argues that, ultimately, the same factors and conditions that lead to underdevelopment exist within and in pre-conflict situations. At the same time, sudden de-development, such as resulting from a financial crisis as in East Asia in 1997, or a state collapse, etc., can have the same impact on people's every day livelihoods and dignity (if not survival) as conflict. While underdevelopment may not directly cause violent conflict, poor social, economic and environmental conditions as well as weak or ineffective political institutions certainly diminish the capacity to manage social tensions in a non-violent manner. Ultimately, research and policy proposals need to focus on the interactions of both greed and grievance to improve understanding of the causes, character, and dynamics of civil strife and move towards more effective policies of conflict prevention and resolution.

Implications and costs of conflict

In all these conflicts, the largest number of people killed, hurt, and maimed have been civilians. Conflicts generate large numbers of internally displaced persons and millions of refugees, most of whom are women. The Gender Development Index ranking for most conflict-ridden states is amongst the lowest in the world. Rehabilitation packages for women have uniformly been less than those for men. In many instances, compensation packages have been usurped by the extended families. Rape and sexual abuse of women has often been used as an instrument in inter-community conflicts. Conflicts orphan children and keep them away from schools. Children caught in the crossfire are killed, maimed, and traumatized.

They are sometimes militarized into child soldiers. In most conflict regions, counter-insurgency measures aimed at destroying the infrastructure support base of terrorists ravage homes, workplaces, and fields of ordinary people or mark them as enemy territory.

Economic, political and environmental costs

At the macro level, war has direct impact on production and trade, government tax revenues, expenditures and inflation, and indirect ones on foreign exchange shortages. Enormous resources are lost in the acquisition and development of arms and armies. For instance, financial losses to Arab countries from the Iran–Iraq, and the Gulf wars and the Lebanese and Yemeni civil wars are estimated at $904 billion. At the end of the 1990s, economists estimated that nuclear weapons production in India would cost at least 300 million rupees a year for the next 10 years, which is 0.5 per cent of the annual average GDP. The same amount could be used for providing elementary education for every child in India, where more than 30 per cent children still remain out of school. Military expenditures in all of South Asia have increased as almost all states face a variety of armed conflicts. Yet South Asia remains a region with the largest number of poor, with 680 million below the poverty line.

War results in declining entitlements, changes in household composition, displacement, increased burden on women, and rising mortality rates. Heavy development costs include the reduction of new investments, destructions of physical land, decline in human resources and social and organizational capital. Conflict leads to brain and human resource drain, internal migration and uneven development. Ties between communities and villages break up, leading to stress and trauma while successive wars pose a 360 degree threat to the communities involved. Disruption of social ties, tolerance and coexistence, the breakdown of families and small communities and the general collapse of social values and normal life are the most enduring consequences of the war, which cannot be mitigated in a short time. All conflicts involve environmental damage, deforestation and poaching, land mines, and uncontrolled waste. The political costs of conflict are also high and involve the collapse of political institutions, institutionalized insecurity, fragmentation of territorial sovereignty and of civil society.

Clearly then, human insecurity is at the base of all these conflicts. A varying mixture of underdevelopment, iniquity, denial of social, cultural and economic rights, denial of political power and representation to individuals and communities leads to resentments and aspirations that get transformed to militancy if they remain unfulfilled. The argument that development alone can alleviate conflict does not work. Many states that continue to be in the low human development regime but have some form of democratic space and ability for power sharing, manage to negotiate conflicts.

War and conflict are not the only reason for mass violence that may have other causes. An examination of the different types of violence becomes necessary that raises questions on the many hidden kinds of violence in societies. Such an examination is necessary for a human security framework since it looks for an overall end to human suffering not restricted to wars and crisis alone.

Covert and overt violence in human society

The idea of personal security and societal peace have been broadened by the human development and human security paradigms, to include not just violence from conflict but the structural, personal and private violence and violence from development. Academic supporters of the human security paradigm like Des Gasper argue that the scale of physical violence and insecurity among the poor, especially women is overlooked (Gasper, 2005a: 115). Evidence shows that many countries have followed growth models that have led to increased structural violence and physical insecurities. Often, even when economic and social changes are recognized to be causes of violence, this is treated as a short-term outcome resulting in a marginalization of the issue. While development is considered synonymous with progress, it fosters violence in many forms. Gasper lists the many types of violence that demand the attention of development and human security analysts. These include: violence against workers; women; children; indigenous people; other civilizations, races or ethnic groups; and against oneself. This reveals a picture of how human nature accommodates the realities of violence in which models of development are grounded and how this can lead to inter-community conflicts at later historical stages.

There are many instances of development models leading to violence and to situations of armed conflicts. Fifteen states in India currently are in the throes of violent Maoist movements that get support from the impoverished peasantry. The so called 'Naxal infected areas' of India are in tribal belts of about 7,000 villages in approximately 19 per cent of India's forests. It is widely acknowledged that the adoption of privatization policies have increased inequality and rural-urban divide in addition to increased exploitation of natural resources; alteration of forest laws leading to the felling of trees and the entrance of exploitative contractors into impoverished tribal communities. The Naxals have mobilized people on issues of environmental and food security and have been sheltered and supported by these communities. The Naxals are in fact filling what former police officers call 'a governance vacuum'. The civil war in Nepal is based on similar lines by Maoist rebels, who have mobilized the peasantry and the poor.

Other examples come from the Yugoslav and Rwanda conflict of the 1990s both of which faced debt rescheduling at a time of political transition and other social stress. As Peter Uvin elaborates in the case of Rwanda:

> [If] we define structural violence as consisting of the combination of extreme inequality, social exclusion, and humiliation/assault on people's dignity ... [then] notwithstanding positive macroeconomic indicators, Rwanda has been characterised for decades by a high degree of structural violence greatly intensified.
>
> (Uvin, 1999a)

These examples indicate that basic economic and social rights and the norms of basic human needs have to be institutionalized to be an integral part of the development agenda without which conflicts and violence will increase. A human security insight into conflict needs to factor in the violence due to structural causes, including violence caused by development patterns through history, in order to adopt a model of development that excludes such violence.

Operational challenges: 'doing' development in conflict situations

Some claim that poverty alleviation and development cannot take root in situations of perennial conflict, and given the negative impacts of conflict on poverty reduction and sustainable development, conflict resolution should therefore become central to effective long-term development efforts. Others contend that reduction of poverty and steady development are the only instruments to avoid the outbreak of civil conflicts. The two approaches start with and refer to completely different essential assumptions and prerequisites. On the one hand is the development-oriented approach, that relies on the active participation of the state in ensuring the protection and empowerment of its citizens. This approach assumes the existence of the state, and includes the proponents of 'democratic governance', drawing upon the tenets of the Bretton Woods institutions, more specifically, the World Bank. Yet, the concern of the World Bank may be more on the relationship between state, market and civil society in countries receiving financial aid than with human security and the trade-offs it requires between equity and growth. In brief, the philosophy behind the interest for good governance is state-centred, but not people centric. On the other hand, the conflict-oriented approach is openly intrusive: it deals with conflict prevention, military intervention or peacekeeping, and assumes the non-existence of the state or its incapability to carry out its basic functions.

Contemporary analyses of security need to factor in systemic, structural, institutional and operational causes of armed conflict. Systemic causes include global and local inequities, negative effects of globalization, arms trafficking, and international organized crime. Structural factors encompass denial of rights, lack of development, country disparities, weak, failing or predatory states, insecurity, oppression, and aspirations for self determination. Malformation of institutions could trigger institutional collapse in the face of crises. Operational aspects therefore would need to include dealing with conflict triggers such as resource scarcity, historical memories of oppression; aspirations for independent statehood; capture of power and resources; small arms, population movements, land redistribution, public health emergencies, sudden and severe inflation. This is not only because the truths of war, do not match the myths of war but also because as Nordstrom points out, that much is invested in erasing the truths of war (Nordstrom, 2004: 32). Unveiling this truth is critical not only for the victim and for those in a conflict context but for the human security approach as well.

Institutionalizing the 'conflict lens'

Development actors, such as the World Bank and the UK Department for International Development (DFID) have increasingly recognized the importance of incorporating safeguards for conflict prevention in all arenas of policy, such as development, trade, investment and foreign policy. Development interventions without a conflict prevention lens may inadvertently exacerbate or reinforce conflict dynamics. For example, it may increase competition for resources, introduce new institutions that challenge existing ones or help to perpetuate structures of dominance. Viewing all policy thrusts through a 'conflicts lens' can provide valuable support to local and national capacities for peace and increase the effectiveness of development assistance. It is important for transition from large-scale, short-term, externally-driven humanitarian and military interventions that are typical in the midst of crisis, to more grass-roots, longer-term, locally-driven development interventions. Three of the main development actors, the Organization for Economic Co-operation and Development (OECD)'s Development Assistance Committee (DAC), the United Nations Development Programme and the World Bank have all expanded their programmes to include a conflict lens since the late 1990s.

OECD/DAC guidelines: integrating development with conflict prevention

The Development Assistance Committee (DAC) is a consultation forum on development cooperation of the OECD, established in 1948 by the recipients of the Marshall plan, and then consolidated as the main club of developed countries. OECD/DAC countries provide $60 billion a year in development assistance. Structured around the basic liberal precepts of trade liberalization and free circulation of capital, the DAC has shown a growing preoccupation with conflict. In 1997, it created ground-breaking guidelines on conflict, peace and development co-operation on the threshold of the twenty-first century. A 2001 supplement looked primarily at collective conflict as also state violence against groups and individuals. It focused on 'fragile' states through EC, DAC, UN and World Bank initiatives on 'learning and advisory process on difficult partnerships'. The guidelines encouraged the donor community to adjust to the local context, move from reaction to prevention, focus on state building, recognize the political-security-development nexus, and act fast but stay engaged long enough to give success a chance.

Given an increase in military spending in the post-September 11 era, the OECD/DAC sought to clarify directives to expenditures related to conflict prevention and peace-building. With no international standard policy on military assistance, 'defence diplomacy' or 'military assistance' is included under the category 'other official flows' (OOF) at the DAC. Assistance for the supply or financing of military equipment or services, training of military personnel, even in non-military matters, even in emergencies is not reportable as ODA. Only the additional costs of military personnel delivering humanitarian aid is included in ODA. The OECD/DAC review in 2004 however was prompted by pressure to incorporate military assistance expenditure (called Southern peacekeeping) into ODA budgets. OECD/DAC consultations reached consensus on technical cooperation and civilian support for six items which could constitute as ODA: first, Management of security expenditure through improved civilian oversight and democratic control of budgeting, management, accountability and auditing of security expenditure; second, enhancing civil society's role in the security system; third, supporting legislation for preventing the recruitment of child soldiers; fourth, security system reform to improve democratic governance and civilian control; fifth, civilian activities for peace-building, conflict prevention and conflict resolution and finally, controlling, preventing and reducing the proliferation of small arms and light weapons. DAC consultations concluded that training the military in non-military matters, such as human rights, and extending the coverage of peacekeeping activities were not appropriate use of ODA budgets. Unlike the six items agreed on which expenditures were relatively modest, these items involved large sums, mostly from defence budgets, and could not be reported as ODA.

World bank: early warning tools and post-conflict development

While the work of the OECD DAC has focused on conflict prevention, the World Bank has institutionalized policies with regards to post-conflict development. Since 1980, the World Bank lending to post-conflict countries increased over 800 per cent to $6.2 billion. In 1997, the World Bank adopted a new policy statement that evaluated nine case studies that analysed first, the World Bank's strengths or comparative advantages in this field, second, its partnerships with other international organizations and NGOs, third, its role in reconstruction strategy and needs assessment, fourth, its role in rebuilding the economy and government institutions, fifth, its management of resources and process and sixth, its monitoring and evaluation experience (Kreimer *et al.*, 1998). The study identified five areas of focus for further improvement: clarifying World Bank policy, defining the Bank's role, sharpening the World Bank's comparative advantage and performance, considering the problem of some conventional wisdom and making appropriate institutional arrangements. After this study, the World Bank endorsed a 'framework for World Bank involvement in post-conflict reconstruction'. To improve further operational policies in post-conflict situations, the World Bank created a post-conflict unit, which serves as a centre for policy development, cross-country learning and expertise development, and develops programmes on demobilization, reintegration of ex-combatants, reintegration of displaced population, and removal of land mines.

In the meantime, the research on economic causes of war which the World Bank published in a report *Breaking the Conflict Trap: Civil War and Development Policy*, led to the development of a conflict analysis framework (CAF) as a tool for *ex ante* evaluation of countries at risk. The CAF used nine indicators as early warning indicators to capture the deteriorating environment in a country. In addition to the more traditional causes of conflict, such as political indicators and militarization (high defence spending, large armies, availability of arms, etc.), the CAF drew on the recent debates of greed and grievance to include social issues, economic indicators, history, as well as presence of active regional conflicts.

UNDP: mainstreaming conflict in operations

For UNDP, the merging of security and development meant a focus on guiding principles for development interventions in crisis countries. This thinking led to a process of re-examining the role of the institution in conflict prevention, a consultation among its 135 country offices and the creation of a bureau for conflict prevention and recovery in the early 2000s. The bureau led UNDP's work in new areas such as post-disaster recovery, risk reduction, mine clearance, peace-building, transitional justice and security sector reforms among other initiatives. UNDP consequently developed an assessment toolkit for its country-level assistance, a conflict-related development analysis (CDA) which built on conflict assessments undertaken in Guatemala, Nepal, Nigeria, Guinea-Bissau and Tajikistan, and a series of analytical tools on the role of conflict analysis in peace building. In some countries, UNDP regularly issues early warning reports based on a set of interrelated indicators to monitor the overall economic, social, political, religious and ethnic environment. In Bulgaria, the information was based on monthly opinion polls, data from governmental institutions, and information in the press.

UNDP also developed a set of guiding principles for the institutions' operations in conflict prone regions, extending the development initiatives to all stages of pre-, during and post-conflict. It warned that at whatever stage of crisis, whether before, during or after open conflict, work to sustain livelihoods must be pursued as vigorously as life-saving endeavours, and throughout a crisis, opportunities for rehabilitation and reconstruction must coexist with acute relief. It also proscribed to work on a culture of disaster management and mitigation and on the analysis of the root cause of the conflict.

On the thorny issue of coordination, both UNDP through its resident representative system and the World Bank sought to cooperate with the increasingly numerous actors that came to crowd in post-conflict situations.

The human security challenge to peacebuilding

In recognition of the reality of mutual vulnerabilities and inter-dependence of threats, the international community is increasingly willing to deal with risks of humanitarian crisis, terrorism, organized crime trafficking (people, arms, narcotics), uncontrolled migration, increased impoverishment, growth of epidemics and other threats to the security of the international community and people worldwide which often stem from weak or failed states. Rich donor countries are also increasingly made aware of their own responsibilities, outlined in the eighth goal of the Millennium Development Goals, to help countries abide by their responsibilities to protect people from economic crisis, humanitarian disasters, epidemics and gross violations of human rights. These efforts are being carried out under the general umbrella of 'peacebuilding' efforts.

Peacebuilding refers to a long-term process that occurs after violent conflict has slowed down or come to a halt. It is a complex notion, encompassing various postwar activities aimed at avoiding re-escalation of violence, reducing conflict, promoting justice and assisting economic recovery. It is a multi-sectoral and multifaceted concept, which includes several components, including providing for security, both external (territorial) and internal (human), institution-building and good governance; strengthening the rule of law; and sustainable economic development.

In 1992, the former UN Secretary General Boutros-Ghali, in *An Agenda for Peace*, defined post-conflict peace-building among other UN roles and strategies, such as prevention, peacemaking, and peacekeeping. The document presented peacebuilding as a phase of the peace process, taking place after peacemaking and peacekeeping and focusing on capacity building, reconciliation, and societal transformation. There are nuances between peace building and the more traditional strategies of peacemaking and peacekeeping. Peacemaking is the diplomatic effort to end the violence between parties in conflict, move them towards dialogue, and eventually reach a peace agreement. Peacekeeping is a foreign engagement, usually, though not necessarily, military, to assist the transition from violence to peace by separating the fighting parties and keeping them apart. The peacekeeping operations not only provide security, but also facilitate other non-military initiatives. One certainly can connect post-conflict peace building with peacekeeping, as it often involves demobilization and reintegration programmes, as well as immediate reconstruction needs. Meeting immediate needs and handling crises is no doubt crucial. But while peacemaking and peacekeeping processes are an important part of peace transitions, they are not enough to meet long-term needs and build lasting peace. Long-term peace building techniques are designed to address the underlying substantive issues that brought about violence. Various transformation techniques aim to move parties away from confrontation and violence, and towards political and economic participation, peaceful relationships, and social harmony. The new intervention modalities, in terms of early and long-term engagement by various actors, show the breakdown of the walls between prevention, peacemaking, peacekeeping and peace building – indeed they are not exercised necessarily in a linear sequence, rather in a circular sequence with peace building resembling conflict prevention.

The international community is increasingly seeking to respond more effectively both to the immediate crisis at hand, and to planning out post-crisis responses in the context of long-term stabilization and peace-building strategies. Multiple challenges are especially apparent during post conflict stages. Post conflict situations, such as those of the Balkans, East Timor, Afghanistan, Sierra Leone, Mozambique and Iraq, each require different tools. Yet each case, successful or not, has provided the international community with a better understanding of what needs to be improved in how they are handled, case by case, as well as in aggregate terms. The multiplicity of threats and actors have forced national and international organizations to develop a more coherent policy, integrated approach to stabilization and peacebuilding. In recognition of the need for integrated approaches to peacebuilding (humanitarian aid, military assistance, economic reconstruction, aid to governance, stabilization, support to the civil society, etc.), a number of donor countries active in post-crisis situations have created trans-ministerial organizational units as a platform for permanent dialogue and for the preparation of coordinated interventions in situations that potentially need 'interventions'. International institutions, including the United Nations, the European Union, the World Bank and the North Atlantic Treaty Organization, are initiating approaches to insecurity on behalf of the international community. These aim to build and maintain peace, promote security, development and stabilization, and tackle challenges in specific regions. These efforts are in the recognition that military force alone cannot achieve long term security. Thus, the US, the UK and Canada are leading the way in creating trans-ministerial/trans-agencies/multi-disciplinary bodies to improve capacity to deal with immediate post-conflict stabilization by integrating civilian and military policy, planning and operations. In creating these units, governments seek to ensure that contribution to post conflict recovery is better designed, faster, and more flexible.

The question, however, is how do we evaluate their success in applying an 'integrated' approach? First, different actors have different approaches to peace building mission. 'Peace-building' is recognized in its various forms by various actors. The UN defines peace building as efforts to assist countries and regions in their transitions from war to peace. Other actors use the term to describe a long term process of reconstructing a society's physical, political, economic and social infrastructure. Others, such as the United Kingdom's Conflict Reconstruction Unit (PCRU), use the term to cover recovery and stabilization immediately after conflict. Stabilization describes the process of achieving an effective transition from immediate responses to an insecure situation, to long term development. Different models for the design and implementation of these missions are based not only on differences in resources, capacities, personnel and geo-strategic interests, but also on differences in principles, for example, minimum interference with national sovereignty (ASEAN way), the use of civilian forces (EU doctrine for Europe), use of force (American doctrine), the use of sociologists and anthropologists in the design and implementation of missions (Nordic countries), linkages with conflict prevention and development interventions (British approach), etc. The differences, hence, may not only be technical, but based on underlying assumptions about what is best needed for post-conflict situations, which are at best, political/conceptual understandings and constructs of the situation. Hence the first question to be probed by a human security framework is to what extent are differences in the modality of intervention based on technicalities (capacity, mandate, legitimacy, resources, personnel, theatre of operation), or cultural norms/assumptions (based on historical experiences, internal dynamics, interests, etc.).

Second, many peacebuilding missions lack coordination and coherence between sectors (military, economic, policy, what should come first and what sequence mutually reinforcing) and timing (focus on short-term stabilization, mid-term or long term). If, in previous times, the post-conflict operational zones, the military was involved in stabilization, the humanitarian aid workers in providing for relief immediately after the conflict paving the way for development actors for longer-term strategies, and the diplomatic community engaged in political resolution of conflicts, it is becoming increasingly clear that all these actors are operating in the same zone at the same time, often distinguishing the boundaries of when their work starts and finishes. The involvement of the military in delivering humanitarian aid and reconstructing local infrastructures, as seen by the PRTs in Afghanistan, brings the military into relief and development mandates of others. Economic actors, such as IFIs often engage in reconstruction and state-building even while the conflict may be ongoing. Poorly conceived economic and political models and distribution of aid in fragile countries can exacerbate the very reasons that conflict occurred in the first place. Bottom-up strategies that work with local populations can weaken the state, which may be needed to legitimize the political construction of a state and its further fragmentation. All these multi-sectoral challenges require better coordination between economic, political, civilian and military forces. It is also becoming clear that state-building cannot be alienated from the stabilization agenda.

Third, the failure of interventions in the long term can also be caused by the large gap that exists between the perception of people who are willing or unwilling recipients of the intervention, and those of the external partners, as to what constitutes an adequate, satisfactory 'intervention'. This gap in perception is both on the basis of differences in intentions, the modalities, the management, the interests and visions that local populations may have with external actors. In Afghanistan, for example, UNAMA's priorities include strengthening Afghan institutions and building the capacity of the Afghan Administration at all levels, including the development of institutions of good governance, of law and order, and of security. Emphasis is also given to increasing employment and cash for work schemes, which provide income to families. Yet, there are large gaps between the perceptions of the donors and recipients, the 'interveners' and the local population on questions pertaining as to why intervention is necessary, its modalities, leadership, sequencing, etc.

A human security approach can be useful in probing into new ways of evaluating the success of peace-building efforts of the international community. How do we appreciate the integration of efforts? Is success to be viewed from the point of view of the intervening actors, the overall macrocoordination, or from the point of view of the local population? What should be the prerequisites for success for designing a peace-building process in an efficient, effective and satisfactory way (for example, local strategies, leadership, ownership, credibility, the political economy of the country, etc.)? Can human security, viewed from the position of local populations, be the ultimate evaluation tool for measuring progress and success? How can external actors gauge with local demands for security, basic and strategic needs?

Ultimately, 'achieving' human security in a post-conflict situation requires integrated solutions which allows the 'interveners' to check interventions against their potential unintended consequences by stressing on the distributional impacts, and using a multi-disciplinary framework to understanding causes and consequences. The framework can be used to examine experiences of peace-building, both from the point of view of 'interveners' (external actors) and those of local populations (domestic actors), in order to contribute to knowledge about evaluation on the one hand, and to deduce suggestions on how to design successful sustainable peace building process in such a way that conflicts does not recur again and that the maximum levels of satisfaction, coherence and effectiveness are reached.

Conclusion

With its stress on understanding the socio-economic, political and cultural causes of conflict, the human security approach tries to analyse both the objective reality of opportunities (greed) and subjective perception of the motives (grievance). Important issues like how these inequalities are turned into militarized nationalisms have not figured in the models of greed and grievance. Tamils were seen as 'outsiders' by Sinhalese nationalists in Sri Lanka. Right-wing forces in India propagate that the Muslims are outsiders loyal to Pakistan. In Indonesian ethnic riots the Chinese were seen as outsiders, and as alien to 'national cultures'. An analysis of the currently unresolved armed conflicts shows that conflicts rise out of human insecurities where the interplay of development patterns, denial of rights, exclusions, and rising aspirations combine to aggravate inequalities that ultimately lead to conflicts. The human security approach shows this interconnectedness.

Conflict data only qualifies to be counted as such if at least a thousand people are killed in a year. This means that a number of small-scale but long-term conflicts such as sectarian conflicts do not get reflected. Further, repressions and human rights violations by states are not included in such data. A human security approach takes note of such conflicts and broadens the meaning of conflict from just armed conflict to include other structural violence as well. Conflict data also does not fully reveal the socio-economic dislocations caused by the integration of conflict regions into the global economy. Development assistance for millions of dollars in most conflict regions has been given to states who themselves are partisan in the conflict and biased in disbursing funds. Clearly then, alternate methods of development assistance have to be thought out and the aid donor and receiver have to be made more accountable.

A human security approach to conflict has a people-sensitive lens to viewing conflicts to understand what led to societal violence and who the victims are. The gendered aspects of conflicts should be taken seriously, as many conflicts studies (unless done by feminists) do not emphasize the special implications that conflicts have on women and the marginalized. A human security approach would take into account the inter-related nature of threats that make up conflicts and move from the myths that wars create to see the deep links between local conflicts and the specific way the global economy impacts on the country or region. The arms trade, the funders of conflicts and the structural causes would be included in such an analysis. The human security model of conflicts is important as it would show the way to pre-empting conflicts, peace maintenance and reconstruction, all of which should involve the local people, including the poor, women and marginalized who are normally excluded, as partners. A human security approach would look into fiscal revenues to ensure not only social expenditures on vulnerable groups, but also, people oriented development rather than a mere growth focus. Since it has been argued that inequalities and poverty are inputs into conflicts, development patterns should support equity and fair distribution of resources. A sustainable human development strategy that would stress on gendered and equitable development within and between regions, classes and ethnic groups is possible in an environment of overall human security, where political, social and economic institutions work towards such goals.

7   The state and its domestic responsibilities

The paradigm shift away from national or international security to the security of people has far reaching implication on actors and institutions at the domestic level. The perceived inadequacy of the traditional security theory after the end of the Cold War and the acceleration of the globalization process led to the idea that security is a concern not only for states but also for individuals and society. Yet, the human security concept emphasized the role of the state as the 'fundamental purveyor' (CHS, 2003: 2) for the protection of its citizens in order to 'develop their resilience to difficult conditions' (CHS, 2003: 10). The state, understood here in Weber's term as a 'human community that successfully claims the monopoly of the legitimate use of physical force within a given territory' (Weber, 1946: 78), is the ultimate organizational institution at the national and international level, and remains the dominant security referent even within the human security framework. It remains the most legitimate actor for providing traditional security to its people, in the traditional Hobbesian social contract. Indeed, at an international level, the state remains the most legitimate actor, if only because only states are admitted to the United Nations, overall guardian of collective peace and security. Furthermore, the democratic state remains the fundamental actor on the international scene, because unlike representatives of the civil society, NGOs or other groups, it represents the majority of people on a given territory, and this provides ultimate legitimacy, provided the majority is not predator to a minority, and that the democratic institutions function properly. As a paradox, such enhanced expectations emerge at a time when the accelerating process of globalization appear to decrease or at least rearrange the capacities of states to protect and provide.

At the domestic level, what are its responsibilities *vis-à-vis* the people whose human security is at risk? How does a human security framework increase or change the nature of these responsibilities? How does, ultimately, state security complement human security?

This chapter first outlines the responsibilities of the state before dwelling on the nature of strong and weak states viewed from the human security framework. It then provides a general framework of what types of policies and institutions would enable the state to provide, protect and empower its citizens. The analysis is limited to a focus on the state, although it is imperative that future research extends the analysis to that of non-state actors in ways they can support or hamper the state in fulfilling its roles and responsibilities.

The state and its human security responsibilities

The notion of human security does not replace but ultimately supplements that of state security. The International Commission on Intervention and State Sovereignty took a strong position on this issue with its 2001 report *The Responsibility to Protect* (RTPR): 'The commission believes that responsibility to protect resides first and foremost with the state whose people are directly affected' (ICISS, 2001: para 2.30). To quote Keohane and Nye, 'order requires rules, rules require authority, and authority is exercised on behalf of people by states' (Keohane and Nye, 1998). The focus on human security, therefore, does not mean an end to the role of the state; rather, it reinforces its roles and responsibilities.

The role of the state with regard to human security and to the people is highly ambitious. Human security seeks to reject looking at security in terms of regional stability and territorial security for nation states. The guarantor of national security is no longer military power, but favourable social, political and economic conditions, promotion of human development, human rights and inclusive policies. For the operationalization of these human security goals, the institution of the state remains fundamental. The absence of the state or its lacking effectiveness can be detrimental to human security. On the other hand, states are not a sufficient condition for human security, they can even be an obstacle, as is the case of failed or weak states.

Tan See Seng criticizes the human security discourse for attempting 'to solve a complex human dilemma by recourse to the very institution (i.e. 'the state') – or the discursive commitment to its ontology – that in part created that dilemma in the first place' (Tan See Sang, 2001: 4). An approach which continues to base its argumentation on the centrality of the state to security processes and on the primacy of state interest in the achievement of security thus may seem problematic. Yet, while human security proponents demand that states make greater accommodations to the contributions of non-governmental and civil society organizations (Van Rooy, 2000), the challenges of human insecurities are nonetheless related primarily to the state (Wesley, 1999: 28). The state is most apt at protecting human security because of a combination of capability, will, knowledge, and admissibility in international forums such as the UN. Thus human security transforms, rather than replaces the national security discourse and is not an alternative to state security. It argues for changes in statecraft to adopt a human security framework within policy orientation to offset inequalities and provide social safety nets for people ensuring 'freedom from fear', 'freedom from want' and human dignity and rights. By intervening where the market cannot ensure equal opportunities for people, states hold the capacity to transform market forces for the good of the people towards ensuring economic stability and ensuring essential social services. While non-state actors can assume some of the state's functions, they cannot replace the state in its primary responsibilities.

Defining responsibility

Agents of the state are responsible for their actions and accountable for their acts of commission and omission towards social and economic policies which can help in reducing poverty, mitigating fear of conflict, violation of human rights, war crimes, torture, genocide, rape, terrorism and initiating and sustaining development processes. The state has the fundamental role in providing the legal framework for a liberal, pluralistic society. In the perspective of 'freedom from fear', the state obviously protects its population against any armed attack from outside, and assures domestic peace and physical well-being of its citizens by fighting against violence and crime and assuring law and order. In the concept of 'freedom from want', the state guarantees basic social justice which is, in some states, is institutionalized in a welfare state model with a complex system of redistribution. Furthermore, the state sets standards for every human's well-being by assuring the maintenance of labour and environmental standards. From the perspective of 'dignity', the state ensures that laws are created, abided by, and that the human rights of individuals and communities are guaranteed.

The primary responsibility is to provide traditional security, and by extension, prevent threats and protect people from them. The state therefore should not and cannot withdraw from its obligations in the field of security. Political security includes legitimacy of the state's authority from both the domestic and international viewpoints. Hobbes's solution to the problem of personal security was the construction of a sovereign state to protect people. He equated security with the state and insecurity with its non-existence. The state therefore is a security arrangement of prime importance (Jackson, 2000: 186).

The second responsibility is to 'provide', a notion embedded in the upholding people's basic rights and freedoms as well as delivering on social services in an equitable manner. The state providing for its citizens has been historically experimented in the welfare states of the 1960s and 1970s, but which began dismantling with the liberal models introduced in the 1980s. India, for example, adopted the welfare state model with a large public sector to ensure infrastructure development and equitable distribution to its citizens, 60 per cent of whom were below the poverty line. This strategy contributed to the growth of a middle class and sustained democracy.

The responsibility to 'empower' comes next. The strength of the state rests in its responsiveness to people and their needs by enhancing 'people's ability to act on their own behalf' (CHS, 2003). People are not only passive recipients of security, or even mere victims of its absence, but active subjects who can contribute directly to identifying and implementing solutions to the dilemma of insecurity. Human security as public good entails a responsibility and conscious willingness to be given by the state, but also has a corresponding duty of engagement by people – the capacity to be requested and assumed. If those in a position of power have a responsibility to protect, provide and empower, for those in a position to receive (people and communities), this responsibility entails assuming, engaging and demanding. Supporting people's ability to act on their own behalf means providing education and information so that they can scrutinize social arrangements and take collective action. It means building a public sphere that tolerates opposition, encourages local leadership and cultivates public discussion. This responsibility flourishes in a supportive larger environment, with freedom of the press, and information, freedom of conscience and belief, and freedom to organize, with democratic elections and policies of inclusion. Societal groups can give people a voice and the state needs to be responsive to them. Yet, if the state is too weak, certain societal groups can kidnap the state and seek to use it for their own purposes or to undermine its governing capacity.

By-products of the responsibility

The by-product of discussions on the responsibilities of states towards human security is the reopening of two questions for the state: one is the transformation of the notion of 'sovereignty', the other is the question of 'legitimacy' of state building.

Transforming sovereignty: if sovereignty once meant monopoly over the use of violence and protection of territory from external threats, it now has to percolate to the level of responsibility to protect and to empower. As RTPR firmly stated, 'Sovereign states have a responsibility to protect the population from the effects of avoidable trauma or disasters.' A state must acknowledge the dual nature of its sovereignty: it is an autonomous actor, exercising supreme authority within its boundaries; at the same time, it is also responsible for the protection and well-being of its citizens. Yet, to critics of a narrow vision of human security, opening up the definition, nature and responsibilities of sovereignty is hypocritical at best given an international arena that has seen a number of interferences in the domestic affairs of weaker states. Since the end of World War II, violation of sovereignty has ranged from the simplest financial support of political groups and factions, to military assistance, to direct supply of weapons, to assassination of political leaders, cooperation and support in the organization of military coup and overthrowing of governments, direct violation of territorial integrity (e.g. direct military interventions in Afghanistan (by the USSR), Panama (the USA), Lebanon (Israel) and Iraq (the USA and UK), to mention only the most blatant cases. Paradoxically, it is exactly at a time of the crisis of the traditional notion of the nation-state resulting from both the end of the Cold War and the acceleration of the globalization process, that sovereignty has transformed into a responsibility not only towards external aggressors, but internal demands.

Legitimacy: actors and institutions hold a responsibility for the people, just as they also have to be accountable to the people. It is thus in its response to the people that the state will find its meaning and moral legitimacy. The *raison d'être* of any actor or institution rests with their contribution to the well-being of the very people which brought about these institutions and actors in the first place. Buzan argues that states 'can claim their own right of survival over and above that of their individual citizens' (Buzan, 2000). Their *raison d'état* is rooted in their alleged defence of the national interest. Yet, the 'national' is a 'moral' construction (Campbell and Shapiro, 1999:7). It is the imaginary 'national' which tends to serve as the source of moral legitimacy for states. Scholars have for example highlighted the deployment of the rhetoric of 'national security' by governments for perpetuating forms of 'structural violence' against segments of their own citizenry (Alagappa, 1998: 30–1). The national interest needs a radical re-definition so as to be fully compatible with the higher good of human security.

State building presumes the consent of the people who voluntarily delegate some of their freedoms and rights onto the state. Within the human security perspective, state-building, however, is not an end in itself. Institutions, governmental, as well as judicial, will not alone serve their purpose. People need to relate to these structures. They need to agree with the spirit of these institutions and fill them with life and meaning through participation and support. The state can enhance people's capacities and give way to protection from 'external' threats and mediation of 'internal' conflicts of redistribution. States can give people a voice. The strength of the state needs to be founded in its responsiveness to people and their needs. Ideally people are not only empowered through the security provided by the state, but also empowered by the state to contribute to human security in their daily lives at the local level. In transition or post-crisis countries, for example, peace and state building should thus be 'owned' by the local people who should be the ultimate beneficiaries. When states are heavily dependent on foreign funding, the legitimacy is endangered as they become accountable to the demands of external actors as opposed to their own constituencies.

Types of states

What type of state can uphold these responsibilities? Despite their responsibility, states do not always manage to fulfil their human security obligations. A state can open up its markets without providing people with social safety nets, or an authoritarian state can suppress human rights and establish a reign of fear. In these cases, instead of being a protector of human security, the state turns into a source of threat to the security of its own people. States may also not be able to provide human security due to dearth of institutional capacity and resources or the breakdown of order or even ongoing conflict, which can be observed for example in Somalia. The state therefore appears as an ambiguous actor regarding the provision of human security: first guarantor of human security, it also probably constitutes the first violator. In the sections that follow, we identify different types of states from the perspective of human security and evaluate the challenges they face in fulfilling their responsibilities.

'Strong' states

According to Hampson, the 'strong state' has the capability to assure human security for its population by providing freedom from want, freedom from fear and protecting the dignity of the individual human being against human rights abuses (Hampson *et al.*, 2002: 16–18). The strong state should in fact be most apt at protecting human security because of a combination of capability, will and knowledge of its nation that few other actors (International Organisations, NGOs, private companies, etc.) would have. Thus, the ideal 'humanly secure state' would be a fully sovereign democracy with a functioning administration and social, political, economic, and legal institutions and a strong and focused developmental agenda. To borrow from Sorensen, the role of the 'developmental state' depends on three factors: first, state autonomy, second, state bureaucracy controlled by an elite that gives priority to development, and third, statecraft: the ability to formulate proper policy responses to development challenges (Sorensen, 2000). It should also be able to develop and implement a disaster management strategy that mitigates against harms of natural disasters.

However, the conception of 'strong states' has a number of problems. First, do such types of strong states exist that assure all the three dimensions of human security, namely freedom from fear, freedom from want, and assurance of human dignity and well-being for all their citizens equally? Even in rich 'strong states', many groups of people, such as immigrants or jobless people, live at the margins of society. The US, for example, has very strong inequalities in its society despite a high per capita income. The second problem is of normative nature. Can we talk of communist societies as the perfect model for assuring the human security as they care for every aspect of people's life and assure a 'right to work' but not the right to participate? The balance between protection and empowerment is clearly not achieved under Communist regimes. A third problem is that we have in history several examples of dictatorships that combined every feature of a strong state but tyrannized their own population or parts of it, for example in Nazi Germany. Fourth, even strong states cannot exercise control over multinational firms and their policies, or other non-state actors which may be stronger than the state in terms of resources, outreach, network, etc. Fifth, a state can concentrate all its resources to become 'strong' from the point of view of its domestic responsibilities but would have to make trade-offs that would mean decreasing expenditure and ability to protect itself from external aggressors. Even strong states may not be able to protect themselves from global and regional economic or political crisis. Finally, a strong state may create dependencies in its population and rob them of the long-term ability to fend for themselves in the long term. It may raise expectations that in the long term would be unsustainable.

In a true democracy, state interests reflect the interests and welfare of its residents, individuals and groups, through promoting military defence, stability of the government and national economic development and social distribution. Yet, state interests often become entangled in those of power holders instead, bent on maintaining regimes and ideology. In a number of East Asian countries for example, the economic development model was for growth first, distribution later. The model however often failed to trickle down to the labour that had created the wealth as elite groups ended up as beneficiaries of resources. In such strong states, suffering is often caused or aggravated by the governments' incapacity, unwillingness, inefficiency or corruption in implementing fair policies. No matter how strong they are, such governments then fail to respond to overpopulations, economic disparity, famines and environment disasters.

The 'weak states' (unwilling or incapable states) of human security

Thus, even though the strong state is the desirable state of human security, it may remain as an utopia. On the other side of the spectrum are the 'fragile states' or 'quasi-states', a relatively recently analysed phenomenon in international relations (Jackson, 1990). Jackson applied this term to states with a colonial past and featuring a combination of formal juridical sovereignty (that is, constitutional independence) with a lack of substance in empirical statehood (Jackson cited in Sörensen, 2000: 2). These states exist mainly because they are recognized to exist. Their problem lies with domestic weaknesses, and they are not 'threatened by hostile external powers' (Stohl, 2000: 6). Stohl adds that even when a state is incapable of fulfilling its sovereign responsibilities *vis-à-vis* its population, it is often capable of 'trampling the rights of individual citizens and/or of murdering them' (Stohl, 2000: 5). The worst form of a 'weak state' is one that cannot assure its basic functions for its population but uses its remaining forces and infrastructure to threaten its own population.

It is however important to distinguish between two types of weakness: intentional and unintentional. In the first category are 'unwilling states' that have the capacity to provide and protect but withhold from this responsibility. If states are unwilling to protect human security, the social contract can fail. For Mack, 'in theory, states are responsible for protecting their citizens; in reality, they often violently repress them. Indeed, in the last one hundred years, far more people have died at the hands of their own governments than have been killed by foreign armies' (Mack, 2004). Repression by the state in its various manifestations has been a significant source of insecurity. The unwilling state is one where people fear official security forces, the state and the police, where corruption is rampant and riches are not distributed intentionally, and where dictatorships prefer to strengthen their own subsistence.

The second category of 'incapable states' includes those that have become incapacitated, either by man-made practices, such as wars or globalization, etc. or those at perpetual risk of natural disasters. By human security definition, a weak state is one that cannot implement or enforce the law, is unable to formulate and implement development policies, has ineffective institutions, cannot collect taxes and is unable to provide its citizens with the most essential public services or the means to participate in public life. A weak state is a state which cannot exercise its primary function of social control and therefore fails in its duty to protect and care for its citizens. Weakened states are characterized by lack of capacity and resources. Inevitably, they erode trust between government and the citizens by being a non-performer in terms of delivery or protection. The state, by failing to perform required functions, opens the way to anarchy and abuse, and leaves its citizens exposed to new types of risks and insecurities. It subsequently suffers from a proliferation of paramilitary groups and has high levels of crime and corruption.

What characterizes many of these failed states is the experience of colonization and subjectification of a historical 'divide and rule' policy. Colonial governments drew borders purely through negotiations among the European countries, often ignoring the local demographics. For example, Sykes–Picot Agreement and Berlin Conference in late nineteenth century were intended to divide the Middle East and Africa respectively among European powers. The local economies were also crippled to the point that they had no choice but to rely on their colonial rulers. For imperialist powers, colonies existed to exploit the riches and resources in the South to export European products (Fanon, 1963: 152). When these countries became independent, many of them were left with a devastated economy, irregular borders, and ethnic antagonism. After independence these countries often lacked the capability 'to command loyalty – the right to rule – to extract the resources necessary to rule and provide services, to maintain that essential element of sovereignty ...' (Holsti, 1996: 82). Thus, they were often incapable of protecting their citizens from the violence by rebels or local warlords or the necessary capacity to provide public services such as social welfare, employment, and social infrastructure.

Weak states have implications, in that their very weakness can 'spill over' and threaten neighbours, in the classic security dilemma. This can be in the form of refugees or armed soldiers coming over the borders, or by problems like food shortages, natural disasters like floods or diseases, all of which create instability. The crisis in sub-Saharan Africa is a classic example where refugee movements and inter ethnic conflicts have spilled over to neighbours. Stohl makes out a case for intervention in weak states because they threaten regional security (Stohl, 2000). As Chapter 8 will examine, however, interventions because a state is unable to provide for the 'want' of its own population are much more difficult to justify and carry out.

The human security perspective, in the meantime, casts the focus on the domestic responsibilities of the state. A weak state is defined as one that cannot uphold the Hobbesian contract for providing not only security, but also and especially developmental goods and human rights imperatives for its own citizens. State weakness is judged not only on the basis of problems that threaten the security of other regions, or the state itself (such as through armed movement or ethnic strife), but conditions that threaten the physical integrity, welfare, self-determination and opportunities for citizens. In weak states, the 'freedom from want' perspective is perhaps the most lacking: there is either no or an insufficient social protection, complete welfare system comparable to that in strong states and health and educational systems are highly incomplete and insufficient. Such states have little capability to control external capital, such as through Multi-National Corporation on whom they are mostly directly dependent.

An example of weakened states are those that have endured transition processes in the atermath of the break-up of the Soviet Union. For the post-Communist countries of Eastern Europe and the Commonwealth of Independent States (CIS), 'transition' from centrally planned economies to market ones involved a restructuring of political and economic management that led to stronger states in terms of democracy but weaker in terms of the ability to provide for the human security of their citizens. The societies became increasingly characterized by social and economic insecurity, which was a trade-off between the basic social security provided by the old regimes and the political freedom and new economic opportunities in the new regimes. Under the pressure of resource constraints, many states withdrew from their responsibilities in the sphere of the economy, environment, and health. In Albania, for example, the adoption of new liberal models meant that the state rapidly relinquished many of its welfare and protective functions, which in turn created an institutional vacuum. The de-capacitated minimum state that replaced the socialist welfare state evolved into refocusing of its activities to personal security (fight against crime), social security (social insurances) and external security. Yet, the experience of most of the former CIS countries showed that the withdrawal of the state from social sectors led to much misery and insecurity of large numbers of people, sometimes leading to situations of conflict.

Challenges in weak states: militarization of underdevelopment and privatization of security

Weak states are much more susceptible to the machinations of the arms trade and they use and disperse small, illegal arms and land mines. At the same time, the potential conflict situation of these states makes them high risk areas for procurement of more arms. The prevailing concept of security as that of inter-state relations and state security and the protection of territories by military means has resulted in proportionally high military expenditures in most countries. South Asia has, ironically, become the world's largest arms bazaar and is expected to spend upwards of $130 billion in the next decade on arms.

The 1990s have witnessed a rise in an international private military and security industry with clear corporate structures, an area that has seen very little research so far. According to Holmqvist, this rise is due to an increase both in demand and supply. The reasons for the mushrooming of private security companies are: first, the domination of post-Cold War free market models of the state and the outsourcing of traditional government functions; second, the global downsizing of national militaries, providing vast poll of trained former military personnel for recruitment; third, the gradual disengagement of major powers from parts of the developing world, especially unemployed personnel from the former socialist bloc who are ready to be mercenaries; and finally, the privatization of milliard goods production in Europe (Holmqvist, 2005). In addition, the breakdown of Cold War secrecy and the outbreak of smaller regional conflicts has led to the privatization of security. Private security companies provide operational support in combat, military advice and training, arms procurement and maintenance to logistical support. In post-conflict societies like Afghanistan, private security plays a key role. Private security facilitates peace operations, and is useful within broader political process. It has been used as a resource to help delivery of humanitarian aid.

Yet, the privatization of security however also comes with a serious set of problems. First, there is confusion about the nature of their services since they replace the state role in providing security. Second, there is the lack of transparency about the strategies and motivations of private security groups. The motivation of profit leads them to be more accountable to shareholders and not to the state or citizen. In weak states, where the state does not have the capacity to provide security, but also parallel or 'shaded' structures of power and authority, private security becomes a symptom of state weakness and reinforces such deficit in three ways. First, by creating a false image of security in the short term that can lead to the overthrow or further conflicts within the state. Second, private security can lead to skewed distribution of security among the population, with the elite and powerful benefiting and the poor remaining insecure. Third, weak states can crowd out the establishment of legitimate and functioning state institutions, which do not receive enough support for training and institutionalization from donors. The Private Militaries Corporations (PMCs) are not bound to respect or adhere to human rights and humanitarian law. The rules of engagement thus remain unclear and often they end up causing more insecurity than providing long-term security.

As is apparent in the case of Afghanistan, in a militarized society, where even coalition forces engage in reconstruction and rehabilitation through regional provincial teams (PRT), and the US provision of food aid is carried out under independent military authority, the distinctions between legitimate and effective human rights and humanitarian action by the UN and NGOs and a military campaign is blurred (Tadjbakhsh *et al.*, 2004). Research for UNDP's *Human Development Report* for Afghanistan between 2002 and 2004 showed that three years after the international community had decidedly engaged in the country, the slow record of change and lack of delivery on promises of security and development had gradually created public distrust in the weak state institutions and a fear that the existing peace may only be partial or temporary. In the eyes of the Afghan, the new government had to play an all encompassing lead role for sustained political commitment, institution building, massive resource allocations, attitudinal changes and social transformations. While the presidential and parliamentary elections were a first step towards the establishment of a rule-based state order, there were nonetheless concerns about the environment in which they were organized. Despite success in holding elections, the electoral system suffered lack of clear data on population figures, security, organized and experienced political parties, and, especially, lack of understanding of the electoral process.

In addition, the first years of the transitional government were also mired by perceptions of threats to survival and dignity, because of ethnic repression and political exclusion. Political exclusion continued to be visible in the form of stereotyping entire ethnic, linguistic or religious groups; monopoly of power and inadequate ethnic representation in higher ranking government positions; denying the right to employment to certain groups, such as the disabled; restricted access to higher education; unequal distribution of resources; and the monopoly of the public media by one group. Threats also included the perception that people had about the relationship between the state and warlords and narco-mafia bosses.

As the transitional government was unable to hold the monopoly of power in Afghanistan in the first post-Taliban years, its authority was challenged by a number of competing factions. Armed regional and local warlords together with their armed followers, established their own rules of provision of welfare and security, collection and distribution of wealth and clientalism. The security dilemma meant that the elections had to be 'insured' through expensive private security companies contracted by the UN, the US-led coalition forces and NATO. As a consequence, everyone was fearful, powerless and defenceless. Such a climate gave rise to vigilantes, which made it difficult to know who genuinely was involved in working for the government (both Afghan and US) and who was not. US private security firms were guarding the President, and contractors were used by the CIA to interrogate detainees in Afghanistan. The private security personnel may not always have been accountable to the standards of international human rights, a fact that has been evident from investigations of prisons in Guantanamo Bay, Abu Ghraib and Afghanistan.

What therefore should be the ideal political, economic, and social responsibilities of the state?

Having identified the general responsibilities for a state towards human security, as well as the types of state that could respond to the challenge, we turn to a general framework that identifies the areas that a state should be engaged in. As we have argued in this book, if the security of people becomes the ultimate end, then all other entities become means for allowing that security to blossom. What kind of policies are needed for human security to be achieved? We present a number of ideals that institutions should aim at, whether in post-crisis countries, developing countries, and industrialized countries as well. These collectively consist of the responsibilities of the states from a human security point of view, not only because of ethical principles, but also because human security is indivisible and threats make states and societies mutually vulnerable, both within a country and across.

The state building process

The role for the state and a state-building process should be founded on a fair and efficient governance system and the rule of law to equalize opportunities. The capacity to 'provide' human security requires a strong state that can generate and distribute public goods. It must therefore take up a provider role in addition to a regulatory one, regulatory in order to ensure safe conditions for development and providing sufficient security for markets to function. But it should play a provisionary and active role in providing social services, basic health care, education, and job security to all the population, not only to diminish threats but especially as a matter of rights. The state can delegate some of the activities to commercial and non-government organizations, but it still bears the ultimate responsibility.

In all situations, post-conflict or developing, the responsibilities of the state should increase rather than decrease. These new responsibilities do not mean that the state should dictate the directions of the economy, but that it should intervene in the areas where markets cannot ensure an efficient allocation of resources or equal access to assets and opportunities for all people. Even the market, therefore, needs a new state which is responsive, transparent and open to widespread public participation, one that serves the wishes of the majority while protecting the interests of the minorities. The viability and legitimacy of the state depends heavily on its capacity to take care of the needs of the population and able to resist threats from peace spoilers from within and from external forces. Hence, the role of the state in the state-building process is threefold: first, to guarantee that the reconstruction process is equitable, efficient and empowering, second, to promote investment in human capabilities, and third, to equally distribute the resources.

State–society contract

A shift to a human security vision requires the involvement of people as agents of change and opportunities, and not as vulnerable groups for whom projects and policies are designed. The principles of democracy can provide the best environment for securing political and social freedoms especially in post-conflict situations. Empowering and inclusive governance systems provide security better than military defence measures. Enlisting the support of civil society in the promotion of human security by helping in early detection, providing feedback into policy making processes, partnering with the state to provide protection and assistance, and in influencing public opinion is a key element of credible governance. Civil society advocacy groups ensure that the issues and concerns of socially, economically and politically marginalized groups are placed on the policy agenda.

Finally, participation constitutes contributing to development, benefiting from development and taking part in decision-making about development. Empowerment of the people is thus a crucial aspect of honouring the state–society contract. For this, the prerequisites are an informed and mature civil society, and freedom of choice as well as freedom of action, provided through information and consultation, which allows people to voice grievances and discontent. Participatory planning raises commitments, enables people to ensure focus on their human security needs, and to contribute their own human and financial resources. Ultimately, sharing power and responsibility lightens the burden for all involved, thereby accelerates development.

What kind of democratic system?

There is no denying that democracy and the respect for human rights could build security in society. A representative democracy, where all social groups have access to political decision making process and benefit from equal representation, satisfies the goals of equity and justice, but does not necessary lead to efficiency. However, emphasis should not be on narrow definitions of democracy *per se*, but on democratic values, the quality of democracy, as well as absorption capacity.

The question however is on the quality of democracy. The new global outlook of recent years is the assumption that democracy and accountability are prerequisites for economic development. As a result, building democracy was seen as a goal of transition in post-Soviet countries for example, when it really should have meant better lives; emphasis was on building its institutions, rather than promoting its values. The democratization process, especially as it applied to the post-Soviet world, focused mostly on holding elections, reforming the judiciary system and, increasingly, decentralization of decision-making, with power shifting from the centralized government to localities. That people took advantage of these channels in increasing numbers is not disputed. Whether this actually led to participation in decision making or better livelihoods, however, deserves scrutiny.

Liberal democracies and market-oriented economies open up the system to a multiplicity of interests, but are not the answer to all types of development operations, nor the surest foundations of peace. Democracy and capitalism, both encouraging social competition, can exacerbate social conflicts in war-shattered states that lack the institutional structures required for conciliation. Fledgling democracies therefore have to face political hurdles that hamper economic and social development. Democracies can also be too dependent upon special interest groups that all too often win at the expense of favourable conditions for economic growth. The dilemma for post-conflict and transition countries would be to reconcile competing interests and to create a democracy that does not exacerbate inequalities.

The best security against crises and downturns is democracy and broad public participation. A country that has a constitution but which neither allows dissent nor listens to dissenting voices is not sufficiently democratic to ensure human security. Sen illustrates the Indonesian case:

> The victims [of 1997 financial crisis] in Indonesia may not have taken very great interest in democracy when things went up and up. But when things came tumbling down for some parts of the population, the lack of democratic institutions kept their voices muffled and ineffective. The protective umbrella
> . of democracy is strongly missed exactly when it is most needed.
>
> (Sen, 1999: 32–3)

Economic growth models

Human security, as well as peace and stability, require a different set of tools and policies than economic-growth only agendas. To create economic stability and ensure 'downturns with security', human security requires social safety nets and politically responsive governance, whereas raising GDP is a technocratic task calling for a different set of economic measures. For this reason, not only should development adopt a human-security orientation, but also human security should be pursued for its own sake and regardless of improvements in economic development (Sen, 1999: 26).

Investments in physical infrastructure (especially roads, water and electricity), agricultural markets, skills development, financial services, good governance and education are all expected to play a key role in laying the foundations for sustained and broad based economic growth. However, freedom from economic insecurity and hunger requires the translation of growth into an assured basic income either from waged employment, self-employment or social transfers (formal or informal). The challenge remains to ensure that inclusion in a dynamic economy results in the needs of economically vulnerable people being addressed through self-reliance or effective public action. Thus, distribution issues need to be integrated in economic policy models to significantly improve the 'absolute' as well as 'relative' condition of the poor through land reform, universalization of basic education, and widespread employment generation among low-skilled workers. 'Equity-based' growth can be achieved through a variety of strategies, which obviously depend in part on each country's initial conditions. Economic growth should have a pattern that directs resources disproportionately to the sectors in which the poor work (such as small-scale agriculture), the areas in which they live (such as underdeveloped regions) or the factors of production that they possess (such as unskilled labour or land).

When the capacity of the state to meet the social needs of the population is limited, individual self-employment and private entrepreneurship appear as new individual strategies for ensuring economic security, as an instrument of self-preservation. In Moldova, data from household budgets in 1999 showed that over 40 per cent of incomes in the country overall and 60 per cent in rural areas came from self-employment, individual activities, the shadow economy, and the entry of women into the shadow economy (UNDP, 1999c). While shadow economies mean the creation of jobs, they also mean that the state budget fails to get revenue, the sectors are hampered by disorganization, and workers do not benefit from legal avenues for job security.

From the human security point of view, social equity and distributive justice, both as instruments and ends in themselves, are an integral part of the debate on economic development, not an add-on when existing economic policies are inadequate. Researchers have argued that 'traditional causes' of inequality, such as land concentration, urban bias and inequality in education may not be as responsible for widening inequalities as are 'new causes', linked to the 'excessively liberal economic policy regimes' (Cornia and Court, 2001). Exacerbated inequality is hence not inevitable, and should be mitigated through specific policies addressing not only traditional causes, such as education, land reform and regional policies, but also new causes, such as the impact of new technologies and trade, avoiding sharp recessions through stabilization and adjustment policies, correlating national and international financial liberalization and regulation, progressive tax policies, and enacting equitable labour market policies.

The question remains whether the liberal paradigm of economic growth, which seems to form consensus in economic planning in many countries and is part of the policy package of the IFIs, is good for human security. The liberal paradigm argues against government interventions in market results, which could lead to ineffective use of available scarce resources. The paradigm places the mechanisms of the free market, rather than centrally planned government interventions, at the centre of the economy, and changes the role of the government from that of a decider and a provider to that of a facilitator, responsible for the creation of an enabling environment for the private sector. According to this neo-classical economic paradigm, a healthy economy can be restored only if distortions in the market resulting from government intervention are removed and a level playing field for the domestic and international private sector is created. This is achieved by eliminating subsidies and regulations, privatizing state-owned enterprises, reducing or abolishing import controls such as tariffs and quotas, and introducing market-based interest rates. The resulting increased competition will force the private sector to reach higher levels of efficiency in the use of scarce resources, resulting in economic development. Economic development is expected to create more economic opportunities, increase employment and reduce poverty through a trickle-down effect.

But neo-liberalism, although hegemonic today, has had a poor performance in the last quarter of century in both developing countries, as well as post-crisis ones. Compared to the performance of post-colonial policymaking in developing countries, roughly from the 1950s through the mid-1970s, neo-liberal conditionality-based policies have performed poorly, in terms of first, slowing economic growth, second, greater economic instability, third, rising inequality, fourth, widening underemployment and fifth, persistently pervasive poverty (McKinley, 2004). As was well documented in the late 1980s and early 1990s (cf. UNICEF's *Structural Adjustment with a Human Face* and UNDP's *Human Development Reports*), structural adjustment imposed heavy social costs in the countries on which it was imposed. While priority was given to economic liberalization and building of institutions of representative democracy, problems such as poverty, inequality, health, education degradation and social exclusion could intensify. The neo-liberal orthodoxy of state withdrawal is mostly blamed for the transformation of the communist welfare state into the post-communist 'farewell state'. Yet, principles of traditional economic-growth based development, embodied in the neo-liberal paradigm, may bring about new insecurities. Neo-liberalism, with its emphasis on growth at the expense of people, may be good for a few, but the model is not fool profit for the poor. Inequality is accepted as part of the competition theories. The state is rolled back to free the market, in the redefinition of the role of the state as protector of the poor only.

Afghanistan, for example, although a post-crisis country, followed the path of many other Asia-Pacific countries, as well as the path of all the transition countries of the former Soviet satellite shedding their central planning models. Under the guidance of the World Bank and IMF, it initially undertook short-term measures, such as devaluating the currency and cutting public expenditure to reduce fiscal deficits. These measures were followed by longer-term measures, such as deregulation of trade and industry, and liberalization of international trade, investment and exchange rates. As the guiding principles for reconstruction in Afghanistan, the standard neo-liberal paradigm for internationally-supported reconstruction in postwar situations that had developed during the 1990s was adopted. This standard paradigm based on market-driven growth, an open economy and a minimalist regulatory state, recognized economic growth, especially through the private sector as 'the engine of growth', as the principal strategy for economic growth combating poverty. The government's National Development Framework in 2003 for example presented a vision of social and economic reforms based around macroeconomic stability and private sector led growth. All reforms were premised on the government's adopted economic policy of market integration, a liberal trade position, the promotion of the private sector as an engine for growth and a key 'enabling' role for the state.

Yet, human security requires that alternative models could be considered, especially in post-conflict countries. To begin with, root causes of conflict need to be factored in when designing policies. Liberal democracy and market-oriented economy are not always the answers to all types of development operations, not the surest foundations of peace. Democracy and capitalism, both encouraging social competition, can exacerbate social conflicts in war-shattered states that lack the institutional structures required for conciliation. Adopting a strategy that ignores the differences in participation in the political and economic agenda can lead to inequalities. Even if the GNP can become higher within a few years, chances are that there would be more poverty owing to rising inequality. The higher the level of inequality, the less impact economic growth has in reducing poverty – for any rate of economic growth, and inequality not only represses growth, but also has underlying political and social impacts on crime and political stability (Cornia and Court, 2001).

Social policy making

If human security is a priority, then governments must increase public expenditure through a stronger public administration towards renewed restructuring of social policy financing and provisions to permit everyone to survive with dignity. Targeting social policy to the poorest is administratively complex and vulnerable to arbitrary decisions of officials. The combination of public guarantees with private insurances may help those in well-paid employment, but can marginalize those in the informal sector.

Cuts in public expenditures could in fact stifle economic growth. If human security is a priority, then governments must instead be looking to increase public expenditures through a stronger public administration that can gather taxes and contributions efficiently, and use them well. For this, a renewed restructuring of social policy financing and provisions is required. The welfare system should permit everyone to survive with dignity. Many countries have tried to reduce costs by limiting benefits to the very poorest through means testing. However, many people lose out on these schemes through ignorance, fear or social stigma. Targeting is also administratively complex and vulnerable to arbitrary decisions of officials. The combination of public guarantees with private insurances may help those in well-paid employment, but can marginalize those in the informal sector.

In the case of transition economies in the post-Soviet space after independence in 1991, shortfall in revenues put an enormous pressure on public expenditures, health, education and social services. The consequences of the cutback of expenditures and the adoption of reactive rather than preventative measures exacerbated not only poverty and rising income gaps, but also population and health crises in Central Asia. In the education and health sectors, expenditures cutback led to infrastructure breakdown, decline in quality and quantity of services, and a widening gap between rural and urban areas. In the area of social welfare, most governments tried to cut welfare spending, increasingly linking benefits to income as opposed to universal benefits. However, unemployment benefits were extremely low, and there was a marked increase in the number of pensioners due to forced early retirement coupled with a decrease in contributions from large enterprises because of economic recession. Lack of financial security and the breakdown of the care support system posed increased care-related challenges, with additional burdens on the unpaid informal sector, which happened to be dominated by women in Central Asia.

States have to play an interventionist role for weaker sections of society. For example, economic and social pressures in countries like India and China where the populations have reached almost a billion people in each country has led to pressure on couples to reduce the size of their families. In patriarchal societies like India, where the male child is valued over the female and the girl is seen as a burden, families have resorted to female foeticide after gender tests. As a consequence, over a million girls are 'missing' and the births of boys far exceed those of girls in India. Such aspects can be addressed only by gender sensitive and human security approaches where the state and civil society work in partnership to change laws and social imagination.

Unemployment is a major cause of social distress in many societies. One major step taken in this direction is the most ambitious pro-poor scheme launched by an Indian government, in a country where nearly 70 per cent of the population lives in villages. Under the National Rural Guarantee Scheme, one member from each of India's 60 million rural households in 200 poorest districts is guaranteed 100 days of work each year. They will receive a daily minimum wage ($1.35) or an unemployment allowance if there is no work. People employed on the scheme will work on projects such as building roads, improving rural infrastructure, constructing canals or working on water conservation schemes. However, critics say the scheme is too expensive and question whether the government will be able to support it. Others say there is little transparency, which may lead to red tape and corruption. It is however the biggest social security net ever provided in India and the programme is expected to be extended to the entire country in the coming years.

An effective social protection oriented towards human security principles will mean growth in real terms of social expenditure. Enlisting and integrating NGOs could supplement state policy implementation efforts. A fair social system built on the basis of universalism providing everyone with human and income security would rely heavily on inclusive and fair social policies, based on social consensus, and implemented through partnership mechanisms between the state and civil society. This would require the development of the state's capabilities at the central and local level to mobilize social resources through partnership with NGOs, CBOs, local communities and the private sector. Such social policies should concentrate on poverty eradication, job creation, care provision, and community development.

Conclusion

As it has been argued in this chapter, the human security approach does not bypass the state. The state has the primary responsibility for the provision of human security for its citizens. This is an important point that may work to mitigate criticisms that implementation of human security would dangerously destabilize international relations, would entail a revolution in international relations and/ or is a utopian and hence unrealizable project. Moreover, the recognition in the human security framework that the state continues to play a fundamental role may help to overcome the suspicion of some states that human security is little more than a thinly veiled attempt to encroach on their sovereignty.

Although the role of non-state actors has been beyond the focus of this chapter, a human security approach recognizes that where the state is able to provide human security, it is not the sole provider. The ideal-type human security approach envisages the state to be part of a dynamic and seamless policy network with non-state actors, including NGOs and civil society, international and regional organizations as well as individuals and their communities. From a human security perspective, non-state actors do not compete but complement the state in their common objective of promoting human security. An empowered citizenry can demand respect for their dignity when it is violated. They can create new opportunities for wealth through their aspirations and address many problems locally. They can mobilize the security of others, that is, by publicizing food shortages early, preventing famines or protesting human rights violations. Supporting people's ability to act on their own behalf implies provision of education and information so that they can scrutinize social arrangements and take collective action. A public space that tolerates opposition, encourages local leadership and cultivates public discussion fosters a democratic environment and practices policies of inclusion.

This chapter focused on the quality of the state and how it fulfils its social contract. It reviewed the responsibility of the state in protecting and empowering citizens in order to ensure human security. It tried to provide a general framework of the domestic structures and policies that could respond to the human security needs of the population without dwelling on a detailed blueprint for action. The next chapter will look at what happens in cases where the state is unwilling or unable to fulfil its responsibility. The literature on the residual role of the international community in intervening in such cases is abundant. What clearly lacks in human security literature however is the focus on the domestic responsibilities of the state. If, as Chapter 1 has noted, states such as Canada and Japan have adopted the human security concept as their foreign policies, no state so far has applied it as the organizing vision of its own domestic policies. This omission deserves considerable analysis which we hope would engage future human security researchers.

8   Intervention, engagement and the responsibilities of the international community

The human security framework focuses on two pillars of the role of the international community when a state is unwilling or unable to assume its proper functions: one is a responsibility to protect civilians in a given country, coupled with maintaining collective security. The other is a responsibility to provide, through effective engagement (which this chapter will peruse) and aid (which will be examined in Chapter 9). The protection role stems from both an ethical responsibility towards the well-being of individuals whose rights have been systematically violated as well as a functional responsibility, given that threats are increasingly inter-linked across borders and regions. This role has been extensively debated, as this chapter will show, in discussions on the means and motivations of interventions. The human security framework is used to examine the shift from the duty to intervene to a responsibility to protect, and what this shift has meant in rethinking collective security arrangements.

The chapter first argues that if human security can be seen as a global public good, there are specific responsibilities for the international community. We then examine how an expansion of the threats agenda changes the means and ends of interventions in the name of collective security and responsibility. Finally, we argue for a transformation from humanitarian interventions to human security engagement. What are the 'new' responsibilities and what is the effectiveness and legitimacy of the different actors? What kind of institutional reform is necessary to match this responsibility?

Human security as a public good?

The first question to examine is can human security be a framework for international cooperation to deal with global threats? In other words, should human security be viewed as a Global Public Good (GPG)? According to the International Task Force on Global Public Goods, which was created through an agreement between France and Sweden signed on 9 April 2003:

> International public goods, global and regional, address issues that: (i) are deemed to be important to the international community, to both developed and developing countries; (ii) typically cannot, or will not, be adequately

addressed by individual countries or entities acting alone, and, in such cases (iii) are best addressed collectively on a multilateral basis.

(International Task Force on Global Public Goods, 2004)

The concept of public good may be derived by looking at the opposite concept of private good. A private good is something that is traded in markets. Once the buyer and seller agree on a price, the ownership or use of the good (or service) can be transferred from one to another and subsequently this good cannot be enjoyed by someone else. As opposed to private goods, public goods are non-excludable and non-rival in consumption. Global public goods' benefits also reach across borders, generations and population groups.

Human security can be considered as an inclusive good that benefits everyone, in contrast to the traditional definition of security that is non-joint and excludable. As Reich explained: 'one state's security can only be achieved at a cost to all states because the measure of security in this case is the distribution of power. Power, being finite, can only be redistributed between states and cannot be enlarged' (Reich, 2004). Human security, however, focuses on a different conception of power. One's security benefits others, but one's insecurity affects others negatively. The value added of considering human security to be a global public good is a useful way to conceptualize the difference between state-centred and individual-centred security: If traditional definitions of security focusing on state integrity in global public good terms are 'non-joint' and 'excludable' i.e. security is relative and competitive as it is measured in terms of the distribution of power between rival states, human security is indivisible and non-excludable and puts the emphasis on universal, absolute and inviolable rights. One individual's security from violence or poverty does not cost another's; on the contrary an increase in an individual's human security increases everybody else's human security. Associating the two concepts then reinforces the idea of our mutual vulnerability and the necessity for multilateral cooperative action.

If human security is a GPG, there is a *duty* to provide it at the global level because its benefits are universal while its disadvantages can negatively impact everyone in the mid and long run. Though domestic in nature, each of the components of human security can be considered as global public goods as they affect the citizens not just of one country, but also others through the inter-connectivity and mutual vulnerability of threats (Chenevat and Kohn, 2005). Kaul argued as much:

The 1994 *Human Development Report* analysed threats to world peace in terms of a series of trans-border challenges: unchecked population growth, disparities in economic opportunities, environmental degradation, excessive international migration, narcotics production and trafficking, and international terrorism. The report argued that the world needs a new framework for international cooperation to deal with global threats of this kind … a theory of global public goods would be an essential part of such a new framework, providing a new motivation for a different type of development assistance.

(Kaul *et al.*, 1999: foreword)

The added value of assimilating human security to a GPG is to underline the interdependency of everyone's security, soliciting legitimization for political action. Human security as a public good entails a responsibility for the state to protect people from underdevelopment and to provide empowering measures; and a corresponding duty of individuals and communities to assume, engage and demand what is owed to them. Most importantly, human security as a global public good puts the ultimate responsibility for its provision on the international community and gives rise to demand for new policy infrastructures and solutions. Human security threats may be transnational and therefore can best be addressed by collective response.

The freedom from fear approach to security for example is a global public good, since fear and insecurity generate conflicts with regional and international consequences. Similarly, the development approach could also be considered as a GPG. Models of growth that do not ensure equity will, in the long run, lead to deep inequalities between classes of people, genders, and communities. Rejecting that development needs are global and, by extension, narrowing threats to the security of some societies, means prioritizing intentional threats to their security. Yet, it is clear that non-intentional threats such as global warming may be more dangerous than intentional ones, such as terrorism, with which global society seems to be increasingly concerned today. Even human rights can be considered as a global public good. With the widespread support for human rights, the notion of equality of all human beings is increasingly recognized, and it has become harder to justify the difference in killing human beings in war as 'collateral damage' or in other circumstances. Kaldor notes that such a role played by human rights has led people to think about developing 'an alternative strategy to bring the 'inside' out, to extend domestic peace globally' (Kaldor, 2003).

Associating human security with public goods however is not devoid of risks. First, it implies using an 'economic' lens. If human security is a good, it involves market mechanisms, especially those conceptualized in the context of neo-liberal economics. Thus, Grayson argues that a new theory of public goods would be needed, one that stems 'as the result of political factors rather than market conditions' (Grayson, 2001). The privatization of security and of social insurance in both developing and industrialized countries for example reveals that states are often unable (or unwilling) to provide GPG in their area of sovereignty. Mixing the concept of human security that underlines the failures of the states to protect individuals, with an economic theory based on market mechanisms would be a risky strategy that could open the door to a conceptual legitimization of the intervention of markets and private actors to provide the good named 'human security'. Furthermore, there appears to be a bias in the concept of GPGs that sets a universal objective that does not take regional, cultural, social conditions into consideration and is constructed mainly on the basis of Western values (Chenevat and Kohn, 2005). Though GPG are supposed to represent an aggregation of individual preferences, they often become instead the main reasons for conflicts between different countries and economic actors. For instance health or environment are not considered as public goods by many countries that have commercial interests on these topics, as illustrated by the struggles in the World Trade Organization on the TRIPS Agreement, especially patents for medicines and property right. Many countries would not agree with the idea that human security is a Global *Public* Good, as it would be a justification to the fact that they do not provide enough of it for their people.

There are also a number of limitations to the concept of GPG which would not benefit the human security goals. First is a risk of oversimplification and reductionism. The tendency would be to focus on transnational threats, which fit readily within the global public good definition. However, not all human security threats are transnational in character. Threats at the regional, country and community levels require responses at the corresponding level. If threats are not global in character, does this undercut the responsibility of the international community for certain forms of human security? Second, the GPG debate may overlook the crucial question of specificity. Individuals may not require an identical basket of global public goods. How can global public goods be tailored to meet local needs and aspirations? Finally, the conceptualization may risk entanglement with the question of power politics: who decides and how is the decision made to define a global public good? The danger may be that richer, powerful nations will be able to impose their definition of human security as a global public good to suit their own needs and interests.

Thus, associating human security to the basket of global public goods would be by itself inadequate unless it was clearly linked to notions of justice. A human security approach would be more judiciously served by arguments that are seen to be and are based on global justice instead.

Revisiting international responsibility: from collective security to global justice

Kaldor recalls that the idea of managing security as a global good is attached to the fact that historically, there used to be what was called a 'great divide' between the way conciliation of interests was sought based on the rule of law inside nation states, and the way national interests were pursued through whatever means available in the unregulated international arena. But 'globalization, based on the spread of new technologies, has eroded the Great Divide' (Kaldor, 2003): the sources of insecurity have changed (insecurity arises from the 'new wars', from global terrorism or organized crime networks, etc. ...); the usefulness of conventional military forces for dealing with these new threats is limited; finally, the rule of law and domestic norms have extended outside national borders. Since the threats have evolved to trans-border ones, dealing with them has become a global issue for every state, and then for all of them together. If security can be seen as a GPG, it is because improving the level of security in one place should not prevent from improving it in another place, and it will benefit everyone, not only those directly facing the threat. This view requires the strengthening of international humanitarian and human rights law, which must be applied impartially.

In addition, however, Kaldor also calls for a commitment to global social justice. Even if global public evils are not the cause of violence (poverty and inequality, environmental irresponsibility, spread of global pandemics, etc. ...), their continuing existence at a high level in our globalized world is both an argument and an incentive to violence – and consequently a threat to peace and security. In order not to always use the example of terrorism, one may also see that mafias and all other international criminal organizations thrive locally on unemployment and other forms of social exclusion. The process of globalization has first raised global concerns, which in turn have demanded to be globally addressed, and this geographic globalization has extended to a global social justice approach, which can be the instrument, together with collective security, to provide effective human security.

A point recurrent in the definitions of human security is its commitment to multilateralism to address multiple threats. According to Lodgaard, human security 'is also a matter of defending international rules, norms and standards in support of human beings at risk [...] a distinct tendency to restrict the sovereignty of states and enhance the salience of international norms' (Lodgaard, 2000). Collective security then is one of the foundations for such networked action. The idea of collective security, embedded in Woodrow Wilson's fourteen points, the interwar period and the League of Nations, was a system aimed at preventing state aggression: states would join together and pledge that aggression against one was against all, and commit themselves in that event to react collectively. Peace in the international community could be maintained through binding pre-determined agreements that took collective action to preserve it (Miller, 1999). Ideally, aggression would not reflect a balance of power but a community of power. In the far less than perfect real world, however, power politics and perceived national interests tend to prevail over concerns for the safety and welfare of individuals.

The UN and the League of Nation were created by the victorious great powers, and made themselves the principal agents of collective action. They did a balancing act that contained each other and attempted a status quo of the international system. An internal bipolar rivalry emerged and the US became the principal agent of military and economic sanctions. Instruments of enforcement also varied and a shift of less to more coercive sanctions emerged as instruments of enforcement. Collective security and humanitarian intervention has been viewed by many states and people as motivated intervention for national interest of some powerful states. Can a human security paradigm of intervention change such a vision? If during the Cold War, collective security was narrowly conceived in state-centric military terms, it has increasingly been endorsed by the UN, the ultimate guardian of this responsibility, as a collective commitment to uphold the rights, freedom, and dignity of individuals as well as state security. This thinking was echoed in a number of major UN reports in the first half of the twenty-first century: *Responsibility to Protect* (2001), *A More Secure World: Our Shared Responsibility* (2004), *In Larger Freedom* (2005), etc., all of which tried to redefine the concept of collective security and to convince nation-states that a human security approach is not only a moral obligation but also, and perhaps especially, in their best interests.

Revisiting sovereignty as responsibility

The principle of state sovereignty and the notion of universal human rights and the international obligation to protect involve a principle contradiction if understood within their traditional conceptualization, as explained in the earlier chapters. On the other hand, there has been the simultaneous development of certain ethical principles like international human rights and an increasing unwillingness of the international community to tolerate extensive violation of these principles. The 1648 Peace of Westphalia had posited the major underlying principles of the international order: the sovereign state had absolute and unconditional power over its territory and citizens, and no supra-national organization or state could have authority above the state. Interventions in the name of humanitarian principles seem to be shaking the foundations of this realist conception of the state. The emergence of human rights in 1948, where rights of the individual are meant to be overriding over power and state politics, may be seen as a direct contradiction with the principle of sovereignty when the state is unable or unwilling to protect an individual's rights.

The reconciliation of these two seemingly contradictory principles has led to a revision of sovereignty as a responsibility of the state towards its citizens (Schmitt *et al.*, 2004). It is crucial to point out, however, that the different UN reports do not challenge the legitimacy of statehood itself. The individual sovereign state remains the fundamental organizing unit of international relations and has the primary responsibility for providing human security to its citizens by remaining the 'front-line actor' for dealing with threats (ICISS, 2001: 11). Accordingly, it would be problematic to claim that these UN reports constitute a 'paradigm' shift in global security. They are best seen as efforts to reconcile state security with human security. One of the ways this is done is by redefining the meaning of and responsibilities implied by the term 'sovereignty' to make it conditional on the state's ability and willingness to protect and provide for its own citizens.

Even the strongest supporters of state sovereignty do not support any claim of the unlimited power of a state to do what it wants to its own people. In this context, the term 'dual sovereignty' of a state, namely externally – to respect the sovereignty of other states, and internally, to respect the dignity and basic rights of all the people within the state, has evolved (ICISS, 2001: para. 1.35). The 2001 report *Responsibility to Protect* (RTPR) for example considers that aspect. Sovereignty for a state should mean protection of its population, and if for some reason it cannot or will not work, the international community has the residual responsibility to intervene. Sovereignty, upheld and celebrated by states and confirmed by international law, is thus gradually being viewed as conditional, specifically on the ability to provide security to the individual. That is to say to abide by its social contract.

From duty to intervene to responsibility to protect: a shift in ends and means of interventions

If human security is a global good and the international community has a responsibility towards ensuring the protection and security of individuals, what role should its institutions play in ensuring this? Should it intervene to uphold human rights and prevent mass killing? What about in cases of mass famine as in Sudan or natural disasters, as the Tsunami? As both stated in the *Responsibility to Protect* report and in the High Panel report of December 2004:

> The Panel endorses the emerging norm that there is a collective international responsibility to protect, exercisable by the Security Council authorizing military intervention as a last resort, in the event of genocide and other large-scale killing, ethnic cleansing or serious violations of humanitarian law which sovereign Governments have proved powerless or unwilling to prevent.
>
> (High Level Panel on Threats, Challenges and Change, 2004, proposition 55 out of 101)

Human security, because of its broad scope, could serve some powerful states as an excuse for intervention in weaker ones. The RTPR sought to overcome this controversy by approaching intervention, in all its stages, from the perspective of individuals instead. It redefined humanitarian intervention as a responsibility rather than a right, arguing that the 'right to intervene' was unhelpful because it upheld the claims of the intervening state rather than the 'urgent needs of potential beneficiaries of actions'. The report thus tried to negate the fears around interventions in a number of ways.

The RPRT, for example, focused on strict criteria for intervention to prevent the abuse of the human security paradigm for power politics. The Report's primary goal was to establish clear rules, procedures and criteria of humanitarian intervention, especially those related to the decision to intervene, its timing and its modalities. According to Acharya, 'no other policy document has gone further in specifying the criteria for humanitarian intervention' (Acharya, 2002: 374). Clear guidelines for intervention would guarantee an apolitical and 'impartial' involvement, guided by the concern of the protection of human security. For this purpose, the RTPR set down six specific and important conditions for intervention for human security purposes: right authority, just cause, right intention, last resort, proportional means and reasonable prospects. The RTPR argued that military intervention for human protection was justified in two sets of circumstances, namely in order to stop or prevent:

> large scale loss of life, actual or apprehended, with the intent of genocide or not, which is the product either of deliberate state action, or state neglect or inability to act, or a failed state situation, or large scale 'ethnic cleansing,' actual or apprehended, whether carried out by killing, forced expulsion, acts of terror or rape.
>
> (ICISS, 2001: para. 4.19)

These conditions in general include, amongst others, those actions defined by the framework of the 1948 Genocide Convention that involve large scale threatened or actual loss of life, but also overwhelming natural or environmental catastrophes, where the state concerned is either unwilling or unable to cope, or call for assistance, and significant loss of life is occurring or threatened. However, the report does not define 'large-scale' casualties in numeric terms since it thinks that most cases will not generate major disagreement. This means, however, that the 'cold blooded question ... how many dead and dying are enough to require intervention?' remains unresolved (Acharya, 2002: 375). At the same time, as Rawls argues:

> Even in a just war, certain forms of violence are strictly inadmissible; and when a country's right to war is questionable and uncertain, the constraints on the means it can use are all the more severe. Acts permissible in a war of legitimate self-defence, when these are necessary, may be flatly excluded in a more doubtful situation.
>
> (Rawls, 1971: 379)

The RTPR set out a number of additional conditions for interventions which diffuse the controversy around human security as an excuse for interventions. First, was the principle of right intention, 'to halt or avert human suffering'. This meant that interventions were not justified if aimed at the alteration of boundaries or supporting claims of self-determination or regime change through military or other coups. Acharya stresses that: '[...] humanitarian intervention thus defined can be usefully separated from the West's ideologically charged democratic 'enlargement' campaign.' Nevertheless, the Report recognized the possibility of mixed motives behind intervention decisions, because the financial costs and human risks involved in military action might make it necessary to claim some degree of self-interest. Where crisis in faraway countries could generate worldwide problems (refugee outflows, health pandemics, terrorism, etc.) it is in the interests of every country to contribute to its resolution. Second, was the principle of 'last resort' characterized by the failure of 'every ... non-military avenue for the prevention or peaceful resolution of the humanitarian crisis'. Interventions thus could take many different forms, from sanctions in the military (arms embargo, ending military cooperation and training programs, etc.), economic (financial sanctions, restrictions on income generating activities, etc.) and in the political and diplomatic arena (restriction in diplomatic representation, restrictions on travel, etc.). A third condition for intervention identified in the report was the 'proportional means' principle which implied that the scale, intensity, and duration of military action must be commensurate with the provocation. Fourth, there had to be reasonable prospects, that is, tangible chance of success in stopping atrocities and suffering that acted as a trigger for the intervention. Fifth, was the criterion of right authority, i.e. in case of state failure in providing human security, the international community, under the leadership of the UN, could fill in the responsibility. In cases where the UN Security Council was unwilling to act, the report suggested the establishment of a 'code of conduct' for the permanent five to govern the use of the veto in intervention decisions. It called on the permanent members to resort to 'constructive abstention'.

A shift from duty to intervene to responsibility to protect had significant implications as it changed the notion of intervention as hitherto understood. The International Commission on Intervention and State Sovereignty (ICISS), by changing the language of intervention from right or duty to intervene to responsibility to protect, put the focus on those who needed support. It asked the Security Council to face up to the consequences of inaction: pressures of intervention for wrong reasons by ad hoc coalitions or states would intensify, and in the process, threaten the legitimacy and credibility of the UN. It also called for the need for a responsibility to prevent and rebuild after conflicts as complimentary to the responsibility to protect.

Analysing the responsibility

Though the ICISS claimed to draw its inspiration from human security as such, it in fact abandoned the specificity of the concept, equating it in its report to more traditional views on human rights, humanitarian intervention and international politics (Keren, 2005). When it explicitly addressed human rights and human security (ICISS, 2001: 14–15), it only used the concept as a way to bypass state sovereignty, insisting on the fact that security should be people-centred rather than state-centred. Yet, the Commission overlooked the all-encompassing nature of the notion, which takes into account *all* threats to human lives, whatever they may be. The ICISS preferred a narrow, freedom from fear approach to human security. According to its report, the two threshold criteria of the just cause, justifying a military intervention were:

> large scale loss of life, actual or apprehended, with genocidal intent or not, which is the product either of deliberate state action, or state neglect or inability to act, or a failed state situation; or large scale ethnic cleansing, actual or apprehended, whether carried out by killing, forced expulsion, acts of terror or rape.
>
> (Ibid.: 32)

In those criteria, the entire range of human development, freedom from want side of human security, is neglected. Among the seven categories of the 1994 HDR, for example, only personal, political and community insecurity were considered as threats grave enough to the 'core of all human lives' to justify intervention in the Final Report. Economic, food, health and environmental security were overlooked.

As Owen pinpointed, the innovation of the human security paradigm is that it does not appraise threats according to their causes but their severity, immediacy and scope (Owen, 2004). Yet, the ICISS evaluated threats according to their causes as well as severity. Human security does not concentrate on issues that demand a response, military or otherwise, but on the 'severity, immediacy, and scope' of those issues, making no distinctions as to whether people are killed by militias or by chronic poverty. This means that whether we are dealing with ethnic cleansing or massive poverty, whether they are due to human agency or natural causes, the responsibility to protect of the international community remains similar. It is not worse if people get killed by militias or by a tsunami than by chronic poverty. Yet, it can be argued that, though it might seem relevant to intervene militarily to stop ethnic cleansing, an army may not be the best way to stop poverty (Keren, 2005). It is true, but not because one cause is more just than the other, i.e. not because ethnic cleansing is worse than massive poverty; or, put in Michael Walzer's terms, because we have a right, internationally acknowledged, to be protected from ethnic cleansing, but we are not from pervasive poverty (Walzer, 1992) . It is true because, in the just war theory, war should always, first, be the last resort; second, have reasonable prospects of success regarding the just cause (in our example, stop poverty). It is likely that, if the international community had the will to stop massive poverty in one country, they would find many more effective ways to do so than military intervention, and it is likely that the authorities of the country in question would more than welcome such a surprising and generous initiative. But if, for example, the government of a state was impoverishing the inhabitants of one region on purpose in order to tame a particularly rebellious minority, and was accordingly closing all public services (health, education, etc.), cutting all subsidies, stopping all development programmes, prohibiting foreign investments, etc., then, it is our contention that, if that government persisted in spite of the international community's condemnations and sanctions, it might be a case for intervention. One could argue that this reasoning would multiply to infinity the cases for intervention. It would indeed increase the cases when intervention is considered. But if we keep in mind Owen's three criteria (severity, immediacy and scope), and the criteria of the ICISS, (last resort, proportionality, reasonable prospects), human security is the most relevant touchstone for evaluating the justice of causes when the prospect of a military intervention is debated, because it is based on actual human suffering (whatever its cause may be).

Second, the RTPR put inadequate focus on prevention and engagement. The report's RTPR's primary objective was to provide practical and morally tenable guidance to the why, how, and when of military humanitarian intervention. It focused on how to respond to an urgent crisis, where large-scale loss of life was imminent or occurring. *Responsibility to Protect*, dealt, therefore, with the response to a situation where human security had failed. While it insisted that there was a complimentary responsibility to prevent and to rebuild after interventions had happened, it failed to recognize the real difficulties of devising and implementing comprehensive strategies for conflict prevention. One of the major constraints of conflict prevention is the difficulty to predict a conflict and the assessment of early warning structures. Until now, for example, the UN does not have a central capacity to manage and use effectively the information it receives on potential crises. It is more difficult to obtain funding for preventive missions than for missions once the conflict has broken out (Kittani, 1998: 100). The report also ignored the fact that the three elements of prevention that it identified, i.e. early warning/analysis, preventive toolbox and political will, were heavily influenced by relations of force among various countries. It also failed to recognize the outcomes of economic pressures, such as 'adjustment' programmes imposed by conditionalities, which often weaken the states' capacities to provide for the 'wants' of their populations or manage conflicts when they do happen.

Third, the report may have underestimated the difficulties of implementing rebuilding policies. Military interventions often destroy domestic capacities for rebuilding strategies. Reconstruction policies are usually bound with models of development. This is illustrated by the gap between the pledges donors make for reconstruction and the resources they actually provide. In other cases strategies are often 'imposed from the outside'.

Ultimately, the criteria set out by the RTPR, from a human security point of view, failed to separate the humanitarian from the political rationale. They failed to alleviate the fears of the motives, i.e. the 'ends' of interventions as well their means. We argue that the fear persists for three specific reasons.

First, apolitical and impartial engagement is not possible. The international community cannot limit humanitarian interventions to saving lives without getting implicated in the political aspirations of the victims. As Duffield points out, no act is neutral: 'Aid is no *substitute* for political action because it *is* the political action' (Duffield, 2001: 88). In other words, actions are not considered right in themselves but are judged against their outcomes. Within this framework, human security gives an ideal end point against which the 'good' of an intervention has to be measured. The responsibility to protect discourse ignores the problem of the relation of force between developing countries and developed/intervening countries before the intervention, such as the push toward the expansion of markets for Western economies, and so on. Additionally, the lines between a 'right intention' and a 'moral cause' depend on perspective.

Second, no matter how much the notion of responsibility to protect sought to put brakes on trigger happy interventions, the fact remains that its association with the needy's perspective meant that human security is increasingly seen in the South as 'yet another attempt by the West to impose its liberal values and political institutions on non-Western societies' (Ul Haq, 1998), an excuse for intervention in states' domestic affairs and for conditionality on ODA. Attached to their sovereignty, their 'home-grown notion of comprehensive security' (Acharya, 2001) and their values, a number of Asian governments were willing to look at only the freedom from want aspect of human security, which was not part of dilemmas of the responsibility to protect, and resist freedom from fear because of its close connection with the idea of human rights and humanitarian intervention. Some Asian countries such as Myanmar and North Korea thus encouraged the G77 to reject the RTPR, while others rejected it as excessive moralism.

Third, there is ultimately, a subjective view of where insecurities are born. The links between human security and different levels of intervention depend on the estimation of the human security deficits. Hampson argued that human security could be a means of emphasizing the need 'to address the serious distributional inequalities that arise from the operation of the global markets and the forces of globalization' (Hampson *et al.*, 2002: 53). This understanding of the root causes of human insecurities points towards a need to change not just the political, but also the economic environment (Duffield, 2001: 40). An intervention by countries of the core in countries of the periphery, no matter the justification for a responsibility to react, would not solve the structural causes which led to inequalities between the core and the periphery in the first place. Looking at the question from the North–South perspective, Hampson concluded:

> Human Security as the 'North's' development establishment understands it, is interventionist when it comes to the policies and practices of states in the South, but essentially laissez-faire and status quo regarding the role of the market and global governance arrangements.
>
> (Hampson *et al.*, 2002: 169)

Since interventions can never be attempted against powerful states, international action in the name of human security risks turning into a prerogative of the strong against the weak. Clearly, then, the notion of 'responsibility to protect' will be acceptable only when the faith of the South is restored by a manifestation of good intentions on equitable terms, rather than with the persistence of examples such as interventions in Iraq.

Just war for human security?

Ultimately, the RTPR may have provoked more anguish than reassurance because of its focus on the conditions of military interventions instead of developing alternative avenues for global justice and collective responsibility. In the narrow sense, a humanitarian intervention is a short-term military engagement to save lives. As a reactionary tool, it fails to address the complexity of structural causes of insecurities. Additionally, it can be considered as an expression of power politics under the guise of altruism. Whether interventions failed to occur, as in Rwanda in 1994, or did occur, as in Kosovo in 1999, their morality, modalities and efficiency were issues of major debates in international relations.

It was Secretary-General Kofi Annan himself who explicitly linked human security and intervention together, when in his statement to the fifty-fourth session of the General Assembly of the United Nations (UN) in 1999, he made clear his intention to 'address the prospects for human security and intervention in the next century.' The report of the ICISS obviously borrows a lot of its main conclusions from the just war theory – without explicitly paying it the tribute it owes (Keren, 2005). 'Just war' was systematically examined by Aquinas in his *Summa Theologica* in the thirteenth century, where he discussed not only the justification of war (jus ad bellum), but also the kinds of activities permissible in war (jus in bello). Later theorists including Hugo Grotius (1583–1645), Samuel Pufendorf (1632–1704), Christian Wolff (1679–1754), expanded this notion, with the most important contemporary text being Walzer's *Just and Unjust Wars* (1977, reprinted 1992).

The guidelines the RTPR set forth (just cause, right intention, proportionality, right authority and reasonable prospects) are all, without exception, directly taken from the just war doctrine. Its organization itself, which distinguishes between 'the responsibility to react', 'the operational dimension' and 'the responsibility to rebuild' as chapter headings, reminds one of the traditional distinction between 'jus ad bellum', 'jus in bello', and 'jus post bellum' in the just war doctrine. As the Commission tried to link human security and intervention, it resorted naturally to the theory of just war (Keren, 2005).

Human security takes into account what actually kills people, not only war, but also poverty, famine, political repression, disease, and environmental degradation. In fact, war (whether it is just or unjust) is one of the main causes of human insecurity. Yet, supporters of just war have argued that when human insecurity within a state is such that it 'shocks the moral conscience of mankind' (Walzer, 1992: 107 also used in the RTPR, ICISS, 2001:31) and when the authorities of this state either do nothing about it or worse, are the very cause of human suffering, it is necessary for other states or the international community to intervene, possibly with military force. Yet, all international interventions so far have been mired in controversies: Kosovo was a questionable intervention. In Rwanda there was no intervention in the face of genocide. In Somalia there was an unconditional withdrawal, and in Iraq, intervention was used for military occupation.

The 1999 NATO intervention in Kosovo was undertaken to achieve human security goals, i.e. to stop the ethnic cleansing in Kosovo. Yet, as Thakur noted, it 'remains hotly disputed in terms of whether it triggered more carnage than it averted' (Thakur, 2002). Chomsky, a critic of the US-led war against Yugoslavia, argued that far from stopping the violence, the bombing 'greatly accelerated [the] slaughter and dispossession' of the Albanian Kosovars (Chomsky, 1999: 81). The consequences of war included unintended unfortunate collateral damage such as refugee flows, as well as more long-term consequences stemming from the fragmentation of the Yugoslav state, the destruction of the economic space, and ensued dependency. On the other side of the spectrum, the Rwandan case showed the risks of selective interventions. Analysts have underlined that an intervention that would have used all feasible force to halt large-scale killing and military conflict in Rwanda would have saved the lives of about 275,000 Tutsi (Kuperman, 2000). The Clinton administration at the time avoided using the term genocide (which would have created an obligation to intervene according to the Genocide Convention), since there were no important national interests at stake in the country, which, was a prerequisite for the United States to consider action (DiPrizio, 2002: 148). Beyond military action, however, there were other responsibilities that the international community could have considered well before the genocide was underway. It is also well established that the majority of Rwandans lived in extreme poverty and inequality between the ruling elites and the rest. At the same time the International Monetary Fund and the World Bank demanded that Rwanda implement a programme of structural adjustment, and the government's budget for 1989 was slashed nearly in half at a time of famine.

Rwandan society had approximately four years (between the time where the first signs of genocide appeared at Kibilira to the massacre triggered by the shoot down of the President Habyarimana's plane) to stop the genocide.

Such incidents of selective humanitarian intervention have made much of the South, especially civil society, cynical of the concept to the extent of rejecting it. Bello argued:

> Most of us, at least most of us in the global South, recoil at Washington's use of the humanitarian logic to invade Iraq. Most of us would say that even as we condemn any regime's violations of human rights, systematic violation of those rights does not constitute grounds for the violation of national sovereignty through invasion or destabilization. Getting rid of a repressive regime or a dictator is the responsibility of the citizens of a country.
>
> (Bello, 2006)

Galtung who conducted a cost benefit analysis of intervention in Iraq on the basis of 'basic human needs (BHN)', warned against self-interest legitimacy and the dominance of military culture, despite the labels of 'humanitarian' and human security attached to such interventions. His general conclusion on the intervention in Iraq was: 'neither security, nor human'. While opposing such methods, however, he argued that 'doing nothing is not an option'. In his view, the requirement was a responsibility for the international community to 'fulfill basic needs of people + soft intervention in cases of genocide + conflict resolution' (Galtung, 2003).

From humanitarian intervention to human security engagement

Thus, the establishment of internationally accepted norms for military humanitarian intervention is vitally important. Interventions by international and regional organizations tend to focus on promoting 'freedom from fear' and human rights by seeking to prevent, or more often bring to an end, to man-made mass loss of life. This idea is reinforced by the criteria given under the heading of 'just cause' in the report on the *Responsibility to Protect*, setting the bar for international intervention at 'large-scale loss of life' or 'large-scale ethnic cleansing'. Similarly, in the report of the UN High Level Panel on Threats, Challenges and Change, five of the six clusters of threats involve physical violence, for example from nuclear weapons or terrorism. All other types of threats to human security are crowded together under the heading of 'poverty, infectious diseases and environmental degradation'. Although to some extent such a categorization responds to political pressure operating within the UN structure, it is still an indication that UN intervention tends to be very much focused upon these violent punctual threats.

A key way in which human security engagement can go beyond humanitarian intervention is by addressing a broader range of threats to individuals' security. Thus, a human security engagement approach would give a more prominent role to the pursuit of 'freedom from want' and would always make clear the interactions between different forms of insecurity. This applies not only to ongoing, long-term efforts to alleviate insecurity but also to the types of crises that are considered. For example, economic crises such as in South-East Asia in 1997/8 and natural disasters such as the Tsunami in 2004 could be seen as triggering responsibilities on the part of the international community. In short, one way of looking at the broadening of threats as one moves from a humanitarian intervention to a Human Security engagement approach is that not only acts of direct violence are taken into account but also acts of structural violence (Galtung, 1969: 170), and indeed threats to security that lie beyond the control of human beings. Humanitarian intervention does not solve the problem of who is responsible for protecting human security against structural violence – poverty, disease, etc. – or natural disasters and economic downturns.

Additionally, the focus of a broader human security engagement would be on prevention rather than dealing with crises that are already under way. If noting is done more than fire-fighting then the crises will keep returning. This therefore implies a commitment over the longer-term that should be based on ongoing needs rather than wherever media attention is focused at any particular moment in time. Effective prevention avoids the kind of life-threatening emergency situation that must be dealt with militarily which renders individual empowerment virtually impossible. However, the colossal problem is that avenues for effective prevention, particularly in relation to conflict situations, remain unexplored and since politicians receive little credit for having prevented something from happening, prevention is rarely a political priority. Even if it does stress the responsibility to rebuild, humanitarian military intervention is always going to be, by definition, an ad-hoc response to an emergency crisis. This response will always be (at least to some extent) determined by political decisions and media interest. human security, by contrast, entails long-term engagement, which takes place away from the spotlight and media headlines. Military humanitarian intervention requires a disaster to galvanize the international community into action and alert them to their responsibilities. Arguably, though, the responsibility of the international community or responsibilities between states is not just 'residual' and sporadic.

Achieving human security entails long-term engagement and commitment, combining issues of development, conflict prevention and human rights in a holistic strategy and banner. Human security engagement would provide means like prevention (early warning systems, the search for root causes); protection (social safety nets, provide downturns with security, protection from sudden change) and empowerment measures (development, education, democracy, etc.). It should be noted however that this 'maximalist' human security approach required for human security engagement is not without its critics. Duffield sees in this trend a risk to the very ideal of humanitarianism. For him, the danger is that 'the new humanitarianism involves a shift in the centre of gravity of policy away from saving lives to supporting social processes and political outcomes' (Duffield, 2001). He goes on to suggest that this implies an assumption that suffering and loss of life today is a price worth paying for a 'better tomorrow' and as such the process has the effect of normalizing violence and complicity with its perpetrators. This is a valid criticism of a process of substituting longer-term engagement for humanitarian intervention in crisis situations. However, the human security approach does not necessarily need to replace existing measures but rather improve them and complement them.

By way of summary, and in order to highlight the differences between a humanitarian intervention approach and a Human Security engagement approach the indicative Table 8.1 compares the potential differences in terms of actors, means and goals of the two approaches.

Beyond the state, who is responsible for protecting human security and when?

Ultimately, protecting human security, when the state fails to do so, requires multiple actors, at multiple levels, because the threats in the very same way can be local, national, regional or global. While a large variety of actors can provide human security, including most notably NGOs or even individuals through empowerment, ultimate responsibility for organizing and coordinating these efforts at levels above that of the state fall upon international or regional organizations.

Is the UN adequate?

The United Nations certainly has responsibility as regards the protection of human security, a responsibility that the Secretary General called a 'special burden' in his report *In Larger Freedom*: 'Our guiding light must be the needs and hopes of peoples everywhere … United Nations, while it is an organization of sovereign States, exists for and must ultimately serve those needs. To do so, we must aim, as I said when first elected eight years ago, to perfect the triangle of development, freedom and peace' (Annan, 2005a). Even though the report does not explicitly use the term 'human security', the references to its discourse are all too clear, if only in the name of the chapters, that is to say 'Freedom from fear' (security), 'Freedom from want' (development), and 'Freedom to live in dignity' (human rights). Article 24 of the UN Charter confers upon the Security Council, the 'primary responsibility for the maintenance of international peace and security'. According to the RTPR, the provisions of Chapters VII and VIII constitute a formidable source of authority to deal with security threats of all types.

If the United Nations, through the *In Larger Freedom* Report, the Commission on Human Security or the UNDP Report of 1994, clearly expressed the will to further human security aims, the Secretary General also clearly acknowledged a need for reform to enhance the capacity of the UN in furthering these aims. The *In Larger Freedom* Report, based in part on the High Level Panel's Report, offered for example a number of proposals on how to realistically reform and strengthen the UN (realistically as both recognize the constraints it has to abide by, for example the veto of the P5 in the Security Council). *The Responsibility to Protect* Report also offered proposals of reform of the UN, although these were more specific to furthering humanitarian intervention.

Table 8.1 Humanitarian intervention and human security engagement

	Members	Agency	Instruments	Obligations	Threats	Timescale
Humanitarian intervention	UN member states	Security Council	Military peace support operations	Responsibility to protect	Large-scale loss of life/ethnic cleansing	Short-term crises
Human security engagement	UN member states, regional organizations, NGOs, civil society, individual	Security Council, Network of actors from members of the Security Council as well as countries where the engagement will take place Peacebuilding commission Collaboration with local population, etc.	Peace support operations Development Humanitarian aid Upholding of HR (conventions, sanctions, shaming, naming, etc. Military interventions as last resort	Responsibility to protect, prevent and also to empower	Survival but also threats to livelihood and dignity	Mid- to long-term commitment to treat root causes

The reforms proposed both by the High Level Panel Report and the *In Larger Freedom* Report were generally based on the will to achieve 'better system coherence', allowing the UN to work in a more efficient, integrated, and coordinated manner, coordination that should be enhanced not only between UN institutions, but also between the UN, Member States, regional organizations, and civil society. These reforms were guided by four underlying principles: first, to increase the involvement in decision-making of biggest contributors in financial, military and diplomatic terms (also to promote the attainment of the 0.7% of GNP aim on ODA), second, to have a more representative, broader membership especially developing countries, third, to enlarge the Security Council without diminishing effectiveness of the council and fourth, to increase the democratic and accountable nature of the body.

Among the many suggestions tabled by the reform documents, proposals for a Peacebuilding Commission would undoubtedly serve to further human security aims. The Peacebuilding Commission's core functions were said to serve the freedom from fear as well as the freedom from want aspects of the human security agenda. They were: first, to identify countries under stress or which risk sliding towards state collapse; second, to organise proactive assistance, in cooperation with national government, to prevent further deterioration; third, to assist in planning for transitions between conflict and post-conflict peacebuilding and fourth, to marshal and sustain international peacebuilding efforts. Furthermore, the Peacebuilding Commission would allow for great intra-UN and inter-organization coordination as the High Level Report recommended that it should include representation from the Economic and Social Council, from the IMF, the World Bank, and regional development banks, from national representatives of the country concerned, from major donor and troop-providing countries, and finally from regional and sub-regional groups strongly involved in the country.

Even if the proposed Peacebuilding Commission could take a big step in furthering human security aims and achieve better efficiency and coordination, it is also clear that creating commissions and councils to alleviate suffering and peacebuilding, human rights, development or other matters can also create extra bureaucracy and inefficiency, in an institution that generally lacks financial capabilities, as well as independence from member states.

What may be needed for human security purposes is not a council for everything, but rather one small, efficient 'umbrella' council, a human security council, which would bring together, in close coordination, existing UN institutions, such as the Security Council (security), the UNDP (development) and the proposed Human Rights Council. Various proposals have been forwarded for an ideal global architecture by Mahbub Ul Haq in 1995 and the Commission on Human Security in 2003. Naturally, however, strong resistance from member states make these proposals idealistic at best for now, similar to the failure to pass a human security resolution at the Security Council or the General Assembly. The UN, as an organization of member states, which upholds and reaffirms their sovereignty, remains constrained in attempts to further human security and to reform its institutions, most visibly at the Security Council, where power politics and geo-strategic concerns still have the upper hand. Slow change of Member States' attitudes (with forerunners such as Canada, Japan, and Norway) might in the end be the best way to assure bold reform of the UN towards furthering HS aims.

Are global institutions the answer anyway?

Many states, especially from the developing world, remain sceptical of the role of the international community in ensuring human security because, in their view, international organizations are relatively powerless in promoting a neutral vision of the world order and are still dominated by national interest and power politics. Ultimately the UN reflects political sensibilities and rivalries of member-states. Human security can only become a global agenda if key member-states endorse the concept. For example, it is difficult to imagine the US endorsing human security and responsibility to protect. This is itself a threat to human security when powerful states do not comply with norms.

But criticism is not the onus of power politics only. The Realist School also doubts the role of international institutions in international politics. Even if human security is considered a GPG, the classical realist position is that such goods can only be provided by a hegemonic leader or a group of states as only they can offer or withhold the necessary side payments to get others to join the regime. The liberal point of view considers international organizations legitimate but not well suited to ensure human security. They face conflicts of interests among their most powerful members, are thwarted by resource problems, and are unable to provide public goods. Formal institutions suffer from a lack of political leadership at the top and bureaucratic inertia or opposition from below, that stifles progress in meeting human security needs (Hampson *et al.*, 2002: 53). Thus, the onus of responsibility could shift to regional institutions.

Regional solutions?

What are the relative strengths and weaknesses of regional organizations? It is widely acknowledged that regional organizations are often better placed to act than the UN (ICISS, 2001 para. 6.31). An advantage of regional actors is that they understand the dynamics of strife and cultures more intimately than outsiders do. Regional blocs such as the Organization of African Unity (OAU), NATO, OECD, Shanghai Cooperation Organization (SCO), ASEAN, the Southern African Development Coordination Conference are increasingly influencing the geopolitics of the international political system. Local knowledge and expertise, enhanced capabilities, and obvious self-interest, can make regional institutions longer-term, prevention-inclined, specifically-adapted actors in the protection of human security. This is especially true in intervening in region-specific threats, either in times of crises such as natural catastrophes (droughts, earthquakes, tsunamis, etc.), environmental disasters (oil slicks, radioactive disasters) or financial crises, or on the longer term, either in post-disaster rebuilding and development or more generally creating safety nets in preparation for the future.

Another potential benefit of a regional approach is centred on the idea that regional entities have a greater degree of legitimacy in intervening in countries that are members of a similar organization. An example of this can be seen in the refusal of the Sudan government to accept any other presence other than that of African Union forces on its territory. Taking a regional approach in promoting human security beyond crisis situations could also provide an effective response to many critics of the concept. This is particularly true in relation to the claims by states such as Cuba and India that human security is yet another means of imposing Western values upon developing nations. If human security were promoted by other developing nations within the same regional grouping, this criticism would of course less readily apply. Involvement by regional powers is also less likely to be perceived as illegitimate interference (MacFarlane and Weiss, 1994: 283).

The question of the scope of the responsibility of regional organizations in promoting human security also needs to be raised. In other words, should regional organizations be able to act in countries that are not members of the organization? In Europe, for example, the question of human security is often cited as that of the insecurity of its neighbours or the spill over from human insecurity in the form of illegal migrants from conflict/poor countries, and also the spread of threats like bird flu, SARS, AIDS. The interconnection of threats under globalization is also recognized. An expert group from London School of Economics (LSE) presented a proposal, *The Human Security Doctrine for Europe* (HSDE) in 2004 at the Barcelona Forum of the European Union (EU). The report was produced to reinforce the needs of addressing growing insecurities beyond the borders of Europe. Human security was defined as to the freedom for individuals from basic insecurities caused by human rights violations, what the *Human Security Doctrine for Europe* Report refers to as a 'bottom-up approach'. Within the doctrine there is an almost implicit assumption that a collective European response to situations of human insecurity would be much more likely to apply to states lying outside EU boundaries rather than to member states themselves (Study Group on Europe's Security Capabilities, 2004). Indeed, one can infer from this that the document's authors have a fairly narrow conception of human security, implying that actions such as structural funds for recently joined Eastern European countries do not fall under the human security umbrella, but that it is instead something particularly focused upon intense crisis situations. The document does however present a credible solution to the issue of how countries might fulfil their responsibilities to former colonies in terms of protection against insecurities. The suggestion was that such activities be carried out under an EU banner, thus diminishing the risk of conflicts of interest and a hostile response from populations in the relevant country. Furthermore, the European Neighbourhood Policy (ENP), proposed in May 2004, the umbrella policy of programmes such as TACIS or the Barcelona Process, seeks to strengthen 'stability, security and well-being for all concerned [Eastern and Southern neighbours of the EU]' (European Commission, 2005). Indeed, even if the ENP is based on partnership with states through action plans, these cover 'a number of key areas for specific action: political dialogue and reform; trade and measures preparing partners for gradually obtaining a stake in the EU's internal market; justice and home affairs, energy, transport, information society, environment and research and innovation; and social policy and people-to-people contacts' (EC, 2005).

The rationale for acceptance of this doctrine by the EU was many-fold. First, it would reinforce the image of the EU as a successful example of peaceful development based on cooperation, and on core values of respect for diversity, rule of law, human rights, democracy, and citizen participation. It reflected the changes in the strategic environment after Iraq and September 11, where Europe hoped to play a more active role in global security. It recognized threats as a nexus between conflict, insecurity, and poverty and called for the need to tackle root causes and emphasis on good governance. Yet, *Human Security Doctrine for Europe*, despite its misleading title, was essentially a defence and security strategy for Europe laying out criteria for intervention, in contrast to what could be referred to as the 'idealism' of the original human security concept which would largely reject military intervention in favour of non-military human security engagement. While it did insist on the primacy of human rights and the importance of locally led peacebuilding – as opposed to classical peacekeeping – it did not discuss, for example, long-term development policies. The HSDE thus identified clear factors determining priorities for intervention, even if it emphasized the overriding need for prevention and reconstruction.

The ASEAN presented another case for the dilemma of interference in the name of human security in member state. South East-Asian countries, except for Thailand, initially saw the 1994 UNDP definition of human security as a critique of the region's comprehensive security approach. This approach, 'sogo anzen hosho' or 'comprehensive national security', was introduced in the 1970s by Japan, shaken by the US defeat in Vietnam and the oil shock of 1973, to pre-empt economic and strategic threats to national security given its dependence on overseas material and energy resources (Ezrati, 2000: 144). The approach called for cooperation within the region, based on sovereignty and a policy of non-interference and de-militarization. The ten ASEAN countries, although set apart by their histories, political systems, and varying patterns of trade, sought regional development through creating a region-wide market and through strengthening regional competition.

The inter-connectedness of the regional economies was tested by the Asian financial crisis of 1997, which had a deep impact on the people of the region, leading to increased poverty, inflation, and unemployment. The crisis sparked debate concerning a human security approach. Thailand's Foreign Minister Surin Pitsuwan at the time of the 1997 crisis proposed a 'flexible intervention' policy, that would allow member states to engage in discussions about sensitive political, economic, and social problems with neighbouring states encountering difficulties, without however interfering with their sovereignty. The purpose of the of 'flexible engagement' was to create a ASEAN regional community in which individual members had responsibilities as well as rights and could discuss sensitive economic, social, political issues. But the discussions on adopting a human security approach, coupled with flexible engagement, were rejected by countries such as Myanmar among others. Yet, since the 1997 crisis, other non-military threats such as the SARS outbreak, bird flu, human trafficking, the tsunami, and cross-border smuggling have revived the debate. Although no single regional approach to human security has been proposed, ASEAN Vision 2020 adopted as goals 'freedom from want and freedom from fear for future generations'. In the meantime, significant literature on human security continues to be produced by South-East Asian scholars. Most of these observers recognize that the lack of human rights, the neglect of the quality of life as well as non-military threats such as environmental degradation, could undermine the stability of both the state and society, adversely affecting the people. They differ, however, as to the solutions: some suggest increased participation by NGOs, while others propose regional cooperation among 'like-minded countries'.

In theory, regional approaches are effective in managing a number of regionally specific problems. Providing indications for when and where regional institutions are best placed to promote human security does not however address the issue of when they will have the capability and resources to do so. On the other hand, regional organizations are structurally weak and are reluctant to intervene in the name of sovereignty. One potential solution to this problem is that international organizations such as the UN or regional organizations with substantial resources such as NATO or the EU provide financial and logistical support to organizations such as the African Union in supporting human security. A second possibility is that proposed by Acharya in the context of Asia, whereby regional organizations would leave military intervention to the UN in situations where sovereignty is used as a barrier to intervention, and that the region should focus on conflict prevention and the responsibility to protect (Acharya, 2002: 378). A combination of these two propositions is perhaps the best approach, bringing the benefits of regional expertise and legitimacy over the long term and the unique legitimacy of the UN in terms of intervention along with a potential means of meeting resource shortfalls.

Conclusions

In conclusion, human security can be instrumentally used by states in the name of intervention, but the human security approach is one of engagement with security issues on a long term basis, and equal engagement with a multiple issues that range from inequality to democratic institutions, to safeguarding minority and excluded communities. As one moves from a humanitarian intervention to a human security engagement approach, not only are acts of direct violence taken into account but also acts of structural violence and indeed threats to security that lie beyond the control of human beings.

By linking conflict, human rights, and development, human security offers an analytical framework for a shift in the means and ends of intervention. International action would not remain restricted to securing the rights and safety of humans in selected countries, but would aim at creating conditions favourable to social justice and equity. The concept of human security has significantly changed the notion of international intervention. Sovereignty is now considered a responsibility and human security could easily serve as 'an excuse' for the international community to intervene in other countries' internal affairs. Given the failure of the 'new humanitarian intervention' to fully address human insecurities, there is a need to search for legitimate and acceptable methods to achieve this. Proposals have been made for reform of the UN and reports have been written for rules of engagement. But many of these proposals continue to resort to fire-fighting in case of severe threat, rather than seeking structural change.

In today's world, regional organizations as intermediate structures are gaining importance and their inputs are crucial at the international level. Because of their growing influence, the advocacy work of many civil society organizations is focused on them. These moves have to be supplemented by continuous engagement on a human security basis rather than compartmentalization, neglect, and then intervention. If human security is a collective responsibility then this responsibility lies in the coordinated action of actors at all levels who must act in the framework of international law. At the same time, one must recognize, as Badie does, that 'It is not merely to satisfy a moral need that we promote human security; it is also because this is the only chance for humanity to survive in the face of the challenges confronting it.' '[Human security] is not only an ethical discourse [...] it is also a utilitarian discourse' (Badie, 2001). The main challenge is not to try to convince state authorities to be moral, even though their self-interest is not at stake, but to change the way they think and make them realize that problems cross borders in multiple ways. Human security threats are global in scope, which is why governments around the world ought to understand that it is in their, and in everybody's interest, to achieve it.

9 Externalities of human security

The role of international aid

In militarized language consistent with the post-September 11 world, international aid is said to be one of the most powerful weapons in the war against poverty. But as UNDP argued in its 2005 *Human Development Report*, 'that weapon is underused and badly targeted' (UNDP, 2005: Chapter 3). The international community has repeatedly enunciated its willingness and responsibility to help those whose human security is endangered. Foreign aid plays a crucial role at the intersection of short-term humanitarian relief and long-term economic development. It can work as a catalyst or reinforcement for the efforts of the people, the institutions and the governments on the issues of human security. Unfortunately its record has been less satisfactory than its stated intentions.

In this chapter, we first define the practice and politics of aid before exploring the positive and negative externalities of interventions on human security. We end the chapter with a few recommendations on what donors of 'good human security assistance' may want to consider.

Defining foreign aid: quantum

When the leaders of international governments met at the Earth Summit in Rio de Janeiro in 1992, they adopted a programme for action, entitled Agenda 21, which included an Overseas Development Aid (ODA) target of 0.7 per cent of GNI (gross national income) of 22 rich members of the OECD/DAC. The commitment was reaffirmed in the Monterrey Consensus Declaration at the UN Financing for Development Conference in April 2002, when world leaders agreed to make aid one of the building blocks of a new 'global partnership' for poverty reduction. Official development assistance increased by $12 billion from 2002 to 2004 and in March 2005, donors agreed to review not just the quantity of aid, but its quality: effectiveness, harmonization, coordination and country ownership, in what came to be known as the Paris Declaration on Aid Effectiveness.

According to the OECD, Japan had been the largest donor of aid during the 1990s, but as Japanese aid dropped by nearly $4 billion, the US retook this position in 2001. This was due to the United States' 600 million disbursement to Pakistan for economic support in the aftermath of September 11 coupled with a 12.7 per cent depreciation of the Yen. While Japan and the United States both pledged increased aid, they would still have spent only 0.18 per cent of GNI on aid in 2010, lower than any other donor country (UNDP, 2005). By 2005, the US was the world's largest provider of development assistance but its ratio of aid to GNI had increased from a base of 0.10 per cent in 2000 to only 0.16 per cent in 2004, placing it well behind other donors. The United States had approved an $8 billion bill for increase in development assistance, although the increase included large aid transfers for Afghanistan and Iraq (UNDP, 2005: Chapter 3).

The EU's 15 richest countries agreed in 2005 to meet a minimum target of aid to GNI of 0.51 per cent by 2010 as an interim step to meeting the 0.7 per cent commitment by 2015. Denmark, Luxembourg, the Netherlands, Norway and Sweden had consistently met or surpassed the 0.7 per cent target, while France and the UK plan to reach that goal by 2013. Canada was uniquely well-placed to set an early target date for raising aid to 0.7 per cent of GNI. Aid flows touched $100 billion in 2005 and ODA to developing countries from member countries of the OECD/DAC rose 31.4 per cent to a record high $ 106.5 billion. It represents 0.33 per cent of the Committee members' combined GNI in 2005, up from 0.26 per cent in 2004. Aid in the form of debt relief grants increased between 2004 and 2005, while other aid increased 8.7 per cent in the same period. The rise in debt relief for Iraq and Nigeria as well as relief aid in the aftermath of the tsunami were the main factors for the increase in aid.

Yet, the UNDP HDR 2005 assessed that assistance received by poor countries continued to be unpredictable, uncoordinated, hedged with conditions, and was tied to purchases in donor countries. Unpredictability of aid made it difficult for developing countries to plan ahead for such expenditures as teachers' salaries and infrastructure building. Weak donor coordination, a preference for operating outside government systems, and excessive reporting requirements had driven up transaction costs and reduced aid effectiveness. Tied aid cost developing countries up to 20 per cent more than buying the same goods on the open market.

The politics and politicization of aid: motivations in donor assistance

We propose to examine three political practices in development assistance which can be considered as harmful for the long-term achievement of human security. One such practice is the politics of conditionality which may weaken the states' capacities to provide human security. Another is the global consensus based on liberal peace as the rationale for development assistance which can exacerbate inequalities which can in turn weaken countries' capacities to prevent and manage conflict. Finally, a third 'nemesis' of human security can be considered as the post-September 11 emphasis on military expenditure at the detriment of development assistance. For an analysis of aid from the human security point of view, it would not be enough to look at the quantity of aid, nor only its quality. Comparisons of aid flows from the US, Japan, and the European Union reflect that much aid is still caught up in geopolitics despite a call to address the human security and development needs of all affected people.

Nemesis 1: conditionalities

Aid conditionality can range from explicit contractual arrangements on budgetary accountability to more implicit notions of what type of institutional, political, economic, and increasingly military conditions are necessary (Barakat, 2002). It can include punitive measures of suspending aid to require specific types of economic and political reforms, or human rights principles, which can be imposed through sanctions, such as was witnessed during the Taliban years in Afghanistan. It can also include positive approaches of rewarding compliant countries that reform their institutions and policies according to a prescribed policy agenda. In the view of the World Bank, for example, policy and institutional reform is imperative for increasing absorptive capacity of aid and creating better prospects for achieving the Millennium Development Goals. Conditionalities in the form of *ex-ante* prescriptions of policy associated with a programme of assistance were introduced by the IMF in the 1950s. The logic was based on a banking tradition: the client country had to ensure that it was able to reimburse the support received before receiving subsequent tranches of financial support (Browne, 2004). IMF conditionality traditionally focused on fiscal, monetary and exchange rate policies. From the 1980s, however, the scope of conditionality expanded to cover more fundamental structural concerns and public sector reform with the World Bank focusing on structural adjustment programmes. The numbers of conditions reached a peak during the Asian crisis of the late 1990s, when the IMF programme for Thailand incorporated 73 structural conditions, for Korea, 94, and for Indonesia, 140. However, as the number increased, the rate of compliance and success of the programmes declined (Browne, 2004).

Although conditionalities are necessary in order to assure that assistance goes towards the 'right policies' of 'good governance', or that loans are paid back and investments safeguarded, they can enforce the asymmetry of power and voice between the donor and the recipient country. Conditionality in war-torn societies can be even more problematic when viewed from the extreme vulnerability of populations and from the lack of bargaining powers of weakened administrative structures. From an efficiency point of view, evidence points to the limitations of aid conditionality as an instrument of policy reform. As the 2004 study by Brown argued, there are several reasons why conditionality has worked poorly as an instrument of reform. The first is that donors cannot agree on a single set of conditions. Second, implementation is not always feasible, given that conditionalities are often removed from local political realities. The process of imposing conditionalities reinforces traditional hierarchical relationships by failing to open up policy discussions to consultations about economic management, governance or human rights. It undermines open dialogue that is central to democracies and in the final analysis, it renders governments answerable to foreign remote parties. From a human security point of view, conditionalities can be especially detrimental to the well-being of the population as the case of the transition economies in the post-Soviet space shows.

Conditional aid in Central Asia: Kyrgyzstan in transition

With independence in the 1990s, post-Soviet countries were caught in debates between shock therapists who advocated reforms and rapid transformation in the wake of 'success stories' from Eastern Europe and Baltic states, and gradualists who argued for the Chinese model, with high growth rates and step-by-step approaches that prevented recession (Popov, 2001). The statist approach of the 1980s planned economies gave way to the other extreme of a minimalist state and free market. With the support of the IFIs, reforms were adopted first in Russia, and then in Kyrgyzstan, Kazakhstan, and with less success in Tajikistan, which had already undergone a debilitating civil war by then. Uzbekistan and Turkmenistan opted for closed economies.

Far-reaching structural adjustments in the economy were a condition of financial support from international financial institutions. In its 1996 *World Development Report*, 'From Plan to Market', the World Bank stated that differences in economic performance had to do with good and bad policies, particularly with the progress in liberalization and macroeconomic stabilization, with market reforms having better chances of limiting reduction of output and recover from transformation (World Bank, 1996). Thus, the package of economic reforms proposed to the transition countries consisted of macroeconomic conditionalities of the IMF (reducing budget deficit, devaluation, reducing domestic credit expansion) and structural conditions of the World Bank (freeing controlled prices and interest rates, reducing trade barriers, privatizing state enterprises, and providing property rights and promoting competition as a way of improving quality of investment). Initial reforms focused on macro-stabilization, price liberalization and the dismantling of the institutions of the communist system. Macroeconomic strategy emphasized restrictive fiscal and monetary policies, wage controls and a fixed exchange rate. Micro-strategies relied on price liberalization, while a number of key prices like those of energy, housing and basic consumer goods remained controlled. Macro and micro strategies were accompanied by institutional reforms that would ensure the functioning of a market-oriented economy.

The social sector, in the meantime, was deemed unsustainable as it had been maintained via massive direct and indirect transfers from the Soviet Union and through the provision of services by public enterprises. The states were encouraged to transfer responsibility for social assets such as housing, utilities, clinics and kindergartens from enterprises to local government, which, however, lacked the necessary resources or skills to deliver. Given that social sector spending had proven vulnerable to the cuts mandated by adjustment measures, governments and donor agencies began to design programmes intended to reduce the social cost of adjustment, such as social funds or safety nets, and poverty eradication programmes, like the World Bank-led Poverty Reduction Strategy Papers (PRSPs) required for concessional loans from the IMF.

All the countries suffered from the collapse of the Soviet Union, but some, which had followed advice on the shock therapy, may have declined further than those who chose to refuse such advice and opt for a gradual transition strategy.

Most countries underwent a process of de-industrialization, with decline in employment and wages. Development was in effect thrown into reverse as the share of agriculture in GDP rose and share of industry in GDP plummeted in all the countries. The debt averages grew from zero in 1992 to an average 73.5 per cent of the GDP of five countries (Armenia, Georgia, Kyrgyzstan, Moldova and Tajikistan) in 1999. The transition meant economic depression and the rise of new insecurities as well as the exacerbation of old problems in Central Asia. During its first phase, collapsing output, soaring inflation and cutbacks on social expenditures plunged people into poverty, and when people needed it most, governments withdrew crucial forms of support. While priority was given to economic liberalization and building of institutions of representative democracy, problems such as poverty, inequality, health, education degradation and social exclusion intensified with a speed rarely seen in a single region of the world (UNDP, 1999a). The increase in poverty and inequality in the region over the past decade, noted by the World Bank in a 2000 Report, was 'as striking as it is unprecedented' (World Bank, 2000).

Among all the countries of the region, Kyrgyzstan was the fastest to open up its economy and political systems. Privatization and trade liberation were completed by the mid-1990s, and the country was rewarded by accession to the WTO in 1998. Small-scale privatization was also completed rapidly, while large-scale privatization slowed after the mid-1990s. The period until 1996 was characterized by macroeconomic instability. With advice from the IFIs, structural reforms concentrated on price liberalization, currency reform, and the restructuring of loss-making public enterprises. Yet, as real GDP plummeted, inflation was high and the extent of the problem faced by the authorities, and their inability to respond sufficiently was underestimated by the IFIs. The period from 1996 to 2000 saw a resumption of growth and a decline in inflation, but the country was subjected to a large external shock stemming from the Russian financial crisis in 1998. Living standards fell, the currency declined sharply. Externally funded investment programmes had low outputs and the government relied heavily on borrowing, amassing large external debt. The period since 2001 saw relatively more successful macroeconomic stabilization, with some progress on structural reform, albeit at a pace slower than the IMF expected. The growth rate became stable at around 5 per cent per year. Inflation was reduced and sustained in low single figures, and privatization continued with most state owned banks liquidated or privatized (IMF, 2004).

Throughout all stages Kyrgyzstan continued to be considered a darling of the West, an 'IMF Protectorate'. The slow growth rate and stalled reforms were attributed by the IMF both to the external environment that remained weak (such as the spillover effects of the 1998 Russian crisis as well as internal weaknesses: weak governance, failure to return to the public investment program, the insufficient reforms in public administration and overall lack of implementation of reforms, and rampant corruption). And yet, if the IMF deemed the reforms as insufficient, the fact remained that Kyrgyzstan had adopted very ambitious structural reforms which had led to serious negative externalities. For example, it had liberalized rapidly its trade regime, slashing average tariffs. Cheap goods flooded in, a considerable number from China, undermining local production (Vaux and Goodhand, 2001). The Kyrgyz export base, in turn, remained narrow and un-diversified, with gold accounting to up to 80 per cent of exports to non-CIS countries by 2003. Industrial enterprises were unable to compete with the flow of imports and the agricultural sector had to concentrate on import substitutes, such as wheat, instead of increasing exports. In order to boost investment, Kyrgyzstan became more dependent on the inflow of external capital and increased its external debts, which, by the end of 2001, had reached a whopping $1.7 billion, 91 per cent of the Gross National Income. Two-thirds of the long-term public debt was owed to multilaterals such as the World Bank, IMF, ADB, while bilateral debt was owed primarily to Russia and Turkmenistan. By the end of 2004, the net value of public debt was over 160 per cent of exports and over 300 per cent of budget revenues.

The rapid and indiscriminate implementation of adjustment policies, such as privatization, financial liberalization and trade liberalization, had left the Kyrgyz economy in disarray, with a shrunken industrial base, lower real wages and more extensive unemployment and underemployment. While the state's debt rose, the structural changes had already had a devastating toll on the population of the country. The proportion of the population in poverty rose from 44 per cent in 1996 to 48 per cent in 2001. The World Bank estimated in 2004 that 55 per cent of the population in Kyrgyzstan stood below the national poverty line in 1999, up from 37 per cent in 1988, and reaching 55 per cent in 2004. The real GDP growth went from an average of –10.8 per cent in 1990–1995 to 5.6 per cent in 1996–2000. Inflation went from an average of 324.4 per cent (1990–1995) to 24.1 per cent (1996–2000) and the Gini Coefficients for income per capita for Kyrgyzstan went from 0.31 (1987–1990) to 0.47 (1996–1999). Ten years of transition widened the gap between the urban and rural population, men and women, the poor and the rich, and those able to take advantage of the changes, and the most vulnerable groups, like children and pensioners, for whom the care system significantly collapsed.

In Central Asia, the international organizations may have had an unrealistic expectation about the speed with which transition from a planned economy to the recovery of growth and living standards could be achieved. The policy advice provided by multilateral agencies to Central Asia was based on standard advice and instruments from other post-socialist countries, although each country in Central Asia was choosing its own path. Tajikistan was undergoing a bitter civil war. Kazakhstan's economy was primarily resource based, dependent on Russia and energy sufficient, while Turkmenistan opted to declare its neutrality and refuse IFI advice. What constituted as 'sound policies' for the donor and the international community did not always coincide with the policies of the governments, which were progressively more reactive as outputs and living stands fell and measures had to be taken to avoid the further regression of human development, avoid social tensions and conflicts and consolidate sovereignties at the same time. In the meantime, aid to the region was much less than needed and loaded with conditionalities to break up a central planning system (to ensure the irreversibility of reforms) and, after September 11, to join the war on terrorism. These conditionalities created the perception, among Central Asian governments and increasingly the public, that aid serves the interests of the donor, including, institutional interests, trans-national interests (IFIs promoting international accounting firms and banks), commercial interests (British and Canadian interest in gold), a combination of political and commercial interests (for countries looking to the oil and gas fields) and, more recently, political interests (US interest in political allies in regional wars).

Nemesis 2: a political model for the state based on the liberal peace model

The break-up of the Soviet Union, and with it the end of the Cold War, saw a demise of alternative criticisms of the liberal economic model. The triumph of liberalism meant an assumption, among policy makers and academics, that development would act as a de facto security strategy by preventing conflicts. War became identified as a 'de-developing' phenomenon and peace was seen through promoting intensified inter-dependence and economic linkages among states. The liberal peace model born within the context of the merging of development and security, came to argue for the accountability of liberal economic instruments and democratic practices of 'open' societies as a means of enforcing peace. The consensus among international organizations, be they the UN or IFIs by the mid-1990s, was based on the Kantian call for the simultaneous opening of political and economic systems and the interaction between growing economic interdependence and mutual democracy as a fundamental instrument of promoting international peace (Kant, 1983). By the mid-1990s, democracy as the best form of governance to fight poverty and encourage development, and therefore promote peace and stability (given that democracies do not fight each other), became a norm by itself within the UN system. If underdevelopment was dangerous, the type of development that was needed was based on the liberal model: a transformative development, conceived as the self-management of liberal markets, transforming social processes.

It is within this context of changing global norms and paradigms that development assistance in Central Asia was carried out. As the five republics of Uzbekistan, Tajikistan, Kyrgyzstan, Kazakhstan and Turkmenistan, broke from the Soviet yoke and away from a centrally planned economy and a closed political system to a liberal model of "open societies" in 1991, the doors were cast open for the increased engagement, both in terms of technical assistance, policy advice and direct investments through loans and grants, of the United Nations system, IFIs, inter-government bodies, bilaterals and INGOs (International NGOs). These models promoted the liberal peace approach of the dual goal of 'marketization' and 'democratization'. 'Marketization' was based on the neo-liberal or monetization models, which dictated macroeconomic stability, privatization and liberalization as shown above. The 'democratization' project was based on limited concepts of electoralism, multi-party systems, growth of civil society, freedom of the press, and, in more recent years, decentralization and devolution of power. The liberal peace consensus was based on two motives: to make sure that reforms would be irreversible and to avoid conflicts with other countries, based on the assumption that interactions between growing economic interdependence and mutual democracy (of open society, open markets) would bring long-lasting development to the region while avoiding conflicts. Yet, while the liberal model may have decreased chances for inter-state conflicts, it may have indeed exacerbated the potential for intra-state violence.

If the political and economic systems are more open in 2006 in Central Asia than they were a decade ago, standards of living plummeted with poverty and inequality breaking new ground in the region. While international policy strongly favoured free market economics and privatization, these policies had, in the short-term at least, pushed up prices and created high levels of unemployment. Structural adjustment policies led to a decline in the quantity and quality of state services. The radical transformation of the economy and public and political life of the countries of Central Asia was accompanied by a chaotic situation for law and order. The shadow economy, corruption and bribery, which became the most profitable ways to survive amid poor socio-economic conditions, grew, while the unlawful acts of officials became part of increased criminality as a whole. Personal grievances, namely poverty, disease, crime and repression, and personal crisis could be seen as sources of violence, conflict and instability, which became manifest in the March 2005 Tulip Revolution in Kyrgyzstan. High levels of poverty among the Kyrgyz population and inequality between resources available in the north and south of the country, coupled with high rates of unemployment led to a situation whereas mobs took their grievances to the street, toppling President Akaev. As Vaux and Goodhand (2001) argued, Western involvement also created its own set of potential conflict dynamics. For example, Kyrgyzstan's position as spearhead or symbol of Western modernism cost the country dearly, alienating powerful regional neighbours and decreasing the share of the pie available to average people (Vaux and Goodhand, 2001). The failure to control corruption and the monopolization of power by elites helped create a class of predatory interests, which employed extra-legal and illegal means to secure their ends. They were able to use external support, such as aid programmes, to further consolidate their position.

What led to such regression within ten years in Central Asia, especially among countries that 'best' implemented the reforms prescribed by the IFIs? The World Bank argued that the emerging poverty and the subsequent rise in inequalities were attributed to the 'social and economic dislocation of transition, the resulting drop in output, government revenues and household incomes' (World Bank, 2000: 10). Others, however, argued that the speed and extent of the reforms themselves, the rise of premium in education and healthcare, and state withdrawal were the reasons for increasing poverty, insecurity and inequality in the region (UNDP, 1999a). The debate over the cause of insecurity as an *outcome* of transition social and economic policies, or the original *input* into reform models, is an ideological battle between neo-liberal economic models and alternative models of social and human-focused development. Beyond this battle, global research now shows that rising poverty and inequality, regardless of its root causes, is not only potentially dangerous as it leads to potential grievances among groups (horizontal inequalities), but also to inefficiencies in the overall system.

The case of Central Asia shows that the liberal model could in fact increase corruption, competition, inequalities and poverty, and diminish the powers of the state when they are needed most. It questions whether economic development, devoid of its human outcome, provides in actuality a tool for avoiding conflicts – or whether competition for resources and markets may in fact result in an increased likelihood of conflict among a dissatisfied and marginalized people as well as a decrease in the society's potential to manage tensions peacefully.

Nemesis 3: conditionalities based on military cooperation

If conditionalities based on specific economic and political models could be detrimental to states' capacities to protect and provide for human security, those based on military imperatives have even a more direct consequence. Debates about military expenditure *versus* investment in human development and social programmes, or 'warfare' and 'welfare', raise the question whether development and security, in a narrow sense, are two independent variables, locked in a zero sum equation. With the expansion of the notion of security to human security, this debate was supposed to have become obsolete.

The end of the Cold War bipolar rivalry initially brought forth hopes that sufficient military security could be achieved at far lower levels of spending. By reducing global military spending, demilitarizing societies, and developing concrete plans for regional conflict prevention, global security in the twenty-first century could be preserved and enhanced. With savings from reduced military spending, developing nations could implement related reforms, such as conversion, land-mine clearance and the reintegration of demobilized soldiers. Ideally, industrialized nations would exchange debt forgiveness for military conversion efforts, promote full transparency and reductions in military budgets, and bring about the end of military involvement in the civilian economy. However, the post-September 11 increase in military spending, both in industrialized and developing countries, did not realize these hopes. Instead of the expected peace dividend, military expenditure at the beginning of the new century increased as the war on terror competed with the war on poverty and inequality for funds.

Since 2002, much of the focus on national military spending debates has continued to be on the need to increase military spending. According to SIPRI, military expenditure today is twenty times larger than aid outlays (SIPRI Yearbook, 2004). In 2001, the combined military spending of OECD countries was slightly higher than the aggregate foreign debt of all low-income countries and 10 times higher than their combined levels of official development assistance in 2001. In 2002 and 2003, world military spending increased by about 18 per cent in real terms, with high-income countries accounting for about 75 per cent of this spending. The increased attention on the war against terrorism raised concerns that development policies risk being subordinated to a narrow security agenda, with aid allocated according to geo-strategic priorities. The main reason for the increase in world military spending has been the massive increase in the United States, which accounts for almost half of the world total. The 'coalition of the willing' for example, was heavily rewarded in 2003, with economic aid allocated to Turkey ($1 billion), Jordan ($0.7 billion) and Egypt ($0.3 billion). Such aid was surpassed by an immense increase in military assistance to new allies of the US in its war against terrorism, including the new Central Asian republics, and in the Caucasus, and joint military exercises in both India and Pakistan.

One of the most damaging consequences of the September 11 phenomenon can be argued as the ensuing political and military conditionalities. In this case, aid provided by the US government has been contingent on the willingness of developing countries to join 'the war against terrorism'. In Central Asia, for example, support for countries was based on their allegiance to the coalition military interventions in Afghanistan beginning in 2001. By 2004, the website of USAID classified each country according to the extent to which they were supporters of the war in Afghanistan. Ironically, two of the countries that were not sufficiently well disposed to the economic reforms proposed by the IFIs, namely Uzbekistan and Turkmenistan, proved better friends of the US' war on terrorism. Turkmenistan allowed a 30 per cent of aid delivery to Afghanistan through its territory, and Uzbekistan, together with Kyrgyzstan, allowed the deployment of American troops on its territory. In the case of the former, significant aid was promised for this deployment in the Khanabad air base, not only by the US ($1,6 million), but also by Turkey (military support to the amount of $1.5 million), NATO (promised to help restructure Uzbekistan's armed forces), and even countries like China which wanted to insure their influence in an increasingly popular field ($600 thousand). This generous support reversed the order of countries receiving financial aid from the US, and put Uzbekistan on top of Kazakhstan. Until then, Uzbekistan had faced international criticism when it had refused the IFI recommendations to open up its economy. In October 2001, following agreements on the deployment of US troops in Uzbekistan as part of the war against terrorism in Afghanistan, the Uzbek government went from the status of a 'non-reformer' to a key ally of the United States. It drew an Agreement on Strategic Partnership with the US government in March 2001, followed by a Staff Monitored Programme (SMP) with the IMF, promising major reforms in agriculture, banking, trade liberalization and foreign exchange convertibility. Both these agreements were heralded as a window of opportunity for political and economic reforms in a state-controlled system. By July 2002, however, Uzbekistan failed to deliver on its promise, prompting the departure of the IMF staff in September 2002, and a subsequent renewal of criticism by the international press.

Critics argue that tying development assistance to narrow security agendas makes aid vulnerable to short-term attention span, with interest disappearing as soon as the emergency is over. This new type of conditionality also means that development assistance is increasingly confused with the politics of bilateral support and foreign policy priorities, instead of being based on social justice and enlightened self-interest in shared prosperity and collective security. Since 2003, OECD/DAC had been responding to US pressure to open the door for re-defining aid to include expenditure related to a donor-driven counter-terrorism agenda. The pressure to include military assistance as part of ODA, prompted OECD to examine the question at a DAC High Level Meeting of Ministers and Heads of Aid Agencies in March 2005. The DAC sought to clarify directives to expenditure related to conflict prevention and peace-building, specifying in particular that military aid could be included in ODA only when it was used to improve civilian control over the security system, civilian peace-building, child soldiers, and small arms. According to UNDP, in the meantime, for every $1 invested in development assistance, another $10 was spent on military budgets. No G7 country has a ratio of military expenditure to aid of less than 4:1. The UK has a ratio of 13:1 and the US 25:1 (UNDP, 2005). The UNDP argued that between 2000 and 2003, there had been a $118 billion increase in military spending, while only 3 per cent of this increase in spending was needed to finance basic heath intervention that could prevent the deaths of 3 million infants a year. The amount that rich countries spend on HIV/AIDs, a threat that claims 3 million lives a year, represents three days' spending on military hardware (UNDP, 2005).

Given that the governments of developing countries are usually threatened by internal unrest originating in social deprivation, poverty, marginalization, environmental degradation and ethnic exclusion, the rationale of spending more money on defence as opposed to social programmes remains an enigma. The challenge does not cease to be with just determining the quantum of development aid a rich country is willing to spare. In fact it is just the beginning of a long journey of transforming these resources to real benefits at the grassroots. While human security advocates argue that a better guarantee of security would be to use the cost for one modern jet fighter to offer schooling to a million children, the operational challenges posed to evaluating need gaps and channelizing this money to creating functional schools in remote areas of the developing world are complex.

Making aid an effective tool for development: the human security framework

Assessing needs

There are different ways to assess the basis for aid: aid based on needs and rights, on costs and on supply. From a human security point of view, determining who needs aid means improving needs assessment for greater consistency in the way problems are framed, causes of insecurity recognized, and risk factors assessed. Such an approach fuses the basic-needs approaches with the rights-based approach. It also means defining thresholds or minimum requirements which are ultimately urgent: insecurities should be addressed not only because they are threats to survival and dignity, but also because they could lead to renewed conflicts or inefficiencies. In conflict situations, monitoring of outcomes of interventions should be based on an assessment of the external environment and the changing nature of risks rather than the typical focus on the outputs–input equation of project management (Darcy and Hofmann, 2003).

Aid based on the needs (basic needs approach) or the entitlements (rights based approach) of a population are the pillars of a human security approach. These include 'core elements' of humanitarian needs, such as protection of life, health, subsistence, and physical security as well as freedom from violence or fear, from coercion, and from deprivation of the means of survival. Such a needs-based assessment is value-neutral. A more normative approach would be to base aid on the rights and entitlements of the population, regardless of their actual needs. Such an approach, although more controversial (which fundamental rights? which priorities?), would nonetheless by-pass the difficulties in assessing properly the needs of post-conflict countries, where logistical, security as well as capacity problems hamper the collection of data.

Aid based on costs of meeting long term targets is determined by the estimated operational and implementation costs of various national institutions undertaking relief or development programmes. It presumes trust in the institutions of the state in delivering development. The government of Afghanistan for example presented a $27 billion bill to donors in Berlin in March 2004 for sustaining the state in its peace-building efforts until 2015. If direct budgetary support is challenged by trust in the capacity of the state institutions to deliver, other mixed project and budget support tools are applied in the rationale of aid based on costs. For countries that have undertaken a costing exercise of the Millennium Development Goals for example, aid can also be based on the assessment, often conducted by donors, of what it takes for the country to reach agreed upon targets of development by the year 2015. Focus on the MDGs often transforms the discussion of aid from the short-term context of postwar reconstruction to the longer term concerns of development more generally.

Perhaps one of the least productive, from a human security point of view, but most realistic ways that aid can be based is on what donor countries are willing to contribute, often in the haste of a post-crisis situation, as it was demonstrated in the tsunami of 2004 and in post regime changes in Iraq and Afghanistan. When a country is in the media spotlight, pledging conferences are organized to draw investments into its peacebuilding or recovery efforts. Assessments are then conducted in the context of appeals for funds, putting into question both the objectivity of analysis and the successes of implementation. Needs assessment is then typically subsumed within a process of resource mobilization, conducted by agencies in order to substantiate funding proposals to donors. Such assessments often encourage supply-driven responses, and the lack of independent 'reality checks' makes it difficult to ensure that responses are appropriate, proportionate and impartial. In such circumstances, the political interests of the international community, or the capacity of specific agencies, national or international, to 'market' their interests may introduce biases in the situation analysis. One can argue that the reconstruction project in Afghanistan for example did not begin on the basis of established real needs assessment or a carefully planned process based on agreements among all parties to the conflict. On the contrary, it was initiated as part of a rushed 'knee-jerk reaction' by external actors to the sequence of events that followed September 11, 2001. In these types of reactions, the country's absorption capacities are often overlooked, leading to short- and long-term deficiencies in the delivery and impact of the aid.

A first imperative for development intervention in conflict or crisis situations is therefore to give greater priority to needs assessment, as a necessary condition for effective prioritization and appropriate response. A needs assessment based on the concept of human security should identify the threats faced by various groups of the population, the link between these threats, their causes and consequences, and, ultimately, the dynamics of the political economy within which any intervention takes place. The answers to these questions should inform decisions about whether and how to provide assistance.

Evaluating the impact of aid: externalities

The human security framework can be useful in an evaluation of aid (both development and relief-oriented) by keeping the focus on the intended beneficiaries: people. In all development situations, donors have responsibilities to ensure that their actions are not directly benefiting powerful factions or exacerbating existing tensions. While evaluation of development in conflict contexts has been limited for example, humanitarian assistance has seen a number of assessments since the 1990s, spearheaded by the Dutch activities in Somalia and the Danish-led multi-agency evaluation of humanitarian action in Rwanda. The Overseas Development Institute (ODI) sought to improve the consistency and quality of evaluation methodologies to enhance accountability and institutionalizing lessons learnt for monitoring the performance of humanitarian aid operations (Hallam, 1998). Evaluating the impact of aid from the human security point of view must begin by looking at motivations for the interventions, methods, possible externalities, etc., in a complex multi-sectoral analysis. Only then should more secondary questions of effectiveness, capacity, coordination and distribution be evaluated.

As an evaluative framework, human security poses the questions needed to understand the ultimate impact of development or relief interventions upon dynamics of other fields and on human welfare and dignity. Using the human security framework therefore requires policy coherence and coordination to tackle every intervention from a broad spectrum in order to accentuate positive externalities while reducing negative ones. Box 9.1 shows for example a number of possible human security interventions to tackle threats to the seven components outlined in the 1994 Report of UNDP, against the possible positive and negative interventions. Interventions outlined are not exhaustive but indicative, the purpose being to show the possibilities of influences in other fields of action.

From the examples highlighted below, we can deduce that securitizing human needs in different fields can have negative impacts in others. Coherence is therefore needed between different interventions in order to avoid negative outcomes while choosing multiplying effects of positive interventions. As an example, we propose here to draw lessons from diverse situations to assess positive and negative consequences that aid can have for human security.

Box 9.1 Positive and negative externalities of human security interventions

Economic security

Threats stem from poverty, unemployment, indebtedness, lack of income, etc.

Possible interventions and assistance by international donors

- Relief aid and public aid.
- Micro-credit projects (self-employment).
- Poverty eradication strategies.
- Safety nets and social welfare programmes.
- FDI and long term investments.
- Trade facilitation.
- Debt relief: low interest rate or cancellation of loans.

Possible positive externalities in other domains

- Increases in income (linked to food security).
- Social inclusion (linked to personal security).
- Empowerment of women (community security).
- Boosting the private sector (political security).
- Reducing inequality (community and personal security).

Possible negative externalities in other domains

- The state can become more dependent on foreign donors and is no longer accountable to the population (political insecurity).
- If solely targeting women or IDPs or other vulnerable groups, there are risks of marginalization in the community (link to community insecurity).
- Conditionality and politicization of aid could affect the political system (political insecurity).
- Unregulated private sector can increase gap between rich and poor (linked to personal and community insecurity).
- Increase competition between groups (community insecurity, political, and personal insecurity).
- Quick fix projects can harm the environment (linked to environmental insecurity).
- Relief aid can have negative long-term consequences for sustainability (linked to food insecurity).

Food security

Threats stem from hunger, famines and the lack of physical and economic access to basic food

Possible interventions and assistance by international donors

- Public food distribution system.
- Crop distribution and improved farming techniques.
- Midday meals in schools.
- Food-for-work programmes.

Possible positive externalities in other domains

- Hunger relief (responding to immediate need).
- Increased and improved agriculture (linked to economic and environment security).

Possible negative externalities in other domains

- Discourage local agriculture (decreased livelihoods and job security for farmers).
- Affect the population metabolism by changing what they eat (linked to health insecurity).
- Crops might not meet the soil condition (linked to environmental insecurity).
- Food distribution may be inequitable (linked to community insecurity).

Health security

Threats include inadequate health care, new and recurrent diseases including epidemics and pandemics, unsafe environment and, unsafe lifestyles

Possible interventions and assistance by international donors

- (Re) building the public health care system.
- Technical cooperation.
- Health education programmes.
- Safe and affordable family planning.
- Primary care.
- Prevention strategies.
- Regulating private health care.

Possible positive externalities in other domains

- Balance (re)attained in mortality/fertility rates (linked to personal and community security).
- Equal access to health care (personal, community security).
- Gender empowerment (personal, community security).
- Healthy environment (linked to environment security).
- Healthy labour force (linked to economic security).
- Nutritional programmes that are sustainable (linked to food security).

Possible negative externalities in other domains

- Replacement of the state's responsibility in providing healthcare (lack of trust in institutions, political insecurity).
- Family planning may go against local cultures (community insecurity).
- Stigmatization of disease and isolation of patients (community, economic and personal insecurity).

Environmental security

Threats stem from environmental degradation, natural disasters, pollution and resource depletion

Possible interventions and assistance by international donors

- Installing environmental sound management practices.
- Environmental awareness programmes.
- Implementing strict environment laws.
- Cleaning community water sources.

Possible positive externalities in other domains

- Recovering waste and polluted renewable resources (linked to economic and health security).
- Introducing environment-friendly technologies (linked to economic, food and health security).
- Mitigating the negative impact of man-made disasters (community, economic and personal security).
- Poverty eradication (economic security).
- Improved water (health security).

Possible negative externalities in other domains

- Ignoring agricultural traditions (linked to community insecurity).
- Exacerbating land disputes (linked to community, economic and political insecurity).

Personal security

Threats include crime and violence

They include threats from the state (through physical torture inflicted by the military or police), from other states (such as wars, cross-border terrorism, etc.), from other groups of people (such as ethnic or religious conflicts, street violence, etc.). They can be directed against women (such as domestic violence, abuse or rape), or against children (such as child abuse, neglect, child labour, or child prostitution).

Possible interventions and assistance by international donors

- Law and order.
- Peace negotiations.
- Crime prevention.
- Demobilization of soldiers.
- Curbing domestic violence through education, gender just laws, etc.

Possible positive externalities in other domains

- Freedom from fear, want and indignity (with impacts on all human security concerns).
- Domain development resource (economic security).
- Law and order (which has positive externalities for all security types).
- Strengthening human rights monitoring (tied to economic, community and political security).
- Demilitarization (community and political security).
- Employment (economic security).
- Gender empowerment (community security).

Possible negative externalities in other domains

- Replacing the state (linked to political insecurity).
- Militarization and increasing of policing (tied to political and community insecurity).

- Privatization of security (linked to community, political and economic insecurities).
- Creating stereotypes of ethnic/religious communities (linked to community security).

Community security

Threats stem from discrimination and abuse of various groups (including ethnic, gender, language, racial, religious, etc.), from group armed conflicts, from oppression by traditional practices. They also include threats to the integrity of cultural diversity.

Possible interventions and assistance by international donors

- Gender empowerment.
- Human rights interventions.
- Good migration policies.
- Quotas and affirmative action policies within donor projects for most vulnerable groups.
- Secular education.

Possible positive externalities in other domains

- Social harmony (leading to the security of all components).
- Culture of non-discrimination (economic, political, personal security).

Possible negative externalities in other domains

- Exacerbating tensions between communities.
- Cultural interference (linked to political, personal security).
- Exclusion if targeting specific groups such as women, refugees, etc. (linked to personal, economic and political insecurities).
- Racist policies (with consequences on economic, personal and political insecurities).

Political security

Threats can come from political or state repression, including torture, disappearances, human rights violations, detention and imprisonment. They can also stem from mistrust in the capacity of the state to provide and protect.

Possible interventions and assistance by international donors

- Support for transition to democratic practices.
- Reduction of corruption policies.
- Promoting democratic culture.

Possible positive externalities in other domains

- Reduction of political exclusion (linked to community and economic security).
- Reducing corruption and implementing good governance (linked to community, economic and personal security).
- Impact on a democratic evolution of political institutions (economic, political, personal security).
- Respect for human rights (impact on all securities).
- Improving the functioning of markets (economic security).

Possible negative externalities in other domains

- Imposing a particular type of governance system (linked to potential community and economic insecurities).
- Risk of creating new inequalities in distribution of power (linked to economic, political, personal insecurities).
- Lobbying and financial pressure by some groups (linked to community insecurities).

How aid can harm

Too little aid does not build the capacity of states to provide for human security public goods. Yet, too much aid can lead to lower domestic savings, and higher exchange rates which lower the competitiveness of national enterprises in domestic and foreign markets. Though aid is a key component of financing for poor countries, the spectre of debt from private and public financial aid is one of the most harmful burdens that countries have to bear (Ahounou *et al.*, 2004). For transition post-conflict states, which are heavily dependent on international money, this practice creates accountability to international financial institutions and taxpayers in other countries. Large amounts of aid means that both donors and the recipient states could be tied to the culture of financial accountability required for the management of short, fixed term budgets measured by indicators of expenditures. Donor funds are usually bound to tight disbursement schedules for budgetary reasons, which can create conflict with long-term planning and measuring of effectiveness through social impact evaluations. The notion of absorptive capacity refers to a 'saturation point' of aid, which would imply that after a certain amount, the marginal impact of another dollar in aid is zero (a very strong version of diminishing returns to aid). In fact this 'capacity' depends on the institutional and policy framework in each country which is not flexible in the short run. If absorption capacities are not there, countries cannot meet their development targets even with better policies, institutions and additional external resources.

Tied aid or bilateral aid presents two main drawbacks. First, aid is used as a tool of external politics, which means that countries concerned have political, diplomatic, and strategic interests helping certain countries. Second, 'tied aid', means that beneficiaries have to use it to buy material and expertise from the donors' financing of huge projects such as, factories, roads, or dams. Often projects are not integrated into the overall development strategy, not necessarily profitable for the country nor a priority. An example is food aid, 10 per cent of which is usually earmarked for relief to victims of war or drought. The other 90 per cent represents institutional aid automatically distributed, allowing US or Europe to dump surplus food stocks.

Aid that is not well targeted, implemented, monitored and coordinated could increase dependency, power and patronage of certain groups, and have negative impacts on coping mechanisms. Critics of securitization of aid point to the potential hazards of large-scale, uncoordinated, ineffective humanitarian aid. An instrumental approach to aid as a tool of peacebuilding,is also contested by those who argue that this inevitably leads to the distortion of humanitarian mandates and principles, particularly those of neutrality and impartiality.

One of the most important critiques of aid is the illusion of neutrality. Because in humanly insecure situations (such as conflict), aid is introduced in a political environment, it may create incentive systems, both positive and negative. Aid ultimately affects not only the size of the resource pie and how it is sliced but also the balance of power among the competing actors and the rules of the game by which they compete.

Langenkamp explains how aid in the post-World War II era was initially meant to be neutral and impartial, but the experiences of the 1970s and of the 1980s demonstrated that it was unavoidably political. In situations of conflict, he claimed:

> Neutrality (defined as taking no position that could be seen as favouring one side or another) and impartiality (defined as providing assistance to anyone in need regardless of affiliation) were seen as working at cross purposes in some cases, particularly where governments sought to take advantage of aid agencies.
>
> (Langenkamp, 2003)

That was the case in Cambodia, Ethiopia, Sudan or Bangladesh. Langenkamp also demonstrated that the decision of aid itself was linked to the interests of donors. In the late 1990s, the justifications for providing aid had grown 'increasingly political' (Langenkamp, 2003: 11) endangering the credibility, impartiality, neutrality and independence of donors. In his studies on Afghanistan, Langenkamp shows how aid programmes during the period 1996 to 2001 were undermined by politically contradictory goals regarding the amount of coordination with the Taliban regime and highlighted the major 'classic problems related to the provision of aid in violent conflict': poor coordination between aid providers, indirect or direct assistance of warring factions, encouraged displacement, dependencies of populations, etc. A UNDP 2005 study on human security and human development in Afghanistan argued that these discrepancies were not limited to the state of war and continued unabated in the post-Taliban period where international assistance became the main backbone of existence and sustainability for the new government (Tadjbakhsh *et al.*, 2004).

Anderson also underlines how aid can never be neutral, especially in a violent conflict. Aid agencies are often delivering implicit messages which contradict their statements on neutrality and impartiality because of different interpretations that can be made. For example, arms that aid agencies need for their own protection can mean in a war zone that arms determine who gains access to food and medical supplies, that security and safety derives from them. The fact that aid workers have better food or enjoyment can transmit values of inequality as well as the message that control over resources is used for personal purposes and pleasure, etc. In conflict situations, as Andersen (1999) argues, aid runs the risk of being illegally diverted to fund war efforts. It could distort economies by creating dependency. Distributional consequences could aggravate tensions between groups. It could lead to warlords foresaking their responsibilities for civilian welfare completely, and finally aid agencies could be legitimizing militaries through payments of taxes and fees levied by regimes in the areas where they serve.

Massive and sudden aid may exacerbate conflict if appropriated by military groups. In Afghanistan, for example, Western aid during the Soviet occupation (1980–1991) and subsequently during the Mujaheddin rule from (1991–2001) became an integral part of the war economy by nurturing armed groups, both directly and indirectly. Aid can also increase competition if the institutional mechanisms for equitable distribution have not been established. Aid agencies target specific groups, focusing on the greatest needs when they have limited resources. This can accentuate tensions between ethnic or social groups, rival factions, men and women in communities, and settled populations and repatriated refugees, which become the focus of interventions.

The distribution of massive amounts of relief aid such as food can create market distortion and substitution as it creates a strong competition with local supply. High profile relief programmes such as food distribution can be prone to corruption with aid feeding clientalist networks while replacing local responsibility for welfare. Aid can affect markets and distort economies by creating its own industries, jobs and wages. Humanitarian agencies hire guards to protect their goods and staff, leading to distorted salaries. They also import and distribute at no cost goods that could be produced locally. While aid is supposed to be temporary, it can compete with local economies and create dependency. Aid can have a substitution effect *vis-à-vis* a state which cannot provide for food, health, and other social services throughout the country, thus contributing to the crisis of legitimacy of post-conflict states. Assistance strategies, which bypass central government and work directly with regional administrations controlled by warlords risk heightening tensions between the centre and the provinces and potentially skewed distribution of assistance to favoured regions. Aid that solely focuses on a centralized state also risks not reaching target beneficiaries if a fair distribution is not planned or implemented by the government.

These arguments do not mean that aid should be withheld but that it should be better designed and targeted for human security purposes.

How aid can help

Aid that is well managed, evaluated and monitored can effectively avoid negative externalities. Practical interventions at the local level which integrate people from across factional lines for the management of common resources such as irrigation or grazing, trading networks, rehabilitation of infrastructure, support to the media, etc., achieve positive outcomes of peaceful and cooperative co-existence. Education programmes raise not only the levels of literacy but also have a host of positive externalities ranging from improved household health management, to decision-making capabilities, informed resource management, etc., which significantly improve human security. Infrastructure investments made possible by aid can improve economic performance, and aid can give incentives to private sector development. The involvement of NGOs and CBOs can increase both the efficiency of delivery and the accountability to ensure that aid, in fact, does no harm. Aid can also have positive impacts on more intangible factors like ideas, relationships, social energy and individual leadership. It can promote social capital, counteracting the social compacting which warlords create and use to mobilize groups (Anderson, 1999).

Replacing 'bad donorship' with 'good human security assistance'

Aid therefore is a double-edged sword. If effectively used, it can clearly help overcome development issues, conflict situations, poverty and insecurity. Otherwise, it can erase past efforts, increase underdevelopment and poverty, create instability and insecurity.

With a human security approach to aid and assistance, the aim is in fact to integrate the different phases of relief, reconstruction, development and prevention to iron out transition problems, eliminate contradictions and minimize negative externalities.

In crisis situations, although such activities may not always 'bring peace', they do play a role in supporting community coping strategies and providing alternatives to the war economy. At best, aid agencies should be simultaneously providing a mixture of humanitarian-, rehabilitation- and development-orientated assistance, in partnership with a range of actors including central government, regional authorities, local commanders and community-based entities. At the very least, there will be a need to ensure that aid (both humanitarian and development assistance) does not undercut peace building efforts and other policy instruments attempting to (re) build the institutions of the state.

Seamless development entails consultation and coordination of all levels and sectors. It calls for sensitive, well-planned action safeguarding against risks of politicization or manipulation by interest groups. A holistic approach cannot be limited to the field. In order to battle human insecurity in all its manifestations worldwide, the donor community needs to transform both domestic as well as external policy approach towards ethical responsibility and radical reform of the international financial architecture. Human security aid therefore starts with an ethnical responsibility. In Afghanistan, for example, given that its insecurities are a result of conflicts compounded by foreign interference, the ethical responsibility was to restore the long denied human security of the people of Afghanistan. Yet, a document called *Securing Afghanistan's Future* prepared for a donor conference in Berlin in 2003 argued that unless the international community provided adequate assistance, Afghanistan would become a narco-mafia state. Valid as this argument was, a human security approach would have put the emphasis on meeting the needs of the Afghan population, not the potential cost a narco-mafia state would have on the traditional security concerns of international and regional regimes. In Afghanistan, the interest of the West was for many years based on what many would consider opportunities and self-interest, often bypassing democratic principles in the interest of engaging with this or that regime. This was evident both during the Cold War, which saw the politicization of aid to overthrow the Soviet-backed regime, to its post-Taliban interest in winning the 'war against terrorism' and the successful outcome of an Afghanistan project designed through the Bonn process, even if this required the blurring of certain humanitarian principles and codes of practice (Barakat, 2002). The pursuit of short-term military and stabilization objectives in Afghanistan, i.e. eradicating the remaining Al Qaeda and Taliban groups through arming militias in the south, from the human security view point could for example endanger the peace. When the international agenda for action is based on a minimalist position of attempting to ensure the country no longer harbours terrorists, the more durable needs of the population can be overseen (Tadjbakhsh *et al.*, 2004).

We therefore propose that 'good' human security assistance requires the following five elements:

Evaluating aid and interventions from the viewpoint of the population

The most important added value of applying a human security approach is to 'evaluate' donor objectives and interventions against the needs and sensitivities of the local population. This requires an understanding of the expectations of the populations concerned by the aid provided, and thus taking into account their needs as well as aspirations. It requires the act of listening to communities and recognizing their resilience, which may have been eroded when the security focus was on the state.

In post-conflict situations, the first step towards reconstruction and development would be to recognize and value people's existing resilience to survive in conflict situations and to nurture coping skills in the absence of state. Adequate consultation in post-crisis situations is often neglected in situations where funding proposals have to be submitted to international conferences on a short timescale, while insecurity prevents consultation with various regions, and where the infrastructure for consultation has not been put in place. Consultations for effective consensus building on the elaboration of anything from development strategies to negotiations over small projects are imperative to disengage from state-based interests in security and design and implement a human security agenda. In most post-crisis situations, despite decades of violent conflict, there are community level structures and parts of a civil society which have not only survived but also continued to grow. Too often the international community does not recognize or value such local initiatives and insists on creating new structures instead of building on these. It is therefore also important that in such politicized environments, space is given for civil society to mature and to contribute positively to any ongoing peace negotiations or processes. By shifting the focus to the needs of the population, a human security approaches propagates then that civilians be centre-stage in the decision making on reconstruction and recovery processes.

Inter-dependence of threats means taking holistic not sectoral approaches

Even where sectoral approaches may be easier to implement, they may not be the best way to deal with development in conflict situations, not only because they may lead to fragmentation and contradictions, but especially because they fail to take into account the inter-connection between various 'insecurities'. Instead, an integrated approach to planning, budgeting and monitoring to avoid negative externalities is needed. For example, if food aid (relief assistance) is not correlated with food security (agriculture and rural economic recovery), it could hamper postwar agriculture recovery. Similarly, agriculture recovery needs to be correlated with mine clearance and the employment sector. The reintegration of refugees and IDPs should not be dealt with in isolation from the reintegration of demobilized combatants, given that they are likely to be returning to the same rural and urban communities. Although many agencies work on mainstreaming gender issues into their programmes, women are singled out as a 'category' in isolation from their wider social, cultural and family context. A macroeconomic framework based on market incentives may lead to inequalities and the proliferation of needy individuals.

Taking a long-term view instead of quick fixes

The tensions between a long term approach and a mid-term/short term approach are particularly strong in the field in terms of human security where development aid agencies are focused on long-term development, while humanitarian NGOs specialize in short-term relief. The former often accuse the latter of prolonging war and exacerbating conflict. Media coverage on the large amount of aid that pours into on-going crisis and post-crisis situations, such as in Afghanistan, Iraq and Sudan, makes it difficult to resist the temptation of quick fix projects that demonstrate quick results. As such, the problem in these countries is not the shortage of the funds but absorption capacities and policy priorities. To build the bridge between quick impact and longer term human security is to involve people in the recovery and reconstruction process so that they have a vested interested towards sustaining peace. Capacity building of local institutions is a slow process, which cannot be expected to grow overnight. It is imperative not to rush with externally imposed blueprints and template solutions. From the human security viewpoint, people and institutions must be given the necessary respect and the time-frame that suits them best, and not the constraints of budget deadlines determined by donor governments.

Strengthening and not interrupting the state-society links

When the international community takes the lead in determining interventions in a crisis situation, the danger is not only that a state's weak transitional structures will be overwhelmed and marginalized in the decision-making processes, but it may also undermine the role of people as agents of change. It is therefore crucial to support institutions at the national and local levels that enhance the top-down/bottom-up linkages. It is mostly through the state that people relate to the international community or to the international system. The international community can forgo the state and cooperate directly with sub-national societal units of the population. In this case it risks replacing the state, which would not necessarily enhance human security perspectives in the long-run. Human security efforts need to be locally sustainable and hence require an effective, legitimate, accountable and participatory political structure as well as an economically viable government able to generate its own resources. External interference is unlikely to enhance local capacities if it does not build upon pre-existing efforts and capabilities of those directly affected.

Applying a political economy approach

Perhaps the greatest and most crucial challenge facing international aid agencies is to start asking new types of questions. Currently, a great deal of relief programming is primarily short-term and technical. In essence, it has asked the 'what' questions: 'What groups are facing food insecurity, and what commodities are being exchanged at what price?' A political economy approach centres much more explicitly on asking *why* and *how*. How have patterns of relative vulnerability and power come about? If a group is facing acute food insecurity (or poverty), for instance, why is this? How have political, economic and other processes contributed to that group's predicament?

Any project in a conflict situation needs to be assessed against the background of an understanding of conflict as transformation. A potential conflict situation is a highly complex and rapidly changing reality. Although many problems existed before the outbreak of a conflict, consequences of violence can radically alter the political, demographic and economic structure of a country. For example, the gender balance changes when women become household heads in the absence of men. Migration of educated classes negatively impacts human capital. Displacement creates new ethnically polarized zones. Hence, changes brought about by conflicts need to be identified and incorporated in rehabilitation and assistance strategies. It is not only necessary to be aware of dividers but also of links between communities to improve the effectiveness of aid. The questions that therefore should be asked are: 'How does development impact on the risk factors for conflict, and how does conflict impact on development?' Such an approach would require awareness of the negative externalities that misguided or misused aid could incite. This includes, first, sensitivity to equitable benefits, second, flexibility in terms of planning and implementation, third, monitoring and evaluation which includes some form of peace and conflict impact assessment and fourth, strong linkages with society. An understanding not only of the issues around which the conflict became politicized (i.e. ethnicity and religion) but also on the prior failures of governance is important. This requires aid actors both to think historically and to plan ahead over the long-term based on knowledge and the willingness to learn lessons.

Conclusion

A human security approach starts with an assessment of who is at risk and how much aid is needed in a particular country. It fuses the basic-needs approaches with the rights-based approach to quantify a need gap that demands bridging. In a conflict situation, an analysis of the country's history, especially concerning aid and the conflict, is needed to know the root causes of the conflict. If the assessment process is not comprehensive, the aid programme design may be both inadequate as well as inappropriate.

Once the assessment exercise is satisfactorily completed, a human security aid approach demands a long-term commitment to reconstruction and development rather than military intervention and temporary relief. This entails proper targeting of large funds, implementation of programmes and close monitoring of impact from the point of view of the population targeted. The process of ongoing transformations should be people – rather than market – oriented. Aid has the capacity, in the very long term, to correct behavioural patterns and push for socio-economic change that dispenses justice. Hence, expectations of quick results in these areas would be sadly misplaced. Nor can donor countries set deadlines on the recipient state for radical systemic transformation. Ultimately, a balance should be kept between bottom-up and top-down approaches to guarantee an even distribution of aid and of peace dividends across regions and groupings. Sectoral approaches in general lead to fragmentation and contradictions because they do not take into account the linkages between the various insecurities. For a holistic human security approach, the planning, budgeting and monitoring of different interventions across sectors and levels should be integrated.

The wrong kind of aid runs the danger of creating perverse incentives leading to conflicts or exacerbated human insecurities. Hence, donors and aid agencies must be self-critical and aware of the potentially negative effects of aid. Direct assistance for peace-building development is only one of the responsibilities of the international community, and in many circumstances not the most important. Beyond aid, there are other responsibilities, such as stemming the flow of proliferation of weapons, promoting fair and equitable trade, and encouraging regional cooperation and the flow of investments and know-how. To meet the ultimate challenges of human security requires thinking beyond aid, since sustainable peace and development will, in the final analysis, not be the result of development assistance, but of home-grown policies and individual agency.

10 Concluding thoughts

Whither human security?

Human security in theory

We have argued in this book that despite lack of consensus on definitions, human security is useful as an agglomerate of interconnected concepts because it propagates an integrated and comprehensive analytical and political agenda. Human security finds its true potential not just as an addition to the existing fields of international studies, but also as a transformational synthesis incorporating security, development and human rights into a single framework, deepening, reinforcing and critically evaluating existing concepts and their interconnections. It allows us to analyse insecurities on a long-term basis and aims at addressing underlying structural factors and norms as they exist today in international relations. Because it encompasses a broad range of issues, it allows for an inter-sectoral approach, acting like a bridge (Thomas, 2004) where all different fields can encounter and use a common language to cooperate and integrate their actions.

Human security is a combination of major innovations in the security field that culminate in the shift from understanding international relations and security from the state's standpoint to individual perception. It allows for a continuum from prevention to emergency through a practical merger and reconciliation of human rights, human development and security. It comes within the scope of Mill's insight that no people can really be free unless they themselves fight for this freedom. It is, indeed, the means by which people shall be empowered and regain dignity, freedom from fear and from want that will leave them free to strive for democracy and rights. It is the guaranteeing of the Sen's 'functionings and capabilities' that shall habilitate them to advance towards 'democratic peace' stressed by Doyle. It is a rejection of decades of humiliation flowing from Strauss's 'doctrinal imperialism' according to which democracy and civilization need to be imposed. Rather, human security is the means to expand both sides of Berlin's typology of freedom (Berlin, 1969): the 'negative freedom' flowing from protection against state or community oppression in guaranteeing the limits of a private sphere and the 'positive' freedom to realize the socio-political nature of humanity by taking part in public debate and the elaboration of law. Human security consequently makes it possible to think of freedom outside the dogma of liberal democracy:

freedom as empowerment, as directing one's own destiny, as being one's own master (Reve, 2004a).

Human security thus represents a necessary widening and deepening of traditional notions, given the new imperative to respond to the challenges of globalization, weak and predator nation-states and new actors in international relations. Changing the lens of security to people as referent objects allows for recognizing insecurities beyond wars and violence, to what matters to people in their everyday existence and dignity. As such, it expands to non-military threats, or structural violence, such as inequalities or poverty, that are embedded in social, political and economic structures at all levels from local, to national, and global. Finally, the advantage of the concept of human security for revisiting security studies is that it incorporates a wide range of actors as potential providers of security, multiplying the opportunities for coordinated, international responses within a normative network as well as for new institutional arrangements.

If human security is an expansion of insecurity to new threats and of security providers to new actors, it also allows a revamp of human development to include the downside risks, thus helping to secure human development gains while building preventive measures, if not against the shocks themselves, then against their impacts on people. As such, it complements 'growth with equity' by the idea of 'downturns with security'. Achieving human security means securing daily living through provisional measures such as setting safety nets and political participation to mitigate any threats against lives, livelihoods and dignity.

By highlighting the relationship between security and development, human security sets strong grounds for more comprehensive and integrated development policies that can serve as preventive action. That underdevelopment and/or badly distributed development can, in some cases, aggravate tensions within a society underlines the vital necessity to promote an inclusive and equally distributed development. By encouraging the study of structural violence at all levels, human security allows an analysis of causes of internal conflict, such as how horizontal inequalities, which are inequalities among groups in economic, political and social spheres, launch a vicious cycle of disaffection and mobilization (Stewart, 2000). Beyond intra-state conflicts and military diplomacy, it addresses inter-state causes of conflict: hunger, disease, crime and repression, and personal crises caused by decades of war, thus attempting to pre-empt full-fledged eruption of conflict and the consequent military interventions through timely, stratified and gradual preventive measures. Once conflict has evolved, its resolution needs to be appropriate. Reconciliation should not be about stopping wars only, but also about preventing future conflicts and building lasting peace.

In common with the human rights framework, human security adopts a holistic approach to violations. The two enclose similar content, the first generation of humans rights corresponding to freedom from fear, the second generation corresponding to freedom from want and the third to a life of dignity. In fact, human rights, with their large and developed normative and legal framework could be the operational tool for human security. Human security, in turn, strengthens human rights by highlighting them as not only a moral necessity, but also a means for achieving global security, and allows a deep examination of the potential sources of threats to these rights as well as the structural conditions for their improvement.

In the final analysis, human security is a normative concept with a specific ethical goal that does not aim to 'idealize security as the desired goal' (Buzan, 2004) but to enhance individuals' capabilities through a better perception of their rights to well-being and quality of life. Human security does not limit itself to defining its goal by what it aims to eradicate. It rethinks peace beyond the classical understanding as 'non-war'. It espouses the cause of peace as defined by Annan 'the absence of war and economic development, social justice, environmental protection, democratization, disarmament, respect for human rights and the rule of law' (Annan, 2001) and by Galtung, 'positive peace' presupposing the elimination of 'structural violence'.

The criticism concerning the broadness of the concept is refuted in this book when we consider that the multidimensional approach of human security is both an advantage and a necessity – an advantage because it offers scope for an integrated approach and transverse analysis as opposed to the current, compartmentalized studies on security, development, human rights, peace, etc. It is a necessity because without this integrated approach, it would be impossible to efficiently counter threats which are intrinsically linked. The concept is resolutely ambitious and this is one of its strongest points.

Human security in practice

After presenting the competing definitions for human security and the critiques that the new concept provokes, we argued for the desirability of human security as a normative concept for a evaluating policy frameworks. While being relevant to all nations – rich and poor – human security remains context and structure specific (Hampson, 2004). For some countries insecurities encompass hunger and disease, while for others, they include trafficking, drugs and urban crime. However, while insecurity threats are context specific, consequences of insecurity in one part of the world can have widespread implications transmitted across the globe. Famines, ethnic conflicts, social disintegration, drugs, terrorism, pollution and drug trafficking are no longer confined to national borders. Their consequences travel the world, leading to inter-connectivity and inter-dependence among states and international systems on one hand, and mutual vulnerability among communities on the other. Human security is, at the same, time an independent and a dependent variable, and the interaction between the threats is mutually reinforcing – capable of spiralling into either a virtuous or a vicious circle of interlinkages and consequences.

A human security approach gives rise to a host of policy implications and challenges. The first is the central question of responsibility: human security by whom? This policy issue cannot be separated from normative considerations. Considering human security as the fundamental and inviolable right of all individuals – regardless of state citizenship – automatically impacts upon the question of responsibility, paving the way for the provision of human security in terms of an obligation incumbent upon on a wide range of actors above and beyond the state. However, this by no means implies a destabilization of international relations, for, as we have argued in Chapter 7, the human security approach does not bypass the state. In the human security perspective, the individual sovereign state remains the fundamental organizing unit and actor in international relations. The state has the primary responsibility for provision of human security to its citizens. Moreover, the recognition in the human security framework that the state continues to play a fundamental role may help to overcome the suspicion of some states that human security is little more than a thinly veiled attempt to encroach on their sovereignty.

Whilst accepting that the state is the primary provider of human security, a human security approach identifies three provisos to this role. First, in contrast to the realist paradigm, it considers the democratic, rights-based state to be the most effective and legitimate provider of human security. Second, sovereignty is redefined in terms of responsibility, and is, therefore, conditional upon the state's willingness and ability to provide human security. This raises the issue of failing or failed states, which in turn brings to prominence the linkages between conflict and underdevelopment. Typically, post-Cold War conflicts occur and recur within the world's poorest states; civilian populations are targeted and regional destabilization is common. We showed how a human security perspective is well placed to address the challenge of recurrent intra-state conflict. Third, a human security approach recognizes that even where the state is able to provide human security, it is not the sole provider. The ideal human security approach envisages the state as part of a dynamic and seamless policy network with non-state actors, including NGOs and civil society, international and regional organizations, as well as individuals and their communities. From a human security perspective, non-state actors do not compete, but complement the state in their common objective of promoting human security.

Given the definitional expansiveness of human security and the multifaceted policy framework within which it is ideated and implemented, it is unlikely and indeed undesirable that a human security approach could provide a detailed blueprint for action. Ideally, the human security approach should adopt a practical framework for cooperative action in which different actors work according to their capabilities to achieve different, but ultimately compatible, human security goals. A key consideration must also be how, if and where possible, to involve the individual in the promotion of his/ her own human security after all; individual empowerment is both a means as well as an objective of human security.

We argued, following Hampson, that a convincing way to operationalize human security within such a framework is by conceptualizing it as a global public good (Hampson *et al.*, 2002). Considering human security as a global public good brings into sharp focus the duties and responsibilities of the international community and organizations. Conversely, if human security is not considered a global public good, there can be no expectation from international organizations (namely the United Nations) towards upholding human security. We argued in Chapter 8 that the duty of the international community in providing human security is residual, in that it becomes primarily responsible only if the state abdicates responsibility, but fundamental in that it has the ultimate responsibility for providing human security. International efforts are being made as testified to by a series of recent high-level reports to redefine the concept of collective security and to convince nation-states that a human security approach is not only a moral obligation but also in their own best interests. A key insight of these reports is that only a collective, cooperative and multidimensional response can meet the challenge of today's interconnected, transnational and/or global threats. A persistent theme of these reports is that we cannot simply pick and choose which threats to respond to, nor can we prioritize them; they must be dealt with holistically and in a coordinated fashion. It is thus that human security identifies new sets of opportunities and interconnections that would enable us to respond to new challenges. As Sen points out, while the nature of today's challenges has become increasingly complex and diverse, so too have the instruments to respond to them (Sen, 2000b). Lodgaard, in this context, distinguishes between *foundational* prevention (to address deep-seated causes of human security through long-term strategy for equitable, culturally sensitive, and representative development) and *crisis* prevention (Lodgaard, 2000: 51–2).

The key question is whether this enhanced capacity can be translated into effective policy, which would require a degree of institutional reform within international and regional organizations, as well as political commitment. While the language and objectives of human security are increasingly establishing themselves within the lexicon of the United Nations, institutional changes to promote human security remain negligible. Even allowing for the fact that the concept is only a decade-old and that it takes time for institutional arrangements to develop around a new approach, the limited progress by UN agencies in integrating a human security approach is also a reflection of political sensibilities and political will or the lack thereof of member states. The question thus remains: can the network of human security actors, heterogeneous in both capacities and interests, work in a way that promotes human security, be it the broad or the narrow definition? Without a universally accepted definition, or a universally accepted coordinator (refuting the UN's capacity to play that role) it seems at first difficult to conceive how policies could be set, let alone be implemented. However, we can consider human security as a framework for cooperation and complementation, where the different actors act within their capacity and their interest together, but sometimes towards varying goals. The solutions so offered would be far from idealistic, but better than making isolated, uncoordinated forays into the field. Furthermore, even in such a scenario, the UN can be seen as centralizing agent, grouping together various international institutions that have different agendas (UNDP for development, FAO for food, Security Council for peace to name a few), states, and a great number of international NGOs (which are represented at the UN, and which are often co-opted by the UN for their expertise and capacities). Finally, even though the role of the UN is indispensable due to its unique ability to provide long-term engagement, prevention and early warning, an important provider of human security is the individual himself, who, through empowerment, can fulfil his own as well as others' potential and aspirations (Ul Haq, 1995).

A key obstacle to the operationalization of human security is the resistance of major states, particularly within the G77. Key players, like China and India, who would be vital to a global provision of human security, perceive the human security approach as a 'Western' attempt to impinge on their state sovereignty. Meanwhile, those states that have embraced human security, namely Canada and Japan, have championed competing definitions of the concept and have worked unilaterally to promote it. The reasons why certain states wilfully ignore the 'human' in the human security equation and maintain an attachment to a Westphalian concept of sovereignty were briefly described in this book but deserve a more nuanced analysis. However, the accusation levelled at human security that it provides the guise of universalism for the imposition of a 'Western' agenda cannot be ignored. Even if, as Acharya points out, human security can 'claim a significant Asian pedigree' (Acharya, 2001), human security interventions must be careful to avoid the perception of paternalism. In order to do this, human security policies must follow their own prescriptions, and wherever possible, strive to forge local partnerships. Ultimately, if each country has to decide what its own insecurities are and how it will deal with them, the idea of human security would be democratized and it would not be seen as a nemesis of Northern intervention into Southern countries.

The book does not advocate the use of military force for humanitarian interventions. Instead, it argues for a responsible engagement of the international community. Such human security engagement for international aid should be scrutinized for its ownership, impact, efficiency, coordination, political agenda, etc. Human security is an inter-disciplinary problem, and as such, requires an inter-disciplinary solution, which seems rather beyond the scope of present-day international organizations and government bureaucracies with their multiplicity of mandates for the various issues such as security, development, financial management, human rights, children, or women. Coordination is often hampered by 'turf' protection and lack of knowledge of how inter- (and not multi-) disciplinary approaches should be designed and implemented. The implementation of a human security vision requires reconciliation of the military, political and development objectives of the international community.

It also requires consensus at the global level for a new framework of development cooperation with a common agenda for priorities, strategic partnerships based on mutual benefit and trust, correlation of activities between international donors, linkages between domestic and international events and responses, and overall coordination between multiple approaches, including those of non-state or sub-state actors, nation-states and multilateral or international systems. Human security provides the framework to assess both the positive and the negative impacts of relief or developmental interventions and their secondary effect and externalities. Interventions that are not well targeted, implemented, monitored and coordinated could increase dependency, power and patronage of certain groups, and have negative impacts on coping mechanisms. There have been too many examples of fragmented and uncoordinated interventions that have actually led to more problems down the line. The best that international organizations can do for the cause of human security is actually not to increase insecurities by failing to coordinate properly between partners and between sectors. The ultimate challenge is to make sure that interventions do no harm.

The unfinished agenda: human security for future research

Human security as a concept needs to be flexible enough to adapt to changing situations and levels of understanding. The practical remedies to human insecurities should be geared towards analysis of root causes, comprehensive and holistic policies, and appropriate measurements for monitoring. Thus, human security can be constituted as a space of research that cannot be narrowed, not at least in during the times of paradigmic wars. It expresses the concern to relate or articulate specific findings resulting from classic disciplines such as economics or political science into a broader picture or coherent framework for a specific objective by means of a network of scholars interested in this approach. Despite the booming research that the human security paradigm has generated, there still remains a large body of questions that require further analysis that this introductory book has not been able to tackle.

The most urgent research agenda, in our opinion, is the study of human security indicators and by extension the identification of thresholds of insecurity below which life is unbearable to human beings and should not be tolerated by those who can do something about it. Thresholds and measurements of human security are especially complicated, given the distinction between objective (real) and subjective (perceived) fear, because security, on any scale, will remain a feeling, and because thresholds of tolerance can be different and culture/space/time/circumstance specific. Yet, research can determine measures of vulnerability, both objective and subjective, which are common to everyone and are universally valued. In the same way, among the many possible components that the Human Development Index could have included, the three most basic and universal were chosen to calculate: longevity, measured by life expectancy, knowledge, measured by a combination of adult literacy and mean years of schooling, and standard of living measured by purchasing power, based on real GDP per capita adjusted for the local cost of living (PPP). Although a number of scholars such as King and Murray (2001), Booysen (2002), Lonergan *et al.* (2000) have attempted to construct a Human Security Index, the idea of a composite index remains problematic as it would mean narrowing the scope of definitions, choosing among dimensions to include, identifying appropriate scale and weighing elements, and finding adequate reliable data. Ultimately, a Human Security Index may present unwelcome elements of ranking and as Mack recognizes,

> It would be deeply resented by poorly rated states. A low ranking would signal that the governments concerned were either incapable of, or unwilling to, protect their citizens. *Any* ranking exercise that reflects badly on governments will generate both resistance and resentment – the reason why UN agencies have long been discouraged from creating a Human Rights Index (HRI).
>
> (Mack, 2002b)

Beyond a human security index, however, it may be appropriate to devise a set of measurable indicators, both qualitative and quantitative which could allow scholars and policy makers new tools for identifying human insecurities, probing the relationships and causalities of threats, and ultimately, measuring the impact of policies.

Another area of research is the study of region-specific threats and menaces. Human security, like human development, varies widely along regional lines, thus cannot be understood and applied, let alone politicized, in the same way across all regions. Regional approaches to human security were spearheaded by a series of UNESCO studies. By mid-2005, the Social and Human Sciences Sector of UNESCO had commissioned independent reports on the 'Promoting Human Security: Ethical, Normative and Educational Frameworks' in the Arab States (2005), Latin America and the Caribbean (2005), East Asia (2004) and Central Asia (2006). It was also in the process of preparing reports for Eastern and Western Europe. Each analysed the multifaceted complex of human security issues in their regions. In the Arab world, for example, the major human insecurity is not only lack of political freedoms but also military interference by other states. In Africa, food security, conflict and gender inequalities may be the most pertinent insecurities. In Latin America, insecurities stem from the pace of reforms and the changing nature of democracies in the region. In South Asia, given the close connections and integration between the economies, insecurities at the local level are often the result of external shocks such as financial crises, globalization, etc. In Eastern Europe, insecurities resulted from the transition to market economy and democracy. While a small set of countries enjoyed a relatively successful transition, for others, it coincided with the beginning of violent conflicts, poverty, ethnic problems, etc., that have evolved into present day frozen conflicts, economic crises, border disputes, human rights problems, human trafficking, and the arms and drugs trades. Insecurities in India may be the result of overpopulation. Within each region, country cases differ. Within each country, insecurities for communities differ. Within each community, people are affected differently according to their entitlements, aspirations, wealth, capacities, etc. What can be learnt from these varied contexts in terms of social, economic and political models and how they relate to the capacity for providing human security and the way that insecurities impact societies? How are threats connected from the local to the national, to the regional, and to the global?

Research is also needed to see how human security can be applied to domestic policies. Japan, Canada and the EU for example, by adopting the concept in their external affairs, have taken as their point of departure the premise that the security of these states/regions is associated with the insecurity of people outside their borders. Yet, it is clear that human security needs also relate to the demands of people within industrialized nations. The implications of adapting a human security lens to socio-economic policies in all societies, developing or 'developed', call for fresh research. Similarly, as the effects of human security in each regional space is a function of both sub-national and trans-national forces. Regional conglomerates need to be studied with a special focus on their unique, region-specific characteristics and hence human security challenges. Human security is not a problem confined only to the developing world, and the North does not have all the 'solutions' for it through interventions, financial assistance, or responsibility to protect. The concept easily extends itself to Western societies threatened as they are by urban violence, job insecurities, epidemics, privatization of social delivery, militarization of societies, etc. The challenge of studying the scope of human security issues in Western societies is, perhaps, more than before and more than in other areas of the world, an imperative.

Beyond regional case studies, there are a number of other sectoral areas that can elicit vigorous research interest. What does interdependence of threats really mean and how can we analyse the cause and effects of insecurities across different fields, such as economic, environmental, personal, etc.? How are these variables connected? The study of causalities remains a widely unexplored field of research.

Finally, if human security was a window of opportunity that came after the end of the Cold War, what do the changes post-September 11 and post-Iraq mean? Will there be an impetus to keep focus on the peace dividend at a time of heightened attention to national and state security and escalating defence expenditures? Pessimists would argue that the window of opportunity for human security may have indeed shut, that the post-Iraq world is witnessing a breakdown of order, chaos, turbulence and random violence and a return to national/ethnic/religious/ clan identities as a counterbalance to an increasingly militarized unilateral world. On the other hand, however, the turbulence of times, the cult of war and Western superiority have also given rise to dissenting public opinion. Global changes after September 11 have been dealt with through increasingly military solutions, the negative 'securitization' of anything from a war against terror to a war against poverty.

We should perhaps respond instead by inventing a new non-military term, such as 'human dignity', if, ultimately, 'human security' is unable to move away from its negative connotations or association with 'securitization'. A new geography of the human dignity can be devised, with thresholds as the borders of tolerance. The focus would be first on the individual's physical security, then on his/her dignity of being, related to such variables as empowerment, pride, self-confidence, education, equality, culture, etc. Once these are violated, then the culprits should be sought at other levels outside the imaginary border, i.e. the community, the state, the region and the international community, not necessarily in a linear order, but as satellite entities around the human being.

In the final analysis, from the dark ages of war, only one thing survives: the thirst for new ethical norms to regulate the follies of global society. Despite the frequent and often legitimate characterization of the human security approach as too broad or ambitious a concept or a policy agenda, it is a call to reason. Its core objective is quite humble: to ensure that the situation does not become worse and that our lives are worth living.

Bibliography

Acharya, A. (2000) 'Human Security in the Asia Pacific: Puzzle, Panacea or Peril?', *CANCAPS Bulletin*, 27.
—— (2001) 'Debating Human Security: East Versus West', paper presented at 'Security with a Human Face: Expert Workshop on the Feasibility of a Human Security Report', Cambridge, MA: Harvard University.
—— (2002) 'Redefining the Dilemmas of Humanitarian Intervention', *Australian Journal of International Affairs*, 56(3): 373–81.
—— (2004) 'A Holistic Paradigm', in P. Burgess and T. Owen (eds), 'What is Human Security? Comments by 21 authors', Special Issue of *Security Dialogue*, 35(Sept.): 355–6.
Adler, E. (1997) 'Seizing the Middle Ground: Constructivism in World Politics', *European Journal of International Relations*, 3(3): 319–63.
Ahounou, M., Sayed, H.E., Antunes Dos Santos Rego, J. (2004) 'Financing and Assisting Human Security', unpublished paper, Human Security Class, Sciences-Po, Paris.
Alagappa, M. (1998) *Asian Security Practice: Material and Ideational Factors*, Stanford, CA: Stanford University Press.
Alesina, A. and Dollar, D. (2000) 'Who Gives Foreign Aid to Whom and Why?', *Journal of Economic Growth*, 5(1): 33–63.
Alkire, S. (2002) 'Conceptual Framework for Human Security', prepared for the Commission on Human Security. Available at http://www.humansecurity-chs.org/doc/frame.pdf (accessed 25 April 2006).
—— (2004) 'A Vital Core that Must be Treated with the Same Gravitas as Traditional Security Threats', in P. Burgess and T. Owen (eds), 'What is Human Security? Comments by 21 authors', Special Issue of *Security Dialogue*, 35(Sept.): 359–60.
Alpes, J.M. (2004) 'Thinking and Implementing Human Security in a World of States-"State"ments About the Potential Impact of Human Security on Global Politics', unpublished paper, Human Security Class, Sciences-Po, Paris.
Amouyel, A. (2005) 'What is Human Security?', unpublished paper, Human Security Class, Sciences-Po, Paris.
Anderson, M. (1999) *Do No Harm: How Aid Can Support Peace – or War*, Boulder, CO: Lynne Rienner.
Andersen, R. (June 2000) 'How Multilateral Development Assistance Triggered the Conflict in Rwanda', *Third World Quarterly*, 21(3): 441–56.
An-Na'im, A.A. (2001) 'The Legal Protection of Human Rights in Africa: How to Do More with Less', in A. Sarat and T.R. Kearns (eds), *Human Rights Concepts, Contests, Contingencies*, Ann Arbor, MI: University of Michigan Press.
Annan, K. (2001) 'Towards a Culture of Peace', lecture delivered at UNESCO. Available at http://www.unesco.org/opi2/lettres/TextAnglais/AnnanE.html (accessed 5 May 2006).
—— (2005a) *In Larger Freedom: Towards Development, Security and Human Rights For All*, Report of the Secretary-General, 21 March 2005. Available at http://www.un.org/largerfreedom/ (accessed 25 April 2006).

—— (2005b) 'Managing Risk', *Global Agenda: The Magazine of World Economic Forum Annual Meeting*, 2005 Edition: Available at http://www.globalagendamagazine.com/2005/kofiannan.asp (accessed 5 May 2006).

Annen, B. (2005) 'What Is Human Security?', unpublished essay, Human Security Class, Sciences-Po, Paris.

Axworthy, L. (1997) 'Canada and Human Security: The Need for Leadership', *International Journal*, 52(2): 183–96.

—— (1999a) 'Introduction to Human Security: Safety for People in a Changing World', Concept Paper of the Department of Foreign Affairs and International Trade (April).

—— (1999b) Interview with *Canada World View*, Special Edition, (Fall). Available at http://www.international.gc.ca/canada-magazine/special/se1t3–en.asp (accessed 7 May 2006).

—— (2001a) 'Introduction', in Robert Grant McRae and Don Hubert (eds), *Human Security and the New Diplomacy: Protecting People, Promoting Peace*, Montreal: McGill-Queens University Press.

—— (2001b) 'Human Security and Global Governance: Putting People First', *Global Governance*, 7: 19–23.

—— (2004) 'A New Scientific Field and Policy Lens', in P. Burgess and T. Owen (eds), 'What is Human Security? Comments by 21 authors', Special Issue of *Security Dialogue* 35(Sept.): 348–9.

Ayoob, M. (2004) 'Third World Perspectives on Humanitarian Intervention and International Administration', *Global Governance*, 10: 99–118.

Badie, B. (2001) 'Opening Remarks: UNESCO, What Agenda for Human Security in the Twenty-First Century?', First International Meeting of Directors of Peace Research and Training Institutions, Paris, 27–28 November.

—— (2002) *La diplomatie des droits de l'Homme: entre éthique et volonté de puissance*, Paris: Fayard.

—— (2004) *L'impuissance de la puissance*, Paris: Fayard.

Bain, W. (1999) 'Against Crusading: The Ethic of Human Security and Canadian Foreign Policy', *Canadian Foreign Policy*, Spring: 85–98.

—— (2000) 'National Security, Human Security, and the Practice of Statecraft in International Society', paper presented at the Conference on Global Governance and Failed States, Purdue University, Florence, 6–10 April.

Bajpai, K. (2000) *Human Security: Concept and Measurement*, Occasional Paper 19, The Joan B. Kroc Institute for International Peace Studies, University of Notre Dame, August.

—— (2004) 'An Expression of Threats Versus Capabilities Across Time and Space', in P. Burgess and T. Owen (eds), 'What is Human Security? Comments by 21 authors', Special Issue of *Security Dialogue*, 35(Sept.): 360–1.

Baldwin, D.A. (1997) 'The Concept of Security', *Review of International Studies*, 1(23): 5–26.

Barakat, S. (2002) 'Setting the Scene for Afghanistan's Reconstruction: The Challenges and Critical Dilemmas', *Third World Quarterly*, 23(5): 797–816.

Barakat, S. and Chard, M. (2002) 'Theories, Rhetoric and Practice: Recovering the Capacities of War-torn Societies', *Third World Quarterly*, 23(5): 817–35.

Bello, W. (2006) 'Humanitarian Intervention: Evolution of a Dangerous Doctrine', speech delivered at the conference on Globalization, War, and Intervention, International Physicians for the Prevention of Nuclear War, Frankfurt, Germany, 14 January. Available at http://www.focusweb.org/content/view/818/26/ (accessed 5 May 2006).

Berdal, M. and Malone, D. (2000) *Greed and Grievance: Economic Agendas in Civil Wars*, International Peace Academy, Boulder, CO: Lynne Rienner.

Berlin, I. (1969 [2002]) 'Two Concepts of Liberty', in *Four Essays on Liberty*, London: Oxford University Press.

Betram, C. (1995–6) 'Multilateral Diplomacy and Conflict Resolution', *Survival*, 37(4): 65–83.

Boer, L. and Koekkoek, A. (1994) 'Development and Human Security', *Third World Quarterly*, 15(3): 519–22.

Booth, K. (1995) 'Dare To Know: International Relations Theory Versus the Future', in K. Booth and S. Smith (eds), *International Relations Theory Today*, Philadelphia, PA: Penn State University Press.

—— (1998) 'Introduction', in K. Booth (ed.), *Statecraft and Security: The Cold War and Beyond*, Cambridge: Cambridge University Press.

Booysen, F. (2002) 'The Extent of and Explanations for International Disparities in Human Security', *Journal of Human Development*, 3(2): 273–300.

Boulding, K. (1991) 'Stable Peace Among Nations: A Learning Process', in E. Boulding, C. Brigagao and K. Clements (eds), *Peace, Culture and Society: Transnational Research and Dialogue*, Boulder, CO: Westview Press.

Brecher, M. and Harvey, H. (2002) *Conflict, Security, Foreign Policy and International Political Economy*, Ann Arbor, MI: University of Michigan Press.

Brown, M., Lynn-Jones, S. and Miller, S. (eds) (1995) *The Perils of Anarchy, Contemporary Realism and International Security*, Cambridge, MA: MIT Press.

Brown, N. (1989) 'Climate, Ecology and International Security', *Survival*, 31(November/ December): 519–32.

Browne, S. (2004) 'Beyond Conditionality: UNDP's Policy Opportunity', unpublished paper, internal document for UNDP, New York.

Bruderlein, C. (2001) 'People's Security as a New Measure of Global Stability', *International Review of the Red Cross*, 842: 353–66.

Bull, H. (1977) *The Anarchical Society: A Study of Order in World Politics*, New York: Columbia University Press.

Burke, N. (2005) 'Using the Human Security Paradigm to Guarantee Human Rights', unpublished paper, Human Security Class, Sciences-Po, Paris.

Burnell, P. (1997) 'State of the Art: The Changing Politics of Foreign Aid – Where to Next?', *Politics*, 17(2): 117–25.

Burnside, C. and Dollar, D. (2000) 'Aid, Policies, and Growth', *American Economic Review*, 90(4): 847–68.

Buzan, B. (1983) *People, States and Fear: The National Security Problem in International Relations*, Chapel Hill, NC: University of North Carolina Press.

—— (1997) 'Rethinking Security after the Cold War', *Cooperation and Conflict*, 32(1) (March): 5–28.

—— (2000) 'Human Security in International Perspective', paper prepared for the ISIS Malaysia 14th Asia-Pacific Round Table on Confidence Building and Conflict Reduction, Kuala Lumpur, 3–7 June.

—— (2001) 'Human Security in International Perspective', in M. Anthony and M.J. Hassan (eds), *The Asia Pacific in the New Millennium: Political and Security Challenges*, Kuala Lumpur: ISIS.

—— (2004) 'A Reductionist, Idealistic Notion that Adds Little Analytical Value', in P. Burgess and T. Owen (eds), 'What is Human Security? Comments by 21 authors', Special Issue of *Security Dialogue*, 35(Sept.): 369–70.

Buzan, B., Wæver, O. and de Wilde, J. (1998) *Security: A New Framework for Analysis*, Boulder, CO: Lynne Rienner.

Byers, M. (2005) 'New Threats, Old Answers', *Behind the Headlines*, 62(2): 8–15.

Caballero-Anthony, M. (2000) 'Human Security (and) Comprehensive Security in ASEAN', *Indonesian Quarterly*, XXVII(4): 413–22.

Caillonneau, N. and Hamill, O. (2005) 'Underdevelopment as Dangerous Greed and Grievance: Underlying Causes of Conflict?', unpublished paper, Human Security Class, Sciences-Po, Paris.

Campbell, D. and Shapiro, M.J. (eds) (1999) *Moral Spaces: Rethinking Ethics and World Politics*, Minneapolis, MN: University of Minnesota Press.

Canagarajah, C. and Sethuraman, S. (2001) *Social Protection and the Informal Sector in Developing Countries: Challenges and Opportunities*, Social Protection Discussion Series Working Paper, no. 0130, Washington, DC: The World Bank.

Capeling-Alakija, S. (1994) 'Shared Vision: Women and Global Human Security', *Development*, 2: 44–8.

Carim, X. (1995) 'Critical and Postmodern Readings of Strategic Culture and Southern African Security in the 1990s', *Politikon*, 22(2): 53–71.

Carnegie Commission on Preventing Deadly Conflict (1997) *Preventing Deadly Conflict* Final report of the Carnegie Commission, New York: Carnegie Corporation. Available at http://www.carnegie.org/sub/research/index.html (accessed 5 February 2006).

Carillo, J., Djebbi, S. and Röder, A. (2005) 'Financing and Development Assistance for Human Security', unpublished paper, Human Security Class, Sciences-Po, Paris.

Carothers, T. (2003) 'Promoting Democracy and Fighting Terrorism', *Foreign Affairs*, 82(1) (Jan./Feb.): 84–97.

Carr, E.H. (1945) *The Twenty Years' Crisis, 1919–1939*, New York: Harper and Row.

Carter, D. (2004) 'Human Security and Human Rights', unpublished paper, Human Security Class, Sciences-Po, Paris.

Carter, J. and Rubin, R. (2002a) 'Human Security and the Future of Development Cooperation', Development Cooperation Forum, Atlanta, GA: The Carter Centre. Available at http://www.cartercenter.org/documents/950.pdf (accessed 4 May 2006).

—— (2002b) 'Mapping and Explaining Civil War: What to do About Changing Paradigms', *Journal of Peace-building and Development*, 1(1).

Castillo, L., Miller, K. and Zelenovic, J. (2005) 'Human Security and Human Rights Compared', unpublished paper, Human Security Class, Sciences-Po, Paris.

Checkel, J.T. (1998) 'The Constructivist Turn in International Relations Theory', *World Politics*, 50(2): 324–48.

Chen, L., Fukuda-Parr, S. and Seidensticker, E. (eds) (2003) *Human Insecurity in a Global World*, Cambridge, MA: Harvard University Press.

Chenoy, A. (2001) *Militarism and Women in South Asia*, New Delhi: Kali Books.

—— (2005) 'A Plea for Engendering Human Security', *International Studies*, 42(2): 167–79.

Chenoy, K.M. (2001) 'Human Rights Violations in Kashmir: A Report', *Social Action*, (India), 51(April–June): 192–209.

Chenevat, L. and Kohn, J. (2005) 'Human Security as a Global Public Good', unpublished paper, Human Security Class, Sciences-Po, Paris.

Chomsky, N. (1999) *The New Military Humanism: Lessons from Kosovo*, Monroe, ME: Common Courage Press.

Chourou, B. (2005) 'Promoting Human Security: Ethical, Normative and Educational Frameworks in Arab States', Paris: SHS/FPH/UNESCO. Available at http://unesdoc.unesco.org/images/0014/001405/140513E.pdf (accessed 5 May 2006).

Christian Aid (2004) 'The Politics of Poverty: Aid in the New Cold War', April. Available at http://www.un-ngls.org/politics%20of%20poverty.pdf (accessed 25 April 2006).

Colard, D. (2001a) 'La doctrine de la Sécurité humaine. Le point de vue d'un juriste', *Arès*, XIX(47): 11–25.

—— (2001b) 'A propos de la sécurité humaine', *Arès*, 47(1).

Collier, J.F. (2001) 'Durkheim Revisited: Human Rights as the Moral Discourse for the Postcolonial, Post-Cold War World', in A. Sarat and T.R. Kearns (eds), *Human Rights Concepts, Contests, Contingencies*, Ann Arbor, MI: University of Michigan Press.

Collier, P. (1999) 'Economic Consequences of Civil War', *Oxford Economic Papers*, 51: 168–83.

—— (2000) 'Doing Well Out of War', in M. Berdal and D. Malone (eds), *Greed and Grievance: Economic Agendas in Civil Wars*, Boulder, CO: Lynne Rienner.

—— (2001) 'Economic Causes of Civil Conflict and Their Implications for Policy', in A.C. Chester, F.O. Hampson and P. Aall (eds), *Turbulent Peace: The Challenges of Managing International Conflict,* Washington, DC: United States Institutes of Peace Press.

Collier, P. and Dollar, D. (2004) 'Development Effectiveness: What Have We Learnt?' *The Economic Journal*, 114: 496.

Collier, P. and Hoeffler, A. (1998) 'On the Economic Causes of Civil War', *Oxford Economic Papers*, 50: 563–73.

—— (2000) 'Greed and Grievance in Civil War', *World Bank Policy Research Group Working Paper Series* 2355, Washington, DC: The World Bank. Available at http://www.worldbank. org/research/conflict/papers/greedgrievance_23oct.pdf (accessed 3 May 2006).

—— (2002) 'Military Expenditure: Threats, Aid and Arms Races', *The World Bank Policy Research Working Paper Series* 2927, Washington, DC: The World Bank.

Collier, P., Elliot, L., Hegre, H., Hoeffler, A., Reynal-Querol, M. and Sambanis, N. (2003) 'Breaking the Conflict Trap: Civil War and Development Policy', *A World Bank Policy Research Report*, Oxford: World Bank and Oxford University Press.

Commission on Human Security (CHS) (2003) *Human Security Now, Final Report of the Commission on Human Security*, New York: United Nations Publishing: Available at http:// www.humansecurity-chs.org/finalreport/ (accessed 25 April 2006).

Constantin, F.O. (ed.) (2002) *Les Biens Publics Mondiaux: Un mythe légitimateur pour l'action collective?* Logiques Politiques, Paris: l'Harmattan.

Coomaraswamy, R. (1986) 'Nationalism: Sinhala and Tamil Myths', *South Asia Bulletin*, VI(Fall): 21–6.

Cornia, G.A. and Court, J. (2001) *Inequality, Growth and Poverty in the Era of Liberalization and Globalization*, Policy Brief no. 4, Geneva: UNU/WIDER.

Cornia, G.A., Jolly, R. and Stewart, F. (1987) *Adjustment with a Human Face*, Oxford:Oxford University Press.

Cortright, D. and Lopez, G.A. (2000) *The Sanctions Decade: Assessing UN Strategies*, Boulder, CO: Lynne Rienner.

Cramer, C. (2005) 'Inequality and Conflict A Review of an Age Old Concern', *Identities, Conflict and Cohesion Programme Paper*, Number 11, October 2005, UN Research Institute for Social Development.

Dalgaard, C.-J., Hansen, H. and Tarp, F. (2004) 'On the Empirics of Foreign Aid and Growth', *The Economic Journal*, 114(496): 191–216.

Dallmayr, F. (2002) 'Asian Values and Global Human Rights', *Philosophy East and West*, 52(2) (April): 173–89.

Darcy, J. and Hofmann, C.A. (2003) 'According To Need? Needs Assessment and Decision-Making in the Humanitarian Sector', Humanitarian Policy Group Paper Number 15 (September), Overseas Development Institute.

Daudelin, J. (1999) 'Human Security and Development Policy', Concept Paper Prepared for the Canadian International Development Agency Policy Branch, Ottawa: Strategic Planning Division.

Degnbol-Martinussen, J. and Engberg-Pedersen, P. (2003) *Aid: Understanding Development Cooperation*, London: Zed Books.

Del Rosso, Jr, S.J. (1995) 'The Insecure State (What Future for the State?)', *Daedalus: Journal of the American Academy of Arts and Sciences*, 124(2) (Spring): 175–207.

Department for International Development Report, (2005) 'Why We Need to Work More Effectively in Fragile States', London. Available at http://www.dfid.gov.uk/pubs/files/ fragilestates-paper.pdf (accessed 3 May 2006).

De Soto, H. (2000) *The Mystery of Capital: Why Capitalism Triumphs in the West and Fails Everywhere Else*, New York: Basic Books.

—— (2001) 'Dead Capital and the Poor', *Sais Review*, 21(1) (Winter/Spring): 13–43.

DiPrizio, R.C. (2002) *Armed Humanitarians: U.S. Interventions from Northern Iraq to Kosovo*, Baltimore, MD: The Johns Hopkins University Press.

Donnelly, J. (2002) *Universal Human Rights in Theory and Practice*, Ithaca, NY: Cornell University Press.

Doyle, M. (1983) 'Kant, Liberal Legacies, and Foreign Affairs, Part I', *Philosophy and Public Affairs*, 12 (Summer): 205–35. Part II, ibid.: 323–53.

—— (1986) 'Liberalism and World Politics', *The American Political Science Review*, 80(4) (December): 1151–69.

Duffield, M. (2001) *Global Governance and the New Wars: The Merging of Development and Security*, London: Zed Books.

Dumenil, G. and Levy, D. (2004) 'Neo-Liberal Dynamics: A New Phase?', in L. Assassi, K. van der Pijl and D. Wigan (eds), *Global Regulation, Managing Crisis After The Imperial Turn*, London: Palgrave.

Dutt, A.K. (ed.) (2005) *International Handbook of Development Economics*, Cheltenham: Edward Elgar Publishers.

Easterly, W. (2002a) *The Elusive Quest for Growth. Economists' Adventures and Misadventures in the Tropics*, Cambridge, MA: MIT Press.

—— (2002b) 'What did Structural Adjustment Adjust? The Association of Policies and Growth with Repeated IMF and World Bank Adjustment Loans', Centre for Global Development, Institute for International Economics, Yale University.

Esping-Anderson, G. (1990) *The Three Worlds of Welfare Capitalism*, Cambridge: Polity Press.

European Commission (2005). *European Neighbourhood Policy: Strategy Paper*, Brussels, 12 May. Available at http://europa.eu.int/comm/world/enp/policy_en.htm (accessed 25 April 2006).

Evans, P. (2003) 'Asian Perspectives on Human Security: A Responsibility to Protect?', July 23, paper for UNESCO Conference on Human Security in East Asia, 23 June, Seoul, 35–61. Available at http://unesdoc.unesco.org/images/0013/001365/136506e.pdf (accessed 25 April 2006).

—— (2004) 'A Concept Still on the Margins, but Evolving from Its Asian Roots', in P. Burgess and T. Owen (eds), 'What is Human Security?' Comments by 21 authors, Special Issue of *Security Dialogue*, 35(Sept.): 363–4.

Evans, T. and Thomas, C. (2001) *The Politics of Human Rights: A Global Perspective* (Human Security in the Global Economy), Sterling, VA: Pluto Press.

Evans, P., Jackson, H.K. and Putnam, R. (eds) (1993) *Double-Edged Diplomacy: International Bargaining and Domestic Politics*, Berkeley and Los Angeles, CA: University of California Press.

Ezrati, M. (2000) *Kawari: How Japan's Economic and Cultural Transformation Will Alter the Balance of Power Among Nations*, Massachusetts: Perseus Books.

Fanon, F. (1963) *The Wretched of the Earth*, New York: Grove Weidenfield.

Finnemore, M. (1996) 'Norms, Culture, and World Politics: Insights from Sociology's Institutionalism', *International Organization*, 50,(2): 325–47.

Finnemore, M. and Sikkink, K. (1998) 'International Norm Dynamics and Political Change', *International Organization*, 52(4) (Autumn): 887–917.

Florinin, A.M. and Simmons, P.J. (1997) 'The New Security Thinking: A Review of the North American Literature', Rockefeller Brothers Fund Project on World Security, New York: Carnegie.

Foucault, M. (2000) 'Lemon and Milk', in J. Faubion (ed.), *Power*, New York: New Press, 435–8, translated by Robert Hurley.

Fuentes, C, and Aravena, F.R. (2005) 'Promoting Human Security: Ethical, Normative and Educational Frameworks in the Caribbean', Paris: SHS/FPH/ UNESCO. Available at http://unesdoc.unesco.org/images/0013/001389/138940e.pdf (accessed 5 May 2006).

Fukuda-Parr, S. (2003) 'The New Threats to Human Security in the Era of Globalization', in L. Chen, S. Fukuda-Parr and E. Seidensticker (eds), *Human Insecurity in a Global World*, Global Equity Initiative, Cambridge, MA: Harvard University Press.

—— (2006 forthcoming) 'International Cooperation for Human Security: A Coherent Agenda for Development and Conflict Prevention', *Kokuren Kenkyu Journal* (Journal of UN Studies) Japan.

Fukuda-Parr, S. and Shiva Kumar, A.K (eds) (2005) *Readings in Human Development: Concepts, Measures and Policies for a Development Paradigm*, New Delhi: Oxford University Press.

Fukuyama, F. (1992) *The End of History and the Last Man*, New York: Penguin.

Furtado, X. (2000) 'Human Security and Asia's Financial Crisis: A Critique of Canadian Policy', *International Journal*, 55(3).

Galtung, J. (1969) 'Violence, Peace, and Peace Research', *Journal of Peace Research*, 6: 170–1.

—— (2003) 'Human Needs, Humanitarian Intervention, Human Security and the War in Iraq', Keynote Speech, Sophia University/ICU, 14 December, Tokyo. Available at http://www. transnational.org/forum/meet/2004/Galtung_HumanNeeds.html (accessed 5 May 2006).

Gasper, D. (2005a) *The Ethics of Development: From Economism to Human Development*, New Delhi: Vistar Publications.

—— (2005b) 'Securing Humanity: Situating "Human Security" as Concept and Discourse', *Journal of Human Development Special Issue*, 6(2) (July): 221–45.

George, J. (1993) 'Of Interaction and Closure: Neorealism and the New World Order', *Millennium*, 22(2): 555–92.

Giacomazzi, M. (2005) 'Human Rights and Human Responsibilities: A Necessary Balance?', Markkula Center for Applied Ethics, Santa Clara University. Available at http://www.scu.edu/ethics/practicing/focusareas/global_ethics/laughlin-lectures/balance-rights-responsibilities. html (accessed 25 April 2006).

Gilpin, R. (1981) *War and Change in International Politics*, Cambridge: Cambridge University Press.

Glendon, M.A. (2000) 'Rights from Wrongs', in H.J. Steiner and P. Alston (eds), *International Human Rights in Context: Law, Politics, Morals*, Oxford: Oxford University Press.

Goldstein, J. and Keohane, R.O. (eds) (1993) *Ideas and Foreign Policy: Beliefs, Institutions, and Political Change*, Ithaca, NY: Cornell University Press.

Gómez Buendía, H. (2002) 'Human Development: An Introduction', unpublished basic text prepared for the Los Andes University Course on Human Development, Bogotá, Colombia.

Goodhand, J. (2002) 'Aiding Violence or Building Peace? The Role of International Aid in Afghanistan', *Third World Quarterly*, 23(5): 837–59.

—— (2003) 'Enduring Disorder and Persistent Poverty: A Review of the Linkages Between War and Chronic Poverty' *World Development*, 31(3) (March): 629–46.

Gordon, C. (1991) 'Governmental Rationality: An Introduction', in G. Burchell, C. Gordon and P. Miller (eds), *The Foucault Effect – Studies in Governmentality*, Chicago, IL: University Of Chicago Press.

Gordon, S. (2004) 'Understanding the Priorities for Civil-Military Co-operation (CIMIC)', *The Journal of Humanitarian Assistance*, 13 July. Available at http://jha.ac/articles/a068.htm (accessed 5 April 2006).

Graham, D.T. and Poku, N.K. (eds) (2000) *Migration, Globalization and Human Security*, London: Routledge.

Grayson, K. (2001) 'Human Security In The Global Era', in D. Drache (ed.), *The Market or the Public Domain: Global Governance and the Asymmetry of Power*, New York: Routledge, 229–52.

—— (2004) 'A Challenge to the Power over Knowledge of Traditional Security Studies', in P. Burgess and T. Owen (eds), 'What is Human Security? Comments by 21 authors', Special Issue of *Security Dialogue*, 35(Sept.): 357.

Gurr, T. (1968) 'A Causal Model of Civil Strife: A Comparative Analysis Using New Indices', *American Political Science Review*, 62(4): 1104–24.

Haftendorn, H. (1991) 'The Security Puzzle, Theory-Building and Discipline-Building in International Security', *International Studies Quarterly*, 35(1): 3–17.

Hallam, A. (1998) 'Evaluating Humanitarian Assistance Programmes in Complex Emergencies', *Good Practice Review*, 7. London: Overseas Development Institute (ODI).

Hampson, F.O. and Aall, P. (eds) (2001) *Turbulent Peace: The Challenges of Managing International Conflict*, Washington, DC: United States Institute of Peace Press.

Hampson, F.O. with Daudelin, J., Hay, J., Reid, H. and Martin, T. (2002) *Madness in the Multitude: Human Security and Word Disorder*, Oxford: Oxford University Press.

—— (2004) 'A Concept in Need of a Global Policy Response', in P. Burgess and T. Owen (eds), 'What is Human Security?', Comments by 21 authors, Special Issue of *Security Dialogue*, 35(Sept.): 349–50.

Hart, A. (2004) 'What is Human Security: And Does it Matter?' unpublished paper for Human Security Class, Sciences-Po, Paris.

Hasenclever, A., Mayer, P. and Rittberger, V. (1996) 'Interests, Power, Knowledge: The Study of International Regimes', *Mershon International Studies Review*, 40(2): 177–228.

Harshe, R. (2005) 'Gramscian Hegemony and the Legitimation of Imperialism', in K. Bajpai and S. Mallavarapu (eds), *International Relations in India: Bringing Theory Back Home*, New Delhi: Orient Longman, 172–222.

Haut Conseil de la Coopération Internationale (2002) *Biens Publics mondiaux et coopération internationale, nouvelle stratégie pour de nouveaux enjeux*, Paris: Karthala.

Henkin, L. (1990) 'Epilogue: Human Rights and Competing Ideas', in *Age of Rights*, New York: Columbia University Press, 81–193.

Higate, P. and Henry, M. (2004) 'Engendering (In)security in Peace Support Operations', *Security Dialogue*, 35(4): 485–6.

High Level Panel on Threats, Challenges and Change (2004) 'A More Secure World: Our Shared Responsibility', December. Available at http://un.org/secureworld/report.pdf (accessed 25 April 2006).

Holmqvist, C. (2005) 'Private Security Companies: The Case for Regulation', *SIPRI Paper*, no. 9, January. Stockholm International Peace Research Institute.

Holmstrom, N. (2004) 'Security and Global Justice', *Logos*, 3(2) (Spring). Available at http://www.logosjournal.com/issue_3.2/holmstrom.htm (accessed 5 May 2006).

Holsti, K.J. (1996) *The State, War, and the State of War*, Cambridge: Cambridge University Press.

Homer-Dixon, T. (1999) *Environment, Scarcity, and Violence*, Princeton, NJ: Princeton University Press.

Homer-Dixon, T. and Blitt, J. (eds) (1998) *Ecoviolence: Links Among Environment, Population, and Security*, New York: Rowman and Littlefield.

Hough, P. (2005) 'Who's Securing Whom? The Need for International Relations to Embrace Human Security', *St Antony's International Review, Special Issue on Human Security*, 1(2) (November): 72–88.

Hubert, D. (2004) 'An Idea that Works in Practice', in P. Burgess and T. Owen (eds), 'What is Human Security? Comments by 21 authors', Special Issue of *Security Dialogue*, 35(Sept.): 351–2.

Hudson, H. (2005) 'Doing' Security As Though Humans Matter: A Feminist Perspective on Gender and the Politics of Human Security', *Security Dialogue*, 36(June): 155–74.

Human Security Council (1999–2000), *Ottawa Law Review*, 31(2): 214–41.

Humphreys, M. (2003) *Economics and Violent Conflict*, Cambridge, MA: Harvard University. Available at http://www.preventconflcit.org/portal/economics (accessed 2 February 2006).

Huntington, S. (1993) 'Clash of Civilizations', *Foreign Affairs*, 72: 22–49.

Independent Commission on Disarmament and Security Issues chaired by Olaf Palme (1982) *Common Security: A Blueprint for Survival*, New York: Simon and Schuster.

Independent Commission on International Development Issues (1980) *North–South: A Programme for Survival (Brandt Report)*, London: Pan Books.

International Commission on Intervention and State Sovereignty (ICISS) (2001) *The Responsibility to Protect*, Report of the Commission. International Development Research Center. Canada. Available at http://www.dfait-maeci.gc.ca/iciss-ciise/pdf/Commission-Report.pdf (accessed 5 May 2006).

International Crisis Group (2001) *Uzbekistan at Ten: Repression and Instability*, Osh/ Brussels: International Crisis Group.

—— (2002) 'The OSCE in Central Asia: A New Strategy', ICG Asia Report, no. 38, September.

—— (2003) *Cracks in the Marble: Turkmenistan's Failing Dictatorship*, Osh/Brussels: International Crisis Group.

International Peace Research Institute, Oslo, The World's Armed Conflicts site. Available at http://www.jmk.su (accessed 25 April 2006).

International Monetary Fund (2004) 'The Kyrgyz Republic: Ex Post Assessment of Longer-Term Program Engagement – Staff Report', 5 November.

International Task Force on Global Public Goods (2004) 'International Cooperation in the National Interest: Across-Cutting Approach to Enhancing the Provision of Global Public Goods with Specific Focus on Global Commons'. Available at http://www.gpgtaskforce.org/bazment.aspx?page_id=147 (accessed 7 May 2006).

IPA/FAFO (2001) 'Private Sector Actors in Zones of Conflict: Research Challenges and Policy Responses', IPA Workshop Report, April. Available at http://www.fafo.no/nsp/ipa-report.pdf (accessed 5 May, 2006).

Irwin, R. (ed.) (2001) *Ethics and Security in Canadian Foreign Policy*, Vancouver: UBC Press.

Jackson, R.H. (1990) *Quasi-states: Sovereignty, International Relations and the Third World*, Cambridge: Cambridge University Press.

Jackson, R. (1998) 'Surrogate Sovereignty? Great Power Responsibility and Failed States', Institute of International Relations Working Paper No. 25, Canada: University of British Columbia. Available at http://www.iir.ubc.ca/pdffiles/webwp25.pdf (accessed 5 May 2006).

—— (2000) *Global Covenant – Human Conduct In A World Of States*, Oxford: Oxford University Press.

Japan Ministry of Foreign Affairs (2000) 'Section 2, Human Security and ODA', in *ODA Annual Report*, Ministry of Foreign Affairs of Japan, February. Available at http://www.mofa.go.jp/policy/oda/summary/1999/ov2_1_04.html (accessed 25 April 2006).

Johnson, M. (1987) 'The Contributions of Eleanor and Franklin Roosevelt to the Development of International Protection for Human Rights', *Human Rights Quarterly*, 9: 19–48.

Kaldor, M. (2003) 'Perspectives On Global Governance: Why the Security Framework Matters', paper presented at the Conference Taking the Initiative on Global Governance and Sustainable Development, Paris: IDDRI, 13–14 April. Available at http://www.iddri.org/iddri/telecharge/G8/kaldor.pdf (accessed 5 May 2006).

—— (2004) 'A Human Security Doctrine for Europe and Beyond', *International Herald Tribune*, 30 September.

Kaldor, M. and Vashee, B. (eds) (1997) *New Wars: Restructuring the Global Military Sector*, London: Pinter.

Kaldor, M., Gladius, M. and Anheier, H. (eds) (2002) 'The State of Global Civil Society Before and After September 11', in *Global Civil Society*, Oxford: Oxford University Press, 3–22.

Kanbur, R. (2000) 'Aid, Conditionality and Debt in Africa', in F. Tarp (ed.), *Foreign Aid and Development*, London: Routledge.

—— (2003) 'The Economics of International Aid', paper prepared for Serge S. Christophe-Kolm and J. Mercier-Ythier (eds), *Handbook on The Economics of Giving, Reciprocity and Altruism*, North-Holland, July 2006. Available at www.arts.cornell.edu/poverty/kanbur/HandbookAid.pdf (accessed 5 May 2006).

Kant, I. (1983) *Perpetual Peace and Other Essays on Politics, History and Morals*, Indianapolis, IN: Hackett Publishing Company.

Katzenstein, P.J. (ed.) (1996) *The Culture of National Security: Norms and Identity in World Politics*, New York: Columbia University Press.

Kaul, I. (2000) 'Global Public Goods: A New Way to Balance the World's Books – What is a Public Good?', *Le Monde Diplomatique*, June.

Kaul, I., Grunberg, I. and Stern, M.A. (1999) *Global Public Goods: International Cooperation in the 21st Century*, Oxford: Oxford University Press.

Keck, M.E. and Sikkink, K. (1998) *Activists Beyond Borders: Advocacy Networks in International Politics*, Ithaca, NY: Cornell University Press.

Keen, D. (1997) 'A Rational Kind of Madness', *Oxford Development Studies*, Special Issue, 25(1): 67–74.

Keller, K. (1996) 'Unpacking the Environment', *World Policy Journal* (Fall): 11–23.

Keohane, R.O. and Nye, J.S (1987) 'Power and Interdependence Revisted', *International Organization*, 41(4): 725–53.

—— (1998) 'Power and Interdependence in the Information Age', *Foreign Affairs*, 77(5) (September/October): 81–92.

Keohane, R. and Martin, L. (1995) 'The Promise of Institutionalist Theory', *International Security*, 20(1) (Summer): 39–51.

Keren, C. (2005) 'Human Security and Just War', unpublished paper, Human Security Class, Sciences-Po, Paris.

Kermani, P. (2004) 'The Human Security Paradigm Shift: from an "Expansion Of Security" to an "Extension of Human Rights"', unpublished paper for Human Security, New York: Columbia University.

Khong, Yuen Foong (2001) 'Human Security: A Shotgun Approach to Alleviating Human Misery?', *Global Governance*, 7: 231–6.

King, G. and Murray, C. (2001) 'Rethinking HS', *Political Science Quarterly*, 2001–2, 116(4). Available at http://gking.harvard.edu/files/hs.pdf (accessed 25 April 2006).

King, G., Keohane, R.O. and Verba, S. (1994) *Designing Social Inquiry: Scientific Inference in Qualitative Research*, Princeton, NJ: Princeton University Press.

Kittani, I. (1998) 'Preventive Diplomacy and Peacemaking: The UN Experience', in O.A. Otunnu and M.W. Doyle (eds), *Peachmaking and Peacekeeping for the New Century*, Lanham, MD: Rowman and Littlefield.

Kleschnitzki, S. (2003) 'Human Security Debates with Realism and Neorealism', unpublished paper, Human Security Class, New York: Columbia University.

Krause, K. (2004) 'The Key to a Powerful Agenda, if Properly Defined', in P. Burgess and T. Owen (eds) 'What is Human Security?' Comments by 21 authors, Special Issue of *Security Dialogue*, 35(Sept.): 367–8.

Krause, K. and Jütersonke, O. (2005) 'Peace, Security and Development in Post-Conflict Environments', *Security Dialogue*, 36(4): 447–62

Krause, K. and Williams, M. (1996) 'Broadening the Agenda of Security Studies: Politics and Methods', *Mershon International Studies Review*, 40: 229–54.

Kreimer, A., Eriksson, J., Muscat, R., Arnold, M. and Scott, C. (1998) *The World Bank's Experience with Post-Conflict Reconstruction*, Washington, DC: The World Bank.

Kuhn, T. (1962) *The Structure of Scientific Revolutions*, Chicago, IL: University of Chicago Press.

Kuperman, R. (2000) 'Rwanda in Retrospect', *Foreign Affairs*, 79 (Jan./Feb.): 105–8.

Lachal, A.-C. (2005) 'What Is Human Security?', unpublished paper, Human Security Class, Sciences-Po, Paris.

Langenkamp, D. (2003) 'The Aims and Impacts of Aid in Afghanistan', The Institute of Human Security Working Paper No. 1, Tufts University, Boston. Available at http://fletcher.tufts.edu/humansecurity/pdf/Langenkamptotal.pdf (accessed 25 April 2006).

Leaning, J. (2004) 'Psychosocial Well-Being over Time', in P. Burgess and T. Owen (eds), 'What is Human Security?' Comments by 21 authors, Special Issue of *Security Dialogue*, 35(Sept.): 354–5.

Leaning, J. and Arie, S. (2000) 'Human Security in Crisis and Transition: A Background Document of Definition and Application', CERTI Project, Payson Center for International Development and Technology Transfer, Tulane University, December. Available at http://www.certi.org/publications/policy/human security-4.htm (accessed 21 April 2006).

Lee, Shin-Wha (2004) 'Promoting Human Security: Ethical, Normative and Educational Frameworks in East Asia', Paris: SHS/FPH/PHS/UNESCO. Available at http://unesdoc.unesco.org/images/0013/001388/138892e.pdf (accessed 5 May 2006).

Leone, F. (2004) 'Human Security to the Rescue? How the international community can save itself from Development', unpublished paper for Human Security Class, New York: Columbia University.

Levin, V. and Dollar, D. (2005) 'The Forgotten States: Aid Volumes and Volatility in Difficult Partnership Countries', paper prepared for the DAC Learning and Advisory Process on Difficult Partnership Countries Senior Level Forum, London, 13–14 January.

Lind, M. (1994) 'In Defense of Liberal Nationalism', *Foreign Affairs*, 73(3): 87–99.

Liotta, P.H. (2004) 'A Concept in Search of Relevance', in P. Burgess and T. Owen (eds), 'What is Human Security?' Comments by 21 authors' Special Issue of *Security Dialogue*, 35(Sept.): 362–3.

Lodgaard, S. (2000) 'Human Security: Concept and Operationalization', paper presented for Expert Seminar on Human Rights and Peace, Geneva, December. Available at http://www.upeace.org/documents/resources%5Creport_lodgaard.doc (accessed 25 April 2006).

Lonergan, S., Gustavson, K. and Carter, B. (2000) 'The Index of Human Insecurity', *AVISO Series, GECHS Project*, vol. 6.

Lucarelli, G. (2003) 'Law, Fear and Efficiency: Challenges and Intersections for Human Security and Human Rights', unpublished paper for Human Security Class, New York: Columbia University

Lumsdaine, D.H. (1993) *Moral Vision in International Politics: The Foreign Aid Regime, 1949–1989*, Princeton, NJ: Princeton University Press.

MacFarlane, S.N (2004) 'A Useful Concept that Risks Losing Its Political Salience', in P. Burgess and T. Owen (eds), 'What is Human Security?' Comments by 21 authors, Special Issue of *Security Dialogue*, 35(Sept.): 368–9.

—— (2005) 'The Pre-History of Human Security', *St Antony's International Review, Special Issue on Human Security*, 1(2) (November): 43–66.

MacFarlane, S.N. and Khong, Yuen Foong (2006) *Human Security and the UN: A Critical History*, Bllomington, IN: United Nations Intellectual History Project Series.

MacFarlane, S.N. and Weiss, T.G. (1994) 'The United Nations, Regional Organizations and Human Security: Building Theory in Central America', *Third World Quarterly*, 15(2): 277–93.

McKinley, T. (2004) 'The Macroeconomics of Transition: The Comparative Experience of Seven Transition Economies', paper prepared for the Initiative for Policy Dialogue, New York: UNDP.

McLean, G. (1999–2000) 'The Changing Concept of Human Security: Coordinating National and Multilateral Responses', Canada on the Security Council, 1999–2000. Available at http://www.unac.org/en/link_learn/canada/security/perception.asp (accessed 5 May 2006).

McLean, G. (2002) '(Re)defining Security Policy: Canada's Human Security Initiative', in D. Mutimer (ed.), *A New Canadian International Security Policy?*, Toronto: Centre for International and Security Studies.

McRae, R. and Hubert, D. (eds) (2001) *Human Security and the New Diplomacy*, Montreal: McGill and Queen's University Press.

Mack, A. (2002a) 'Civil War: Academic Research and the Policy Community', *Journal of Peace Research*, 39(5): 515–25.

—— (2002b) 'Report on the Feasibility of Creating an Annual Human Security Report', Program on Humanitarian Policy and Conflict Research, Harvard University, February. Available at http://www.hsph.harvard.edu/hpcr/FeasibilityReport.pdf (accessed 25 April 2006).

—— (2004) 'A Signifier of Shared Values', in P. Burgess and T. Owen (eds), 'What is Human Security?' Comments by 21 authors, Special Issue of *Security Dialogue*, 35(Sept.): 366–7.

Mack, A. (ed.) (2005) 'The Human Security Report 2005: War and Peace in the 21st Century', Human Security Centre, British Columbia. Available at http://www.humansecurityreport.info/HSR2005/Part5.pdf (accessed on 5 May 2006).

Mackinder, H. (1904) 'The Geographical Pivot of History', *Geographical Journal*, 23(4): 421–37.

Maier, N. (2000) *This House has Fallen, Nigeria in Crisis*, London: Penguin.

Makaremi, C. (2004) 'Human Security: Definitions and Critics', unpublished paper, Human Security Class, Sciences-Po, Paris.

March, J.G. and Olsen, J.P. (1989) *Rediscovering Institutions: The Organizational Basis of Politics*, New York: The Free Press.

Marchal, R. and Messiant, C. (2000) 'De l'avidité des rebelles. L'analyse économique de la guerre civile selon Paul Collier', *Critique Internationale*, no. 16.

Mastanduno, M. (1998) 'Economics and Security in Scholarship and Statecraft', *International Organization*, 52(4): 825–54.

Mearshimer, J. (1994/5) 'The False Promise of International Institutions', *International Security*, 19(3) (Winter): 5–49.

Miller, L. (1999) 'The Idea and Reality of Collective Security', *Global Governance*, 5(3) (July–September): 303–32.

Mitter, S. (1986) *Common Fate, Common Bond, Women in the Global Economy*, London: Pluto Press.

Møller, B. (2000) 'The Concept of Security: The Pros and Cons of Expansion and Contraction', Copenhagen Peace Research Institute, Norway, 2000.

—— (2001) 'National, Societal and Human Security', in '*What Agenda for the Human Security in the 21st Century?*', Proceedings, UNESCO, pp. 41–63. Available at http://www.unesco.org/securipax/whatagenda.pdf (accessed 25 April 2006).

Momsen, J. (1991) *Women and Development in the Third World*, London: Routledge.

Monshipouri, M. and Welch, C.E. (2001) 'The Search for International Human Rights and Justice: Coming to Terms with the New Global Realities', *Human Rights Quarterly*, 23: 370–401.

Moravcsik, A. (1997) 'Taking Preferences Seriously: A Liberal Theory of International Politics', *International Organization*, 51(4) (Autumn): 513–53.

Morgenthau, H.J. (1960) *Politics Among Nations: The Struggle for Power and Peace*, New York: Alfred Knopf.

Mosely, P., Hudson, J. and Verschool, A. (2004) 'Aid, Poverty Reduction and the New Conditionality', *Economic Journal*, Royal Economic Society, 114(496): 217–43.

Myers, N. (1989) 'Environment and Security', *Foreign Policy*, 74: 23–41.

Naidoo, S. (2001) 'A Theoretical Conceptualization of Human Security', paper presented at 'Peace, Human Security and Conflict Prevention in Africa', UNESCO-ISS Expert Meeting, South Africa, 23–24 July. Available at http://www.iss.co.za/Pubs/Books/Unesco/Naidoo.html (accessed 5 May 2006).

Naidu, M.V. (2001) 'State Sovereignty, Human Security and Military Interventions', in *State Sovereignty in the 21st Century, Concepts, Relevance and Limits*, New Delhi: IDSA, 49–73.

Nayyar, D. and Chang, H. (2005) 'Towards a People-Centred Approach to Development', in E. Hershberg and C. Thornton (eds), *The Development Imperative: Towards a People-Centered Approach*, New York: Social Science Research Council.

Nef, J. (1999) 'Human Security and Mutual Vulnerability The Global Political Economy of Development and Underdevelopment', 2nd edition, Canada: International Research Development Centre. Available at http://www.idrc.ca/en/ev-9383–201–1–DO_TOPIC.html (accessed 5 May 2006).

Nehru, J. (1961) *India's Foreign Policy: Selected Speeches*, September 1946–April 1961, New Delhi: Government of India Press.

Newland, K. (1991) 'From Transnational Relationship to International Relations: Women in Development and the International Decade for Women', in R. Grant and K. Newland (eds), *Gender and International Relations*, Buckingham: Open University Press.

Newman, E. (2004) 'A Normatively Attractive but Analytically Weak Concept', in P. Burgess and T. Owen (eds), 'What is Human Security?' Comments by 21 authors, Special Issue of *Security Dialogue*, 35(Sept.): 358–9.

—— (2005) 'Human Security: Mainstreamed Despite the Conceptual Ambiguity?', *St Antony's International Review, Special Issue on Human Security*, 1(2) (November): 24–37.

Nicholson, M. (2000) 'Globalization, Weak States and Failed States', in Globalization and the Failed States: A Conference, Florence, Italy, April 7–10, 2000. Available at http://www.ippu. purdue.edu/failed_states/1999/papers/Nicholson.html (accessed 25 March 2006).

Nordstrom, C. (2004) *Shadows of War, Violence, Power, and International Profiteering in the Twenty-First Century*, Berkeley, CA: University of California Press.

O'Neil, H. (1997) 'Globalization, Competitiveness and Human Security: Challenges for Development Policy and Institutional Change', *European Journal of Development Research*, 9(1) (June): 7–38.

Onuf, N. (1995) *World of Our Making. Rules and Rule in Social Theory and International Relations*, Columbia, SC: University of South Carolina Press.

Oberleitner, G. (2002) 'Human Security and Human Rights', European Training and Research Center for Human Rights and Democracy, Human Rights and Security – The Two Towers Centre for the Study of Human Rights Discussion group, published in European Training and Research Center for Human Rights and Democracy, issue no. 8 (June). Available at http://www.lse.ac.uk/Depts/human-rights/Documents/Security_and_human_rights.pdf (accessed 25 March 2006).

Obuchi, K. (1998) 'Opening Remarks by Prime Minister Obuchi at the Intellectual Dialogue on Building Asia's Tomorrow', Tokyo, 2 December. Available at http://www.mofa.go.jp/policy/culture/intellectual/asia9812.html (accessed 25 March 2006).

Ogata, S. (2005) 'Human Security: Theory and Practice', *St Antony's International Review, Special Issue on Human Security*, 1(2) (November): 11–23.

Organization for Economic Cooperation and Development (OECD) (2001) 'Helping Prevent Violent Conflict', The DAC Guidelines, Paris: OECD/DAC. Available at http://www.oecd.org/dataoecd/15/54/1886146.pdf (accessed 5 May 2006).

—— (2004) 'The Security and Development Nexus: Challenges for Aid', paper presented at the DAC High Level Meeting on 15–16 April. Available at http://www.oecd.org/dataoecd/7/60/31785359.pdf (accessed 5 May 2006).

Ostby, G. (2003) 'Horizontal Inequalities and Civil War', Centre for the Study of Civil War, Oslo: International Peace Research Institute. Available at http://www.prio.no/files/file40747_gudrun_ostby__thesis_2003.pdf (accessed 5 May 2006).

Ottoway, M. and Mair, S. (2004) 'States at Risk and Failed States', *Policy Outline*, Carnegie Foundation, September.

Owen, T. (2004) 'Human Security – Conflict, Critique and Consensus: Colloquium Remarks and a Proposal for a Threshold-Based Definition', in P. Burgess and T. Owen (eds), 'What is Human Security?' Comments by 21 authors, Special Issue of *Security Dialogue*, 35(Sept.): 373–87.

—— (2005) 'A Response to Edward Newman: Conspicuously Absent? Why the Secretary-General Used Human Security in All But Name', *St Antony's International Review, Special Issue on Human Security*, 1(2) (November): 37–42.

Paarlberg, R.L. (2002) 'Governance and Food Security in an Age of Globalization', Food, Agriculture, and The Environment Discussion Paper 36, International Food Policy Research Institute, Washington, DC.

Pape, R.A. (1997) 'Why Economic Sanctions Do Not Work', *International Security*, 22(2): 90–136.

Paris, R. (2001) 'Human Security: Paradigm Shift or Hot Air?', *International Security*, 26(2) (Fall): 87–102. Available at http://mitpress.mit.edu/journals/pdf/isec_26_02_87_0.pdf (accessed 25 March 2006).

—— (2004) 'Still an Inscrutable Concept', in P. Burgess and T. Owen (eds), 'What is Human Security?' Comments by 21 authors, Special Issue of *Security Dialogue*, 35(Sept.): 370–2.

Paul, J.A. and Akhtar, S. (1998) 'Sanctions: An Analysis', Global Policy Forum. Available at http://www.globalpolicy.org/security/sanction/anlysis2.htm (accessed 25 April 2006).

Pender, J. (2001) 'From "Structural Adjustment" to "Comprehensive Development Framework": Conditionality Transformed', *Third World Quarterly*, 22(3): 397–411.

Picciotto, R., Olonisakin, F. and Clarke, M. (2006) 'Global Development and Human Security – Towards a Policy Agenda', a Policy Review Commissioned by the Ministry of Foreign Affairs, Sweden.

Pogge, T. (2002) *World Poverty and Human Rights*, Cambridge, MA: Blackwell Publishers Press.

Ponzio, R. (2005) 'A Response to S. Neil MacFarlane: Why Human Security *Is* a New Concept with Global Origins', *St Antony's International Review, Special Issue on Human Security*, 1(2) (November): 66–72.

Popov, V. (2001) 'Lessons from Transition Economies: Strong Institutions are More Important than the Speed of Reforms', paper presented at the UNRISD meeting on 'The Need to Rethink Development Economies', South Africa, 7–8 September.

Porter, G. (1995) 'An Ethical Basis for Achieving Global Human Security', *Development*, 3: 56–9.

Power, S. (2001) 'Bystanders to Genocide', *Atlantic Monthly*, 288(September): 84–108. Available at http://www.theatlantic.com/doc/200109/power-genocide (accessed 5 May 2006).

Preiswerk, R. (1981) 'Could We Study International Relations as if People Mattered?', in *Peace and World Order Studies: A Curriculum Guide*, New York: Transnational Academic Program, Institute for World Order', p. 8.

Prieto-Oramas, B. (2004) 'Human Security and the European Union Foreign and Security Policy', unpublished paper, Human Security Class, SIPA New York: Columbia University.

Radelet, S. (2003) 'Bush and Foreign Aid', *Foreign Affairs*, 82(5) (September/October): 104–17.

Rahman, A.T.R. (ed.) (2002) *Human Security in Bangladesh in Search of Justice and Dignity*, Dhaka: UNDP.

Ramcharan, B. (2002) *Human Rights and Human Security*, The Hague: Nijhoff Publishers.

Rawls, J. (1971) *A Theory of Justice*, Cambridge, MA: Belknap Press.

Reich, S. (2004) 'Human Security as a Global Public Good', *The Courier ACP-EU 202*: 33–4.

Renner, M. (1996) *Fighting for Survival: Environmental Decline, Social Conflict, and the New Age of Insecurity*, 2nd edition, New York: W.W. Norton.

Reve, A. (2004a) 'What is Human Security ?' unpublished paper, Human Security Class, Sciences-Po, Paris.

—— (2004b) 'Realist, Liberalist, Constructivist Views of Security', unpublished paper, Human Security Class, Sciences-Po, Paris.

Risse, T., Ropp, S.C. and Sikkink, K. (eds) (1999) *The Power of Human Rights: International Norms and Domestic Change*, New York: Cambridge University Press.

Robertson, G. (2002) *Crimes Against Humanity The Struggle for Global Justice*, London: Penguin.

Rodier, R. (2004) 'Beyond the Egg (Security) and Chicken (Development) Dilemma: A Human Security Approach to Civil Wars', unpublished paper, Human Security Class, New York: Columbia University.

Rothschild, E. (1995) 'What is Security?', *Daedalus*, 124(3) (Summer): 53–98.

Rostow, W.W. (1960) *The Stages of Economic Growth: A Non-Communist Manifesto*, Cambridge: Cambridge University Press.

Roy, O. (2002) *L'Afghanistan, Islam et Modernité Politique*, Paris: Seuil/Esprit.

Rubin, B. (2004) *The Fragmentation of Afghanistan: State Formation and Collapse in the International System*, New York: Yale University Press.

Ruffin, J.C (1992) *Le piège humanitaire*, Paris: Hachette Pluriel.

Ruggie, J.G. (1982) 'International Regimes, Transactions, and Change: Embedded Liberalism in the Postwar Economic Order', *International Organization*, 36: 195–231.

Ryfman, P. (2002) 'Les campagnes globalisées de ONG: les biens publics mondiaux au service de la Société civile?', in F. Constantin (ed.), *Les Biens Publics Mondiaux, un mythe légitimateur pour l'action collective?*, Paris: l'Harmattan, Collection Logiques politiques.

Saether, G. (2001) 'Inequality, Security and Violence', *The European Journal of Development Research*, 13(1): 193–212.

Sagasti, F. and Alcalde, G. (1999) 'Development Cooperation In A Fractured Global Order: An Arduous Transition', Canada: International Development Research Center publications. Available at http://www.idrc.ca/es/ev-9405–201–1–DO_TOPIC.html (accessed 5 May 2006).

Sakai, E. (2004) 'Why is Japan Involved in Human Security?', unpublished paper, Human Security Class, Sciences-Po, Paris.

Scheper, E. (2001) 'On the Right to Development, Human Security, and a Life in Dignity', Weatherhead Center for International Affairs, Harvard University: 4–38. Available at http://www.wcfia.harvard.edu/fellows/papers00–01/scheper.pdf (accessed 25 March 2006).

Schmeidl, S. (2002) '(Human) Security Dilemmas: Long-Term Implications of the Afghan Refugee Crisis', *Third World Quarterly*, 23(1): 7–29.

Schmitt, H., Alpes, J.M. and Cameron, A. (2004) 'Human Security as an "Excuse" For Intervention?', unpublished paper, Human Security Class, Sciences-Po, Paris.

Schraeder, P., Hook, J.S.W. and Taylor, B. (1998) 'Clarifying the Foreign Aid Puzzle: A Comparison of American, Japanese, French and Swedish Aid Flows', *World Politics*, 50(2): 294–323.

Seidensticker, E. (2002) 'Human Security, Human Rights, and Human Development', paper presented at Harvard Kennedy School, February. Available at http://www.humansecurity-chs.org/activities/outreach/0206harvard.pdf (accessed 25 March 2006).

Sen, A. (1988) 'The Concept of Development', in H. Chenery and T.N. Srinivasan (eds), *Handbook of Development Economics*, New York: North Holland, 10–24.

—— (1999) 'Beyond the Crisis: Development Strategies in Asia', Lecture at Sustainable Development and Human Security: Second Intellectual Dialogue on Building Asia's Tomorrow, Singapore: 15–35.

—— (2000a) *Development as Freedom*, New York: Knopf Publishers.

—— (2000b) 'Why Human Security?', Presentation at the International Symposium on Human Security, Tokyo, July. Available at http://www.humansecurity-chs.org/activities/outreach/Sen2000.pdf (accessed 5 May 2006).

—— (2001) 'Global Inequality and Persistent Conflicts', paper presented at the Nobel Peace Prize Symposium in Oslo, published in G. Lundestad and O. Njølstad (eds), *War And Peace In The 20th Century And Beyond*, Oslo: Norwegian Nobel Institute.

—— (2002) 'Basic Education and Human Security', Speech given at Workshop on Education, Equity, and Security organized by the Commission on Human Security, UNICEF/India, the Pratichi Trust, and Harvard University, Kolkota, 2–4 January. Available at http://www.humansecurity-chs.org/activities/outreach/0102Sen.html (accessed 5 May 2006).

Sen, A. and Dreze, J. (1991) 'Public Action for Social Security', in E. Ahmad, J. Dreze, J. Hills and A. Sen (eds), *Social Security in Developing Countries*, New Delhi: Oxford University Press.

Shah, A. (2006) 'The U.S. and Foreign Aid Assistance', *Global Issues*, 26 April. Available at http://www.globalissues.org/TradeRelated/Debt/USAid.asp (accessed 25 March 2006).

Sheehan, M. (2006) *International Security: An Analytical Survey*, Delhi: Viva Books.

Shméder, G. (2005) 'Une doctrine de "sécurité humaine" pour l'Europe?', *Défence Nationale et sécurité collective*, February: 50–60.

Shusterman, J. (2005) 'What is Human Security?', unpublished essay, Human Security Class, Sciences-Po, Paris.

Schwarz, R. (2005) 'Post-Conflict Peacebuilding: The Challenges of Security, Welfare and Representation', *Security Dialogue*, 36(4) (December): 429–46.

Smith, D. and Stohl, R.J. (2000) 'The Evolving Role of Military Forces in Human Security', paper presented at 'Globalization and the failed States: A Conference,' Florence, Italy, 7–10 April.

Smith, S. (2002) 'The Contested Concept of Security', Institute of Defence and Strategic Studies, Singapore. Available at http://www.ntu.edu.sg/idss/publications/WorkingPapers/WP23.PDF (accessed 25 March 2006).

Sogge, D. (2002) *Give and Take: What's The Matter With Foreign Aid?*, London: Zed Books.

Sörensen, G. (2000) 'Development in Fragile/Failed States', paper presented at the Conference on Globalization and the Failed States, Florence, Italy, 7–10 April.

South Commission (1990) *The Challenge to the South: The Report of the South Commission*, New York: Oxford University Press.

Stedman, S.J. (1995) 'Alchemy for a New World Order: Overselling "Preventive Diplomacy"', *Foreign Affairs*, 74: 14–20.

Stewart, F. (1999) 'Horizontal Inequalities: A Neglected Dimension of Development', *Queen Elizabeth House Working Paper no. 81*, Oxford: Queen Elizabeth House. Available at http://www2.qeh.ox.ac.uk/RePEc/qeh/qehwps/qehwps81.pdf (accessed 5 May 2006).

—— (2000) 'Crisis Prevention: Tackling Horizontal Inequalities', *QEH Working Paper Series No. 33*, Oxford, Queen Elizabeth House. Available http://www2.qeh.ox.ac.uk/pdf/qehwp/qehwps33.pdf (accessed 5 May 2006).

—— (2003) 'Conflict and the Millennium Development Goals', *Journal of Human Development*, 4: 3.

—— (2004) 'Development and Security', paper prepared for the Security and Development Workshop, Centre for Research on Inequality, Human Security and Ethnicity (CRISE) Queen Elizabeth House, University of Oxford, 25–26 January.

Stewart, F. and Fitzgerald, V. (eds) (2000) *War and Underdevelopment*, vol. I, Economic and Social Consequences of Conflict, Oxford: Queen Elizabeth House Series in Development Studies.

Stiglitz, J. (2002) *Globalization and its Discontents*, New York: W.W. Norton.

Stockholm International Peace Research Institute (2004) *SIPRI Yearbook*, Oslo: SIPRI.

Stoett, P. (1999) *Human and Global Security: An Exploration of Terms*, Toronto: University of Toronto Press.

Stohl, M. (2000) 'Globalization and the Failed State: The Continuing Tensions Between National Security and Human Security: A Summing Up', paper presented at the onference on Globalization and the Failed State, Florence, Italy, 7–10 April. Available at http://www.ippu.purdue.edu/failed_states/2000/papers/mstohl.html (accessed 25 March 2006).

Stohl, M. and Lopez, G. (1988) 'Westphalia, the End of the Cold War and the New World Order: Old Roots to a New Problem', paper given at the conference on Failed states and International Security: Causes, Prospects, and Consequences, Purdue University, West Lafayette, 25–27 February. Available at http://www.ippu.purdue.edu/failed_states/1998/papers/stohl-lopez.html (accessed 5 May 2006).

Study Group on Europe's Security Capabilities (2004) 'A Human Security Doctrine for Europe: The Barcelona Report of the Study Group on Europe's Security Capabilities', Presented to EU High Representative for Common Foreign and Security Policy, Javier Solana, on 15 September, Barcelona. London: London School of Economics.

Sucharithanarugse, W. (2000) 'The Concept of "Human Security" Extended: Asianizing the Paradigm', in W.T. Tow, R. Thakur and I. Hyun (eds), *Asia's Emerging Regional Order: Reconciling Traditional and Human Security*, Tokyo: United Nations University Press, 49–61.

Suhrke, A. (1996) 'Envrionmental Change, Migration and Conflict: A Lethal Feedback Dynamic?', in C. Crocker, F.O. Hampson and P. Aall (eds), *Managing Global Chaos: Sources of an Response to International Conflicts*, Washington, DC: United States Institute of Peace Press, 113–28.

—— (1999) 'Human Security and the Interests of States', *Security Dialogue*, 30(3): 265–76.

—— (2004) 'A Stalled Initiative', in P. Burgess and T. Owen (eds), 'What is Human Security?' Comments by 21 authors, Special Issue of *Security Dialogue*, 35(Sept.): 365.

Swatuk, L.A. and Vale, P. (1999) 'Why Democracy is Not Enough: Southern Africa and Human Security in the Twenty-First Century', *Alternatives*, 24(3): 361–89.

Sylvester, C. (1994) *Feminist Theory in a Postmodern Era*, Cambridge: Cambridge University Press.

Tadjbakhsh, S. (2004) 'A Human Security Agenda for Central Asia', in F. Sabahi and D. Warner (eds), *The OSCE and the Multiple Challenges of Transition: The Caucasus and Central Asia*, Aldershot: Ashgate Publishing.

—— (2005a) *Human Security: Concept, Implications and Application*, Paris: Etudes du CERI, Sciences-Po.

—— (2005b) 'Paix libérale et assistance en Asie Centrale', in G. Devin (ed.), *Faire la Paix*, Paris: Editions Pepper, Chaos International.

—— (1993) *The Bloody Path of Change: The Case of Post-Soviet Tajikistan*, New York: Harriman Institute Forum, Columbia University.

Tadjbakhsh, S. (ed.), Saba, D. and Zakhilwal, O. (2004) *Security with a Human Face: Responsibilities and Challenges, First National Human Development Report for Afghanistan*, Kabul: United Nations Development Programme.

Taliaferro, J.W. (2000/01) 'Seeking Security under Anarchy: Defensive Realism Revisited', *International Security*, 25(3): 128–61.

Tan See Sang (2001) 'Human Security: Discourse, Statecraft, Emancipation', Working Paper no. 11 (May), Singapore: Institute of Defence and Strategic Studies.

Taylor, V. (2002) 'Realising Socio-economic Rights: An Imperative for Human Security', paper presented at a colloquium of the Socio-Economic Rights Project, CLC, UWC.

—— (2003) 'Human Security = Women's Security?', paper presented at the Feminist Institute of the Heinrich Boell Foundation in Collaboration with the Friedrich Ebert Foundation and the Women's Security Council, Berlin, October. Available at http://www.glow-boell.de/media/de/txt_rubrik_3/Taylor_autorisiert.pdf (accessed 5 May 2006).

Tehranian, M. (1997) 'Human Security And Global Governance: Power Shifts And Emerging Security Regimes', paper presented at the International Conference on Human Security And Global Governance, Toda Institute for Global Peace and Policy Research. Honolulu, Hawaii, 6–8 June. Available at http://www2.hawaii.edu/~majid/draft_papers/hugg_paper/hugg.html (accessed 25 March 2006).

Teschke, B. (2003) *The Myth of 1648: Class, Geopolitics and the Making of Modern International Relations*, London: Verso.

Thakur, R. (2002) 'Outlook: Intervention, Sovereignty and the Responsibility to Protect: Experiences from the ICISS', *Security Dialogue*, 33(3): 323–40.

—— (2004) 'A Political Worldview', in P. Burgess and T. Owen (eds), 'What is Human Security?' Comments by 21 authors, Special Issue of *Security Dialogue*, 35(Sept.): 347–8.

Thayer, C.A. (1999) 'ASEAN: From Constructive Engagement to Flexible Intervention', *Harvard Asia Pacific Review*, 3(2) (Spring): 67–70.

Therien, J.-P. (1999) 'Beyond the North–South Divide: the Two Tales of World Poverty', *Third World Quarterly*, 20(4) (August): 723–42.

Thomas, C. (2000) *Global Governance, Development and Human Security: The Challenge of Poverty and Inequality*, London: Pluto Press.

—— (2004) 'A Bridge Between the Interconnected Challenges Confronting the World', in P. Burgess and T. Owen (eds), 'What is Human Security?' Comments by 21 authors, Special Issue of *Security Dialogue*, 35(Sept.): 353–4.

Tickner, J.A. (1992) *Gender and International Relations*, New York: Cornell University Press.

—— (1995) 'Re-Visioning Security', in K. Booth and S. Smith (eds), *International Relations Theory Today*, Cambridge: Polity Press.

—— (1999) 'Feminist Perspectives on Security in a Global Economy', in C. Thomas and P. Wilkin (eds), *Globalization, Human Security and the African Experience*, Boulder, CO: Lynne Rienner, 41–58.

Tow, W.T., Thakur, R. and Hyun, I. (eds) (2000) *Asia's Emerging Regional Order: Reconciling Traditional and Human Security*, Tokyo: United Nations University Press.

Tucker, R.W. (1977) *The Inequality of Nations*, New York: Basic Books.

Uddin, S. (2004) 'Human Security and the Politicization of Overseas Development Assistance', unpublished paper, Sciences-Po, Paris.

Ul Haq, M. (1995) *Reflections on Human Development*, Oxford: Oxford University Press.

—— (1998) 'Human Rights, Security and Governance', *Peace and Policy Journal of the Toda Institute for Global Peace and Policy Research: Dialogue of Civilizations for World Citizenship*, 3(2).

United Nations (1992) 'An Agenda for Peace: Preventive Diplomacy, Peacemaking and Peace-Keeping', Report of the Secretary-General Boutros Boutros Ghali, 17 June. Available at http://www.un.org/Docs/SG/agpeace.html (accessed 5 May 2006).

—— (2002) 'Outcome of the International Conference on Financing for Development "Monterrey Concensus"', Available at http://www.globalpolicy.org/socecon/ffd/conference/2002/monterreyreport.pdf (accessed 5 May 2006).

—— (2005a) 'In Larger Freedom: Towards Development, Security And Human Rights: Report of the Secretary General of the United Nations' New York. Available at http://www.un.org/largerfreedom/ (accessed 5 May 2006).

—— (2005b) Report of the UN Millennium Project. UN Millennium Project, presented to UN Secretary-General, 17 January, Millennium Report. Available at http://www.ippu.purdue.edu/failed_states/2000/papers/mstohl.html (accessed 25 March 2006).

United Nations Development Programme (UNDP) (1994) *Human Development Report 1994 – New Dimensions of Human Security*, New York: Oxford University Press.

—— (1995) *Estonia National Human Development Report*, Estonia: UNDP.

—— 1998) *Mozambique National Human Development Report*, Mozambique: UNDP .

—— (1999a) *Transition 99*, Regional Bureau for Europe and the CIS, New York: UNDP publication.

—— (1999b) *Central Asia 2010*, Regional Bureau for Europe and the CIS, New York: UNDP Publication.

—— (1999c) *Moldova National Human Development Report*, Moldova: UNDP.

—— (2003a) 'Conflict Related Development Analysis (CDA)', Working Document, October, New York: UNDP Bureau of Crisis Prevention and Recovery (BCPR).

—— (2003b) *Participatory Governance for Human Development: National Human Development Report Kenya*, Kenya.

—— (2005) *Human Development Report 2005: International Cooperation at a Crossroads: Aid, Trade and Security in an Unequal World*, New York: Oxford University Press. Available at http://hdr.undp.org/reports/global/2005/ (accessed 5 May 2006).

United Nations Education, Scientific and Cultural Organization (UNESCO) (1997) From Partial Insecurity to Global Security, UNESCO/IHEDN. Available at http://unesdoc.unesco.org/images/0011/001106/110639e.pdf (accessed 5 May 2006).

—— (1998) *What Kind of Security?*, Paris: UNESCO. Available at http://unesdoc.unesco.org/images/0010/001096/109626eo.pdf (accessed 5 May 2006).

—— (2001) Proceedings of the Expert Meeting on 'Peace, Human Security and Conflict Prevention in Africa', South Africa: UNESCO-ISS. Available at www.unesco.org/securipax/UNESCO_ISSfinal.pdf (accessed 5 May 2006).

—— (2003) International Conference on Contemporary International Security: Consequences for Human Security in Latin America, Santiago, Chile. Available at http://www.flacso.cl/flacso/biblos.php?code=642 (accessed 5 May 2006).

Uvin, P. (1998) *Aiding Violence: The Development Enterprise in Rwanda*, West Hartford: Kumarian Press.

—— (1999a) 'Development Aid and Structural Violence: The Case of Rwanda', *Development*, 42(3): 49–56.

—— (1999b) 'The Influence of Aid in Situations of Violent Conflict. A Synthesis and a Commentary on Lessons Learned from Case Studies', OECD/DAC, Information Task Force on Conflicts, Peace and Development.

—— (2002) 'The Development/Peace building Nexus: A Typology and History of Changing Paradigms', *Journal of Peace building and Development*, 1(1): 5–22.

—— (2004) 'A Field of Overlaps and Interactions', in P. Burgess and T. Owen (eds), 'What is Human Security?' Comments by 21 authors, Special Issue of *Security Dialogue*, 35(Sept.): 352–3.

Vanaik, A. (2005) '1945 to 1989: The Realist Paradigm and Systemic Duality', in K. Bajpai and S. Mallavarapu (eds), *International Relations in India: Bringing Theory Back Home*, New Delhi: Orient Longman, 400–22.

Van Rooy, A. (2000) 'In the Aftermath of Crisis, What Now? Civil Society and Human Security in the Asia Pacific', paper prepared for the ISIS Malaysia, 14th Asia–Pacific Roundtable on Confidence Building and Conflict Reduction, Kuala Lumpur, 3–7 June.

Vaux, T. and Goodhand, J. (2001) 'Disturbing Connections: Aid and Conflict in Kyrgyzstan', The Conflict, Security and Development Group, Centre for Defense Studies, Conflict Assessments 3, July, London: Kings College.

Walt, S. (1991) 'Renaissance of Security Studies', *International Studies Quarterly*, 35(1): 211–39.

Waltz, K.N. (1979) *Theory of International Politics*, Reading, MA: Addison-Wesley.

—— (1990) 'Realist Thought and Neorealist Theory', *Journal of International Affairs*, 44: 21–37.

—— (2001) *Man, the State, and War: A Theoretical Analysis*, revised edition, New York: Columbia University Press.

Walzer, M. (1992) *Just and Unjust Wars: A Moral Argument with Historical Illustrations*, New York: Basic Books.

—— (2004) 'Au-delà de l'intervention humanitaire: les droits de l'homme dans la société globale', *Esprit*, 8 (August–September): 66–79.

Wapner, P. and Ruiz, L.E.J. (eds) (2000) *Principled World Politics: The Challenge of Normative International Relations*, Lanham, MD: Rowman and Littlefield.

Weber, M. (1946) 'Politics as Vocation', in H.H. Gerth and C. Wright Mills (eds), *From Max Weber: Essays in Sociology*, New York: Oxford University Press.

Weiss, T.G. (2000) 'Governance, Good Governance and Global Governance', *Third World Quarterly*, 21(5) (October): 795–814.

Wendt, A. (1987) 'The Agent-Structure Problem in International Relations Theory', *International Organization*, 41(3) (Summer): 335–70.

—— (1992) 'Anarchy is What States Make of it: The Social Construction of Power Politics', *International Organization*, 46(2) (Spring): 391–425.

Werthes, S. and Bosold, D. (2005) 'Human Security And Smart Sanctions – Two Means To A Common End?', *International Review*, 14(2): 111–36.

Wesley, M. (1999) 'Human Security in Development and Crisis: How to Capture Human Security in Regional Institutional Arrangements?', *The Asia-Australia Papers*, no. 2.

Williams, W. (1998) *'Honest Numbers and Democracy'*, Washington, DC: Georgetown University Press.

Winslow, D. and Eriksen, T.H (2004) 'A Broad Concept that Encourages Interdisciplinary Thinking', in P. Burgess and T. Owen (eds), 'What is Human Security?' Comments by 21 authors, Special Issue of *Security Dialogue*, 35(Sept.): 361–2.

'Women's Equal Participation in Conflict Prevention, Management and Conflict Resolution And In Post-Conflict Peace-Building', Commission on the Status of Women, Report of the Secretary-General, March 2004. Available at http://econ.worldbank.org/prr/CivilWarPRR/.

Wood, B. (2003) *Development Dimensions of Conflict Prevention and Peace Building*, An Independent Study Prepared for the Emergency Response Division, New York: UNDP.

World Bank (1996) *From Plan to Market: World Development Report 1996*, Washington, DC: The World Bank.

—— (2000) *Making Transition Work for Everyone: Poverty and Inequality in Europe and Central Asia*. Washington, DC: The World Bank.

—— (2002) *Transition: The First Ten Years: Analysis and Lessons for Eastern Europe and the Former Soviet Union*, Washington, DC: The World Bank.

—— (2005) *Toward a Conflict-Sensitive Poverty Reduction Strategy: Lessons from a Retrospective Analysis*, Report no. 32586, SDV/ESSD, 2005. Washington, DC: The World Bank.

Yeo, R. (2004) 'Whither Human Security? An Argument for Complementarity and Co-operation in Canadian and Japanese Human Security Policies', unpublished paper, Human Security Class, Sciences-Po, Paris.

Index

9/11 (September 11) 3, 12, 27, 46, 205, 208–9, 214, 216–17, 247

Abu Ghraib 176
academic implications 62–3
access issues 46
accountability 31, 133, 159, 169, 178; financial 226; state 131, 168
Acharya, A. 42, 138, 191–2, 206, 240
activism 5,12; judicial 132, 135
Adler, E. 88
Afghanistan: international aid 163, 209, 210, 228, 230; international intervention 12, 27, 217; national development framework 181; post-conflict situation 161, 174–6, 180, 232; privatization of security 174–5; regime change 219; Regional Provincial Teams (PRTs) 163, 175; Soviet military intervention 169; Soviet occupation (1980–91) 228
African Union 206
Al Qaeda 10, 12, 231
Albania: weak state 174
Alkire, S. 42, 49, 106
altruism 196
Amnesty International 135
anarchy 74, 80, 81, 82, 85, 88, 91, 92, 96, 172; international 74, 82; societal 88; systemic 82, 85, 86
Andersen, M. 228
Angola 147; economic intervention 150
An-Na'im, A. 135
Annan, K. 11, 24, 25, 27, 49, 196
Aquinas, T. 196
armed conflicts 15–16, 24, 31, 40, 62, 119, 149, 151, 154, 156, 164, 225
Asian Development Bank (ADB) 213
Asian Model of Development 36

Association of Southeast Asian Nations (ASEAN) 162, 203, 205–6
authoritarianism 16, 153
autonomy 44, 46, 171
Axworthy, L. 30, 31, 42, 49, 51, 63, 139

Badie, B. 207
Bajpai, K. 43, 49
Balkans: post-conflict situation 161
Bangladesh: international aid 227
Barcelona Forum of the European Union 204–5
basic needs (food, shelter, healthcare and education) notion 17, 46, 103–5, 219, 233; material needs 46, 105
behavioural approach to politics 73, 233
Bello, W. 198
Bipolar World 1, 11, 72, 82, 189, 216
Bismarck, O.V. 81
Booth, K. 90
Booysen, F. 67, 241
Bosnia: conflicts 153; international intervention 12; UN intervention 26
bottom-up strategies 163
Brandt Commission, see Commission on International Development
Brandt, W. 35, 76–7, 145
Bretton Woods Institutions 99, 151, 157
Brown, M. 83
Brown, N. 77
Browne, S. 210
Bulgaria 160
Buzan, B. 10, 43, 53, 56, 60, 62, 76, 79, 83, 85, 169

Cambodia: international aid 227
Canada 203; human security initiatives taken 29, 30–1, 38, 48, 183–4, 242
capacity building 148, 161, 232

capital punishment, issue of 29
capitalism 90, 178, 181
care support system 182
Carim, X. 90
Carnegie Commission on Preventing Deadly 153
Central Asia 3, 5, 24, 182, 212–14, 216, 217, 242
Central Intelligence Agency (CIA) 176
Chomsky, N. 197
Chourou, B. 6
citizenship rights 149 (freedom of thought, conscience and religion) 43, 124, 132
civil rights 128
civil society 42, 53, 87, 92, 96, 134, 155, 157, 159, 166, 177, 182–3, 198, 202, 214, 231, 238; actors 25, 87; global 12; organizations 28
civil war 25, 31, 62, 73, 74, 76, 100, 146–7, 151, 154–6, 211
Clausewitz, K.V. 80–1
code of conduct 193
coercion 85, 219
Cold War 1, 2, 4, 11, 20, 21, 23, 36, 42, 72–3, 77, 83, 88, 90, 100, 124, 143, 146, 166, 169, 174, 189, 214, 216, 230, 238, 243; post- 12, 30, 60, 61, 81, 82, 83, 98, 146, 174, 175
collective security 11, 24–5, 62, 73, 78, 185, 188–9, 217, 239
Collier, P. 147–8, 149, 150–1
colonialism 149, 153, 173
Commission on Global Governance 77
Commission on Human Security (CHS) 23, 27–8, 29–30, 42, 49, 106, 114, 122, 202; *Human Security Now* 27–8, 30, 49, 106, 116, 137
Commission on International Development (Brandt Commission) 76–7, 145
common security 36, 63, 73–4, 76–7
Commonwealth Independent State (CIS) 173, 213
communism 1; communist societies 171; post- 180; systems 211
community, communities, 151; based organizations (CBOs) 183, 229; development 77–8, 109–10; exclusion 12; inter-community conflicts 154; security 1, 15, 16; minorities interests 177
conceptual critiques 58–61
conflict(s) 10, 14, 15, 37, 49, 50–2, 64, 72–4, 79, 86, 99, 116, 121, 129, 143, 181, 187, 204, 205, 207, 213, 231; analysis framework (CAF) 159–60; analysis 109,

143, 153, 159; role in peace-building 160; implications and costs 154–7; institutionalizing 158; management 111; post-conflict recovery stage 148, 162, 175–6, 181, 232; prevention 23, 31, 33, 51, 134, 144, 151–2, 157, 158, 160–2, 199, 206, 218; liberal peace approach 152–3; reconciliation 236; related development analysis (CDA) 160; resolution 10, 49, 62, 136, 148, 150, 154, 157, 163, 192, 198; socio-economic, political and cultural causes 164; and underdevelopment 3, 102, 143–4, 146, 238
Congo: UN mission 26
constitution 29, 74, 148, 178
constructivist approach 87–91
consumerism 99
Copenhagen Summit (1995) 23
corruption 31, 172, 215–16, 226, 228
Covenant on Economic, Social and Cultural Rights (CESCR, 1966) 124
crime 14, 24–5, 31 40, 149–50, 157, 162, 168, 172, 174, 181, 188, 215, 224, 236, 237
criminal prosecution 27
critical theory approach 89
cultural, culture 17, 32, 37, 66, 134–9; diversity 16, 91, 225; freedom 104; identity, impact on security policies 88; integrity 50; and perceptions 89; relativism 2, 124, 130, 136, 138; rights 76, 124–25, 130, 136; threats 59

Dallmayr, F. 124, 137–8
debt: crises 37, 103–4, 106, 114; relief 64; rescheduling 156
decentralization 178, 214
decolonization 73, 101
deforestation 15, 136, 155
Del Rosso, Jr. S.J. 77, 79
Demobilization 148, 159, 161, 224
democracy, democratization 4, 12, 24, 26, 36, 42, 77, 82, 86–7, 92, 130, 133, 145, 148, 152–3, 155, 159, 166, 171, 177–8, 180, 181, 183, 199, 205, 212, 214, 215, 230, 235, 237
demographic growth 46
dependency theory 100, 101
deprivation: economic 18, levels of 105; and conflict 113–14, 149
Derrida, J. 90
development 1, 3, 9–11, 17, 18, 20, 21, 25, 27, 36, 37, 48–50, 53, 58, 68–70, 77–9,

92, 99, 100, 116, 122, 143–7, 150, 152, 164–5, 168, 171, 177–8, 195, 199–200, 207, 215, 234, 237–9; assistance 29, 47, 133, 186, 209, 234; in conflict situation, operational challenges 157–60, 218; co-operation 158, 240; costs 117, 121, 151, 155; deficit 66; economics 35, 101–2; international aid, an effective tool 218–20; integration with conflict prevention 157; interventions 143, 158, 160; reconceptualization as conflict prevention 145; securitization 54, 68, 78–9; and security, interconnectedness 117–18; sustainability 11, 105, 146, 221, 228; thinking, evolution towards human development 101–5, 110–11; dictatorship 83, 171, 172

dignity/human dignity 6, 13, 14, 16, 17, 18, 21, 27, 37, 40, 45, 46, 48, 50, 52, 53, 55, 60, 69, 71, 77, 85, 93–5, 105–6, 121, 131–2, 143, 156, 167, 168, 171, 176, 182, 183, 190, 200

disarmament 24

disarmament demobilization and reintegration (DDR) 148

disaster(s) 24; management and mitigation 127, 160, 171; natural or man-made 14

discontent 12, 177

discrimination 15, 19, 29, 38, 76–7, 154, 225

disease 1, 12, 14, 17, 24, 25, 26, 37, 76, 106–7, 144, 197–9

dislocation and displacement 10, 12, 151, 155, 164, 216, 228, 233

distributive justice issues 49, 105–6, 122–3, 179

divide and rule policy 173

domestic violence 10, 15–16, 91

Donnelly, J. 131

downsizing, government role 103–4

downturns, economic 54–5, 57, security and economic downturn 98–9, 105, 107, 113–14, 117, 121–2, 178, 179, 199

Doyle, M. 86, 152, 235

drug related crimes 14, 17, 30, 31, 144

Duffield, M. 195, 199–200

duty and responsibility 133

East Asia 138; financial crisis 30, 139, 154, 171, 242

East Timor: international intervention 12; post-conflict situations 161; struggle for independence, 149

East–West debate 100

economic, economy 50, 65, 104–5, 118, 145, 177; change, 156; costs of conflict 146, 154–6; crisis 30, 35, 54, 99, 117, 161; and social unrest 113, 117; depression 114, 212; development, 24, 74, 104, 109, 113, 136, 172, 208, 216; disparities 13, 172, 186; distress, 50; factors, 46–7, 154, 196; growth 13, 19, 21, 42, 99, 101–5, 148, 179–81, 182; growth only theory 101; growth with equity, 54, 99, 110, 113; inequality and conflict, relation 148–50; insecurity 174; interdependence 214–15; financial security 182; laissez-faire 196; management 99, 173, 210; participation 161; price shocks 148; recession 179, 182; reconstruction 162; reductionism 103, 154, 188; rights 41, 53, 74, 92, 124, 126, 127, 130–2, 137, 138, 140; sanctions 27, 36–7, 64, 189; security 1, 15, 24, 114, 179, 193, 221–2; shadow economy 150, 179, 215; and social factors 25, 37, 150, 182; stabilization measures 162–3; stagnation 117; subsidies and regulations 180; threats 14

education 14, 37, 99, 110, 199, 243; illiteracy 105

electoralism 214

Eisenhower, Dwight D. 141

empowerment 28, 40, 63, 119, 122, 132, 152, 157, 168–9, 171, 177, 184, 199, 200, 243

enforcement mechanisms 134–5

enlightenment 86

entitlements, concept 118, 151, 155

environment/environmental 55, 59, 79, 83, 85, 154; costs of conflict 155–6; degradation 15, 16, 24, 36, 50, 136, 186, 197, 198, 206, 223; disasters 100, 172, 203; scarcity, 1, 14–15, 50; security 1, 15, 193, 223; threats 14–15, 78, 93

equality 91, 116, 128, 129, 243

equity 13, 51, 54, 92, 96, 99, 153, 157, 165, 178, 179, 207, 236

Eriksen, T.H. 47, 49

ethics, ethical norms 2, 6, 7, 19, 20, 61, 72, 93, 104, 108; rupture 20–2

Ethiopia: international aid 227

ethnicity: conflicts 12, 14, 21, 100–1, 113, 148, 149, 150–1, 165, 176; ethnic cleansing 27, 191, 194, 197; and religious divisions 12, 15, 16, 22, 27, 41, 79, 100–1, 113, 124, 146, 147, 148

European Convention on Human Rights, (November 1950) 135, 136

European Court of Justice 135

European Neighbourhood Policy (ENP) 204
European Union (EU) 9, 23, 158, 162, 206, 209, 242
Evans, Gareth 26
Evans, Paul 43
extremism 10, 149

fear 14, 26, 27, 40, 120; objective and subjective, 17, 241; *see also* freedom from fear
federalism 138
female foeticide 182
feminist contribution to engendering security 91
Finnermore, M. 88
Food and Agricultural Organization (FAO) 145, 239
food security 1, 14, 15, 24, 48, 145, 156, 193, 22, 231, 242; food insecurity 117, 221, 232; under-nourishment 49
foreign aid, *see* international aid
foreign policy 2, 24, 28–30, 36, 38, 46, 66, 158
Foucault, M. 90, 133
free market 139, 152–3, 174, 180
freedom(s) 12, 20, 42, 45, 51–6, 59, 66, 68, 74, 106, 119–25, 170–7; of action 11, 177; of choice 177; of conscience, and belief 169; as empowerment 236 ; from fear 14, 15, 17, 21, 23, 24, 30–1, 38, 39, 40, 44, 47, 48, 68, 109, 111, 115, 119–20, 167, 168, 171, 187, 195, 198, 200, 206, 238; to live in dignity, 119, 120, 200; of movement 133; negative, 235; from pervasive threats 28, 30, 48, 106; of press, and information 169; as a social commitment, 105; from want 17, 21, 23, 24, 29–30, 38, 39, 47, 48, 68, 56, 109, 119, 126, 131, 137, 167, 168, 171, 187, 193, 195, 199, 200, 202, 206
Fukuda-Parr, S. 104–5
fundamental rights, 21, 134, 219

G-77 23, 31, 35–6, 65, 195, 240
Galtung, J. 49, 73, 198–9, 237
Gandhi, M.K. iii, 143
Gasper, D. 105–6, 156
gender 11, 149, 150, 165; aspect of conflicts 164–5; empowerment 223–5; inequality 187; relations 103
Gender Development Index 154
Gender in Development (GID) 103

genocide 14, 18, 25, 44, 45, 57, 60, 168, 191, 193, 197, 198; genocide convention 192, 197
geographical factors 147; geopolitics 73, 91, 203, 209
George, J. 89
Ghali, B.B. 24, 161
Gilpin, R. 82
global: commissions to define and discuss intervention 26–9; consciousness 21; economy 150; governance 196; inequality 145, 153; justice 183, 196; rights and national interests 42; security 16, 22, 24, 35, 50, 62, 190, 205, 216; social contract 18, 35, 150, 166, 172, 183, 190; society 139, 187; threats 13, 185, 186, 239, 241
Global Public Good (GPG), 185–8, 203
globalization 1, 2, 12, 25, 27, 86–7, 90, 157, 166, 169, 172, 188, 189, 196, 204, 236, 240
Goodhand, J. 215
Gorbachev, M. 88
governance 21, 148, 152, 205, 210; governance vacuum 156
Gramsci, A. 89
Grayson, K. 43
Great Depression 101, 212
Great Divide 188
greed model 146–9, 153, 164; drawbacks 149–50
grievances 143–4, 148–9, 150–52, 153, 164, 177, 215
Gross Domestic Product (GDP) 151, 155, 179, 212, 213, 241; Gross National Product (GNP) 101, 103, 181, 202
Grotius, H. (1583–1645), 86, 196
Guantanamo Bay 176
Guatemala, peace building initiative 160
Gulf wars, economic costs, 155

Habyarimana 150, 198
Hampson, O. 21, 45, 49, 51, 63, 65, 67, 123, 134, 170, 195–6, 203, 238
health care 15, 48, 99, 105, 176, 222–3
health security 1, 15, 23, 223
Helsinki Accords 1975 132
Hobbes, T. 48, 74, 80, 166, 168, 173; model of state 18
Hubert, D. 43–4
human development 9, 16, 19, 20, 24, 28, 38, 44, 52–5, 68–70, 79, 99–102, 143, 155, 167, 193, 213, 235–6; human security as a pre-condition, 114–16; evaluation of

101–2, 103–5; pre-requisite for human security 109
Human Development Index (HDI) 241
human: freedoms 42, 116; fulfillment 42, 106; needs 49; diversity 104
human rights 4, 9, 10, 16, 18, 25, 28, 31, 38, 43, 45, 47, 49, 74, 94–5, 116, 145, 148, 159, 167, 170, 173, 175, 187, 190, 193, 199, 202, 205, 207, 210, 235–9; denial 134, 155, 164; enforcement mechanisms 134–6; and human security, linkage, operational implications 131–4; Geneva Conventions 74; interdependence 134; and security; of states, and rights of human beings, conflict 21; subsistence rights 124; Universal Declaration of Human Rights (1948) 74, 124, 132–3, 137, 145; violation/abuses 10, 15, 19, 24, 40, 49, 50, 74, 77, 127, 133–7, 168, 198, 204, 226
human security: alternative theories 3, 89–92; convergence 91–2; as a concept 10–11; conceptual distinctions and added value of, 105–6; debates with human development 106–16; chicken and egg debate 107, 111–17, 119; difference/objection 84–6; deficits 195; definitions in comparison to each other 51–3; existing issues and tools 67–9; for future research, unfinished agenda 241–6; and human development, shadow or threshold 98–101; and human rights 123–4; implementation critiques 67–9; minimalist (narrow)/maximalist (broad) debate 40–1, 48–9, 69, 70, 114, 199; as misfit in international relations theory 62; as an organizing concept 60; as a political discourse 23–6; in practice 237–41; qualitative aspects 48; quantitative aspects, 48; radical theory 89–90; reinforcement of global division 65–7; stake of power 23–4; in theory 235–7; a threat to state sovereignty 64; trafficking 206, 242; welfare 6, 46
Human Security Doctrine for Europe (HSDE) 204–5; Human Security Index 43, 241–2; Human Security Network (HSN) 23, 46, 48
humanitarian: aid 162–3, 175; concerns 45, 50, 143, 145; crisis 50, 160, 192; disasters 161; international standards 42; intervention 185, 195, 195–6; to human security engagement 198–200; principles 190–1; relief 47; humanitarianism 30, 49, 50, 199
Humphreys, M. 148
hunger 1, 14, 16, 24, 179, 236

imperialism 65, 90, 235
Independent Commission on Disarmament and Security (Palme Commission) 35, 73, 77; Report 1982, 35, 73
Independent North/South Commission 35
Indonesia: ethnic riots 164; financial crisis 99, 178
industrialization 37, 99, 101
inequalities 49, 50, 103, 113–16, 145, 147–52, 156, 164–5, 180, 181, 187, 196, 198, 206, 212, 216, 226
inflation 157, 205, 212–13
injustice 113–15, 147
insecurity 2, 5, 10–14, 17, 18, 24, 37, 39, 45, 47, 50, 71, 74, 89, 96, 105–10, 113–18, 143, 155, 156, 157, 168, 172–3, 179, 181, 187, 196, 197, 205, 216, 230, 232, 234–6; and underdevelopment 144–6
instability 25, 37, 48, 50–60, 65, 99, 119, 173, 212
institution, institutional: building 175; collapse 157; development 106–8; reform proposals 26
insurgency 10, 12, 155
intellectual: point of view 2, 5, 11, 29, 35, 46, 48, 63, 122; property rights regime 49
internal conflicts 68–9, 144, 170
international aid, conditionalities 12, 27, 100, 116, 195, 210, 213–14, 216–17; evaluation from population point of view 230; harms 226–9; help, 229; impact, externalities 62, 68, 208–10, 240; quantum 208–9
International Commission on Intervention and State Sovereignty (ICISS) Canada, 23, 26, 193, 194, 196–7; *A Responsibility to Protect* 48, 64, 168 *see also Responsibility to Protect*
international community 2, 25, 31, 24, 45, 50, 63–5, 69, 80, 147, 148, 160–2, 175, 185–8, 208, 232–3; engagement and the responsibilities 185–8
International Covenant of Civil and Political Rights (ICCPR, 1966) 125, 132–3
International Covenant on Economic, Cultural and Social Rights (1966), 139
international crime 24, 50
International Criminal Court (ICC) 23, 31, 44, 50, 131, 133, 135

international financial institutions (IFIs) 145, 163, 179, 211–15, 217
international institutions 12, 29, 41, 50, 62, 146, 162, 203 *see also* international organizations
international law 50, 52, 89, 123, 125, 130, 135, 136, 190, 207
International Monetary Fund (IMF) 50, 103, 153, 180, 197, 202, 210–11, 217; Staff Monitored Programme (SMP) 217
international organizations 3, 9, 10, 12, 16, 23, 38, 39, 45, 86–8, 93, 159, 162, 171, 183, 200, 203, 206, 213, 214
International Peace Academy 146
international relations 4, 2, 10–13, 19–22, 35, 36, 42, 46, 58, 62–3, 72, 77, 80, 83, 84–5, 88–93, 100, 183, 190
international security 18, 21, 38, 43, 50, 58, 66, 75, 80, 123, 188–90
international system 17, 18, 20, 21, 46, 62, 76, 80, 82–4, 86–91
International Task Force on Global Public Good 185–6
interstate: conflicts and rivalry 12, 25, 74, 144, 153; cooperation 62; relations 174
Iraq 205; international aid 209; international intervention 12, 27; post-conflict situations 161; regime change 219; military intervention 169, 195–6
Ireland, Northern, secession movements 152

Japan 203, 205, 208; human security concern 1–2, 29–30, 38, 48, 49, 183–4, 203, 205, 208; Trust Fund for Human Security 29
"just war" 66, 81, 194, 196–8
justice, judicial system 6, 27, 37, 150–52, 154, 160, 161, 178, 188, 205; denial of 12; in distribution 153; impunity 37; judicial activism 132; and enforcement of human rights 135; legal rights 124
Kaldor, M. 153, 187–8
Kant, I. 43, 86, 145, 214
Kargil conflict 153
Katzenstein, P.J. 88
Kaul, I. 186
Kazakhstan: international aid 211, 213, 214, 217
Keen, D. 147
Keller, K. 78
Keohane, R.O. 167
Kissinger, H.A. 81
Kosovo: international intervention 12, 26, 196, 197
Krause, K. 44, 48

Kuhn, T. 19; *The Structure of Scientific Revolutions* 19
Kyrgyzstan, international aid 217; transition conditional aid 211–14; Tulip Revolution 215

Langenkamp, D. 228
League of Nations 189
Leaning, J. 44, 49
Lebanon: economic cost of civil war 155; military intervention 169
legitimacy, struggle for 12, 26, 44, 147, 166, 177
liberal peace approach to conflict prevention 152–3
liberalism, liberal values 12, 78, 87–8, 93, 95, 144
liberalization 158, 180–1, 211, 212–13, 215, 217
liberty 12, 45
life expectancy 69, 99
Liotta, P.H. 44
livelihood 51, 68, 77, 100, 104, 106; loss 16, 151; security 48
Locke, J. 74, 133, 216
Lodgaard, S. 18, 83, 189, 239
London School of Economics (LSE) 204
Lonergan, S. 241
Lyotard, J. F. 90

Macfarlane, K. 44, 48
Machiavelli, N. 80
Mack, A. 18, 45, 48, 59–60, 62, 71, 73, 77, 149, 152; *Human Security Report* (2005) 152, 153
Mackinder, H. 73
MacLean, G. 48
Maoist movements, 156
marginalization 12, 50, 99, 110, 152, 218, 221; and exclusion 12, 100; social 152
market(s) 19, 103–4, 187, 196, 214; and private actors, intervention 187
Marshall Plan 158
Marx, K. 5
Mearshimer, J. 85
media role 92–3, 232
methodological rupture 20, 21, 104
Metternich, K.W.V. 81
Middle East 173
middle power states 28–9, 30, 46
migration 12, 14, 16, 48, 100, 161, 186, 233
military, militarism 5, 9; assistance 158–9, 169; balances 1; cooperation 216–18; expenditure of South Asia 12, 155;

interventions 27, 37, 44, 64, 73, 78, 148, 158, 169, 192–5, 197, 205, 234; militarization 65, 79, 92, 153; security 16, 36, 76–7, 90, 96; threats 9, 18, 42, 50, 61, 72, 74, 76–7, 86, 175, 206, 236
Millennium Development Goals (MDGs) 143, 160, 210, 219
minority rights 50, 114, 148, 152
modernity 90
Moldova 179, Council for National Security 113
Monetary Consensus Declaration (2002) 208
morality, moral issues 6, 20, 38, 79, 80, 92, 93–4, 143, 195, 197; dilemma 59; shared political and moral values 45, 48, 71
Mozambique, post-conflict situations 161
multilateralism 20, 26, 37, 74, 95, 189
multinational companies (MNCs) 136, 171, 173; stake in resources of conflict-ridden 150
Murray, C. 48, 241
Myanmar, international community intervention 195
Myers, N. 77
national security 3, 12, 19, 21, 43, 46, 50, 65, 78–80, 100, 113, 132
nations and individuals, interdependence 11; nationalities 5; nationalism 149
natural disasters 99, 130, 171, 191, 199
natural resource: exports 148; exploitation 156; post-disaster recovery 160
Naxalites 156
Nef, J. 16, 17, 18, 62, 65, 85, 100
Nehru, J. 36
neo-liberalism 180–1
Nepal: civil war 156; pro-democracy conflict 149; peace building 160
neutrality in international relations 227
Newman, E. 45
Nigeria: peace building initiative 160
Non-Aligned Movement (NAM) 36
non-governmental organizations (NGOs) 12, 16, 25, 31, 45, 64, 78, 86–7, 132, 159, 166, 171, 175, 177, 183, 200, 206, 229, 232, 241
non-state entities 12
Nordstrom, C. 150, 157
North Atlantic Treaty Organization (NATO) 162, 176, 197, 203, 206, 217
North Korea: international community intervention 195; nuclear proliferation 30
Norway 203; human security concern 29

nuclear: 10, 15; deterrence 82; power 29, 82; proliferation 30; weapons 24, 25, 49, 155, 198
Nussbaum, M. 151
Nye, J.S. 167
Nyerere, J. 36

Oberleitner, G. 123, 125, 130, 134
Obuchi, K. 29
Ogata, S. 27–8
oil shock 1973, 205
Onuf, N. 87
oppression, oppressive power structures 46, 114, 149, 157; inter group 110
Organization for Economic Cooperation and Development (OECD), 144, 158–9, 203, 208–9, 217–18; Development Assistance Committee (DAC), 144, 158–9, 208–9, 218
Organization for Security and Co-operation in Europe (OSCE) 38, 73
Organization of African Unity (OAU) 203
Ottawa Convention on banning anti-personal landmines (1997) 23, 31; Ottawa Process, Canada 29
overpopulation 76, 172, 242
Overseas Development Assistance (ODA) 29–30, 159, 195, 202, 208–9, 218
Overseas Development Institute (ODI) 220
Owen, T. 68, 117, 193–4

Pakistan: foreign aid 208; Mohajir conflict 149
Palestine 149
Palme Commission, *see* Independent Commission on Disarmament and Security
Palme, Olaf 35, 73, 77
Panama 169
paradigm(s) 85; compared 92–3; problems of 98–101; shift 9, 19–22, 166, 191
Paris Declaration on Aid Effectiveness (March 2005) 208
Paris, R. 45–6, 58–60, 67
participation 44, 46–7, 105, 110, 115, 116, 178
peace: peace building 12, 27, 45, 55, 144, 145, 158–60, 161, 163, 202, 218, 219, 234; peace education 122; human security challenge 160–4; peace keeping 92, 134
People's Union for Civil Liberties (PUCL) 132
personal security 1, 14, 15, 16, 24, 50–1, 156, 174, 224–5

Peru 150
physical violence 48, 69, 91, 104, 119, 128, 156
Pogge, T. 124–6
policy, policy issues 11, 43–4, 72, 121, 124, 138, 175; cohesion 90; community 46; formulation/making 17, 48, 177; initiatives 148
political, politics 1, 9, 10, 19, 20, 28, 36, 47, 49, 99, 138, 146, 149, 154, 190; costs of conflict 155; democracy 18–19; discrimination 19; dissatisfaction 154; economy 163, 220, 232; freedom 174; implications 58, 64–6; of human security 11–13, 58; instability, 36; international 1, 12, 21, 23, 203; and politicization of aid: motivation in donor assistance, 209–18; power and representation, denial 155; *realpolitik* 21; repression 115; rights 18, 55, 74, 124, 129, 130; security 1, 15, 16, 24, 168, 225; threats 15; violence 148; will 135, 195
pollution 14, 15, 17, 24, 37, 105, 128, 137, 223
population growth 24, 50, 153, 186; movements 157
post modernism 91
post-conflict 3, 12, 24, 143, 145, 148, 159–63, 174, 176–8, 181, 202, 219, 227, 231
poverty 11, 12, 14, 15, 17, 24, 25, 26, 35, 36, 37, 68, 70, 77, 79, 80, 86, 89, 100, 103, 113, 135, 152, 165, 180, 181, 186, 189, 194, 197, 198, 205, 208, 212, 213, 215, 216, 221, 230, 233; and conflict 144; eradication 124–5, 183; impoverishment 99, 105, 156, 160
power/power relations 23–4, 39, 43, 46, 65, 87; balance 78, 80, 83–5, 91, 189, 227; distribution 186; sharing 178; structures 89, 105
Preiswerk, R. 89
privatization 225, 243; of security 153, 156, 174–6, 187, 225
prostitution 14, 15
psycho-social needs such as identity, participation and autonomy 44
public expenditure 180
Pufendorf, S. 196

quality of life 16, 46, 49, 78, 104, 206

racism, race 150, 226
Ramcharan, B. 123, 134

Rawls, J. 192
realism 20, 72–4, 80–91, 94, 95; neo-realism, 72, 80–2, 83–85, 94–5; neo-realists 21, 81–7
rebellion 149–50, 154; rebel groups 147
reconstruction and recovery processes 231
refugees 16, 76, 154, 173, 225, 228, 231
regime change 12, 100, 153, 192
regional: cooperation 206; integration 91; interests 150; organizations 202, 241; powers 204; solutions 203–6
Reich, S. 186
Responsibility to Protect Report (RTPR, 2001) 169, 189–90, 191, 192, 194–8, 200, 202
risk factors 144, 147, 218, 233
Robertson, G. 138
rogue states 37
Rostow, W.W. 101, 102
Rothschild, E. 77
rule of law, 21, 45, 25, 49, 188, 205; lack of enforcement 15
rural–urban divide 156
Russia 150
Rwanda 150; military conflicts 153, 156–7, 196, 197–8; UN intervention 26

Sahnoun, M. 26
securitization 54–8, 62–5, 78, 79, 85, 146, 227; as responsibilities 65–6
security 4, 10, 18, 24, 73–4; broadening and widening, and implications 76–88; conditional 45; development–security nexus 116–17; dialogue 40, 47; dilemma model 76; expenditure, 159; interdisciplinary point of view 2; physical security 219; public insecurity 40; state-centred and human-centred, difference 40, 41; studies, paradigm shift 72–7
Seidensticker, E. 123, 127, 130
self-determination 129, 133–4, 192
Sen, A. 20, 21, 27, 61, 98, 100, 103, 107, 117–20, 127, 139, 151, 154, 178, 235
Shanghai Cooperation Organization (SCO) 203
Sharif, N. 153
Shell Petroleum Corporation 136
Shiva Kumar, A.K. 104
Sierra Leone 147; post-conflict situations, 162
Smith, S. 10, 23
social 19, 44, 49, 146; arrangements 169; change, 47, 92, 99, 156; cohesion 114, 121; competition 178, 181; conflicts 181;

contract 166, 190; development 113–14, 178; disintegration 237; distress 182; distribution 171; and economic policies 168; and economic values 58; exclusion 156, 180, 189; expenditure 103, 165; harmony 161; institutions 47; integration 77–8; justice 24, 50, 168, 207, 218; norms 67; policy making, 181–3; processes 47, 100, 145, 152, 214; rights 53, 74, 92, 124, 126, 130, 155; safety nets 99, 114, 167, 178, 199; science concept 61–2; security (social insurances) 4, 43, 145, 174, 183, 187; services, lack of, 150; tensions 31, 213; threats 25; transformation 89–90, 145, 175; underdevelopment 65

socio-cultural factors 154; socio-economic issues 14, 101, 103

Somalia 26, 197; conflicts 153, 170; Dutch presence 220

Sorensen, G. 171

South Commission, The *Challenge to the South: Report of the South Commission (1990)* 35, 36

South East Asian concept of security 74

South Korea, economic crisis 99

sovereignty/state sovereignty 2, 13, 18, 21, 23, 27, 36, 42, 43, 45, 58, 62, 64, 66, 74, 78–81, 85–6, 91–4, 131, 133, 136, 138, 162, 168–9, 171, 172, 173, 187, 205, 207; as responsibility, 190

Soviet Union 36, 83, 100, 211; disintegration 1, 84, 153, 173, 211

Sri Lanka: Sinhalese nationalism and Tamil minority consciousness 149, 164

state 1, 30, 101–4, 113–16 149–51, 200–3; accountability 131, 133; aggressiveness 86; autonomy 171; building process 177; legitimacy 169–70; domestic responsibilities 166*ff*; lack of effectiveness 167; failed 13, 26, 77, 160, 173, 192; human security responsibility 167–70; ideal political, economic, and social responsibilities 134–5, 176–83; integrity 186; inter-dependence and economic linkages 144–5; based on liberal peace model, political model 214–16; legitimacy 191, limits of action 131–5; market and civil society, relation 157; shifting priorities 48; security, 45; strong 171–2; society contract 177–8; statehood 13; types, 170–4; weak (unwilling or incapable) 83–4, 114, 150, 161, 172–6; withdrawal from social sectors 174; viability 62

Stewart, F. 103, 116–18, 119, 150–1

structural adjustment programmes 148, 210

sub-Saharan Africa 173

sustainability 41, 105, 107–9, 115, 146, 221, 228, 238

Sudan: international aid 227

Suhrke, A. 46

Sykes–Picot Agreement (1916), 173

Tajikistan, international aid 213, 214; UNDP peace building initiative, 160

Taliaferro J.W. 83

Taliban 10, 176, 210, 228, 230

Tan See Sang 167

territorial integrity 41, 72–3, 84–5, 94, 130, 169

terrorism 12, 14, 17, 25, 26, 30, 31, 35, 36, 37, 46, 49, 53, 74, 76, 113, 153, 160, 168, 186–9, 192, 214, 216

Thailand 23, 205; economic crisis 99; international aid 210

Thakur, R. 46, 49, 197

Third World 4, 13, 35–6, 153

Thomas, C. 46–7

threats 14–19, 24–6, 28, 37, 39, 40, 43, 44, 46–50, 52–3, 54–7, 59, 60–3, 68, 74, 78–9, 84–7, 92–4, 100, 114, 125–9, 133, 144, 161, 162, 170, 176–7, 185, 193, 199–200, 205–6, 207, 221–6; external 74, 132, 170; interconnectedness 16, 47–48, 62, 91, 164; transnational 74–5, 188; types and their relation to traditional security 25, 30, 60; vulnerability 210

Tickner, J.A. 81, 91

Trade Related Intellectual Property Rights (TRIPs) Agreement 188

trafficking of drugs, people and arms 12

transparency 175, 182, 216

tsunami 98, 191, 194, 199, 206, 229, 238

Turkmenistan, international aid 211, 213, 214, 217

Ul Haq, M. 20, 37, 98, 104–7, 111, 136–7, 138, 139, 202

underdevelopment 3, 14, 24, 35, 36, 37, 50, 64, 65, 85, 89, 187, 214; and conflicts, a vicious cycle 143–4; insecurity and 144–6; militarization 174–6

unemployment and underemployment 213; job security 14, 50, 176, 179, 222

UNESCO 6, 23

UNICEF 103, 180

United Kingdom: Conflict Reconstruction Unit (PCRU) 162; Department for International Development (DFID) 158

United Nations (UN) 1, 5, 11, 12, 24, 25, 29, 35, 36, 38, 130, 134, 145, 153, 162, 166–7, 175, 176, 189–90, 196, 214–15; *An Agenda for Peace* (1992) 24, 161; agenda, rethinking collective security 24–6; *In Larger Freedom* (2005) 189, 200, 202; *A More Secure World: Our Shared Responsibility* (2004) 189; responsibility for human security 200–3

United Nations Assistance Mission in Afghanistan (UNAMA) 163

United Nations Development Program (UNDP) 1, 9, 15, 20, 30, 35, 36, 38, 48–9, 50–3, 85, 144, 158, 160, 202, 205, 218; human security as peace dividend 24; *Human Development Report* (HDR) 1, 15, 23, 26, 105–6, 112, 126, 137, 146, 175, 180, 186, 193, 200, 208, 209, 221, 228; mainstreaming conflict in operations 160

United Nations Economic and Social Council 6, 23

United Nations General Assembly (UNGA) 26, 35, 196, 202

United Nations High-Level Panel on Threats 8–9; Challenges and Change 25, 38, 191, 198, 199, 200, 202

United Nations Human Rights Commission (UNHRC) 26, 27, 135

United Nations Security Council (UNSC) 26, 27, 28, 191–3, 202–3

United States of America: economic intervention 153; Federal Reserve Bank 103; international aid to Third World countries 208–9; military interventions 169, 196; September 11 3, 12, 27, 205, 208–9, 214, 216–17

USAID 217

universalism 137–8, 182

utilitarianism 20, 103

Uvin, P. 47, 156

Uzbekistan, international aid 211, 214, 217–18

values 20, 21, 49, 107, 111–3; Asian, 29, 48, 137–8; in human rights and human security 137–8; western 137–8

Vanaik, A. 90

Vaux, T. 215

victims in conflict 135, 147, 151, 164, 195

Vietnam: conflict 205

violence 14, 15, 24, 25, 26, 31, 39, 49, 59, 78, 86, 168, 170, 186, 189, 197, 206–7; as a model of accumulation 146 against

children (abuse, prostitution, labour), 14, 15; covert, 156–7; fragmentation 153; root causes 143, 146–52; street violence 14, 15

vulnerabilities 13, 15, 17, 26, 62, 80, 85, 100, 105, 151, 160, 186, 199, 200, 210, 232, 237

Walt, S. 72, 82

Waltz, K. N. 53, 76, 81–2

Walzer, M. 194, 196

war(s) 3, 11, 82–3, 147; absence of, 11, 24

wartime behaviour 50; economic, social, political and environmental costs 144; economy 148; socio-economic consequences 151; and underdevelopment 144; war against terrorism 12, 36, 37, 217; war crimes 45, 50, 168; warfare 13, 146, 216

weapons of mass destruction (WMDs) 26, 37, 73

Waever, O. 79

Weber, M. 48, 166

welfare state 4, 5, 50, 64, 168, 174

Wendt, A. 87–8

West, Western 36, 58, 65, 99–100, 135–8

Westphalia Peace Treaty (1648), 18, 74, 80, 88, 190, 240

Wilson, W. 189

Winslow, D. 47, 49

Wolff, C. 196

women, women's 182; disempowerment 99; equality 91; rehabilitation 154; movements 93; Women in Development (WID)103

World Bank, 50, 103, 144, 146–9, 153, 157–60, 162, 180, 197, 202, 210–13; *Breaking the Conflict Trap: Civil War and Development Policy* 147, 159; early warning tools and post-conflict development 159; Poverty Reduction Strategy Papers (PRSPs) 211; *World Development Report* 211

World Conference on Human Rights, Vienna (1993) 124, 137

World Trade Organization (WTO) 30, 188, 212

World War II 124, 125, 169, 227

Yemen economic cost of civil war 155

Yugoslav, conflict 156; fragmentation of state 197; minorities, insecurity 114; US-led war 197

CPSIA information can be obtained at www.ICGtesting.com
Printed in the USA
237214LV00002B/23/P